Woodworking Essentials

Timeless Techniques for Woodworkers

CINCINNATI, OHIO
popularwoodworking.com

Contents

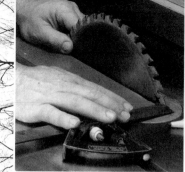

BONUS DOWNLOAD: *For free router and table saw jigs based on this book visit* <u>shopwoodworking.com/ essential-woodworking-jigs</u> *and enter the following discount code when you order:* WWESSENT

Setting Up Shop

The Right Location

by David Thiel

Most woodworkers back their way into woodworking, gathering tools and equipment slowly. Because of this fact most woodworkers also grow their woodworking space slowly as well. They may start out with a corner of the garage or basement dedicated to Saturday projects, but as their interest and skills build, so does the need for space.

That's where we want to start with this first chapter of Setting Up Shop – space. When we poll woodworkers about what they need to improve their pleasure in woodworking, space is the number-one answer, followed closely by more time and less expensive wood.

Given carte blanche to select a "right-sized" woodworking space, most of us would pick something about twice the size of a two-car garage that is heated and air conditioned, has a vaulted ceiling, windows on three sides and a large garage door on the fourth. When you look out any of the windows, there is a bucolic landscaped-view with not another building in sight. Which brings us back to reality.

Most woodworkers use a converted garage or basement space for their woodshop. The lucky few get to convert an exist-ing outbuilding or get to actually build a shop to their own specifications. Each of these options involve compromises, and we'll look at them one at a time to help you avoid complications in setting up your shop.

HOLE IN THE GROUND

Probably the least appealing – but very frequent – location for a woodshop is the basement. The negatives are many. First is deplorable access for moving machinery and lumber into the shop, and for moving finished pieces out. Probably less than half the basements in existence have a walk-out door with straight access. Many more require negotiating steps (whether interior or exterior), and many of those stairwells end in a 90° turn at a wall.

Once you're in the basement shop you are often confronted with ceilings that are less than 7' tall and ductwork for the HVAC system that for some reason had to be run below the ceiling height – not to mention water and electrical lines. Then there's the frequent lack of windows and the likelihood of dampness that is anathema to woodworking equipment.

When you are woodworking, one of the common byproducts is dust. Guess what else is often housed in a basement? The furnace and air conditioner have a bad habit of drawing air from the basement into the rest of the house. Along with that air goes your wood dust and any woodworking-related odors.

So why in the world are people turning basements into woodworking shops? Because that's the only space they have available. Working in a challenging space is a testament to the enthusiasm woodworkers have for their craft.

Now that we've discussed the negatives, there are a couple of positives worth mentioning. Basement shops are much more likely to be climate controlled, making the space an easier year-round workspace. Heat

Woodworker George Jaeger chose his home in northern Kentucky very carefully. The 1,300-square foot detached barn less than 200 feet from his home makes a perfect woodshop with an unbelievably pastoral setting.

Former *Popular Woodworking* publisher, Steve Shanesy had a basement shop in a 150-year-old Victorian house. As you can see, space was a challenge, but Steve still managed to crosscut a sheet of plywood. In a basement shop machinery needs to be stored out of the way when not in use. Materials should be cut down to manageable sizes before being moved into the basement.

Ductwork, piping and the ceiling itself allowed a minimum of head space in Steve's shop. His assembly bench and his most-used machine – the lathe – were positioned near the only window in the workshop to provide as much natural light as possible. Fluorescent fixtures mounted between the ceiling joists provided even light to the rest of the shop, while impacting the ceiling room as little as possible.

is often already in place and if the basement isn't air conditioned for the summer months, the below-ground location helps to keep things cooler.

Security and noise are two other benefits. When you're in the basement, casual passers-by aren't able to see the tools and machinery that are a mere locked door away, which reduces the temptation of theft. Also the noise commonly related with woodworking is muffled in a basement, reducing annoyance to neighbors – though your family might prefer a little more sound insulation.

While a lack of windows in the basement could make lighting an issue, wall space is reclaimed for hanging clamps, jigs and for adding cabinetry for tool and supply storage.

Power is an issue in any shop, but basements have the advantage of usually having electrical service of some type already in place. Garages and outbuildings are less likely to be pre-wired for adequate electricity. There's a good chance the service will still need to be upgraded to meet your woodworking needs, but it's easier to upgrade an existing service than run new service to an unwired space.

Now let's look at how to make the best of the negatives in a basement shop. Short of digging a new entrance to your basement, loading in materials will continue to be a problem if you don't have walk-out access. In some instances longer lumber can be fed through ground-level windows, but more

often than not your best answer will be to cut your lumber and sheet goods to a manageable size before bringing them into the shop. A circular saw and sawhorses set up temporarily in the driveway will help. More important, a little planning will make sure you know the minimum sizes necessary for your project, allowing you to cut darn close to finished size in a more roomy space.

Bringing projects out of the shop poses the same problem. It doesn't mean your woodworking is relegated to jewelry boxes and turning projects though. You'll just have to think modular in your designs. Know the limitations of your stairwell and build any cabinetry in pieces that can be assembled once out of the shop.

Ductwork, piping and the ceiling height will continue to be a problem, unless you're willing to make some radical changes. Ductwork can be redirected, or the ductwork can be changed to a more shallow, wider configuration to reduce height encroachment. This means extra money and extra effort and you'll need to determine how much of a problem the overhead clearance will be.

To avoid pulling your wood dust into the rest of your house, consider isolating the HVAC system in a separate room (building it around the system if necessary). You'll need to make sure that you're following local codes for clearance around the unit, but this is one solid option. At a minimum, replacing the filters used in your HVAC system with High Efficiency Particulate Air (HEPA) filters

Christopher Schwarz, *Popular Woodworking* contributing editor, also has his shop in his basement and has clustered his major machinery around the walk-out door to his driveway. Stock comes in through this door and goes into the racks above the jointer (if it's less than 8' long) and above the planer (if it's longer). After breaking down the stock to manageable lengths with a miter saw (which is positioned to the right of the planer on a rolling tool cabinet), he uses the jointer, planer and table saw to process the rough stock.

Here's the opposite wall of Christopher's basement shop. The bench is below the window to take advantage of natural light for hand work. All of the hand tools for joinery and surface preparation are in the cabinet on the wall, the toolbox on the floor and the drawers beneath the bench. The garbage can at the end of the bench is perfectly positioned to catch plane shavings as he works against the planing stop on the left end of the bench. Notice that even in a smaller basement shop, Christopher has opted to add a sliding table to his table saw to make working with panels, sheet goods (and accurate crosscuts) easier.

(and changing them regularly) will decrease unwanted dust as well as some odors.

Then, of course, there is the option of creating less dust in the first place. All dust-creating machinery (table saws, power jointers and power planers) should be used only with dust collection in place. Whether you choose to hook up a shop vacuum at the source of the dust (such as a random-orbit sander, for example), or work with more hand tools, either will reduce the ambient dust in the air.

GARAGE SHOPS

Garage shops (we're talking about attached garages in this case) offer interesting challenges of their own, mostly space related. While you can set up shop in a one- or two-car garage, you will be limited to a smaller space than in many basements, but the space will be more uniformly arranged. No pillars, or bump-outs to work around and the ceiling height is usually 7'6" or more. Plus the ceiling isn't cluttered with ductwork or pipes. On the other hand, there's usually a garage door running across part of the ceiling.

The first decision is whether or not you expect to park your car in the garage as well as use it as a woodworking shop. The two can co-exist, but there will be compromises. In a

one-car garage, the compromise is likely to be too much to ask for most dedicated woodworkers. Tools and work surfaces will need to be stored away to allow space for the car. This adds a fair amount of set-up and take-down time to your already limited woodworking time. And you're still going to have to squeeze in and out of the car. My honest recommendation is that a one-car garage shop should be a dedicated space. The car will acclimate to the great outdoors.

With a two-car garage you still have the possibility of parking at least one car in the space, sharing it with the tools and machinery. The compromise here is losing the "fourth wall" of your shop to the car. This may seem a small thing, but in practice it can put a real crimp in your storage space. Also, when sharing the garage, you have to consider dirt and damage to your car. A fine coating of walnut dust isn't in the manufacturer's recommendations – let alone a board that slips and takes out a fender or mirror.

Back to the garage door (or doors). This is one of the great aspects of a garage shop. Bringing materials and projects in and out of the shop is greatly simplified with this large opening. In comfortable weather the open door allows fresh air and natural light for your shop. With windows in the garage doors, natural lighting is still available during inclement weather. As to lumber and sheet goods, if you have the room to store them, great. If not, buy for one project at a time.

As I mentioned earlier, you do have an issue with the track system for the garage door, especially if you've added ambient lighting to your ceiling. The door needs to clear that lighting when open, and you need to be able to work without that lighting when the door is blocking those lights. In a perfect world, a two-car garage maintains one garage door and the second door is replaced with sliding glass or carriage doors.

As mentioned in the basement section, climate control and electrical supply can add a challenge to a garage shop. Most garages aren't heated and even fewer are cooled. Most woodworkers opt for heating their shops with space heaters or even small wood-burning stoves (a great option for making use of your wood scraps). Either will take the chill off, but you need to make sure your heating option is safe and that there is no risk of fire.

As for cooling, most woodworkers opt for a T-shirt, a pair of shorts and a couple of well-placed fans.

For power, most garages have a minimum service (a single 15-amp breaker) supplied. This is sufficient for running a single bulb and the garage door opener, but when you start running a planer or table saw, it's just not enough. Consider running a separate sub-panel with four 20-amp breakers and the option of one or two dedicated 220-volt breakers. Once the sub-panel is in place you can split the power off to wherever it's most convenient. This is extra work, but well worth the time and expense.

Lighting in a garage shop is the same as in a basement shop: general ambient lighting throughout, with task lighting over the most commonly used spaces.

I mentioned security and noise as issues with the basement shop. If you're in a garage shop that is visible from the street, you can't help but let the neighbors and the casual observer know you have tools and machinery around. We're not worried about neighbors borrowing tools (though that's an issue in its own right), but rather with theft. Improving the locks on any exterior doors is a worthwhile precaution.

Then there's the noise issue. Make friends with your neighbors and remember to be courteous with your woodworking activities. Planing 12"-wide boards at 7 a.m. on a Saturday will not make you any friends.

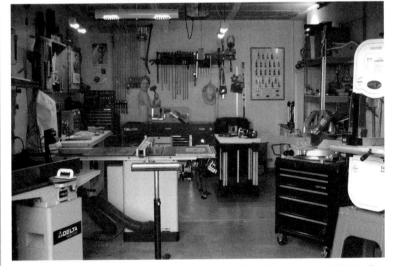

This is my one-car garage shop (attached to my condominium). No, the car won't fit. You'll find a 10" cabinet saw (with dust collector and router table mounted in the wing), 6" jointer, 14" band saw, and 10" sliding compound miter saw. All machines but the table saw are on wheels that allow me to store them against the walls, but quickly pull them out for use. A roller stand makes working with long stock on the table saw easier, while taking up very little floor space. To the right of the table saw is one of two knock-down assembly tables. This is the small one. You'll also notice task lighting over the important areas (unfortunately, no windows). By the way, I did take the bicycles, golf clubs and some gardening tools out of the garage for the photo. Despite no room for my car, it's still a multi-purpose area.

As you move deeper into my shop you'll find the requisite hand tools, a 13" benchtop planer (stored under the bench) and a small benchtop drill press (tucked away under the clamps). There's a benchtop belt/disc sander tucked away on the other side of that cabinet. Out of view to the right are two storage cabinets with five routers, three random-orbit sanders, a fleet of pneumatic nailers and sundry portable power tools. You'll also notice a half-dozen cordless drills stored within easy reach in recycled tennis shoes screwed to the wall. The workbench is still temporary. I'll get around to building the real one any day now.

And even though you're in the garage, dust and smells can still get you in trouble. At the very least, make sure you've got a good floor mat leading into the house to remove some of the dust from your shoes. If possible, add a second door and buffer space to keep things cleaner in the house. Fumes? Just try to be considerate.

OUTBUILDING SHOPS

Most woodworkers would prefer a separate location for their shop to keep noise, fumes and dust away from their home. It also feels more like a "real" shop than a space that's been adapted.

In woodworker Doug Matthews' two-car garage, the walls have been significantly reworked to provide a more comfortable shop. To gain more natural light and to avoid dealing with a garage door track attached to the ceiling, the garage door has been replaced with a pair of sliding-glass doors. This door option still leaves ample room for moving materials and projects in and out. Windows (that open for fresh air) have been added on two walls. Also notice the wood subfloor that has been installed. This helps level out an uneven floor and makes standing in the shop all day much easier on the feet.

Jon Magill's converted garage shop at right shows the best of both shop and garage worlds. This three-car garage has similar space issues to the one-car garage on page 7, but leaves much more room to move around. Multiple machines can be used at one time, rather than one at a time. The garage doors can be opened to bring in fresh air and light, or closed during cool or rainy months. All of the machinery is on mobile bases and collapsible horses. In 20 minutes, two cars can be parked out of the elements by storing the woodworking equipment in the third bay.

But that's not to say that many outbuilding shops haven't been adapted. They may have started as a detached garage or barn, requiring structural changes to make it the perfect shop.

Beyond the benefits of the physical location of the detached shop are the benefits of arranging windows, doors and ceiling space to best accommodate your needs. In addition, when starting with a blank space, ductwork for dust collection and pre-located power access can all be arranged without negotiating around existing impediments.

Also, unlike in many garage or basement shops, you can start from the ground up with your customizing. Ask any woodworker about standing on a concrete floor all day and they'll tell you they'd prefer something softer. With an outbuilding you should have the option of adding a wooden subfloor.

The benefits to a subfloor don't end at just comfort. By stealing 6" from your ceiling height you gain a perfectly flat floor to work on, and you can actually use the space underneath the floor to run electrical conduit and ductwork for dust collection.

If you prefer natural light to fluorescent light (and who doesn't?) an outbuilding gives you the option of cutting skylights in the roof. There's a slim chance you can do that in your garage, but I guarantee it won't work in your basement shop!

Having a wide-open space to bend to your will also allows you the option of dividing the floor plan into dedicated spaces. Most woodworkers are limited in their finishing options in a garage or basement shop, due to fumes and fire hazards. With an outbuilding, these concerns can easily be addressed with a dedicated space that is properly ventilated and protected from fire by using a metal finishing booth.

If you prefer to separate your machining area from your assembly area, again, the larger, unrestricted space offered by an outbuilding makes that division a simple matter of pre-planning.

Outbuildings also give you the chance to move some of the space-intensive and noisy shop equipment outside. Compressors and dust collectors make noise and take up valuable space. Adding a small "mechanical room" to the outside of an outbuilding moves the noise farther away and leaves the interior space available for working.

If your shop doubles as a television studio like my friend Scott Phillips', then you have to worry about the way it looks inside and out. Scott had the luxury of building exactly what he wanted, so he added a front porch for relaxing between projects (and takes). He added offices at the front of the shop, directly off the porch.

As you may have intuited while reading this list of wonderful things available in an outbuilding, it's usually the most expensive of the three options. Beyond the cost of the building itself (if you need to build) there are the concerns of adding water, electrical service and heat to the structure. While you may not need a bathroom, a slop sink is an important feature.

And, of course, adding a subfloor, skylights and all the windows you'd prefer will increase the costs associated with your new shop. But, you will be paying for the chance to set up shop exactly the way you want it – and that's a very happy thing.

WHAT'S YOUR CHOICE?

While we all may have a dream shop in our heads, only a lucky few will have the chance to set up shop the exact way they would prefer. Most of us will make the best of the space we have available, and that's what this section is all about: Helping you make the most of the space you have available.

We'll look closely at providing the best lighting and power options and the best locations for your machinery to make work flow smoothly, and we'll also look at organizing your hand tools and small power tools for maximum efficiency. At the end of the section we'll tackle the topic of dust collection, then look at the best workbenches and workstations to finish out your fantasy shop.

On the inside, Scott designed his shop with the maximum flexibility possible. Lighting is even throughout the shop and electrical connections are everywhere, including junction boxes set flush into the floor. Because he needs to worry about camera angles, many of the heavy pieces are mounted on casters so the layout of the shop can be adjusted by project. A two-car garage door runs across the back of the shop for easy access. While you may not need to worry about camera angles, the planning that went into this shop is definitely something to emulate.

Some stand-alone workshops serve as a place to work and a place to show. Doug Matthews' shop was built to visually fit into the surrounding rural landscape. On the lower level Doug restores and repairs antique furniture, while the upper level of the building houses a showroom for displaying and selling antiques.

Woodworker Charles Caswell built a two-car garage shop at the end of his driveway. The shop offers natural lighting via the open ceiling and skylights, as well as general lighting for less sunny days. The space offers ample room for the European-style combination table saw/jointer with sliding table. The shop's straightforward layout and comfortable, uncluttered work conditions make it a model of efficiency.

Lighting & Power

by Bill Stankus

W hen the workshop has proper lighting, sufficient electrical power and plenty of outlets it is a safer and better work environment.

Whether you are building a new freestanding shop or adapting a garage or basement for your woodshop, determining a plan for your electrical needs is one of the most important steps. Here is where to begin.

EVALUATE YOUR ELECTRICAL NEEDS

Check the electrical service panel and circuit breakers to the workshop location and note the breakers' amp values. If there's only one 15- or 20-amp circuit for the workshop or if the service to your home is 100 amps (or less), then the service will need upgrading.

How you upgrade or install adequate electrical service for a workshop location is dependent on whether you're remodeling

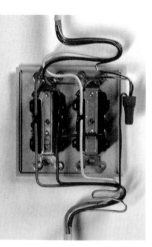

One example of 120v/240v wiring for a two-gang box.

or building a new room. Installing wiring and outlets in a new construction is fairly straightforward compared to remodeling.

Warnings About Electricity

Never attempt electrical work if you have doubts about the wiring layout or the consequences of your effort. Start with your local building departments (usually city and county) and the utility company. Building departments have electrical inspectors who can explain local codes and requirements concerning permits for the work and any necessary inspections. Requirements, regulations and amended versions of the National Electrical Code (NEC) vary from area to area. It is very important to follow the codes and guidelines established for your area. The local utility agencies can assist in the location of underground cables and will recommend the correct approach to any electrical-service upgrades. Find a recommended licensed electrical contractor. Often, it's less time-consuming, more economical and safer to have an expert install new wiring, electrical service panels or other custom work than to try it yourself.

Safety Rules

Upgrading a workshop generally consists of information, common sense, proper tools and supplies. To safely complete an electrical upgrade requires knowing the machinery and tool electrical requirements, code-compliant installation of outlets, use of the proper types and sizes of cables, outlets, etc. If you have any reservations about any of these points, call an electrical contractor.

Never work on a live circuit. Always disconnect the circuit at the service panel. That means switching the circuit breaker to "off" or removing a screw-in fuse. Remember that the electrical power is still live to the service panel from the power utility lines (either below or above ground), so even if you

Above is a typical subpanel installed above the main circuit breaker panel. Below the main panel is a Gen/Tran unit – used for connecting a portable generator to the main panel in the event of a power outage.

This subpanel cover is removed for a better look at the breaker switches and wiring.

Continuity tester

Multitester

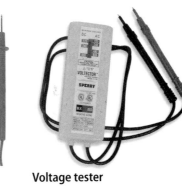

Voltage tester

Circuit analyzer

switch off the main power, the power is still live to the service.

Be certain that the circuit is off by first turning on a light that's plugged into that circuit. If it goes out when the circuit is switched off, proceed with your next steps.

Tell others that you are disconnecting a circuit. This is important when working at some distance from the service panel. Tape a note to the service panel warning others that you are working on the service.

Never work on the service panel or wiring when there are wet spots, moist conditions or standing water. Dry the area as much as possible. Open windows and doors to aid in drying damp basements. If there is moisture on the floor, construct a platform of dry boards over the wet areas.

COMMON ELECTRICAL TOOLS

The following is a list of specialized tools that are typically used for electrical work. Most are commonly available at a local home center.

• **Lineman's pliers:** Use to twist bare wires together and then cut the last ⅛" off so that the twisted wires fit into a wirenut.

• **Diagonal cutting pliers:** For cutting wire; fits in confined locations.

• **Needlenose or snipe-nosed pliers:** For working small parts in confined locations.

• **Wire strippers:** Adjustable to different wire gauges for removing insulation.

• **Multipurpose wire tool:** Combines wire stripper, wire cutter, crimper and bolt cutter.

• **Insulated screwdrivers:** coated with insulation, except for blade tip.

• **Conduit bender:** Use to bend metal conduit.

• **Fish tape:** Thin metal line for pulling cable through enclosed areas.

• **Cable ripper:** For slitting cable sheathing.

• **Electronic metal and voltage detector:** Use to locate metal objects and detect AC voltages within a wall.

• **Continuity tester** – Use to determine if an electrical path is complete. Simple to use when checking fuses, switches and plugs. Only use when the power is off!

• **Voltage tester:** Use to determine if power is present. It is used with the power on. The probes are touched to a hot line and the ground, causing the indicator to light. Also for checking DC/AC voltage, outlets, motors, appliances and fuses.

• **Volt-ohmmeter or multitester:** Use to test a variety of conditions, including voltage, low-voltage current, resistance to ohms and continuity. Also for checking outlets, fuses, wires, plugs, motors and electronic circuits.

• **Circuit analyzers:** Use to determine if there is power to a receptacle, proper grounding or if the wiring is correct. There are more sophisticated circuit analyzers that can check from the receptacle back to the service panel for voltage drops or for current leaks.

ELECTRICAL SUPPLIES

Be certain that the electrical supplies you select are approved or meet local building codes. If you aren't sure about this, then it would be best to consult certified experts. There are too many choices – guessing which part or wire size to use is the wrong approach.

The term "wire" typically refers to a single strand of conductive metal enclosed with insulation.

The term "cord" is used to refer to stranded wires protected by insulation. It can consist of two or three stranded wires

Typical Tool Amperage Draw

10" Cabinet saw	8.3 @ 240v	20-gal. Shop vacuum	10.5
10" Contractor saw	12.8	3½-hp Air compressor	15
14" Band saw (½ hp)	9	Router, 1 hp	6.8
10" Radial-arm saw	11	Router, 3 hp	15
12" Miter saw	13	Belt sander	10.5
6" Jointer	9.5	Plate joiner	6.5
12" Planer	15	Random-orbit sander	1.7
Drill press	6	Spindle sander	3.5
Edge sander	8.4 @ 240v	⅜" Drill	4
2-hp Shaper	16	Bench grinder	6
12" Lathe (¾ hp)	11.4	Strip sander	2.6
Scroll saw	1.3	Jigsaw	4.8
Dust collector (2 bag)	16	Circular saw	13
Dust collector (4 bag)	17 @ 240v		

For tools not included on this list, the National Electrical Code sets minimum amperage capacities:
- Small appliances – 20 amperes
- General lighting – 15 or 20 amperes
- Stationary tools – multiply the machine's amperage by 125%. (A 15-amp planer will require 1.25 x 15 = 18.75, or a 20-amp circuit.)

within the insulation and is used for appliances, lamps, etc.

"Cable" has two or more color-coded insulated wires that are protected by sheathing. In the United States the colors of the individual wires are: black or red is the power, or hot wire; white or gray is the neutral; and green (or green with a yellow stripe) is the ground wire. Sometimes the ground wire is a single uninsulated copper wire.

WIRE SIZE & TYPE

Use the correct wire size and type when upgrading an electrical system. Local codes will specify the types of cable and cable conduits permitted in your area. Here are the common wire types:

• **Type NM (nonmetallic)**, has thermoplastic insulation and is capable of withstanding a wide range of temperatures. It's used for most household circuits.

• **Type UF (underground feed)** is waterproof and is used for damp and outdoor locations.

• **Type USE (underground service entrance)** is used for underground or overhead service entrance and direct burial to garages and workshops.

• **Type THW** is used for outdoor hanging or indoor conduit as service-entrance cables and for conduit to a subpanel.

Of the above types, NM cable is the most common plastic-sheathed cable. It's often referred to as Romex (a trade name). The sheath is usually moisture-resistant and flame-retardant. Normally, there are insulated power wires and a bare ground wire inside of the sheath.

Armored cable (also referred to by the trade name BX cable) has an outer armored layer, usually flexible galvanized steel, that often contains two or three wires wrapped in paper.

Conduit is usually either galvanized steel or plastic pipe. It's generally available in ½", ¾", 1" and 1¼" diameters. The correct size to use in your woodshop depends on the diameter and number of wires inside the conduit.

Wire Size

Wire size is extremely important when upgrading an electrical system. Standard reference numbers, usually printed on the outside of wire insulation, are based upon the American Wire Gauge (AWG) system. Gauge numbers are inverse to their size; that is, the smaller the number, the larger the wire diameter. The maximum current that a wire can safely manage is stated in amperes (amps). Wire diameter and the amount of amperes are directly related. Smaller-diameter wires have greater resistance to electrical current flow; consequently, as the current flow increases so do friction and heat.

Calculating Electrical Usage in the Workshop

When electrical circuits or subpanels are added to an electrical service, the total load must not exceed the service rating. Generally, older homes have 100-amp service and newer homes have 200-amp service. If you are not certain about the service, look at the main circuit breaker in the service panel. If you have 100-amp service, consult with both the utility company and a licensed electrician regarding upgrading to a 200-amp service.

Generally, home woodshops will have one woodworker using no more than two machines at one time (table saw and dust collector, drill press and vacuum). The advantage of this is that the electrical system isn't going to need to support the simultaneous operation of all the woodshop's machinery. As you plan the electrical layout of your shop, make a best guess as to the frequency of use of tools and machines.

Not only will this aid in determining circuit requirements, but it will also aid in planning the placement of outlets. It's often easier to install separate outlets on separate circuits than to have one circuit with multiple outlets. For example, in my woodshop I have three machines requiring 220v service: the table saw, jointer/planer and band saw. Rarely, if ever, are two machines running at the same time. So it's possible for the three machines to have their outlets wired to the same circuit.

However, these machines are located in different areas of the woodshop and it was much easier to install outlets at each of the machine locations and route wires through one or more conduits. Since there was adequate space in the subpanel, it was a straightforward addition of circuit breakers and wire. The exception to this is the dust collector, which is also 220v. Because it's operated simultaneously with each of the stationary machines, there was no choice – it required its own circuit.

The National Electrical Code sets minimum capacities for circuits regarding use and amperage:
- **Small appliances:** 20 amperes
- **General lighting:** 15 or 20 amperes
- **Stationary tools:** multiply the machine's amperage by 125 percent.

The 125 percent factors the electrical surge that occurs when a machine is first switched on. For example, a 12" planer rated at 15 amps (1.25 X 15 = 18.75) will require a 20-amp circuit.

OUTLETS, SWITCHES & PLUGS

When designing a new electrical layout for your workshop, placement of outlets and switches requires planning, guesswork and a bit of luck. Work projects, new machines, relocation of cabinets, stacks of lumber and other fluctuating events will block existing outlets and switches from access. Often, well-thought-out locations aren't that handy once the woodshop is actually used. The ideal situation is never having to use extension cords because you have outlets wherever you work. This can be accom-

Common Copper House Wire & Its Ampere Ratings

No. 18	7 amperes	No. 10	30 amperes
No. 16	10 amperes	No. 8	40 amperes
No. 14	15 amperes	No. 6	55 amperes
No. 12	20 amperes		

plished simply by locating outlets 3' to 5' apart throughout the woodshop, including the ceiling. This may seem excessive, but consider the many work conditions that occur away from the workbench area: Using a vacuum, sander, plate joiner, rotary carving tool or heat gun are but a few.

If the workshop area is a new construction, cables should be installed within the wall framework. If wall coverings are already in place, outlets can be installed on the outside of the wall. Always check your local electrical codes concerning external installations. External conduit adds flexibility to designing and locating outlets because conduit can be routed just about anywhere. Metal conduit pipe can be bent to a variety of shapes and angles and conduit pipe can be cut to length wherever necessary.

Outlets

There are four acceptable plugs for home woodshop use:
- **Grounded three-prong, 120v, 15 amp**
- **Grounded three-prong, 120v, 20 amp**
- **Ground fault circuit interrupter, 120v, 15 amp and 20 amp**
- **Grounded three-prong 220v/240v**

Ungrounded two-prong, 120v receptacles are unacceptable in workshops. If

On the left are 120v, 20-amp receptacles; on the right, 240v, 20-amp receptacles.

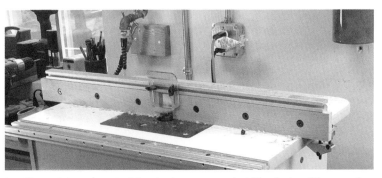

Installing outlets near your tools is not only more convenient, it's safer, too. If, for example, the plug is located near your router table, you're more likely to disconnect it when changing the router bit, which is the safest way to work.

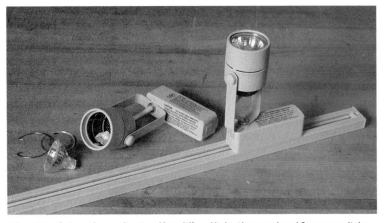

In locations that need more direct and less diffused light, I have replaced fluorescent lights with halogen track lighting. This type of light gives a brilliant white light, lasts about three times longer and uses 65 percent less energy than a standard incandescent light. This particular halogen light requires a 50-watt reflector bulb that is equivalent to the light of a standard 150-watt reflector bulb. It has a built-in transformer that converts 120v to 12v.

A dead-front plug has no exposed wires or screws, and the prongs are surrounded by smooth plastic. Use this type to replace worn plugs on your equipment.

Polarized plugs, commonly found on smaller woodworking tools, have one prong with a wider tip so they fit but one way into a socket.

an existing workshop has ungrounded two-prong outlets, turn off the main power and replace them with grounded outlets. If there isn't a ground wire to the outlet, attach one from the outlet to the receptacle box or the nearest cold water pipe. Check that the ground is functional by using a ground tester. To accommodate most tools, use grounded three-prong 20-amp outlets.

Ground fault circuit interrupter outlets (GFI) are designed to protect you from shock. GFI outlets monitor current; if the incoming and outgoing currents aren't the same, the GFI instantly cuts off the electricity (in 1/40 second). A GFI outlet will trip if there is a ground fault of 0.005 amps. These outlets are generally in bathrooms and outdoor locations where someone may have wet hands and feet. Install GFI units outlets in damp basements or around sinks.

Switches

There are four basic types of switches:
- **Single-pole switches** have two terminals: one for the incoming hot wire and one for the outgoing hot wire. The switch toggle is imprinted with ON/OFF.
- **Double-pole switches** have four terminals and are used primarily for 240v circuits. The switch toggle is imprinted with ON/OFF.
- **Three-way switches** have three terminals. One terminal is labeled COM (common), and the hot wire is connected to this terminal; the other two terminals are switch leads. Two three-way switches are used to control a circuit from two different locations. The toggle has no ON/OFF imprint.
- **Four-way switches** have four terminals and are used with two three-way switches to control a circuit from more than two locations. The toggle has no ON/OFF imprint.

Switches are rated according to amperage and voltage, so choose the correct switch for compatibility with circuits, wire and outlets.

Plugs

Despite the proliferation of battery-powered tools, there are still many tools and machines that have AC plugs. Usually these plugs receive quite a lot of use and wear, often because of the neglectful act of pulling the cord and bending the prongs. When plugs need replacing, replace worn plugs with dead-front plugs. This type has no exposed wires or screws, and the prongs are surrounded by smooth plastic. If there are screws, they are recessed and are only for securing the plug body together.

When attaching wires to a three-prong 120v plug, connect the black wire to the brass terminal, the white wire to the silver terminal and the green wire to the green or gray terminal.

Polarized plugs have one prong with a wider tip. This type of plug is designed to fit into an outlet in only one direction. You'll commonly encounter this kind of plug on smaller appliances and woodworking tools.

LIGHTING YOUR WORKSHOP

There are two types of lighting in most woodshops: fluorescent and minimal use of all other types.

Fluorescent lighting fixtures are probably used the most because they are inexpensive and commonly available. Other lighting types are thought to be useful as house lighting and not for woodshop lighting. While there is some truth to the generalization that fluorescent lights are useful in the woodshop, it is my opinion that their limitations are overlooked.

Unfortunately, few light fixtures seem to be designed specifically for woodshops. Those that are tend to be either sterile-looking white metal devices or cheap-looking clip-on reflector hoods. This simply means that it's up to the woodworker to solve shop lighting questions through both personal experience and research. Trial and error may seem like a difficult path to follow, but it does allow you to customize your woodshop.

When evaluating lights and fixtures, consider that there are several key elements to using light: color, shadow, contrast and reflection. These are the products of lighting that we see in both dynamic and subtle ways. They give usefulness, meaning and emotional connection to woodworking. Many artists refer to the process of their work as "painting with light." Woodworkers should also control and use light for both acceptable room lighting as well as artistic and aesthetic reasons.

Good workshop lighting is more than having a shadow-free environment. Lighting should also assist in artistic and aesthetic evaluations of wood and the subsequent project.

Color is perhaps the most subjective and difficult aspect of light. Fixture location and light source will change color values. For example, an apple in the glow of sunset will look different (warmer) than when it's sitting on a workbench under fluorescent lights (cooler). And a green light will make the apple appear grayish. Imagine the effect that lighting will have if a dark cherry workpiece is subjected to warm or cool lights. Will that "golden oak" stain look yellowish or greenish?

Fluorescent lights and incandescent lamps color objects differently. The cool and warm color differences are a function of wavelength variations.

Warmer light is often thought of as the light at sunset or the light from an incandescent bulb. Cooler light is the light of midday, an overcast sky or fluorescent light.

Degrees Kelvin (K) is the term commonly used for light temperature. The Kelvin scale is invaluable for selecting light to match your needs. Generally, lower degrees Kelvin represents a warmer appearance and higher degrees Kelvin represents a cooler look.

Shadow, Reflection, Contrast

The amount of light required to perform a task is directly related to a person's age. At the age of 40, the light requirement is three times greater than that required for a 10 year old. At the age of 60, the light needed is 15 times that needed for a 10 year old.

In some shops, work-area illumination requires careful light placement so that the area is shadow-free. Generally,

A Regent 300-watt halogen shop light suspended above my table saw provides bright, shadow-free lighting at the saw blade. The housing is 36" in length and features diffused tempered lenses, safety screens and a pull-string on/off switch. This lamp augments the workshop's fluorescent lighting.

A single 50-watt halogen spot light on the ceiling augments the workshop's fluorescent lighting and provides focused brightness at the band saw blade.

it's best to locate light fixtures so that light falls directly over a work area. If there are numerous fluorescent lights throughout a work area, the diffuse light should limit shadowing. Flat lighting can be beneficial to a cabinetmaker wanting to see layout lines clearly. However, flat lighting isn't as useful for woodcarving. Lighting that is 45° to 90° to the carving will create better and more useful shadows that enhance the carving process.

A simple way to brighten the workbench is by clamping an articulated lamp on the corner of the workbench. This gives a spotlight effect, which is ideal for detail work.

Remember: the closer light is to the work area the stronger the shadows. The opposite

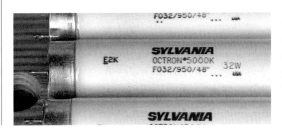

These fluorescent bulbs are rated for 5,000 Kelvin, a color temperature generally referred to as "daylight."

Workshop Lighting Tips

- Use long life, reduced-wattage bulbs whenever possible.
- If color is important, use bulbs that approximate daylight (5,000 K).
- Use zone lighting so that areas in frequent use will be well lit.
- Paint walls, ceiling and other surfaces light colors for maximum light reflection.
- Place incandescent spot lamps at drill press or band saw.
- Put drop lights over workbench if you need spot lighting and less diffused lighting.

Typical 48" Fluorescent Lights

Bulb Name	°Kelvin	Lumens*	Watts	Cri**
Sunshine	5,000 K	2,250	40	90
Daylight Delux	6,500 K	2,250	40	84
SP-35, moderate white	3,500 K	3,200	40	73
SP-41, cool white	4,150 K	3,200	40	42

*A lumen is a unit of measurement that expresses the total quantity of light given off by a light source. For practical purposes, fluorescent lights use much less energy than incandescent bulbs and still produce similar or better light levels.

**Color rendering index (CRI) is a measurement of color shift when an object is illuminated by a light. CRI ranges from 1 to 100, with natural daylight and incandescent light equal to 100. Therefore, lights with a higher CRI produce more natural colors.

NOTE: Foot-candles is a measure of lumens per square foot, as measured on a working surface or floor area. For an office, the general working range is 15 to 70 foot-candles. If you are doing precise work, 100 to 200 foot-candles is recommended. On a cloudless sunny day, the sun gives off 1,000 foot-candles.

is also true: the more distance between light and work area, the weaker the shadows.

TYPES OF LAMPS

There are three main workshop types of lights: tungsten-filament bulbs, halogen lamps and fluorescent lighting.

Tungsten-filament Bulbs

These come in clear, frosted or tinted glass producing warm natural tones. Clear bulbs produce bright and more contrasting light. Frosted bulbs produce diffuse light and tinted bulbs add diffuse warmth to the environment. Spotlights and floodlights are also tungsten bulbs. They are cone shaped with front lenses that either focus or diffuse the light. Light travels outward from spotlights and floodlights in a cone-shaped form and the area of this cone of light with the greatest candlepower is referred to as the beam angle. Generally, beam angle is 15° to 25° for spotlights and 30° to 75° for floodlights. So, for more pin-point lighting, spotlights provide a narrower beam than floodlights.

Halogen Lamps

Halogen lamps are actually tungsten-halogen lamps in two basic types: low voltage and standard-line voltage. Low-voltage halogen lamps require a transformer and operate at both lower voltage and lower wattage than standard-line voltage halogen

This articulated lamp fits into dog holes on a workbench and can be moved as necessary for detail work.

lamps. They are usually designed as reflectors, allowing them to be directed at specific work areas. Low-voltage halogen lamps are relatively small and lend themselves to use in recessed fixtures. Generally, beam angle from the reflector is 5° to 30°.

Standard-line-voltage halogen lamps are more efficient than standard incandescent tungsten lamps but they have the disadvantages of expense and high temperatures. Line-voltage halogen lamps should be kept away from any flammable materials. Follow the manufacturers' use recommendations.

Fluorescent Lamps

Fluorescent lighting is generally low-cost and efficient. Tungsten bulbs have an average life of 750 to 1,250 hours and fluorescent lights have an average life of 20,000 hours.

Fluorescent lamps come in different color sensitivities, ranging from cool to warm white. Before purchasing, make sure that the lamp and the fixture are compatible by checking the size and shape of the end-pins. Also check the lamp's wattage with that of the ballast.

There are at least eight different types of fluorescent lights. Product packaging should furnish lamp designations, including references to color rendering, degrees Kelvin, watts and lumens.

High-intensity-discharge Lamps

This type of lamp wasn't mentioned earlier because it is fairly new and is not commonly used. High-intensity-discharge (HID) lamps include metal halide lamps, mercury lamps and high-pressure sodium lamps. These have primarily been used for industrial purposes but are slowly being accepted for other uses (mostly for architectural and security purposes).

There are disadvantages to using HID lamps: They require warming up and cooling down periods when they are turned on and off, and they produce a bluish light that gives an unfamiliar coloring to most things, including woodworking projects.

Currently, metal halide lamps are the only HID lamps that approach normal colorization. HID lamps, even though they are energy efficient, aren't useful for the woodshop because of their color rendering and fixture configuration.

Placing Machinery

by Scott Gibson

In a much earlier era, cabinetmakers didn't spend much time worrying about where to put machines in their shops. They didn't have much to work with. A small shop might have had a communal lathe turned by an apprentice, but artisans worked mostly at their benches with hand tools. Period drawings of these old shops make it clear just how far we've come.

Anyone setting up shop these days can choose from a tremendous variety of stationary and portable power tools. Manufacturers from Pacific Rim countries, from the United States and from Europe, all competing in a world market, have helped to keep tool prices stable. New designs are safer and more innovative. It's good news for someone just getting interested in the craft.

Finding the right spot to set up shop, covered in Chapter 1 of this section, has a way of helping us decide which tools are most important. Small spaces dictate a very careful selection of essential tools. A larger space invites more freedom. But either way, figuring out exactly where to put those tools is an essential next step.

No two woodworkers are likely to agree on how a shop should be organized. The "best" arrangement depends on a variety of factors – what's being produced, for example, as well as individual work habits. That said, no matter what the shop, machinery should be arranged to eliminate extra steps and extra work while leaving enough elbow room for both safety and comfort.

MACHINERY ESSENTIALS FOR A SMALL SHOP

Woodworking can cover anything from turning wooden pen bodies to building an armoire or a Windsor chair. What we make will help shape the list of machine tools we invest in and how we organize them in the shop.

At one end of the spectrum are woodworkers such as Alan Bradstreet, a Maine professional who turns out a single product – bookmarks made from thin strips of cherry. Every machine in his shop is part of a well-organized progression that transforms blocks of scrap cherry into finished bookmarks. Every tool is devoted to this end, and all of them are precisely placed for efficiency.

Chairmaker Brian Boggs's former Kentucky based shop is a good example of a shop for a woodworker with specialized needs (see photos on page 18).

Most of us, however, are woodworking generalists who might make a dining table one month and a wall cabinet or chair the next.

The basic stationary tools for this kind of woodworking are a table saw, a jointer and a planer. These three tools allow you to turn rough lumber into finished goods, and you really need all three of them. A typical setup for a small shop would include a 10" table saw, a jointer with a minimum capacity of 6" and a 12" thickness planer.

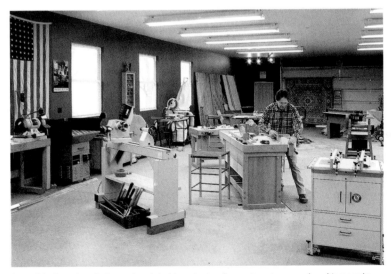

One of the luxuries of a large shop is having plenty of room to set up woodworking equipment without feeling crowded. Smaller shops require more discipline in choosing and placing equipment. This is the nearly 3,000-square-foot shop of Scott Phillips of the PBS television show "American Woodshop."

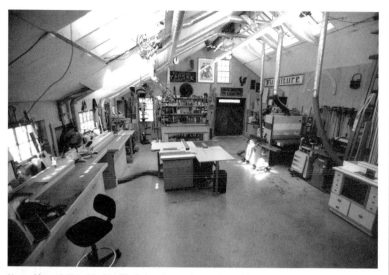

Norm Abram's New Yankee Workshop housed a number of dedicated woodworking machines. The ample floor plan allows this approach, but smaller shops may consider combination machines to save space.

DEDICATED TOOLS OR COMBINATION MACHINES?

If the table saw/jointer/planer combination is to be the tool foundation of most new shops, there's still the question of whether to buy three separate machines or a combination machine that will handle two or more basic functions. There are good arguments for and against each solution.

Dedicated machines are always ready to go – they don't have to be converted from one thing to another – and that saves both time and effort. Separate machines obviously take up more room, but they also can be less expensive and there are more brands from which to choose. There's a brisk market in used tools, so it should be possible to get started on even a fairly modest budget.

Combination machines have some advantages, too. Primarily, of course, they save space. In a very small workshop, a combination planer/jointer eliminates one bulky piece of equipment. And because these tools use a common set of knives for jointing and thickness planing, you'll be able to flatten wide pieces of lumber. That's a very big advantage. The Robland X31, for example, which combines a total of five machines in one, comes with 12" knives for jointing and planing.

The downside to combination machines is that it takes time to switch from one function to another. Key settings – such as the position of the fence – might have to be changed in switching from one job

There are woodworkers who would swap a band saw for a table saw (for one thing, band saws are safer). But even in these shops the basic steps remain the same: Rough lumber must be flattened (face jointed) and straightened on a jointer, then run through a planer to a uniform thickness and finally cut to length and width on a saw. Only then can you make something out of it.

Many woodworkers start with these basics and build on them in time by adding a drill press, stationary belt sander or disc sander, mortising machine, shaper and spindle sander.

The type of work produced in a shop dictates the size and variety of woodworking machinery. Chairmaker Brian Boggs doesn't need a table saw, which is a mainstay in most cabinet shops. For him, a band saw and specialized joint-cutting equipment are more useful.

The assembly room in Boggs' chairmaking shop was nearly devoid of woodworking equipment. Creating a quiet zone away from machinery is worth considering if space allows.

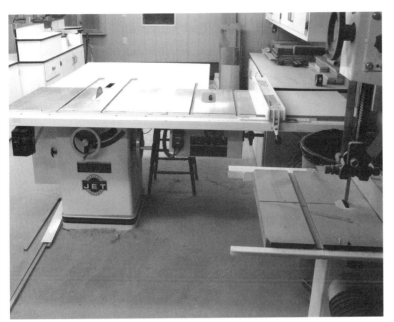

This shop allows plenty of infeed and outfeed room for the table saw. Tom Willenborg incorporated a second table saw in the extension table of his cabinet saw for a dado stack that's always ready to go.

Michigan-based craftsman John Wilson uses a band saw to cut out a canoe paddle in his shop. To cut a piece of stock this long he needs adequate infeed and outfeed room, but the saw could be backed up against a wall and still be effective.

to another. Combination machines also tend to be more expensive than separate machines that do the same jobs. Even with these drawbacks, they're worth considering for very small shops.

FINDING A LAYOUT THAT WORKS IN YOUR SPACE

If you've never set up a shop before, it's going to be hard to visualize the many possible layouts in the space you have to work with. Machines are not only heavy, but they frequently require special connections – a 240-volt receptacle, for example, or a connection to the dust collection system. With that in mind, it makes sense to do as much as you can on paper before pushing machines around the shop.

Start by drawing a floor plan of the shop exactly to scale. Mark on it the locations of windows, doors, electrical outlets and any other features that might affect the operation of a stationary tool. Now make cutouts, also to scale, of each machine you need to find a home for. It's easy to move the machines around on paper.

Each machine requires a certain amount of clearance between it and nearby objects. Think of it as the tool's aura. For example, a table saw must be positioned so that long pieces of lumber can be run over the blade and ripped. Eight feet is a minimum

benchmark for solid lumber (that's also the length of a full-size piece of plywood), so you'll need a space that's longer than 16' in which to place the table saw. It's better to allow a few extra feet on each end. You'll also need space on the left side of the saw so you can maneuver a full sheet of plywood up on the table.

A jointer and planer also need generous allowances of room on both the infeed and outfeed sides. But because you are more likely to cut stock roughly to length before jointing and planing, you may not need quite as much room as you would with the table saw. And you won't need nearly as much width.

In a large shop it won't be a problem locating the saw to provide these kinds of clearances. In a small shop, you may need to take advantage of a window or a door. You might, for example, give yourself 12' of space on the infeed side of the table saw and only 6' on the outfeed side. By positioning the saw near a door, you can always accommodate those extra-length boards when you need to.

Another key element is the relative heights of adjacent tools and fixtures. You might, for example, have plenty of room on infeed and outfeed sides of a table saw to handle long pieces of stock. That part of it works out just fine. But what about potential interference on the side? Maybe you were planning on putting a workbench several feet to the left of the table saw. If it's just an inch or two higher than the saw, the distance between the two becomes the maximum length of stock you can crosscut.

If you weigh these relationships in advance they often can be solved without much trouble. In the case of a nearby bench, raising the saw slightly on blocks or cutting down the legs of the bench a bit may fix the problem.

Taking this idea one step further, consider building simple models of your shop and tools out of cardboard or foam board. Make them to scale and move things around until you're satisfied you've got a plan. It takes more time than working on paper, but you'll get a three-dimensional look at what your shop will look and feel like.

THINK ABOUT WORK FLOW

You'll probably end up buying rough lumber in lengths much longer than what you'll eventually need. You may be building a wall cabinet that's only 3' high, but the rough lumber could easily be 12' or more in length when you get it home. So one of the first steps is to place tools so that you can break the raw material into manageable pieces.

Close to the entry along one side of the shop is a good place to put a long bench, as well as a centrally located chop saw and nearby storage racks for both lumber and plywood. A long board can be cut to rough length before it travels around the shop.

Locating the storage bin for sheet goods close to the table saw makes it easier to cut pieces of plywood or particleboard to size. Sheet goods tend to be quite heavy – a 4' x 8' sheet of Medium-density Fiberboard (MDF) ¾" thick can weigh close to 100 pounds – so it doesn't make sense carrying them any farther than necessary.

What comes next? Usually, the lumber will need to be flattened and straightened on the jointer and then sent through the thickness planer. Locating these two machines (or combination machine) nearby and close to the table saw will save some steps.

These machines can be located very close to one another as long as the stock doesn't bump into anything else while it's being processed. For example, you might group the table saw, jointer and planer in line in the middle of a small shop so that stock runs from side to side, the full width of the space.

A WORKING TRIANGLE FOR THE WOODSHOP

This idea of grouping machines for efficiency and comfort is the same as creating a work triangle in the kitchen. In a kitchen, this is the relationship between the sink, stove and refrigerator. In a shop it might be the relationship between machines that are used most frequently.

Suppose, for example, you expect to resaw stock for bookmatched panels on a fairly regular basis. The process involves a band saw (to slice the full width of a board)

The workshop of Sam Maloof includes a machine room with enough floor area to house a large thickness planer with a jointer parked right next door. These tools are often used in tandem.

This is the assembly area in Maloof's shop. Here, woodworkers use smaller tools and escape the din of the larger machine area.

as well as frequent trips to a jointer so the cut side of the board can be trued up. In a shop like this, the work triangle might include band saw, jointer and possibly a cutoff saw or table saw.

The work triangle in kitchen design is a relatively rigid planning guide. Some designers go so far as to prescribe minimum and maximum distances when you add up all three legs of the triangle. English kitchen designer Johnny Grey favors a much more flexible approach that can be applied to a workshop as well as a kitchen.

Grey starts by accounting for all the important work stations in a kitchen. That includes the sink, food preparation areas, stove, refrigerator and so forth – roughly a dozen in all. Then he thinks of the paths people will travel to get from one function to another. These are not necessarily straight lines that can't be bent. Instead, he thinks of them as rubber bands that have some flexibility but can't be completely severed.

In a workshop, as in a kitchen, no floor plan will perfectly accommodate everything we do. The idea is to think about operations we commonly undertake and design around them. As long as movement around the shop and between machines is unobstructed and logical, the machine layout will probably work most of the time.

SOME MACHINES DON'T NEED MUCH SPACE

It's easy to think of machine placement only in terms of the bigger pieces of equipment. That makes sense because they are the hardest to place and tend to dominate the work environment. But there are many smaller machines that can be worked in around the edges of a shop. They may not need as much room around them because the workpieces we usually bring to them are much smaller.

A bench grinder doesn't take up very much space and can easily be tucked in a corner because the workpieces are short – you sure don't need much clearance for a chisel or plane iron. The same is true of a drill press and a horizontal boring machine. They seldom require the kind of clearances that a table saw, jointer or planer must have.

Smaller tools can sometimes share space. A hollow-chisel mortising machine doesn't have a very large footprint but you occasionally may want to cut mortises in

A power miter saw centered on a bench against a wall can cut be used to cut long pieces of stock into more manageable pieces. By locating the saw near the entry door and storage racks, you won't have to maneuver long pieces of wood through the shop.

This lathe is pushed right up against the wall to the most of a small basement workshop. Some tools don't require much space around them, making them good candidates for overlooked corners and nooks.

fairly long pieces of stock. Housing the tool on the same long bench as a chop saw is one way of dealing with it.

In finding homes for small pieces of equipment, a key consideration is how often they are used. That grinder, for example, may be only an occasional tool for many woodworkers, something we use once a month to regrind edge chisels or plane blades. In that case, it can be housed in a distant corner of the shop, preferably near good natural light, or even mounted to a board that can be put in a storage cabinet when it's not needed.

If, on the other hand, you're going to do a lot of turning, you may need to make frequent trips to the grinder to touch up your

The cabinets in this organized shop have sliding storage shelves for easy access to tools that aren't used every day.

When space is at a premium, tuck infrequently used tools in cabinets, under workbenches or otherwise out of the way until they're needed. They can be mounted temporarily in just a few minutes.

tools. You'd probably want the grinder right next to the lathe or just a few steps away.

Don't overlook out-of-the-way nooks and crannies when trying to shoehorn in all your tools in a shop. There's no reason a compressor has to take up floor space in a small shop when it could just as easily be stored beneath a bench. You may not need a separate router table if you use part of your table saw's extension table for that purpose. In a small shop, consolidate where you can and give up dedicated floor space only to those tools that are used all the time.

MOBILE TOOLS CAN MAKE SMALL SPACES SERVE MANY NEEDS

When the woodshop takes over the garage, the car often winds up outside. But by making some machines mobile, even a single-car garage can accommodate both needs.

Scott Landis, in "The Workshop Book" (Taunton Press), visits one woodworker who has made this arrangement work and no doubt there are countless others. Maurice Gordon, who had only 420 square feet to work with, used a computer-design program to plan his shop. It houses a full complement of tools – everything from a table saw to a scroll saw, and lumber storage to boot. But when it's time to put the car away, the planer, table saw, band saw, jointer and sander can be rolled out of the way.

Gordon's shop is a marvel of good planning and it revolves around good-quality mobile bases for large stationary power tools. Even a full-sized cabinet saw with an extended table can be mounted on a mobile base. When the wheels are retracted, the saw is rock-solid. When it needs to be moved, one person can push it across the floor.

Even if you don't need to make room for the family sedan, mounting some tools on wheels is a great way to create more elbow room in a small shop. Consider a wheeled base for a planer, for instance, which you'll probably use less often than a table saw.

You might want to invest in bases for heavy stationary tools, but a variety of other shop fixtures and tools can be put on bases

Space beneath the long extension table on this full-sized cabinet saw is too valuable to waste. This storage cabinet holds saw blades, a dado set and other table saw accessories.

Even in a very large shop, there's no reason to give up floor space to tools that can work just as effectively under a bench or in an outdoor storage area. Air compressors and dust collectors are two candidates for this treatment.

Dropping a router table into the top of this large, centrally located assembly table is a good way to save space and increase shop efficiency.

of your own making. When looking for casters, invest in models where both wheels and spindles can be locked. Casters with wheel-only locking mechanisms are cheaper but you may find the tool has an annoying habit of moving around while you try to use it.

BE READY TO TRY NEW IDEAS

Even with careful planning, it's tough to get everything in exactly the right spot your first time out. Many woodworkers will continue to tinker with shop layout and machinery locations for as long as they inhabit the space.

The kind of shop you have certainly affects how much flexibility you have to alter machine placements. If you're building a new shop from scratch and plan to start with a concrete slab, you can cast electrical conduit in the floor to get power to exactly where it's needed. That's a big plus, but it also calls for very careful planning and won't allow much tinkering later.

But for those at work in shops with more forgiving floors, experimentation with shop layout is going to be a plus.

Adding a new tool to an existing inventory may require some juggling of equipment. You might borrow an idea from another workshop. Whatever the reason for changes, tool placement is one of those things that's never really cast in stone.

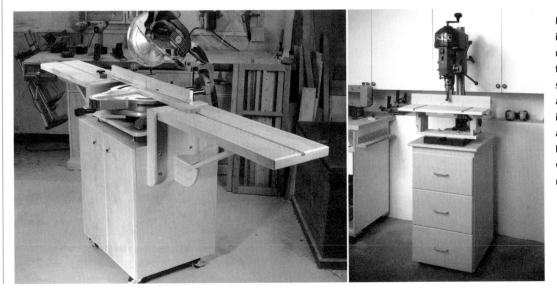

Making a tool mobile is an excellent way of making your shop more flexible. Putting a chop saw or a drill press on a custom stand that includes its own storage allows these tools to be pushed out of the way when they are not needed.

Small Tool Organization

by Scott Gibson

Many of us plan our workshops around big things – workbenches, table saws, planers and jointers. It's a challenge to arrange these large tools so the shop is efficient and comfortable, especially when space is limited. But as we ponder the best layout for these giants it's the small tools that can catch us by surprise.

It begins innocently enough. We typically have so few tools at the start that it hardly seems to matter where we store them; many woodworkers dive in with only a few used hand tools and a couple basic power tools. They all seem to fit handily in a couple of cardboard boxes. But in time, shops and tool collections have a way of getting bigger and more complicated. Eventually we have to deal with a jumble of small tools that accumulated in our shops while we weren't paying attention.

Cardboard boxes won't work any longer. There are too many tools, and they are too valuable to dump together in a box or a drawer where they can bang against each other. Moreover, some of them are used all the time, some only rarely. And mixing layout tools with router bits, or chisels with sandpaper, will seem a lot less than helpful when you're in a hurry to find the right tool for the job.

START BY IDENTIFYING TOOLS YOU NEED ALL THE TIME

For a lot of furnituremakers, the workbench is the hub of the shop, like a traffic circle through which every major road must pass. Dozens of tasks take place here: joinery is laid out and cut, lumber planed and sanded and furniture parts glued and assembled. We might even eat lunch here.

Given this central role for the workbench, one way to organize small tools is by gathering the ones you use most frequently and keeping them nearby. It's not hard to come up with a good list: chisels, planes, a square or two, a hammer or mallet, a marking knife (or a handful of sharp pencils), rules or measuring tapes, scrapers and a few other odds and ends.

These tools should be the first ones that are housed at or near the bench, within arm's reach of where you will be using them. Although it may take a little experimentation, when the arrangement works you will know it. You should be able to reach for exactly the tool you need without spending any unnecessary time scouting for it and without moving your feet.

Tool collections can become more specialized as time goes on, forcing you to make decisions about which tools need a

Most woodworking shops keep dozens of small tools on hand, many of them with sharp or delicate edges. Keeping track of them and protecting them from damage is an organizational challenge.

This traditional European workbench has more than a flat, sturdy top; drawers and cabinets provide abundant storage space for hand and portable power tools.

Racking up frequently used tools near the workbench keeps them close to their point of use and cuts down on wasted steps to distant cabinets or drawers.

front-row seat and which can be relegated to more distant storage. For example, you may routinely need a block plane, a smoothing plane, a small rabbeting plane and a jointer. That's four planes you use frequently. But you use that old moulding plane you picked up at a flea market only once in a blue moon. Why clog up shelves or cabinets near the bench with tools you rarely need?

Virtually any tool category can use the same kind of attention. An adjustable square or try square is something you'll pick up a dozen times a day so keep it close at hand. But a framing square may not be used more than once a month so it can happily live on an overhead rafter or on a nail in the wall some distance away. A little common sense will go a long way in helping you identify what you need close at hand.

No one's list of "must haves" will be exactly the same. Every discipline has its own list of everyday tools, and those needs and habits will become evident with time in your shop as well.

A TOOL CABINET KEEPS IMPORTANT TOOLS CLOSE

Thumb through any book about woodworking shops and you're likely to see all kinds of bins, shelves and cabinets that inventive woodworkers have devised to organize their tool collections. Browsing is an excellent way of getting ideas for your own shop. After all, few ideas are really brand-new.

But a common theme in many shops is a large, wall-mounted tool cabinet. Christian Becksvoort, a Maine artisan specializing in Shaker-style furniture, has just such a cabinet mounted on the wall behind his work-

bench. It's a beautiful piece of furniture in its own right, made from cherry, the wood that Becksvoort uses for virtually all of the furniture he makes.

More important, it holds many if not all of the bench tools he needs to make a piece of furniture. Everything from files to chisels, augers to mallets, is stored neatly behind a pair of folding doors. Even the space on the inside of the doors is put to use. Neatly labeled drawers house drafting tools, bits, a first-aid kit and other small items. Carved into the drawer housing is "C.H. Becksvoort."

Becksvoort has been at it a long time and his collection of close-at-hand tools accurately reflects the sort of work he does. There's a heavy emphasis on hand tools – chisels, planes, scrapers – rather than portable power tools. This formula works for him but he'd be the last person to argue it's the right arrangement for everyone.

Building a first-rate cabinet to hold personal tools is a long-standing tradition for carpenters and furniture-makers. It's part of the curriculum for furniture-making students at Boston's North Bennet Street School. Building a tool chest gives students a chance to develop their furnituremaking and design skills and in the end they have something that will serve them for many years.

Tool cabinets can be infinitely variable, made to house only planes, a collection of chisels and carving tools or an entire suite of hand tools. What may be the most photographed American tool chest ever was made by a Massachusetts piano maker named Henry Studley over a 30-year career. It's a marvel of planning and design, deceptively

As cabinetmaking skills increase, so do the possibilities for building beautiful and unique tool chests. Glen and Malcolm Huey, a father/son team in Ohio, built this one when they moved into a new shop. It's designed for both hand and portable power tools.

small, only 39" high, 9" deep and 18" wide. Yet it holds 300 individual tools packed tightly together but still accessible. A more modern version of a grand cabinet is one built by Glen and Malcolm Huey to celebrate their move into a new workshop.

If you have the space, a wall cabinet can grow into more of a tool locker with space for small power tools as well as hand tools. A larger cabinet not only helps keep shop clutter to a minimum but it also can provide security if you live in an area where crime is a worry.

You might want to leave a tool cabinet of any size and complexity for the future, until individual preferences and needs are a little clearer (to say nothing of develop-

ing the skills required to make one). Start with a more modest wall cabinet for tools. It's an excellent project that doesn't have to consume a lot of expensive materials or take a lot of time. Tool chests can be very simple and as your skills improve you can move on to more complex designs.

DON'T OVERLOOK READY-MADE CABINETS

Another possible route is to buy inexpensive storage cabinets at used office-supply or furniture stores. Older steel cabinets and open shelving units can handle a lot of weight. Even if they need a fresh coat of paint and have a dent or ding here and there, these cabinets will provide a lot of useful storage at a relatively low cost.

Be more cautious about buying used kitchen cabinets. Some of them will be fine as either wall-mounted or free-standing storage, but inexpensive stock cabinets are often made from thin particleboard or plywood and won't stand much abuse.

As libraries convert from paper to digital files they are getting rid of those classic wood card catalogues. If you can manage to get your hands on one, adopt it right away; the small drawers are ideal for storing everything from nails and screws to router bits and collet wrenches.

TOOL BOARDS KEEP EVERYTHING IN SIGHT

If your workbench is against a wall, you can arrange a surprising number of tools directly in front of you on nails or hooks. The down side is that you're not going to squeeze the volume of tools here that you would be able to put in a well-designed cabinet. But they are in plain sight and instantly accessible.

We've all probably been in a highly organized garage or two where one wall was devoted to ¼" perforated hardboard and the outlines of different tools neatly painted in red or white. But driving nails or screws right into the wall works just as well. If your workshop has been clad in drywall, you might want to add a layer of plywood so you can put a nail or screw in wherever you want. T1-11 plywood ⅜" or ½" thick is inexpensive and attractive.

For tools that won't hang (chisels, files, carving tools, screwdrivers and the like), you can make simple racks and attach them

Maine furnituremaker Christian Becksvoort built a large wall-hanging tool chest that's mounted behind his workbench. It neatly holds a variety of hand tools where they can be reached easily.

These very simple, stackable storage boxes are a good example of low-tech ways of organizing tools. Drop-down doors make it easy to find what you need, and the materials list won't break the bank.

A machinist's tool chest includes a tool tray under a hinged top plus a number of drawers that can be protected by a fold-up front piece. Handles make it easy to move.

This rolling tool cabinet holds a lot of tools in bins and drawers. When folded up, the cabinet doesn't take up much room and it can be wheeled out of the way.

to the wall. One easy way to make a rack for chisels or files is to cut a series of slots in a board with a dado blade and then glue another board to it. The width and depth of the slots can be made to suit tools of different sizes. A series of holes in graduated sizes bored through the face of a board will handle chisels or screwdrivers. Magnetic strips will accomplish the same thing. Racks don't have to be fancy to be useful.

For the variety of odds and ends that almost always end up on a bench, drill holes in scrap blocks of wood and put them on a low shelf over the back of your bench. Blocks can store drill bits, nail sets, awls and similarly slender tools with points or sharp edges. You won't lose track of them and their delicate edges will be well protected.

ROLLING CABINETS KEEP LIKE TOOLS TOGETHER

There are two good approaches to making a tool cabinet mobile. One is, in effect, to take the cabinet off the wall and stick a pair of casters underneath it to create a rolling tool garage and workbench. The other is to make one or more rolling workstations dedicated to a single power tool.

Mobile workbenches and tool caddies can be as elaborate or as simple as you want to make them. For example, a design by David Thiel, Popular Woodworking Videos editor, is actually a modular bench consisting of two 21¾"-high rolling boxes and a 6'-long bench that spans them. Adjustable

support assemblies attached to the sides of the boxes can be raised to support the benchtop at a variety of working heights or hold a tool, such as a drill press, router table or a hollow-chisel mortise machine, when it's needed.

It's a good design for a small shop because the boxes can be used alone or together depending on the need, and parked out of the way when it's time to bring the cars in for the night. Another successful design from Thiel and Michael Rabkin incorporates fold-out lids, roomy storage compartments and a series of shallow drawers for fasteners and tools.

In this or a similar work cart, drawers can be built to suit your interests and internally divided in whatever manner makes the most sense for the user. Use a power sander a lot? Devote one of the drawers to your collection of random-orbit and block sanders with separate trays for different grades of sandpaper and other accessories. A heavy bottom shelf could be used for a belt sander. Repair a lot of chairs? Build a mobile tool station that houses just those supplies and can be rolled to any part of the shop where it might be needed.

A rolling cabinet devoted to a single tool saves space in a small shop because it can be pushed into a corner when it's not needed. More than that, having one or more of these rolling workstations helps parcel tools and their many accessories into dedicated spaces where they won't get lost.

Versatile as well as mobile, this modular cabinet design not only houses a variety of tools but also can serve as workbench or portable workstation for a drill press or other benchtop power tool.

As an example, consider the router. Many woodworkers eventually will own several: A laminate trimmer, a mid-size router and a big plunge router all might be found in a single shop. Each has a collet wrench (or wrenches), one or more bases, edge guides and a trammel for cutting circles and curves. Plus there are a lot of bits in one or more shank diameters. It all adds up to a lot of tooling. Building a rolling cart around a router table is a good way of keeping it all straight. Devote a drawer to bits, divided for ¼" and ½" shanks, and another for bases and edge guides. Routers themselves can go in a large enclosure at the base of the cabinet.

TOOLS THAT TRAVEL: TOTES & ROLLS

In addition to working at a bench or around the shop, many furniture makers will also find it necessary to leave the shop once in a while with some of their tools. Maybe it's a repair around the house or construction of a shed or outbuilding or even a working stint a good distance from home. Tools that travel need to be organized and protected from damage just as much as those that never leave the shop.

Depending on how often you need them, carpentry tools can be kept in a separate, out-of-the-way cabinet or segregated on their own shelf. These tools are just as specialized as woodworking and cabinetmaking tools – just a little different. They aren't generally used for woodworking so there's no sense in mixing the two together.

One way of keeping them straight is to build a wooden tote with a handle and keep it in a corner of the shop where it won't get in the way. When you need to fix something in the house – trim a sticky door, for instance, or patch a hole in a drywall ceiling – the tools are ready and waiting.

Totes can be very simple and still very useful; even a box with rope handles made from scraps of plywood or rough lumber and nailed together at the corners will prove practical. Make it long enough to house at least a 2' level and a handsaw. Adding a row of shallow drawers in the bottom of the tote is a good way of organizing small things – drill bits, a compass, drivers and the like – as well as protecting tools with sharp edges that would be dulled if they were thrown in with everything else. Or you can build internal trays and dividers to make it easier to find things as well as protect sharp edges.

Tool rolls are another way of keeping sharp-edged tools safe when you travel. These are simply pieces of leather or canvas with a series of pockets sewn into them. Tools are tucked into a protective sleeve and the whole thing rolled up and tied. Investing in an inexpensive canvas roll is also a good way of protecting sharp edges when the bits have to share drawer space with other tools.

POWER TOOLS DESERVE A SPACE OF THEIR OWN

Portable power tools represent a different kind of organizational challenge; they are not as delicate and easily damaged as many hand tools, but they are generally heavier and bulkier and they often come with a number of accessories of which you have to keep track.

Although they can be kept in cabinets or drawers, heavy power tools will be easier to get if they are stored on a shelf about waist high or in a simple plywood cubby. An open-faced cabinet or set of shelves a couple of feet square and divided into individual compartments is a good way of housing power tools. They can be kept in the same general part of the shop but all given their own space.

The surprising number of accessories, ranging from wrenches for changing blades to replacement motor brushes, should be kept nearby. Devoting one drawer or part of one cabinet to repair and replacement parts for power tools helps to keep these important bits of hardware from getting lost.

In the same general area, keep all parts lists and operating manuals for the tools in the shop. When you need to replace a part or adjust the tool the manual will be invaluable. An expanding plastic organizer, available at any office supply store, makes

A canvas or leather tool roll is a simple way of protecting and organizing tools whether you're in the shop or traveling.

a good library for tool manuals. A separate organizer can be used for small replacement parts, such as O-rings, gaskets and drive belts.

Accessories for larger power tools are easy to find when they are kept as close to the tool as possible rather than in some distant cabinet across the shop. The space beneath a table saw extension is a good place to tuck a small cabinet that can house saw blades, dado blades, wrenches and other supplies. A separate drawer in the same cabinet can also be used for router bits or drill bits. Grouping tool parts in this way makes them a lot easier to find and will protect them from damage.

If you can, try housing cordless tools in the same general area and mount your chargers on a nearby wall. Having all of the tools and batteries in a single location is a plus.

FINDING ROOM FOR ALL THOSE CLAMPS

Most of us apparently believe that old chestnut about woodworking: there is no such thing as too many clamps. If you have a large collection of bar and pipe clamps (and assuming you have the space for it) consider making a rolling or stationary clamp rack. Building in a series of crossbars at different heights makes it convenient to hang clamps of different lengths. The rack should be tapered top to bottom, and in the shape of an "A" when viewed from the side, so the clamps are not easily jounced off as the cart is moved.

Racks can provide two separate sides for storage so they can hold a large number of clamps conveniently. A wall-mounted or freestanding storage rack also keeps long clamps available and out of the way, but when you need a lot of clamps for a big glue-up it's a lot easier to wheel a rack over than it is to make a half-dozen trips across the shop.

If you work in a basement shop, or in any shop with a low, unfinished ceiling, you'll find an ideal storage area for spring clamps and handscrews by looking up; the bottom edge of a joist or rafter will hold many clamps and keep them within easy reach. To store a row of spring clamps beneath a shelf, string a length of heavy wire between two eyescrews so it hangs an inch or two below the shelf. Compress the clamp, pop it over the wire and release it.

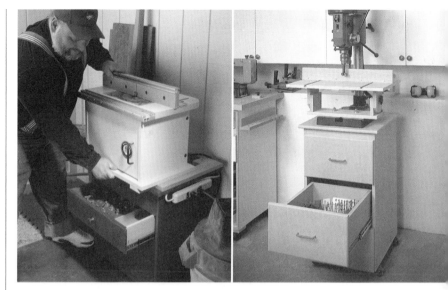

A storage cabinet dedicated to a single tool is one way of ensuring that tool accessories are always close at hand. Making the base mobile is an advantage, too.

KEEPING UP WITH THE CLUTTER

Providing specialized storage cabinets, shelving and rolling racks is certainly a big part of winning the war against shop clutter and keeping small tools organized. These fixtures can represent a significant investment of time and materials, but you don't have to build a shop full of them right away. Let your ideas percolate for a while, take a look at what other woodworkers have done to solve the same problems you have and then set about to fix one storage problem at a time.

The other side of it, of course, is taking the time to keep tools organized once you've made room for everything. Few people return a tool to its proper place the instant they've finished using it. We're more likely to put it aside and get the next tool we need. In the end, though, shops with plans for managing that mountain of small tools will be more efficient, safer and happier places to work.

Many shops have sizeable numbers of clamps, although few will rival the collection of Sam Maloof. A tapered rack keeps them organized. Adding casters would make the rack portable, an advantage in any shop.

Material Storage

by Scott Gibson

Finished work, whether it's a turned bowl or an entertainment center, is at center stage in most woodworking shops. But material storage and handling, such as these racks of lumber in the background, play an important if not as obvious supporting role.

It takes more than a room full of tools to make a productive woodworking shop. Along with stationary power tools and a collection of handplanes and chisels comes a diverse list of materials that must be kept on hand and accessible when you need them.

Not surprisingly, most of us focus on storing lumber. In addition to being the basic raw material that woodshops must have to operate, lumber has its own intrinsic pleasure. We can always make room for it.

Lumber also varies in size, shape and potential use. Rough hardwood that needs jointing and thickness planing before it can be used is nothing like the finished pine we can buy at the local lumberyard. In addition to various kinds of solid lumber, most shops also will need at least a modest inventory of plywood and other panel goods.

And wood is only the beginning. Shops also need everything from stains and finish to boxes of wood screws, pencils and paper, nuts and bolts, glue, cleaning supplies and light bulbs.

It's not hard to find yourself awash in shop clutter. You know you're in trouble when you'd rather go to the hardware store and buy a tube of 5-minute epoxy rather than take the time to look for the tube you know you already have.

Keeping all of these supplies straight is something like the process of organizing tools. By balancing work flow, convenience and safety, you can come up with a quarter-master's plan for your shop. All you have to do is stick with it. But that's another issue.

STORING LUMBER OUTDOORS SAVES SPACE IN THE SHOP

Many woodworkers keep a good deal of lumber on hand – not just enough for the current project but hundreds of board feet tucked away for future use. If you can spare the room, stocking lumber is an excellent approach. It's liberating to have a stack of rough lumber at the start of a project. Resting in those planks is a diversity of grain and range of color that opens many possibilities as a piece of furniture takes shape. You'll have an easier time matching figure in adjacent boards when it really counts or finding a board of exactly the right width when you need it.

A big stack of lumber represents not only opportunity but also responsibility. If properly cared for, those boards will be sound and straight years down the road. I still have some walnut that came from a tree my father cut on the family's southern Maryland farm in 1949.

If, on the other hand, wood is improperly stored you'll have a king-sized headache but nothing you can make furniture with.

It's always better to keep lumber indoors where it's protected from harsh sunlight, rain, snow and insects, than outside. But lumber can successfully be stored outside, too, as long as you're careful about it.

Never store lumber on the ground. It will rot. Start with a sturdy, level foundation of

Layers of boards are separated from each other by narrow stickers that should be aligned with each other vertically. The ends of these freshly sawn cherry boards will be painted with a wax-based product to help prevent end checks.

Careful stacking will help preserve these walnut boards. The wood pile should start on a flat base elevated off the ground.

4x4s spaced 16" to 24" apart. Take the time not only to level each 4x4 individually but also to arrange them so they are all in the same plane. The idea is to create a stable platform that's as flat as you can get it.

The space beneath the bottom layer of lumber and the ground will promote air circulation. If the lumber is just coming from a mill, that will also help it dry. And moving air will reduce the risk of mold. It's also a good idea to put a layer of polyethylene plastic or tarpaper on the ground beneath the 4x4s to keep moisture from migrating upward into the bottom layer of lumber.

Next are the stickers, the narrow pieces of lumber that are used to separate each row of lumber. It's better to use dry material for stickers to minimize the risk of mold. Keep them narrow to get the most air circulation possible; material that's 1" wide and ¾" to 1" thick is more than adequate. Use a consistent thickness throughout each layer.

The key to building a pile is to align the stickers in the pile with one another, beginning with the first ones that are placed directly over the 4x4s at the very bottom of the heap. Here's the sequence: 4x4s, then a layer of boards separated by an inch or so of space between them. Then a layer of stickers placed exactly over the 4x4s, then another layer of lumber, then stickers. As long as the stack is stable and in no danger of toppling, you can make it as high as you like.

Stickers aren't arranged in that way to satisfy some pathological need for neatness and order. They help the lumber stay flat. If you locate stickers without regard to the layer below you run a good risk of getting lumber that dries into a series of delicate

waves – like the pasta that goes into lasagna. The distortion may be too much to joint out of the wood, rendering it useless. If the 4x4 foundation is not flat, it's easy to create a twist in wood that will likewise make it useless for building furniture.

A piece of salvaged corrugated roofing, weighted down with scrap wood or rocks, will keep most of the rain and snow off the lumber. If you buy the lumber green, paint the ends of the boards or use a specialty sealer from a lumberyard supplier to keep the boards from drying at the ends first and splitting.

Just remember that wood that's been stored outside will need to shed some of its moisture before it can be used in furniture. Bring it into the shop and let it acclimate for a couple weeks. If you have a moisture meter, take advantage of it. Also, outside storage probably shouldn't be viewed as an indefinite solution for furniture woods.

INSIDE THE SHOP, BUILD RACKS OR STORE LUMBER VERTICALLY

There are two basic strategies for storing lumber inside a shop: It can be organized in wall-mounted racks, or stood on end vertically and leaned against the wall. Both methods have their pros and cons.

Wall racks can be made from either wood or metal. They don't have to be fancy, just strong and mounted securely to wall framing with adequately sized lag bolts. One advantage of a rack is that lumber can be sorted by width or species or in some other way that makes it easy to find what you want. The closer that supports are to each other vertically, the greater number of shelves the rack will provide. Even when supports are separated only by 12" or so, they can provide lots of useable space.

Another plus is that a lumber rack can be mounted on a wall that otherwise would go to waste. In a shop with a high ceiling, a two- or three-shelf rack above window height is a great way of storing wood you don't need access to very often. When the time comes, get a stepladder and haul down what you need. For the rest of the time, you're saving a lot of floor space.

The downside of a rack is that you usually end up moving lumber to get the board you want. Unless you can slide the board from beneath the stack you'll end up removing a number of boards, retrieving the one you're after, and then restacking the entire pile. At the same time, you can't see everything in this sort of stack. Visibility is limited to the top board and then a series of edges along the side of the stack. For a really good look at what you have, count on taking the boards off the rack.

Another disadvantage is that the space in front of a rack should be kept relatively clear of clutter so getting to a piece of lumber is not akin to running an obstacle course. Avoiding this problem can be tough in many shops where space is at a premium.

The other school of thought is to store boards vertically on their ends and lean them against a wall. George Nakashima, the influential post-war furniture maker whose studio is still in family hands, used this approach to store some of his lumber.

He was a great collector of wood in many forms. Nakashima would buy whole trees and cart them to a mill where they were turned into boards. He had them stacked in exactly the same order in which they came off the saw and banded together so they could dry. That method, storing wood in boule form, is beyond most of us. But vertical storage is not.

In his book "The Soul of a Tree" (Kodansha), there is a wonderful photograph of Nakashima in his wood room, surrounded by a thicket of wide hardwood planks as if he were standing in a grove of trees. All of that beauty in anyone's shop is inspiring. You will be limited, of course, by the height of the room. And the more lumber you collect and store this way, the harder it will be to get to any particular board you're looking for.

But one advantage is that you can easily see all sides of a board once you've found it. By tilting a plank up on one of its lower corners and holding the board in a near-vertical position you can pivot the wood freely to see either the front face or back face.

For shorts and small offcuts – those boards that are left over when you cut a big plank – vertical storage is probably the best solution. They won't easily fit on a rack horizontally and a large number of pieces can be stored on a relatively small amount of floor space. The only caveat here is to remind yourself to sort through the pile periodically and get rid of anything that doesn't serve a genuine purpose. It's easy to hang on to every bit of scrap lumber you create ("I just know I'll use that for something someday") but the truth is that without periodic weeding every garden becomes overgrown.

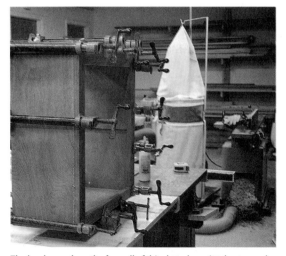

The lumber rack on the far wall of this shop doesn't take up much floor space. But one disadvantage is that the area in front of the rack must be kept relatively free of clutter to make the lumber accessible.

A rack made of 2x4s and pipe lagged securely to the wall makes excellent wood storage. Here, it makes use of wall space that's not practical for other uses.

A lumber shed at the shop of Kelly Mehler provides lots of storage possibilities. This open-ended rack makes it easy to see what's available.

Woodcarver David Monhollen has ready access to lumber that's stored upright. He can easily leaf through what he has on hand.

Another approach for short scraps is to make a storage bin from short lengths of PVC pipe. In these makeshift bins, you can sort short pieces of moulding, lumber and dowel for easy retrieval when you need them.

PANEL PRODUCTS NEED THEIR OWN KIND OF STORAGE

Panel goods are a mainstay of many cabinetmaking jobs and shops often gather a good assortment of them: MDF, veneer-core plywood, high-strength Baltic-birch plywood, particleboard for countertops. A time will come for all of them. And because most panel goods come in 4' x 8' sheets, there is often a good deal of leftover when a job has been completed so you may find yourself the curator of many pieces in different thicknesses and materials.

Their size dictates that panels be stored on edge. Very few shops will have the kind of room you need to store panels flat. And besides, unless you have a lot of one kind of panel, this is probably the least practical of all storage solutions because you'll have to move a lot of material to get the one sheet you need (remember that a 4' x 8' sheet of MDF weighs nearly 100 pounds).

A practical solution is to build a narrow rack, a couple feet wide and 8' long, to hold panels on edge. Locate it so you can pull a full sheet of plywood straight out without running into anything else. The width can be divided into two or more individual bays to help you organize different types of panel

goods – ¾"-hardwood plywood can go in one, a mixed lot of sheet goods in the others. Make the bottom of the rack smooth and flat so the sheets will slide easily and elevate it slightly from the rest of the floor (hardwood plywood is ideal for this). This works especially well if you have a shop with a concrete floor – it's hard work to drag plywood across rough concrete, and it's tough on the material.

Unless you have a very large shop with lots of wall space, try not to store plywood against a wall so you have to approach it from the side. Only the top sheet will be readily accessible (everything else will have to be moved to get to sheets on the inside) and it is virtually impossible not to lean offcuts and shorts against the pile. Before you know it, the sheet of plywood you need is buried beneath a pile of scrap lumber you don't want to handle.

Whenever sheet goods are stored on edge, take care to get them as vertical as possible and rotate unused sheets once in

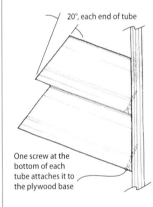

20°, each end of tube

One screw at the bottom of each tube attaches it to the plywood base

Each row of tubes is cut to be 1½" longer than the row above

Metal strap keeps unit together

This storage bin is made from sections of 4" PVC posts. Its graduated rows provide lots of inexpensive storage for just about anything a shop produces, including short scraps.

In Scott Phillips' large workshop, panel goods can be stored upright against a wall. Rotate the panels once in a while if they sit around so they don't develop a bow.

These metal racks, in the workshop of Tom Willenborg, hold a lot of plywood. Storing panel goods on edge, as Willenborg does in the rack in the foreground, saves floor space and makes access relatively easy.

Jigs and patterns are another kind of material that most shops have plenty of. Furniture-maker Troy Sexton is in good company keeping them on a wall over a bench.

a while. If not, the sheet will take on a bow that will make it tough to build straight cabinets and shelves. One way to avoid this if you do store plywood against a wall is to secure it flat against the wall with bungee cords or rope so it can't sag.

LIQUID STORAGE: PAINTS, STAINS, FINISHES & GLUE

The many liquid materials that woodshops accumulate present their own storage and handling challenges. In some cases, liquids can present safety hazards if not handled carefully.

Finishes come in a wide variety, from water-based latex paints to lacquers and shellacs made with volatile solvents. In general, water-based finishes must be protected from freezing temperatures if they are to remain useful.

Solvent-based finishes are not as temperature sensitive, but they are usually more flammable and the powerful solvents they contain can be a fire or explosive hazard in an enclosed space. Companies that specialize in safety equipment sell metal cabinets made specifically for hazardous liquids – it's a good investment if you have a lot of finish on hand and want to protect your shop from the possibility of fire.

Finishes also don't last forever. Polymerizing oils, varnishes and similar finishes have a way of turning into thick gunk over time. It's a good practice to mark the cans with the date of purchase, or the date on which they were mixed if you make your own brew, so that you know when they should

be retired. (When the time comes, don't toss them out the back door or dump them down the drain. Contact your local municipal offices or state environmental office for advice on getting rid of expired finishes.)

Try to store finishes out of direct sunlight and away from sources of heat. They will last longer.

Glue is another material that can be sensitive to time, sunlight and temperature. Yellow and white polyvinyl acetate glues (Titebond and Elmer's Carpenter's Glue, for example) as well as liquid hide glues are happier if they are not allowed to freeze. Even if still in a liquid state, these glues should not be used if they are too cold because the bond will not be reliable – check the label for the specifics. If you have a heated space for water-based finishes, store your glue in there as well.

Epoxy and other two-part adhesives that are not water-based don't need as much

Some materials common to woodworking shops are hazardous if not handled properly. Rags soaked in oil finish can ignite spontaneously if they are not spread out to dry or immersed in a pail of water.

A locker specifically designed for flammable materials is a good investment. Its double-wall construction would help prevent the spread of fire.

This easy-to-build cabinet holds a series of plastic trays – perfect for storing everything from ferrules to rivets.

Wire shelving helps turner Judy Ditmer stay organized. These shelves not only hold a lot of material, their design promotes air circulation.

Ditmer's system includes a labeling system for material stored on shelves. It makes identification and retrieval much easier.

hand-holding although these adhesives do have a limited life span. The manufacturer of West Systems epoxy says this adhesive has a shelf life of about one year from the date of manufacture.

Polyurethane glue and liquid hide glue also are given about a year's shelf life from the time of manufacture before they should be discarded. Glue that comes in powder form can pick up moisture from the air over time. As with finish, it's a good idea to keep an eye on glue containers and get rid of those that are no longer reliable. Glue is one of those things you should buy as you go and use when it's fresh.

NUTS, BOLTS & ALL THOSE OTHER LOOSE ENDS

Most of us have trouble keeping our shops organized. Even with the best of intentions, nails, screws and everything else too small to bother with ends up in a couple coffee cans under the bench. In time, we have absolutely no idea what's in them. The fastener we need is often easier to replace at the hardware store than to find under our haphazard storage system.

Open bins and trays for the fasteners used most frequently can help. With a few hours to spare and a bit of ½" plywood, you can make a stack of sturdy storage containers that will hold a dozen kinds of wood screws in plain view. These stackable containers can be parked on a shelf and pulled out when you need something.

Plastic storage bins – either those with flip-up tops or banks of small drawers – are

an excellent way of organizing very small parts that you don't need many of and don't use all the time.

Sandpaper is another commodity item that's easy to lose track of. A few pieces of leftover hardboard or plywood can be turned into a storage rack with multiple shelves in very little time. Even if your system is as simple as lumping "rough," "medium" and "fine" grits of paper with each other it will save you time.

For bulk storage, there are a variety of low-cost avenues to explore. Used kitchen cabinets are worth looking at (skip cheaply made cabinets because they won't last). Yard sales, used furniture stores and newspaper classified ads all are good places to look.

If all this organization makes you nervous, try to remember that it really will make the shop safer, because it eliminates clutter, and more enjoyable, because it eliminates the frustration of never finding what you need. It's worth a try.

Rules for Workbenches

by Christopher Schwarz

When it comes to building or buying a bench, most woodworkers get wrapped up in what form it should take. Should it be a continental bench popularized by Frank Klausz? A Shaker bench like the one at the Hancock community? How about a British version like Ian Kirby's?

Copying a well-known form is a natural tack to take. After all, when woodworkers buy or build their first workbench, they are in the early stages of learning the craft. They don't know what sort of bench or vises they need, or why one bench looks different than another. So they pick a form that looks good to them – occasionally mixing and matching bits and pieces from different forms – and get busy.

That, I believe, is the seed of the problem with workbenches today. Many commercial workbenches are missing key functions that make work-holding easier. And many classic bench forms get built with modifications that make them frustrating in use.

What's worse, the user might not even know that he or she is struggling. Woodworking is a solitary pursuit, and it's rare to use someone else's bench.

I've built a number of classic bench forms, and I've worked on craftsman-made and commercial benches of different stripes. I've been stunned by how awful some workbenches can be at some tasks, and I've also seen brilliantly realized designs.

And now, after all this work, I've concluded that it doesn't matter what sort of bench you have as long as it performs a set of core functions with ease. I've boiled down these core functions into 10 rules for building (or buying) a workbench. As long as your bench obeys these rules (or most of them), you will be able to hold almost any workpiece for any task with a minimum of fuss.

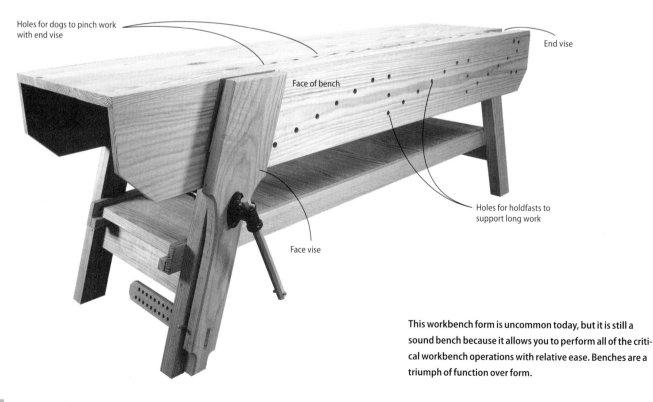

Holes for dogs to pinch work with end vise

End vise

Face of bench

Face vise

Holes for holdfasts to support long work

This workbench form is uncommon today, but it is still a sound bench because it allows you to perform all of the critical workbench operations with relative ease. Benches are a triumph of function over form.

This rig serves as the assembly bench in the *Popular Woodworking* shop, but if you put a vise on it somewhere, it probably could serve as a workbench in a production shop. It is simple and allows great flexibility for clamping. But some basic operations with this setup would be tricky.

This French-style workbench weighs more than 325 pounds. The top is 4" thick. The legs are 5" square. All this mass absorbs vibration and makes every cutting operation smoother.

DO YOU EVEN NEED A BENCH?

Before we get to the rules, it's fair to say that a lot of the best commercial woodworking today is done on benches that disregard many of these rules. In production shops, it's rare to find a traditional bench used in a traditional manner. More often, a commercial woodworker will have something akin to a clamping table, or even a door on sawhorses. And they can turn out high-quality work that will blow you away.

In 2006 I was teaching a class in hand work at a school where Thomas Stangeland, a maestro at Greene & Greene-inspired work, was also teaching a class. Though we both strive for the same result in craftsmanship, the processes we use couldn't be more different. He builds furniture for a living, and he enjoys it. I build furniture because I enjoy it, and I sell an occasional piece.

One evening we each gave a presentation to the students about our work and I showed an image of the enormous French workbench I'd built the year before and discussed its unusual history.

Thomas then got up and said he wished he had a picture of his workbench: a door on a couple horses. He said that a commercial shop had no time to waste on building a traditional bench. And with his power-tool approach, all he needs is a flat surface.

It's hard to argue with the end result. His furniture is beautiful.

But what's important here is that while you can build with the door-off-the-floor approach, there are many commercial woodworkers who still see the utility of a traditional workbench. Chairmaker and furniture maker Brian Boggs uses more newfangled routers and shop-made devices with aluminum extrusions than I have ever seen. And he still has two enormous traditional workbenches that see constant use. Before Kelly Mehler opened a woodworking school, I visited his commercial shop and got a chance to inspect his vintage bench, which saw daily use.

The point is that a good bench won't make you a better woodworker, and a not-quite-a-bench won't doom you to failure. But a good bench will make many operations easier. It's simply a tool: the biggest clamp in the shop.

Rule No. 1: Always Add Mass

Always overbuild your workbench by adding mass. There is a saying in boatbuilding: If it looks fair, it is fair. For workbenches, here's a maxim: If it looks stout, then make it doubly so. Everything about a workbench takes punishment that is akin to a kitchen chair in a house full of 8-year-old boys.

Early Roman workbenches were built like a Windsor chair. Stout legs were tenoned into a massive top and wedged in place. Traditional French workbenches had massive tops (6" thick), with legs that were big enough to be called tree trunks. Later workbenches relied more on engineering than mass. The classic continental-style workbench uses a trestle design and dovetails in the aprons and vises to create

Spindly workbenches are nothing new. This anemic example from the early 20th century is too small and lacks mass. Sadly, there are modern ones that are even worse.

a bench for the ages. The 19th-century English workbench uses an early torsion-box design to create a stable place to work. And good-quality modern workbenches use threaded rods and bolts to tighten up a design that lacks mass.

Many inexpensive commercial benches are ridiculously rickety. They sway and rack under hand pressure. You can push them across your shop by performing simple operations: routing, sawing, planing.

A big thick top and stout legs add mass that will help your work. Heavy cabinet saws with lots of cast iron tend to run smoother. The same goes with benches. Once your bench hits about 300 pounds, it won't move unless you want it to move.

Rule No. 2: Use Stout Joints
Overbuild your workbench by using the best joints. These are times to whip out the through-tenon and dovetail.

If you followed rule No. 1, then rule No. 2 should be no problem. Your joints will be sized to fit the massive scale of your components. If you cannot rely on mass, then you should beef things up with superior joinery. Dovetails and through-tenons work well for a bench.

That's because you are applying racking force to the workbench with typical operations and your vises will do their best to tear apart your bench. All wooden vises need to be overbuilt or they will self-destruct when you cinch them down hard. I've even seen a vise rip a benchtop from its base.

Make your tenons thick and your mortises deep. If you know how to drawbore a

Think big when cutting the joints for your workbench. The small tenons are 1¼" thick and 2½" long. The larger tenons are 2½" thick and 2" long.

mortise-and-tenon joint, this is one good application. Have you ever been in a timber-framed barn? Did you look at the joints? They're massive and pegged. Imitate that.

I think benches are a good place to practice your skills at cutting these classic joints, but some woodworkers still resist. If that's you, you should investigate hardware to strengthen your bench. Threaded rods, bed bolts, Veritas bench bolts or even stove bolts can turn a spindly assembly into something rigid that can be snugged up if it loosens. The hardware won't give you mass, but it will strengthen a rickety assembly.

Rule No. 3: Pick Your Wood Based on Its Stiffness, Not Its Species
Use a stiff, inexpensive and common wood to build your bench. I'd rather have a construction-lumber bench that followed all these rules than a beautiful European beech bench that skipped even one of these concepts.

European cabinetmakers didn't choose beech because of some magic quality of *Fagus sylvatica*. They chose it because it was dense, stiff, plentiful and inexpensive. In the United States, beech is dense, stiff, hard to find and (sometimes) a bit spendy. You can, of course, use it to build a bench, but you will pay a pretty penny for the privilege. And it will have no demonstrable advantage over a bench built from a cheaper species.

Other woodworkers, tacking toward the sensible, use hard or soft maple for their benches, rationalizing that it is like the beech of the New World. And indeed, the maples have all the qualities of a good species for a workbench.

Maple is stiff, resists denting and can span long distances without much of a support structure below it. But so can other species. In fact, if you went by the numbers from the wood technologists alone, you'd build your bench from shagbark hickory, despite its difficult nature. Once you look at the characteristics that make a good species for a workbench, you'll see that white oak, Southern yellow pine, fir or just about any species (excepting basswood and the soft white pines) will perform fine.

Rule No. 4: Use a Tested Design
After you sketch out your workbench design but before you cut any wood, compare your design with historical designs of benches. If

your bench appears to be a radical design or looks unlike anything built before, chances are your design is flawed.

I've seen workbenches with pneumatic face vises. Why? I've seen a workbench that had two twin-screw vises: One vise for the right end of the workbench that was matched to work with two long rows of dogs along the length of the benchtop; and a second twin-screw vise on the face of the bench that was matched to two more rows of dogs across the width of the bench.

Now I'm certain that there are a few woodworkers who would really need this arrangement – perhaps someone who has to work on a circular tabletop on one end of the bench and a Windsor chair seat at the other. But for most people who build cabinets and furniture, this setup is redundant and neglects some critical bench functions.

Rule No. 5: The Overall Dimensions of Your Bench Are Critical

Your bench design cannot be too heavy or too long. But its top can easily be too wide or too tall. I think your benchtop should be as long as possible. Find the wall where your workbench will go (hint: Pick the wall that has a window). Measure that space. Subtract four feet from that measurement and that's a good length for the top. Note: The benchtop must be at least 5' long unless you build only small-scale items. Furniture-sized parts typically range up to 48" long and you want to support these fully with a little room to spare.

It is difficult to make or imagine a workbench that is too long. The same goes for thickness. It is the thickness that allows the top to be that long. If you make the top really thick (4" or more), then it will offer unerring support and allow you to build your bench without any support system beneath. The top can perch on the legs and will not sag under its own weight.

The width is a different matter. You can have a bench that is too wide for a one-person shop. I've worked on benches that are 36" wide and they have downsides. For starters, if you park them against the wall you'll have to stretch to reach the tools hanging on the wall. If you assemble projects on your bench, you will find yourself dancing around it a lot more than you should.

But there's more. Cabinetwork is sized in standard chunks. These sizes come from the human body; they aren't arbitrary. A kitchen's base cabinet is generally 24" deep and 34½" high. This is important for a couple reasons. First: It means you don't really need a bench that's much more than 24" deep to build cabinets. With that 24" depth, you actually get some advantages, including the fact that you can clamp the cabinet to your bench from as many as three sides of your bench. That's dang handy. A deep bench allows you to clamp your cabinets to the bench on only two sides (with a couple exceptions).

Now I'm not going to argue with you if you build really big stuff or have a bench that you share with another woodworker facing you; you might need more depth. But if you are like the rest of us, a 24"-deep bench is a powerful and right-sized tool.

On the issue of workbench height: Many bench builders worry about it and there are a wide variety of rules and advice. The bottom line is the bench must fit you and your work. And in the end, there are no hard-and-fast rules. I wish there were. Some people like low benches; some like them high.

So consider the following as a good place to start. After taking in my crackpot theories, your next stop should be a friend's house or a woodworking supply store to use their benches and get a feel for what is right.

Here is my experience with bench height: I started with a bench that was 36" high, which seemed right for someone who is 6' 3⅝" tall. And for machine woodworking I was right. The high bench brought the work close to my eyes. I loved it. And then my passion for handwork reared its ugly head.

If you get into hand tools, a high bench becomes less attractive. I started with a jack plane and a few smoothing planes. They worked OK with a high bench, but I became fatigued quickly.

After reading the screed on bench heights, I lowered the height of my 36" bench. It seemed radical, but one day I got the nerve up and sawed 2" off the legs. Those two inches changed my attitude toward planing.

The 34"-bench height allowed me to use my long leg muscles to propel the plane forward instead of my arms.

These classic European workbenches were made from fine-grained steamed European beech. Shouldn't you do the same? Not necessarily. Choose a wood that is like beech is in Europe: stiff, inexpensive and plentiful.

Here's proof that odd workbench designs are nothing new. This Hammacher, Schlemmer & Co. bench from an old catalog is a study in tool storage. I've seen one of these in person and I can say this: I would not want to have to build anything using it.

This early 20th-century airplane factory had the right idea when it came to workbench length. With a long bench, you can work on one end and assemble at the other – no need for an assembly bench. Thus, a big bench actually saves floorspace.

Now, before you build your next bench at 34" high, stop for a minute. That might not be right for you. Do you use wooden stock planes? If so, you need to consider that the wooden body planes can hold your arms about 3" to 4" higher off the workbench than a metal plane can. As a result, a wooden plane user's workbench should be lower.

This is as good reason as ever to get to know someone who has a good shop you can visit and discuss your ideas with. It is better not to make this decision on paper alone.

But there are other factors you must consider when settling on the bench's height. How tall are you? If you are over 6' tall, you should scale your bench a bit higher. Start high and cut it down if it's too high. And prop it up on some blocks of wood if it's too low. Experiment. It's not a highboy; it's a workbench.

Here are other things to consider: Do you work with machinery? If so, a bench that's 34" from the floor – or a bit lower – can be good. The top of a table saw is typically 34" from the floor, so a workbench could be (at most) a great outfeed table or (at least) not in the way of your crosscutting and ripping.

Of course, everyone wants a ballpark idea for where to start. So here it is: Stand up straight and drop your arms against your sides in a relaxed manner. Measure from the floor to the place where your pinky joins your hand. That has been the sweet spot for me.

Rule No. 6: Benches Must Hold the Work in Three Ways

All benches should be able to grip the wood so you can easily work on the faces, the ends and the edges. Many commercial benches fail on this point.

Submit your bench to what I call the Kitchen Cabinet Door Test. Imagine a typical kitchen door that is ¾" thick, 15" wide and 23" long. How would you affix that door flat on your bench to level its joints and then sand (or plane) it flat? How would you clamp the door so you could work on the ends to trim the top rail and tops of the stiles so the door will fit its opening? And how will you secure that door on edge so you can rout its hinge mortise and plane off the saw-blade marks without the door flopping around? Does your bench pass this test? OK, now ask the same questions with a door that is ¾" x 15" x 38". And then try a board that is ¾" x 12" x 6'.

How you accomplish each of these three functions is up to you and your taste and budget. To work on the faces of boards, you can use a planing stop, a grippy sanding pad, a tail vise with dogs, clamps or hold-downs.

To work on the ends of boards, you can choose a shoulder vise (especially for dovetailing), a metal quick-release vise, a leg vise or a twin-screw vise. And you can use all of these in conjunction with a clamp across your bench. The vise holds one corner of the work; the clamp holds the other corner.

Working the long edges of boards is tricky with most benches. In fact, most benches make it difficult to work the edges of long boards, doors or face frames. There are a couple ways to solve this. Older benches had the front edge of the benchtop flush with the front of the legs and stretchers so you could clamp your frames and long boards to the legs. And the older benches also would have a sliding deadman (sometimes called a board jack). It would slide back and forth and had an adjustable peg to support the work from below. Another old form of bench, an English design, had a

Here is how high my workbench is compared to my hand, which is hanging loosely by my side. I use hand and power tools in my work, and I've found this height is ideal.

Most benches are easy to set up to work on the faces of boards or assemblies. In this example, a door is clamped between dogs. You can even work simpler and plane against a planing stop.

Working on the ends of boards – especially wide boards – can be a challenge for face vises. Adding a clamp to the setup stabilizes the work for sawing or whatever.

This primitive bench still allows you to work on long edges of boards. The crochet (or hook) grips the board. Holdfasts and a scrap support from below. Simple and brilliant.

wide front apron that came down from the top that was bored with holes for a peg to support long work.

Rule No. 7: Make Your Bench Friendly to Clamps

Your bench is a three-dimensional clamping surface. Anything that interferes with clamping work to your benchtop (aprons, a drawer bank, doors, supports etc.) can make some operations a challenge.

There is a trend in workbench design that I personally find troubling. It's a knee-jerk reaction to a common American complaint: We don't think we have enough space in our shops to store our tools and accessories. And how do we solve this problem with our workbenches? By designing them like kitchen cabinets with a countertop work surface.

This design approach gives us lots of drawers below the benchtop, which is great for storing the things you reach for every day. It also can make your bench a pain in the hiney to use for many common operations, such as clamping things to your bench.

Filling up the space below the benchtop also prohibits you from using any type of holdfast or holddown that I'm aware of.

If you build drawers below the top, how will you clamp objects to the benchtop to work with them? Typically, the banks of drawers below the benchtop prohibit a typical F-style clamp from sneaking in there and lending a hand with the setup. So you can't use a typical clamp to affix a router template to the bench. There are ways around these problems (a tail vise comes to mind) but the tail vise can be a challenge to install, set and use.

You can try to cheat (as I have) and install the drawer bank so there is a substantial space underneath the benchtop for holdfasts and clamps. Or you can give your bench a large overhang to allow clamping (as some Shaker-style workbenches did) but then you have to start engineering a way to hold long boards and assemblies on edge.

Rule No. 8: There are Good Rules for Placing the Vises on Your Bench

Place your vises so they work with your tools. Vises confuse many workbench builders. They're bewildering if you've never spent much time working at a bench to develop a taste for the peccadilloes of all the idiosyncratic forms. There are a lot of weird configurations in the world, from a table with no vises to the bench with a vise on every corner.

Classic workbenches have some sort of vise at the front left corner of the bench. This is called the face vise. Why is it at the left? When we work with hand tools, especially planes, right-handers work from right to left. So having the vise at the left end of the bench is handy because you will always be planing into the vise that is gripping your work, and the work can be braced against the screws of the vise. So if you are a lefty, placing your vise on the front right corner makes sense.

So with that left corner occupied by a vise, where are you going to put the a second vise that is designed to grip boards so you can work on their faces? (The classic vise for this is a tail vise.) Well the right side of the bench is free (for right-handers) and there is no disadvantage to placing it there, so that's where it generally goes.

Messing with this arrangement can be trouble. I've seen face vises on the right

Here's another historical bench that shows some difficulties. The drawers will interfere with clamping things down to the bench. With no dogs or tail vise, this bench could be frustrating to work on.

corner of the bench of people who are right-handed. They said they liked it better for crosscutting with a handsaw. But when and if you start handplaning, that vise will be in the way because it won't be ideal for gripping long stock. It will be holding the tail end of the board and the plane will be trying to pull it out of the vise.

Rule No. 9: No Fancy Finishes

When finishing a workbench, less is more. A shiny film finish allows your work to scoot all over the bench. And a film finish will crack when struck by a hammer or dead-blow mallet. Choose a finish that is easy to apply, offers some protection and doesn't build up a thick film. I like an oil/varnish blend (sold as Danish Oil), or just boiled linseed oil.

Rule No. 10: Get a Window Seat

Try to place your bench against a wall and under a window, especially if you use hand tools. The wall braces the workbench as you are planing cross-grain and sawing. The light from the window points out the flaws in the work that your hand tools are trying to remove. (When I work with hand tools, I turn the overhead lights off. I can see much better with fewer light sources.)

For machine work, I find that placing the bench by a window helps with some operations, though not all. When power sanding, for example, the raking window light points

out scratches better than overhead fluorescents.

In general, when working with power tools, I tend to pull my workbench away from the wall so I can work on all sides of it. When working with routers, you sometimes have to work with odd clamping setups so that you can rout around a template. So having access to all four sides of the bench is handy. Power tool setups thrive on overhead light – and lots of it. So being by the window is nice, but not as necessary.

Most workbench books begin with a grand statement about how the workbench is the most useful tool in the shop. I'm not so sure I agree with that statement as it stands. I think it's correct to say that a well-designed, solidly built and properly outfitted bench is the most useful tool in the workshop. Anything less is only making you struggle.

An oil-varnish blend (any brand) is an ideal finish for a workbench. It resists stains, doesn't build up a film and is easy to apply. Two coats are all I ever use.

You do need to be able to pull your bench away from the wall on occasion. When I am assembling cabinets, I'll clamp them to the benchtop so I'm able to get around the bench. The same goes when I'm routing. Note how I'm harnessing the window light.

With your workbench against the wall, you have the wall and the mass of your bench holding things steady as you saw your workpieces. You also can keep your tools at arm's length. And, the windows cast a useful light on your workbench.

Dust Collection

by Scott Gibson

It's tempting to think of sawdust as little more than a nuisance, a housekeeping problem like mud tracked across a clean kitchen floor. Sawdust is more ominous than that. It does seem to get in every nook and cranny in the shop, clogging machines, filling pockets and eventually finding its way into the house. But sawdust poses real health risks to anyone who regularly spends time in a woodshop.

Exposure to sawdust can cause a variety of health problems, including dermatitis (inflammation of the skin), respiratory problems and a type of nasal cancer called adenocarcinoma. With that in mind, controlling dust is one of those necessary if unglamorous basics of setting up a shop. It's better not to ignore it.

It's hard to eliminate sawdust completely. Unless you do nothing more than whittle spoons with a jackknife, sawdust is an inevitable part of virtually every part of woodworking. Most power tools produce plenty of the stuff but it is the very small particles, those up to about 1 micron in size, rather than big chips that do the most damage. Effects vary by species, with a number of domestic and exotic hardwoods causing the most potential problems.

There are a variety of ways of controlling dust. Strategies can be broken into three broad categories: controlling dust where it's produced, clearing the dust that escapes into the shop air, and, finally, protecting yourself with a good dust mask or respirator.

It's unrealistic to think that dust collection can be covered in a single chapter. We can look at the basics, but it's a topic worth studying in some detail as you're setting up your shop or when you decide to upgrade dust-collection equipment you already have. Look for books on the topic, such as Sandor Nagyszalanczy's "Woodshop Dust Control" (Taunton Press) or visit the U.S. Department of Labor's web site (osha.gov/SLTC/etools/woodworking/wood_dust.html).

It will be worth your time.

BIG MACHINES MEAN LOTS OF DUST AND CHIPS

Almost all woodworking equipment jettisons chips and dust, some of them a surprisingly large amount. The faster a machine is designed to hog through wood, the more dust and chips it will throw into the air unless you're ready to intervene. Really prolific producers such as shapers, thickness planers and jointers tend to produce big, fluffy chips (assuming the knives are sharp) while sanders produce very fine dust. Dust-collection equipment effective for dust may not be as effective with large chips.

The first line of defense is to capture sawdust where it is produced – right at the machine. That's much more effective than trying to clean a shop's worth of air. (That said, room-sized air cleaners can be helpful in collecting what does get away. We'll cover those later.)

Festool's approach makes dust collection an integral part of tool design. Its full line of portable power tools can be connected to a shop vacuum. Even the circular saw has a built-in dust-collection port.

This Fein Turbo III Dust Extractor is typical of a well-designed shop vacuum that can be used for low-volume dust collection. Set to an automatic mode, the vacuum will turn on at the same time as the tool plugged into it.

As much as that seems like common sense, many tools are remarkably ineffective in helping you capture the dust they generate. While many random-orbit and orbital block sanders come equipped with dust filters or bags, for example, some sanders have no dust-gathering capabilities at all, nor is there an obvious way of making one. To take another example, contractor-style tablesaws (the ones with open-frame bases) are notoriously difficult to fit with effective dust collection. There are simply too many ways for the dust to escape.

Conversely, some European tools seem far ahead of their American counterparts on this score. Over-the-blade dust collection on table saws, which is very effective, is readily available on some European saws but is not standard on saws produced here or those made in the Far East and sold here.

Festool makes a line of portable power tools that are designed to work with the company's shop vacuums. Routers, circular saws sanders and even jigsaws all are equipped with dust-collection hoods or adapters that make it easy to connect the tool to the vacuum. Best of all, the systems actually work.

So one rule of thumb is to think about dust collection when you buy a tool. It may not be the only deciding factor, but it's worth throwing in the mix. To go back to table saws, a cabinet saw with an enclosed base and an integral dust-collection port is inherently more effective than a contractor's saw. Not perfect, but a lot better. It's one of the safety features you get by spending a little more money.

In the end, tools that have been designed with this feature in mind tend to do a much better job than those with something that's been cobbled together after the fact.

SHOP VACUUMS ARE BETTER THAN BAGS OR ON-BOARD FILTERS

Shop vacuums do an admirable job of gathering dust from tools that create a low volume of dust, such as sanders, routers and circular saws. They are probably not going to be enough for a table saw and other stationary machines that produce higher volumes of chips and dust. Some tools come with dust-collection adapters, making it easy to take advantage of a shop vacuum for dust collection. But this is not universally true and for some tools you may have to

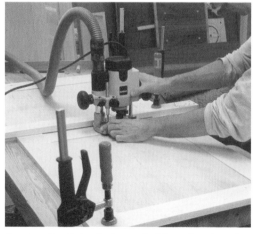

A router with a dust-collection port will keep shop air much cleaner. And without all those chips flying around, it's a lot easier to see what you're doing.

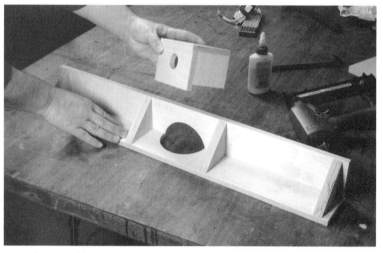

Dust collection can be designed right into jigs and fixtures. This router fence includes a tightly fitted dust-collection hood for efficient pickup.

fashion your own or look for alternate dust control options.

I discovered how effective a shop vacuum can be a couple years ago after I inadvertently stepped on the rigid dust filter that came with my random-orbit sander. I was too cheap to buy a new filter so I connected my vacuum to the sander. If the dust filter was moderately effective, the vacuum was a revelation. It sucked up every speck of dust. Shop air stayed perfectly clean. And it takes a long time to fill up a shop vacuum bag with dust from a random-orbit sander.

The arrangement worked so well that I chucked the dust bag that never worked on my biscuit joiner and switched to the shop vacuum. It's somewhat awkward to be tethered to a vacuum, but the arrangement works beautifully from the standpoint of dust.

Good shop vacuums aren't cheap, but they are more efficient and quieter than bargain-basement machines. Look for one with a feature allowing you to plug the tool directly into the vacuum. The vacuum turns on automatically with the tool and shuts off a few seconds after you release the trigger on the tool. This feature is very useful when the vacuum will do double duty as dust collector as well as shop cleaner.

The other area of concern is the filter. It doesn't do any good to pay for a good-quality vacuum and allow it to spew dust back into the air because the filter's mesh size is too big to trap small particles. Filters can be made from either fabric or paper, or come as a pleated element. Just look for one that traps particles down to about 1 micron. You may have to buy an aftermarket filter, but it will be worth the cost.

A PORTABLE DUST COLLECTOR CAN ROLL TO WHEREVER IT'S NEEDED

When it comes to machines that produce a high volume of sawdust and chips, a shop vacuum will quickly be overpowered. They are not powerful enough or large enough for these tools – you'll have to turn to a dedicated dust collector. A portable, single-stage dust collector may be the right answer for a small shop. These machines, made by a number of manufacturers and widely available, cost about $250 to $350. That's about the same price as a top-quality shop vacuum.

Single-stage collectors draw debris through an impeller and send it into a col-

lector. Typically, the collector consists of a pair of fabric bags, one above and one below a central collar. The idea is that big chips will accumulate in the bottom bag and the upper bag will trap finer dust.

In contrast, a more expensive two-stage dust collector separates chips and dust before debris encounters the fan's impeller. One way of making one-stage collectors more convenient (and behave more like a two-stage machine) is to add a separator in the duct between the tool and the dust collector.

These devices are pretty simple: they consist of a plastic lid that fits over a metal garbage can. The lid has two ports – one for the incoming duct from the tool and the other to carry what's left to the collector. They are designed to separate larger chips from finer dust and reduce the load on the impeller in the collector. They're available through mail order suppliers.

Single-stage collectors typically run on 120-volt (v) current and have 1½ horsepower (hp) motors. They can be wheeled around the shop and connected to whatever machine is running, or connected to a series of closely grouped machines that are equipped with blast gates to control the flow of air. This class of dust collector is really suited to a single machine running at a time, not a shop's worth of tools all generating chips and dust simultaneously.

There are two important benchmarks for dust collectors. One is the volume of air the machine can draw, measured in cubic feet per minute (cfm); the other is how quickly the air moves, which is described in feet per minute (fpm). According to books and magazine articles on the subject, to keep up with a 12" thickness planer (a big chip producer) the dust collector should move at least 600 cfm of air at between 3,500 and 4,000 fpm. A larger planer will require a minimum of about 800 cfm. Some of these machines are capable of that.

Another important factor in dust-collector efficiency is the size of the ducts. Portable, single-stage machines generally have inlet sizes of 4" to 6". Larger-diameter hoses are more efficient because they move a greater volume of air at a lower static pressure (resistance) than small diameter hoses. Performance goes downhill as the number of sharp bends and overall length of the run goes up. Shorter and straighter runs of

This shop-made blast gate for a shop vacuum allows two tools to be connected at the same time. A simple toggle switch opens one inlet port at a time.

Hose and duct diameter is one critical factor in the efficiency of a dust-collection system. Large diameter duct moves more air at a lower static pressure.

duct will make for a happier dust collector so get the collector as close as you can to the machine it's servicing.

Finally, there's the filter itself. As is the case with shop vacuums, unless the filter can capture particles down to about 1 micron in size, a lot of harmful dust will simply be returned to the shop air and, inevitably, delivered to your lungs. Some machines come equipped with a 1-micron bag and some do not, but it is definitely a factor in choosing a machine. If the collector comes with, say, a 30-micron bag you should replace it with a felted fabric bag or a more effective cartridge-type filter. That will add $100 or more to the cost of the collector.

LARGER SYSTEMS COVER AN ENTIRE SHOP

For larger shops, or woodworkers with larger budgets, a central dust collector that handles all tools in the shop through a system of fixed ducts is a big step up in terms of convenience if not efficiency. This is the kind of system you'll find in a production shop, but they also can be sized to meet the needs of a smaller woodshop.

In a central system, a two-stage collector pulls chips and dust through a duct system to a collector where fine dust and larger chips are separated. Chips go into a barrel or similar collector and dust is filtered through one or more cloth bags or a cartridge-type filter. In these respects, a central system is doing just what a portable collector does. But the more powerful motors can pull chips and dust over greater distances while the more efficient collectors (particularly the cyclone collectors) are better at separating debris. And you don't have to move the collector from machine to machine.

A good cyclone collector for a small shop – something like the 2hp model from Oneida Air Systems or Grizzly – is several times the cost of a portable collector. But it has some real advantages, including a large cartridge filter, magnetic controls that can be operated remotely and a blower that can move air at a rate of more than 1,300 cfm.

Duct layout is an important – and complicated – part of designing a system. Everything from the type of duct (smooth metal vs. flexible plastic) to the size of branch and main lines have an effect on the efficiency of the system. Some companies that sell this equipment will also lay out the ductwork – a helpful bonus when spending more money. If not, you'll have some homework to do in designing your own duct system.

However the ductwork is installed, it's important to ground it properly to reduce buildup of static electricity, which can decrease efficiency. Smooth metal pipes offer less resistance to air flow than flexible plastic, and they're easier to ground – good reasons why they're considered a better option.

Central collectors can be located either inside or outside the shop. Getting it outdoors saves floor space in the shop, reduces noise and is cleaner. But in a cold weather climate, such a design will also expel heated shop air. A system located inside doesn't have that problem, but it does make good filtration all the more important.

Blast gates control air flow from a chip-producing machine to the dust collector. They are readily available from woodworking supply dealers, or they can be made with a minimum of material.

Illustration by Matt Bantly

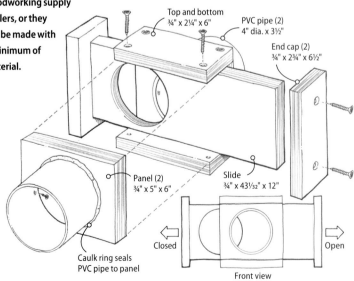

Top and bottom
¾" x 2¼" x 6"

PVC pipe (2)
4" dia. x 3½"

End cap (2)
¾" x 2¾" x 6½"

Panel (2)
¾" x 5" x 6"

Slide
¾" x 43½2" x 12"

Caulk ring seals
PVC pipe to panel

Closed

Open

Front view

AIR CLEANERS, DOWN-DRAFT TABLES AND OPEN WINDOWS

Some tools are just plain hard to connect to a collector. A power miter saw is one of those. Most seem to come equipped with dust bags designed not to capture any of the sawdust these saws produce in such prodigious quantities. Cabinet saws usually have built-in ports for dust collection, but that doesn't pick up the chips and dust thrown from the blade over the top of the saw.

The end result is that even in a shop with a good central collector and a diligent woodworker who's never too busy to use it, some dust is going to escape.

Ambient air cleaners certainly can help. These ceiling-mounted boxes, made by several companies, have two types of filtration: a flat filter that gathers large dust particles as it enters the cleaner and an inner filter bag that picks up finer particles. Fans may have several speeds as well as a remote control so you can flip on the machine from across the shop and control fan speed to suit conditions. It's more or less like using a television remote.

They are quiet enough to be left on while you're in the shop, and some have timers that can be set to clean the air for up to several hours after you're done for the day.

One downside is that filters are not cheap. On the machine I have, for instance, ordinary hardware-store furnace filters don't quite fit the box so I have to mail order the manufacturer's own brand or use shears to cut standard filters down to size. Its inner bag is difficult to clean thoroughly and a replacement costs $40. Even so, these air cleaners are an excellent auxiliary collector and a shop will be cleaner for having one.

If you want some of the same benefits without spending the $250 or so that an air-filtration unit costs, make your own. A $20 box fan and some furnace filters will re-circulate shop air and remove some of the larger debris. Just keep in mind that very small dust particles with the most potential for causing health problems will not be trapped by a makeshift air cleaner. Even spending $250 doesn't guarantee that. Air filtration systems may remove particles only down to the 3-micron size but leave damaging smaller particles suspended in the air.

But prop that box fan near an open window and dust can be jettisoned from the shop completely. Obvious cautions apply

This cyclone collector from Oneida Air Systems efficiently separates chips from fine dust and has a motor powerful enough for most small shops.

George Jaeger put his dust collection system in a bump-out along one wall of his Kentucky workshop. Windows let in the light and a removable panel gives him access for cleaning.

(not a good solution when you live in a cozy neighborhood, for example, or next door to someone with a chronic respiratory problem). But out in the country where a bit of airborne dust will do no harm, this low-tech approach to dust control is very appealing. And cheap.

A down-draft table is an excellent way of controlling sanding dust if the sander doesn't have a collection port for a shop vacuum or if you're sanding by hand. It's simply a working platform with holes drilled in it and connected via duct to your dust collection system. When the collector is turned on, it draws air (and dust) down through the top and carries it safely away.

If nothing else seems to work, use your imagination. Temporarily clamping the end of the duct at your bench with a spring clamp, for example, can be an effective way of capturing dust as it is created.

PROTECT YOURSELF WITH A GOOD DUST MASK OR RESPIRATOR

According to one article I've read, the American Conference of Industrial Hygienists says dust concentrations should be no higher than 5 milligrams per cubic meter – about the concentration you'd get if you dispersed a teaspoon of dust in a 560-square-foot shop.

This Trend Airshield provides a steady flow of filtered air from a battery-powered motor that runs four hours between charges. Turners find this type of respirator especially useful because it combines a full-face shield with respiratory protection.

A down-draft table is a great way of capturing airborne dust. Connected to a portable collector, this table will pick up dust the sander's integral dust collector is bound to miss.

That fact raises the question of why you wouldn't want to invest in a good dust mask or respirator.

At the low end are economical paper dust masks with a single elastic band that fit around the head. These are probably better suited to keeping out pollen or cat dander than the very small dust particles we should be more concerned with. Better versions have two elastic bands for a better fit, and some have small valves in the center of the mask that make it easier to exhale. These masks offer good protection against airborne dust, providing they fit snugly. Look for a mask rated by the National Institute for Occupational Safety and Health (NIOSH) – a N95 mask will remove 95 percent of the particles in the air, but if you're working with potentially hazardous dusts you may want to bump that up to a N100 rating. Throw away the mask when it gets dirty.

A cartridge-style respirator or a dust mask with a rubber gasket that fits against the face will probably provide a more secure fit than most disposable paper masks. These cost more, but the mask itself should last a long time and the filters for dust are not very expensive. Moreover, with different cartridges, a respirator also can be used for a variety of other jobs, like spraying finishes or working with solvents.

Some woodworkers prefer hooded respirators, which work on a different principle than masks. A hood or helmet and clear plastic mask cover the face and create a protected pocket of air that is supplied by a small, battery operated pump and kept clean by means of a filter. This equipment is relatively expensive, and not everyone will like working in the confines of a hood or helmet. Yet many swear by them.

SPECIAL CONCERNS: INDOOR HEATING EQUIPMENT

Dust can create special hazards in shops that share floor space with heating equipment. This is often the case in basement shops where a woodworker might be sanding a tabletop a few feet from a furnace.

By itself, a high concentration of dust can be a fire hazard. Dust also will interfere with the operation of heating equipment that draws combustion air from inside the shop. Dust can clog and ruin the burner, requiring you to call a technician on the coldest night of the year.

Direct-vent space heaters are vented to the outside via a double-walled pipe rather than a chimney. Vent pipes are formed by two concentric layers of steel, creating a pipe within a pipe. Combustion air is drawn through the outer perimeter of the pipe; exhaust gases go out through the middle. The clever design not only keeps the stack cool but it means that no shop air is used for combustion. These heaters typically run on natural gas, propane or kerosene.

If you have a conventional oil or gas furnace in the basement, call your service company and ask for the installation of a duct from the burner to the outside. That will accomplish the same thing. It won't cost that much and will save you a lot of trouble in the long run.

Electric heaters should be inspected regularly and cleaned when the heating elements show a buildup of dust. A blast of compressed air should take care of it.

Routers

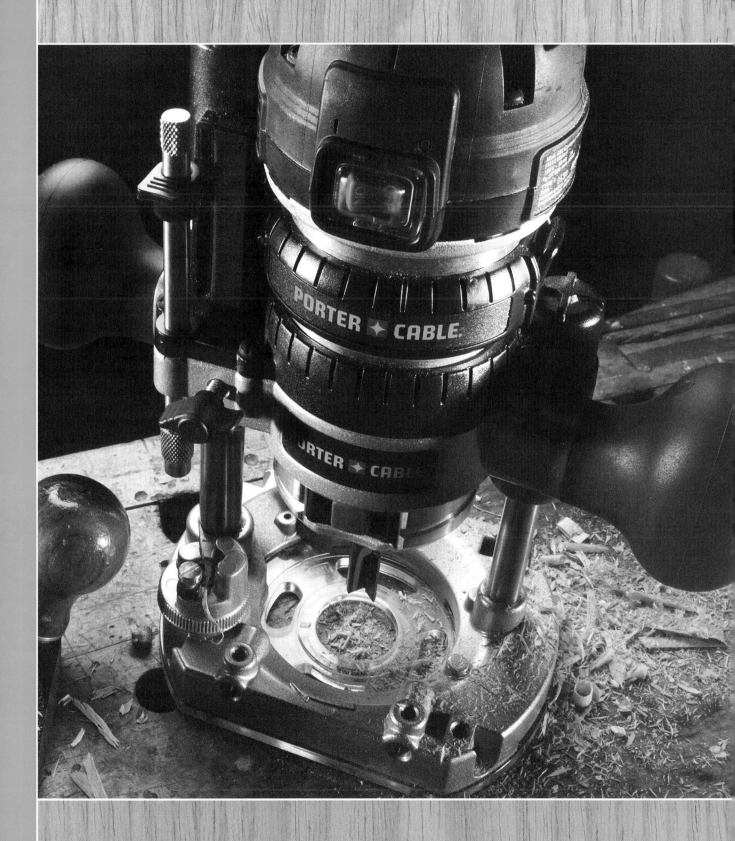

Fixed-base Router

by Nick Engler

The router is perhaps the most versatile tool in your shop. You can rout not only decorative shapes, but also many joints.

Reduced to its simplest form, the router is a motor and a shaft with means of holding interchangeable bits. Once you understand that, using the router becomes a much simpler task. But first, you should know what all those other parts are, and why they're there.

TYPES OF ROUTERS

When you look for a portable router, you will find that they can generally be classified into four categories:

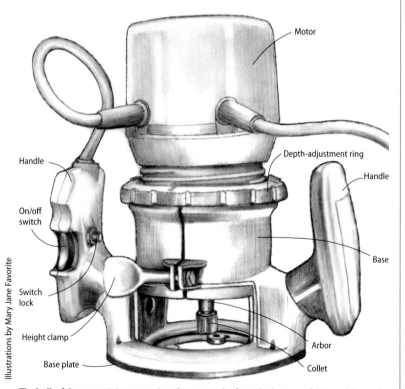

The bulk of the router is its motor. An arbor protrudes from the bottom of this, and the end of the arbor is fitted with a collet to hold a bit in place. These three pieces are mounted in a base, which incorporates a depth-adjustment ring to raise or lower the motor, and a height clamp to secure it in position – these clamps differ for the plunge router, as you'll see in the next chapter. A router also has handles so it can be guided, with a nearby on/off switch. This entire assembly rests on a removable plastic base plate or sole.

Illustrations by Mary Jane Favorite

The Basic Router

Sometimes called a fixed-base router, this is just a motor mounted on a base. Most offer ½- to 1½-horsepower motors, and their collets will accept router bits with ¼" or ½" shanks. The bases are usually 6" in diameter. This is the router we will be discussing here.

The Laminate Trimmer

A scaled-down version of the basic router, this has a smaller motor and base. It has a ¼" collet and is used for trimming laminates and veneers, and is especially handy when you are balancing the tool on thin or narrow workpieces. It's also useful for chores that require finesse, as opposed to strength. Some laminate trimmers come with interchangeable bases that let you work in tight areas or will allow you to rout at an angle, which no full-size router can.

The Rotary Tool

This lets you use very small bits and accessories for more delicate work. It's a carving or engraving tool (such as a Dremel) that can be mounted in a router base accessory. It usually has interchangeable collets for ¹⁄₁₆" or ⅛" shanks. The small size lets you rout inlays, cut mortises for small hardware, make delicate joints or do other jobs where a standard-size router would be too clumsy or difficult to balance.

The Plunge Router

This does all the things that the basic router can do, plus it makes "plunge cuts." Its motor is mounted on two spring-loaded slides above the base, which let you position the motor above the work, push the bit into the wood and begin cutting. The plunge router excels at cutting joints, such as mortises. [*Editor's Note: We will focus more on the plunge router in Chapter Two of this section.*]

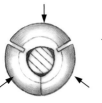

Three segments - three contact points

Multiple segments - many contact points

Collets with just 2-3 segments (left) don't squeeze router bit shanks evenly. In fact, they make contact at just a few points. Collets with multiple segments (right) are more flexible and make contact all the way around the shank, which helps keep the bit from slipping.

ROUTER FEATURES AND CAPABILITIES

No matter what kind of router you opt for, there are several features you need to understand that are important in the operation of the tool:

Collet

Although it might seem small and insignificant, the collet is crucial – a poorly designed one might let the bit slip, ruining the cut. To compensate, many woodworkers overtighten the collet, which only aggravates the problem. Overtightening makes the bits hard to mount and dismount, and can cause excessive wear on your tool.

To avoid this, make sure you get a router with a good collet. You can judge if a collet will give you problems by learning how it works. A collet is a split or segmented collar at the end of the arbor that holds the shank of the bit. Tightening a nut squeezes the collar around the shank, locking the bit.

Generally, the more segments on a collet the better, because these make the collet more flexible so it can get a better grip on the bit shank, as you can see in the drawing above. Routers with multiple-segment collets tend to be a bit more expensive, but the potential headaches they eliminate are well worth it.

Tips & Tricks

Back-routing (climb-cutting)

Occasionally you must back-rout a piece to reduce tear-out on figured wood. This means you cut with the bit's rotation, instead of against it. It's much more difficult to control your work this way, so be sure to take shallow cuts and feed very slowly. Keep the router and the work steady, making sure you don't let the bit chatter.

The Need for Speed

Despite a popular misconception, speed controllers will not harm universal motors (the type of motor found in all routers and most hand-held power tools). However, they can ruin induction motors. If you buy an in-line speed controller, be sure you use it for your portable power tools only.

A Better Bit Goes a Long Way

You should put as much, if not more, care and consideration into choosing bits as you would the machines that run them. After all, it's not the router that does the actual cutting – it's the bit. A mediocre router outfitted with a better-than-normal bit will cut a lot better than the world's greatest router with a mediocre bit.

Offset Baseplates Keep Your Router from Tipping Over

Even with half of the router base in contact with the wood surface, it can be difficult to keep the tool from tipping. When you must hang the router over an edge, as when routing an edge detail, make sure you attach an offset baseplate to the router's base. Keep the offset portion of the plate over a solid surface and press down on it as you work, thereby steadying the tool.

Photo courtesy of Patrick Warner, patwarner.com

Some routers have split arbors, rather than collets. Either way, the same rule applies: the more segments, the better.

Collets come in three standard sizes – ¼", ⅜" and ½", which is the measure of the inside diameter. Most router bits have ¼" and ½" shanks. If you want to take full advantage of all the bits available, you should look for a router with interchangeable collets.

Some routers have only ½" collets, but come with split bushing so you can adapt them to hold ¼" and ⅜" bits. This is OK, but not as desirable as interchangeable collets.

Power

The type of woodworking you want to do with the router will determine the horse-

Router bases come in a variety of sizes and shapes. The round base found on many basic routers (left) is useful for most operations, but may be slightly inaccurate when following a straightedge. If the base isn't perfectly round or perfectly centered on the router bit, turning the base (riding against the straightedge) during operation can change the distance from the bit. The D-shaped plunge router base (middle) has one straight side so you can accurately follow both straight and curved templates without concern of changing the distance to the bit. The laminate trimmer (right) has a square base with rounded corners, so you can follow straight and curved templates no matter how you turn it. You can buy an accessory base for the fixed-base router that has a straightedge, too.

power you need. If you just want to make a few occasional mouldings and joints, a 1-horsepower router should be more than sufficient. On the other hand, if you expect to do a lot of routing or if you want to use bits with large flute diameters, you should look at 2- or 3-horsepower models.

Speed

Most single-speed routers operate between 20,000 and 30,000 rpm. This is adequate for bits with flute diameters of 2" or less. But larger bits should run at slower speeds; otherwise they'll overheat and burn the wood.

If you intend to use large bits often, it might be wise to invest in a variable-speed

tool or a method of altering the speed, such as a rheostat or an electronic speed controller. Rheostats reduce the line voltage, which lowers both the speed and the available torque – the ability of your router to do serious work. Electronic speed controllers, on the other hand, have a feedback mechanism that boosts the available torque at low speeds, which means the tool is less likely to quit when the going gets tough.

Height Adjustment

Most basic routers can be raised or lowered up to 2". If you think you'll need more movement than this, you'll want to look at the plunge router. But whichever router you choose, consider the ease and accuracy with which you can change the height. Because you'll be changing the height quite often, you'll want to make it as easy as possible on yourself.

On some basic routers, the motor housings are threaded in the base so you can screw them up or down. This allows you to make minute height changes accurately. But in some respects, this arrangement is a pain in the neck. Because some on/off switches revolve with the motor, you never quite know where the switch is. And if you mount the router to a table or a stationary jig, the cord can quickly become twisted.

Switches mounted on handles or heights that adjust without spinning the motor remove this concern.

Configuration

For this, you just have to ask yourself how the router feels to you: Is it too heavy or too light when you are holding it and working with it? Can you reach all the controls without taking your hands off the handles? Is it well-balanced or does it seem top-heavy and ready to tip? Does the shape of the base help you see what you're cutting or is your workpiece hidden by the base or baseplate? Will the size/shape of the base help or hinder your work?

ROUTING RULES

The first step in using any tool is to make sure it is properly aligned and adjusted.

For the router, there are only two things you need to check. If you're using it as a portable tool, check the depth of cut (the distance the bit protrudes beneath the sole) and the position of the guide (if there is one).

The shank of the bit must be inserted far enough into the collet for the collet to get a solid grip. If possible, the entire length of the collet should contact the shank. However, don't insert the bit so far that the collet closes around the transition fillet – the portion of the bit where the shank ends and the flutes begin. If the bit is positioned incorrectly – inserted either too far or not enough – the collet may not grip the shank securely and the bit may creep out of the collet when you rout.

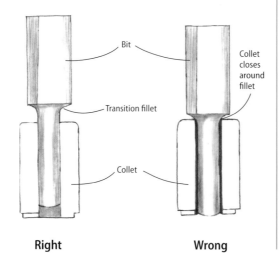

Bit

Collet closes around fillet

Transition fillet

Collet

Right　　　　　**Wrong**

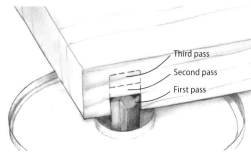

Never "hog" the cut when using a router – the tool is designed to remove only small amounts of stock at any one time. If you need to make a deep cut, rout your piece in several passes, cutting just ⅛" to ¼" deeper with each pass. Generally, the harder the wood, the less you should remove with any one pass.

If your router is mounted in a jig, check the depth of cut (the distance the bit protrudes past the mounting plate) and the position of the fence (if there is one).

Once you've adjusted your router, you'll need to keep a couple of things in mind:

• Before you turn the router on, make sure the bit is properly mounted and the collet is secure. When changing the bits, know that you might have to clean dust out of the collet. A dirty collet won't grip router bit shanks as well.

• Make several test cuts to check your setup; if a job requires several different setups, make sure you have enough test pieces at each subsequent stage to carry you through the entire procedure.

• Remove only a small amount of stock with any single pass. Set your depth of cut to take shallow cuts, usually ⅛" or ¼" deep. The illustration above explains this concept in more detail.

• Keep the router moving as steadily as you can while you cut. If you pause in the middle or move too slowly, friction will cause the bit to heat up and burn the wood. If you feed the router too quickly, it will leave scallops or mill marks in your piece.

• Cut against the rotation of the bit whenever possible, as shown in the drawing at top, right. If you use a fence or a straightedge, use the rotation to help keep the work (or the router) against it.

• Take note of the wood grain direction and rout with the grain as much as possible. When you must rout across the grain, back up the wood where the bit will exit. This prevents the bit from tearing and chipping the wood.

Cutting Direction

Whenever possible, cut against the rotation of the router bit – this will help control the router. If you rout with the rotation, the router or the workpiece will try to pull itself out of your hands. To make sure you're routing against the rotation, just remember that the bit rotates clockwise when the router is used right-side up. To rout the inside of a piece, move the router clockwise within the perimeter; when routing the outside, move it counterclockwise. Treat fences and straightedges as if they were the outside of a workpiece – envision yourself cutting counterclockwise around these guides.

There is one application for routing with the rotational direction. This is known as "climb-cutting" or back-routing. While this action demands better control of the router by the operator, climb-cutting can reduce tear-out when routing highly figured or irregularly grained woods. You must be very comfortable with router use before attempting this.

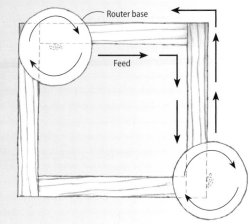

GUIDING THE ROUTER

In addition to those rules, here are some extra tips on guiding the router. You can use these whether you're routing hand-held or with a jig:

• Always hold the router firmly with both hands. Be prepared for the initial jerk when you start it up. (One option is to buy a router with a "soft-start" motor to eliminate this unnerving tendency.)

Tear-out on scrap wood

If your project requires you to rout across the end grain, clamp a scrap to the edge of the board where the bit will exit. This will prevent splintering and tear-out. If routing all four edges of a board, start with a cross-grain edge so the long-grain pass will remove any tear-out.

Tips & Tricks

Loose Tenons for Easy Joints

Instead of cutting perfectly fit mortise-and-tenon joinery on your workpieces, all you have to do is rout two matching mortises – then make a loose tenon to complete the joint. A single loose tenon (easily fit to both mortises) bridges the two mortises. As long as you get a good fit, this joint will be as strong as a traditional mortise-and-tenon joint.

Keep That Piece Clamped Down Tight

Whenever you're routing something, make sure that either your workpiece or your router is stable and secure – they can't both move. If you choose to move the router across the work, clamp the work to your bench. If a clamp interferes with the operation, rout up to it and turn the router off. Then move the clamp to an area on the workpiece that you've already cut and resume routing.

Back Up Your Work When Utilizing a Miter Gauge

Tear-out when routing in end grain can be a real problem. In a router table, when using a miter gauge to rout across the wood's grain, always use a piece of scrap placed behind the work piece to prevent tear-out.

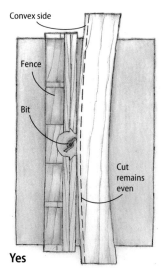

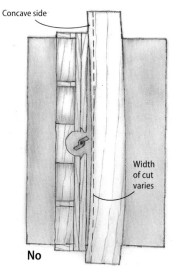

Yes   **No**

If your workpiece is warped or bowed – even slightly – keep the convex side of the bow against the fence or straightedge as you cut. The width of the cut will remain the same from one end of the board to the other (at left).

If you turn the concave side toward the fence (at right), the cut will be narrower toward the middle of the board than it will be at the ends.

• A router motor, like any other spinning body, generates lots of centrifugal force. Because of this, your router will resist any effort to cut in a straight line. As you push it along, it will want to drift to one side or the other, so you have to exert some force against your guide or edge to keep it tracking correctly.

• Make sure the router base is properly supported. When used hand-held, routers are top-heavy. If the workpiece is too narrow, it may be hard to balance the router. Try clamping a wide scrap piece to the work to provide additional support.

• It's not usually a good idea to rout freehand. The cuts won't be very accurate, and the router will try to pull itself all over the workpiece. There are four things you can use to help you guide the router while you cut – a piloted bit, which has a ball bearing guide or bushing to guide the cut; a guide collar, which attaches to the router's base and follows a surface with the bit protruding through it; an edge guide, which is really just a small fence that attaches to the router's base; or a straightedge clamped to your workpiece.

USING A STRAIGHTEDGE OR FENCE

The difference between a straightedge and a fence is all in how you hold the router. A straightedge guides a hand-held router over the work, while a fence guides the work over a table-mounted router. [*Editor's Note: We will focus on the router table in Chapter Three of this section.*]

Whether using a straightedge or a fence, keep whatever is moving pressed firmly against it. Feed the work or the router slowly and steadily – do not pause or speed up if you can help it.

Here are other things to remember:

• Make sure the straightedge or the fence is straight and flat. Otherwise, the cuts won't be accurate.

• Always read the warp or bow in a board before routing (see illustrations on page 54). Keep the convex surface against the fence or straightedge as you cut it.

• If the router sole is circular, paint a spot on the edge of the base plate. Keep the spot turned toward you and away from the straightedge as you rout. The bit is never perfectly centered in the base plate. If you allow the router to turn as you follow the straightedge, the cut will not be straight.

A GAUGE WILL HELP

When guiding the router with a straightedge, make a gauge to help position the straightedge when setting up the cut. To make a gauge the proper width (the distance from the router bit to the base edge), stick a thin piece of hardboard to a scrap piece with double-faced carpet tape, flushing one long edge of both pieces. Position your straightedge against the flushed edges. Mount the bit you plan to use in the router and rout along the straightedge and through the hardboard. The strip of hardboard now functions as your gauge.

Then just lay out the cut you want to make on the work. Position the straightedge on the work parallel to the edge of the cut and offset it the width of the gauge by using your gauge piece to guide you. Secure the straightedge to the work and make the cut, keeping the router firmly against the straightedge.

SELECTING BITS

There are an enormous number of router bits available, many more than can be shown here. But all these cutting accessories can be organized into four simple categories: decorative, used to cut molded shapes; joinery, used to make woodworking joints; trimming/cutting, used to trim or cut various materials; and utility, used to do all three of these tasks.

The cutting edges of the bits are called flutes. Most router bits have two symmetrical flutes, although there are some with just one.

When selecting which bit to use, know that you have a range of diameters to choose from. Router bits vary from a diameter of ¹⁄₁₆" up to 3¼". Some bits, particularly straight bits, are available with different types of flutes for cutting various materials.

CUSTOM ROUTER BITS

If you find yourself looking for a specific kind of router bit and can't seem to find it anywhere, it's possible to have custom router bits made to your specifications. Some places where custom bits are available include:

• **Freeborn Tool Co.:** 800-523-8988 or freeborntool.com
• **Whiteside Machine Co.:** 800-225-3982 or whitesiderouterbits.com
• **Carbide Specialties Inc.:** 800-678-3313 or carbidespecialties.com
• **North American Products:** 800-634-TOOL or www.naptools.com

Most unpiloted router bits have either top-cut or point-cut flutes – flat or pointed cutting edges on the ends of the flutes as well as the sides. This feature lets you cut downward into the stock to make grooves, mortises and other cuts in the interior of a workpiece. For example, a point-cut beading bit (far right) lets you cut quarter-round and half-round shapes in the surface of a piece, not just on the arrises and corners.

A Bit of Advice

A router bit consists of a cylindrical shank (usually ¼" or ½" in diameter) and one or more flutes or cutting wings, usually comprised of a piece of carbide brazed to the metal body of the bit. Throughout this series, we will be providing a closer look at a many of the most common (and

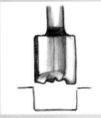

some specialized) bits that you can use with your router.

Straight Bit
The most basic groove-forming bit will give you clean grooves and dados. Diameters range from ¹⁄₁₆" to 1¾".

Rabbet Bit
An often-used bit for edge-forming. Change the bearing size to vary the width of the rabbet. The carbide height is usually ½", with the various bearings making rabbets possible from ⁵⁄₁₆" to ½" wide.

Roundover Bit
This is a great bit for quickly changing the appearance of any project. Depending on the radius of the roundover used (³⁄₁₆", ¼" and ³⁄₈" are common), a sharp edge can be softened or almost entirely rounded over. Add a smaller bearing, and the roundover bit becomes a beading bit.

Chamfer Bit
If you prefer a less-rounded appearance but still want to soften the edges, a chamfer bit is the way to go. Commonly available in 15°, 30° and 45° bevels.

Plunge Router

by Nick Engler

While a fixed-base router is a very versatile tool, there are still some operations that require different abilities. This is where a plunge router proves valuable.

For example, some operations require you to rout the interior of a board without cutting in from the edge. When you rout a mortise, it's best to first make a small hole in the interior of the workpiece, then enlarge it. To make this starter hole, you must lower – or "plunge" – the bit into the wood. While you don't need a plunge router to do this (woodworkers have been plunging with standard routers for years), it does make the operation safer and can be accomplished with greater precision.

The main difference between plunge and fixed-base routers (which were discussed in Chapter One of this section) is that plunge routers can make interior and stopped cuts much more easily. The plunge-base motor is mounted on two spring-loaded posts above the base, which let you position the motor above the work, then lower the bit straight down into the wood and begin cutting.

Similar to fixed-base routers, plunge-base routers are available in multiple sizes and powers. Most will accept both ½" and ¼" collets.

CHOOSING THE RIGHT SIZE FOR YOUR FIRST ROUTER

Plunge routers are available in two main sizes: either a 2-horsepower (or slightly less) or a 3-hp (or slightly more) model. Most larger plunge routers have found happy homes in router tables (we will discuss router tables in Chapter Three of this section), and that's where they belong. They're honestly too large for convenient hand-held routing operations. They can be used this way, but the smaller plunge router is more likely the better choice for hand-held routing.

The smaller plunge routers are easier to use hand-held and will provide an astonishing amount of power for almost all operations. Today's plunge routers often come equipped with variable speed. This is good because the larger-diameter bits cut better when run at slower speeds. Also, many variable-speed routers now offer a type of turbo-boost called electronic feedback control. This feature allows the motor to maintain the revolutions per minute when the router is in use, meaning there's no slowing or stalling during a cut.

So smaller is best when the tool is used outside of a table and larger is likely better for router-table use.

CHOOSING THE RIGHT SIZE FOR ROUTING SPECIFIC PROJECTS

As mentioned above, certain diameter bits perform better at certain speeds. While variable speed can give you a certain amount of leeway in your routing abilities, there are places where the size of your router makes a difference.

In particular, when performing any process that removes a large amount of material in a single pass, a larger plunge router will better meet your needs. This also will indicate that the operation is best

To make sure the collet is safely gripping a router bit, insert ¾" of the length of a ¼" shank bit into the collet and insert a full 1" of every ½" shank bit.

performed in a router table. These operations include rail-and-stile applications for doors, panel-raising for doors and frame-and-panel cabinetry, and large profile work, such as in crown moulding, base moulding or banisters.

In fact, the design of the tool will help you make that decision, too. Most smaller plunge routers will not have an opening in the base that is large enough to accommodate a large-profile bit. If the bit won't fit, you've probably grabbed the wrong router for the application.

HEIGHT-ADJUSTMENT FEATURES

With fixed-base routers, the depth of cut usually is set and adjusted manually by sliding the motor up and down in the base. Some motors will rotate to adjust the height, while others slide straight up and down. When the height is set, the motor is locked in the base and the work proceeds. With plunge routers, the depth of cut also is set by sliding the motor in the base, but there are a variety of ways to set, adjust and fine-tune that height.

Because the plunge router is designed to slide out of the cutting position and then return to the proper depth with a plunge, a repeatable and reliable depth stop is required. The most common and simplest repeatable depth stop on plunge routers is called a "turret stop."

A height-adjustable rod is mounted to the motor housing and aligned parallel to the direction of the plunge. Mounted to the base is a rotating dial with usually three

There is quite an array of router choices. At left, originally designed as a laminate trimmer, this smaller router is used very effectively for a variety of applications. Offering good power and using standard ¼"-diameter bits, it offers many of the benefits of a larger router with easier maneuverability and convenient size. Kits for the trimmers offer fixed- and beveling-base options. The standard fixed-base router in the 1½-horsepower range (middle) will accept ¼" and ½" bits and do almost everything you could need out of a router. The plunge router in the 2½-hp range (right) is able to do everything a fixed-base router can do and more, with extra torque for larger profile work such as frame-and-panel doors.

(but this can vary) stepped-height stops. The depth rod is plunged against the lowest position for the proper height, then locked in place. The other two stops come into play when you are making deep cuts in multiple passes to reduce the strain on the bit and the motor by taking no more than a ¼"-deep cut at one time.

There are a variety of designs for the plunge-rod/depth-stop arrangement, but turret depth stops are the most common height-adjustment system. Many newer plunge routers also offer fine adjustment to the depth setting.

The 1½-hp router, left, has a base opening that is sized for bits appropriate to that size motor. The larger plunge router, right, has a 3-hp motor, appropriately sized for larger bits for panel raising or large profiles. This base has a larger opening to accommodate those bits.

This is accomplished either by adding a fine-thread screw mechanism to the depth rod or by adding a fine-thread screw adjustment to the top of one of the depth rests on the stop itself. Fine adjustment can be very helpful during the initial depth setup, as you frequently can find yourself fighting a balancing act between gravity and the tension of the plunge springs to get the setting right.

The fine-adjustment feature also makes plunge routers a good choice for edge routing and profile work, applications typical for a fixed-base router. In fact, many woodworkers when faced with using only one router (thankfully that's not too often) will choose a plunge router, since it is more versatile.

But can't a fixed-base router be used to make plunge cuts? Sure, but it's not recommended. It's a hazardous operation because the base is supported on only one tiny edge while you tip the tool to plunge. If all you

have is a fixed-base router, there are ways to get the job done, but for most people who will be making more inside cuts, it's well worth it to get that plunge router.

BASE-MOUNTED GUIDES & TEMPLATE GUIDES

Base-mounted guides are available as accessories for most fixed-base and plunge routers. The guide follows the edge of the wood and you can use it rather easily. Instead of holding both router handles, grasp one handle and hold the end of the guide with your other hand. As you cut, keep the guide pressed firmly against the edge of the workpiece. Then just feed the router slowly and easily for a smooth cut.

Template guides attach to the base or sole of the router and follow a straight or contoured edge. These round guides surround the bit and the bit protrudes out through the hole. While template guides can be used to follow along the edges of a workpiece, they were designed to follow templates.

When using template guides, make sure the bit does not rub the inside of the collar. That wear could ruin both the bit and the collar. Also, keep the guide pressed firmly against the edges of the template as you cut.

Don't forget the most simple of router guides – a straightedge clamped to the material you're cutting. This can be a simple piece of scrap found in your shop or one of a number of commercially available guides that have built-in clamping, making their use a lot easier.

Turret stop with fine adjustments

The turret stop is the most common depth stop in plunge routers.

Fine adjustment knobs

Fine adjustment rod

Turret stop

The fine-adjustment knobs make the depth as accurate as possible.

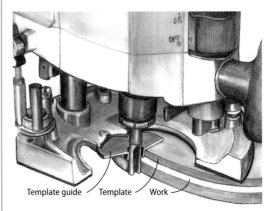

Template guide   Template   Work

Template guides are designed to follow templates. As the guide traces the shape of the template, the bit cuts a similar shape in the workpiece. The routed shape may be a little larger or smaller than the template, depending on the relative diameters of the bit and the guide.

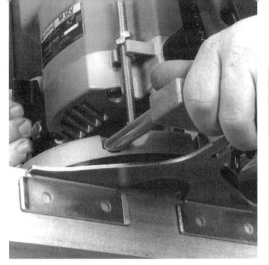

Most base-mounted guides will follow either straight or contoured edges, depending on the shape of the guide. Here, a straight guide – which looks like a small fence – rides along the edge of a board.

HOW TO ROUT A MORTISE

Routing a mortise with a plunge router is an easy operation. First mark the location of the mortise and set up whatever guide system you choose. Your guide system can be as simple as an edge guide, as shown at right, or a jig, as shown in the photo below.

Begin the mortise by making a starting hole. Just position the bit over the work, then push down. Next, enlarge (or elongate) the hole to complete the mortise by moving the router.

OTHER APPLICATIONS

Along with mortising, there are some other operations that plunge routers are ideally suited for:

To rout a mortise with a plunge router, clamp a straightedge or guide to the workpiece and adjust the depth stop. (You also may use a base-mounted guide attached to the router.) Position the router over the work, holding the base against the straightedge (or the guide against the work). Release the height clamp and push the bit into the wood.

The depth stop will halt the bit at the proper depth. Secure the height clamp and rout the mortise, keeping the router against the guide.

Circles and Ellipses

Because cutting these pieces is usually a multi-stage task, the plunge router works best because it can be lowered gradually to make the cuts. You could use a fixed-base router, but it usually takes up more time.

Deep or Large Cuts

If you have a deep cut that is going to be more than one pass or is larger than your bit, break out the plunge router. Even if it means building up support on the outboard side of the router's base to prevent tipping, it's almost always better to use the plunge router.

With a Router Table

Plunge routers are the most popular choice with a table because there are more options in the 3-hp range than fixed-base routers. They're also relatively inexpensive, but there are some problems to be aware of. Because the router's motor is inseparable from the rest of the tool, you can't change the bit easily if the tool is fixed to the tabletop.

A mortising template can be nothing more than a hole cut in a piece of plywood or particleboard. The size and shape of the hole depends on the size and shape of the mortise you wish to cut, the diameter of the template guide in your router and the diameter of the bit you are using. When you make the template, cut it large enough to support the router base.

ROUTER MAINTENANCE

Like many modern portable power tools, the router is a mostly maintenance-free tool. There are, however, a few things you must do to keep it in good working order.

• Keep the motor free of dust. Use compressed air or a vacuum to clean out the housing. Otherwise, the dust will get into the bearings and cause them wear prematurely. The dust also can damage the commutator (a part of the router's universal motor that conducts current) and field of the motor.

• Keep the collet dust-free. Dust in a collet is the most common cause of bits slipping. If you don't keep it clean, the collet also can show wear prematurely.

• Replace the collet immediately if it shows signs of wear. A worn collet changes the shanks of router bits. This may ruin the motor shaft, requiring you to replace the entire armature.

• Wax and buff the base plate and the surfaces of the tool that slide together (such as the plunge bars). This simple act will help these parts move freely and keep the router gliding smoothly across the work.

• Make sure that the plunge bars and sleeves are correctly aligned. If the router is dropped, these parts might need to be inspected. In some routers, the return springs are inside the plunge bars; in others, the spring is fitted externally. Either way, the springs need to be seated properly and cleaned regularly.

• Brushes are blocks of carbon that ride and wear against the commutator in all router motors as part of the motor function. Over enough time, the brushes can wear down enough to require complete replacement. Some, but not all routers, make this a simple task by making the brushes accessible from the outside of the router housing.

Sparking from the motor that is only getting worse is a good indicator that it may be time to replace the brushes. This usually is a simple task that requires removing the brush cover, removing the brush, spring and wire and inserting a new brush. Properly aligning the brushes and leaving proper "play" in the spring will ensure a good fit.

There likely will be a short period where sparking will continue as the new square brush shapes itself to the round commutator. After that there should be no problem.

• Many switches included on routers today are sealed against dust. If you happen to have an older or less-expensive router, you may want to take a look at the switch occasionally as well. After unplugging the router it's simple enough to remove the switch from the housing and use a soft toothbrush (or compressed air) to clean any accumulated dust from the switch and the switch terminals.

Tips & Tricks

Sharpen Cutting Flutes by Using a Diamond Stone

If your cutting edges seem dull, touch up the carbide flutes on a diamond stone. Sharpen only the inside (flat) surfaces of the flutes, leaving the outside (curved) edges alone. If you try to sharpen those, you might change the diameter of the bit.

Wax That Tool; Don't Worry About Wax on Wood

There is a common misconception that if you wax a woodworking tool the wax will rub off onto the wood and interfere with a finish. This is not true, as long as you buff the wax after it dries. Once buffed, the layer of wax remaining on the tool is only a few molecules thick – enough to protect and lubricate the metal but not enough to ruin the finish.

Remove Your Plunge Springs When Routing in a Table

One of the most frustrating things about using a plunge router in a router table is that the plunge springs work against you as you try to increase the height of the bit. Many plunge routers allow you to easily remove the springs. Give it a try.

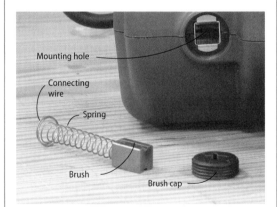

At right is the motor's brush with spring and connecting wire, the cap and the hole in the housing where the brush goes. You can see that the surface of the brush is slightly concave to form to the cylinder of the commutator. When replacing a brush that is already broken in, the shape should be properly oriented to match the motor's round commutator.

To remove the pitch from a router bit, soak it in lacquer thinner or spray it with oven cleaner. Give the solvent a moment or two to work, then wipe off the bit with fine steel wool.

BIT MAINTENANCE

Clean and maintain the router bits, not just the machine itself. After all, a bit is the most important part of your routing system.

- After each use, remove dust and built-up pitch. Then polish the shaft with a piece of steel wool or 3M Scotch-Brite. This will not affect the diameter of the shaft – the tool materials are a lot harder than steel wool and Scotch-Brite.

- If there are any burrs or galling (rough spots) on the shaft of the bit, sand the entire shaft smooth with emery cloth. Carefully check the collet for dust or any signs of wear. Burrs and galling are sure signs that the bit has slipped while you were cutting.

- Lubricate pilot bushings and bearings after every one to two hours of use. Wax and buff the bushings. Apply a dry lubricant, such as powdered graphite, to the bearings – do not use oil or sprays. These mix with sawdust, forming a gummy paste that can ruin the bearing.

USING PILOTED BITS

A piloted bit has either a ball bearing or a bushing to guide the cut. These pilots follow the surface of the work (or the template) and keep the width of the cut consistent, just like you do when using a base-mounted guide.

Usually they're mounted to the ends of the flutes, but some are positioned between the shank and the flutes (called "over-bearings").

When using piloted bits:

- Remember that the pilot is meant to follow the contour of the board. When you set the depth of cut, the pilot must solidly contact the wood surface.

A Bit of Advice

These four bits are great for making interior patterns.

Round Nose Bit
Provides a perfect radius groove and is most commonly associated with producing fluted millwork, signs and decorative designs in cabinet doors.

Beading Bit
A bead is different than a roundover in that it has a shoulder that transitions into the round. Used for decorative edges, it can be used on one side (often with a bearing guide) or two sides to make a double bead.

V-groove Bit
This decorative bit allows you to cut deep or shallow grooves by adjusting the cutting depth. Ideal for making signs and adding decorative accents to furniture and plaques.

Keyhole Bit
This is a very specialized bit that allows you to cut keyhole openings for hanging pictures and plaques. Perfect for use in plunge routers.

Cuts space for the shank

Cuts access hole and space for the nail or screw head

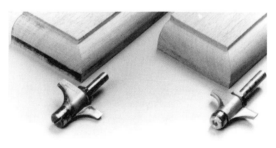

For best results, use pilot bearings, rather than bushings or pins, which turn at the same speed as the bit and rub the edge of the workpiece. The friction causes them to heat up and burn the wood. Bearings turn independently of the bit and won't rub or burn the wood.

- Anticipate the curves and corners of your work to keep the pilot pressed firmly against the board's edge.

- Treat the pilot as if it was a small straightedge or fence when trying to decide which way to move the router or feed the work. With a hand-held router right-side up, cut counterclockwise around the outside of your workpiece. (With the router mounted upside down in a table, feed the work clockwise around the bit.)

- The diameter of the pilot controls the width of the cut. Some piloted bits have interchangeable pilots for you to change the diameter, but not all do, so make sure you're prepared for this.

The Router Table

by Nick Engler

After you've worked with a hand-held router for some time, you'll find that many operations are easier and safer if you pass the workpiece across the bit instead of the other way around. This is especially true when routing small pieces or when making many identical cuts. For these tasks, holding the tool stationary by mounting it in a table or a jig is a good idea.

There are two common ways to mount a router: vertically beneath the work or horizontally beside the work, as shown in the illustration on the next page. Each position offers unique advantages, and there are a number of tools and jigs available that will hold the router in each position. You can purchase or make many different router-mounting jigs and accessories, but the most versatile is the router table. This device holds the router vertically beneath the work, with the bit protruding up through a hole in the table – all you have to do is rest your workpiece on the table's top and guide it over the bit.

There are many commercial router tables on the market, as well as several you can make from a kit. You can make your own from scratch pretty easily. A home-made router table may be a better option in the long run for a number of reasons:

• You can build it to fit whatever kind of router you already own.

• You can make it suit whatever available space you have in your shop.

• If you don't have room for a standalone table, you can customize other fixtures already in your shop to hold a router. A workbench, a table saw or a radial-arm saw all can pull double-duty as a router table.

WHAT ROUTER IS BEST WITH A TABLE?

Choosing which type of router to use in a router table has been the subject of debate for many years. When the plunge router first entered the marketplace, it quickly became the router of choice for table use, offering more precise height adjustment than fixed-base routers.

One problem that arose was when the return spring on plunge routers pushed against the height adjustment, making it a difficult process. It didn't take long for woodworkers to remove the spring from their plunge routers to make the adjustment easier. Manufacturers recently have addressed that problem themselves by offering plunge routers that enable users to "defeat" the return spring.

Another difficulty router tables presented was the need to reach under the table to make height adjustments, change bits and actually turn the router on and off. This led to removable plates in the tabletops to which the routers were attached. Rather than crawling under the table, the router and plate could be lifted free from above the table. These plates soon became even more helpful with the addition of built-in height adjustment. The router-lift plates make it possible to fine-adjust the height of a more-affordable fixed-base router from above the table, providing the best of both worlds.

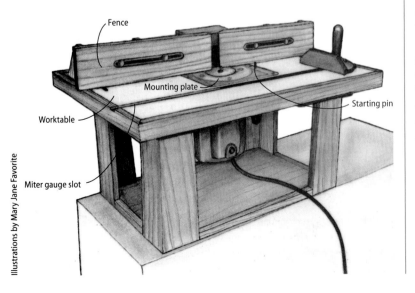

Fence

Mounting plate

Starting pin

Worktable

Miter gauge slot

Illustrations by Mary Jane Favorite

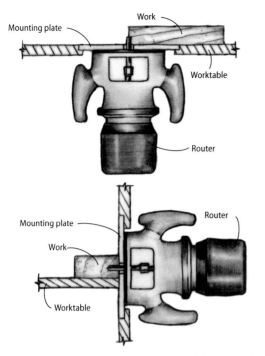

There are two common ways to mount a portable router and hold it stationary. You can mount it vertically under the work (top) or horizontally beside the work (bottom).

Some of the newest fixed-base and plunge routers now offer built-in, through-the-base height adjustment. This makes the router lifts obsolete, though they're still the best option for older (as well as many of the newer and less-expensive) router models.

This brings us back to the question of what router to use in your table. A 1½- to 2-horsepower router can be used successfully in a table, but it will limit you to small- or medium-diameter bits. In general, it makes more sense to use a 2½- to 3-hp router in a table.

The other strong recommendation is to outfit your router table with a variable-speed router. Because your table will support a larger-motor router, you can successfully use large-diameter bits. To get the best performance from these bits, they should be run at slower speeds, so a variable-speed router will give you optimum performance in your table, whether using smaller grooving bits or panel-raising bits for making doors.

That said, with the variety of table-friendly routers and router lifts available, it's impossible to recommend either a plunge or a fixed-base router as best for use in a table. You'll need to determine what your budget will allow and take into consider-

Tips & Tricks

Rout End-grain Edges First To Avoid Any Tear-out
When routing profiles on four edges of a rectangular or square piece, start with an end-grain edge first. If the end of the cut tears out, the following pass on the long-grain edge will most likely remove the torn-out corner.

Titanium-coated Bits Don't Burn Wood When Sharp
Manufacturers sometimes coat the cutting edges of large, carbide-tipped router bits with a gold-colored titanium alloy and claim the bits can be used safely without reducing the routing speed. This is true to an extent. Titanium-coated carbide can be honed to a much sharper edge than the uncoated variety. While the cutting edges remain razor-sharp, the bit will cut cleanly at high speeds. But as soon as the edges dull or load up with pitch, the bit will burn the wood.

Dust Collector Keeps Table's Mess to a Minimum
If possible, make sure your router table has a dust collector to minimize airborne dust as you work. On the table seen here, the collector is part of the fence.

Mount a Power Switch Closer to Table's Front
When a router is mounted in a table, it might be hard to reach the power switch. To solve this problem, mount a combination switch/outlet near the front of the table and wire it to control the power to the outlet. Plug your

router into the outlet and use the switch to turn it on and off.

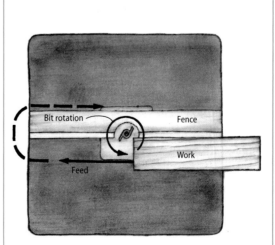

When a router is vertical under a table, the bit spins counterclockwise when viewed from above. Whether cutting the edge or interior of a workpiece, feed clockwise around the fence.

Tips & Tricks

Scrap Piece Helps when Routing Narrow Work

When routing the end of a narrow workpiece on a router table, use a large square scrap to guide it along the fence. The scrap not only holds the work perpendicular to the fence, it also backs up the wood so it won't tear out.

Keep Your Hands Away With Small Workpieces

If a workpiece is very small, your hands may come too close to the router bit as you rout it. In this case, you have two choices – you can rout the work with a portable router using a commercially available foam rubber "routing pad" to hold the work, or you can rout a portion of a larger workpiece and cut a small piece from it, as seen above.

Slide Smoothly with Wax

To help the table slide more smoothly, wax and buff the table surface, the fence faces, the miter gauge bars and the grooves for any miter fixtures.

Scrap

Waste trimmed after router work

A CLOSER LOOK AT ROUTER LIFTS

Router lifts are available in a number of varying designs, ranging from a retrofit kit to replace the spring in a plunge router to heavy-duty mounting platforms that include the table plate. Prices range from $100 to $400, so you should know what you're getting into before you spend any money.

The router lift should adequately support the router underneath the table without any concern of deflection or slipping. Deflection will cause the bit you are using to deviate from a 90° angle to the table, ruining the cut. The lift also should adjust the height smoothly in measurable and repeatable increments, and not interfere with the table surface. Most lifts that are on the market are designed for use with fixed-base routers, which is fine, but you should choose a router with variable-speed control to take maximum advantage of the larger motor and available larger-diameter bits.

Some lifts also will allow you to change bits from above the table. These lifts raise the router high enough through the tabletop (while not running) to use both wrenches (or one wrench and a shaft lock). This is a great feature and highly recommended.

USING THE ROUTER TABLE

When using a router in a router table, you will need to pay extra attention to the tool's feed direction. When your router is mounted upside down under a table, the bit spins counterclockwise (as viewed from above). Whether you are cutting the edge or

ation what routers you already own. With all the choices currently available, there's no reason you shouldn't be able to buy or build a router table that allows you to adjust and operate the router from above the table surface. It's up to you to choose how you assemble the hardware.

When adjusting the position of a router table fence, loosen the clamps at both ends of the fence and slide it forward or back. To make fine adjustments, tighten just one clamp and move the loose end of the fence.

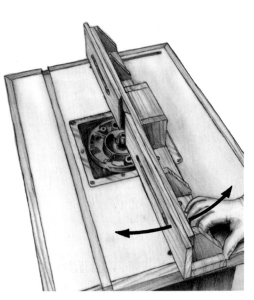

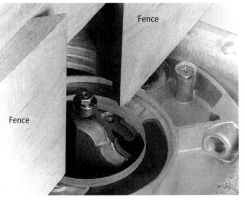

Fence

Fence

When properly used, a fence guides the work and also protects you from the bit. Even when using a bit with a bearing guide, align the fence faces even with the front edge of the bearing and adjust the fence gap as tightly against the bit as possible.

the interior of a workpiece, imagine that you are feeding it clockwise around the fence – right to left as you face the fence.

The rotation will help keep the board pressed against the fence, making it safer to make the cut. When using a fence, you also need to check that the router is properly aligned and adjusted in the table. There are two things you need to check – the depth of cut (the distance the bit protrudes past the mounting plate) and the position of the fence.

Other things to remember when using a router table with a fence include:

• Keep the workpiece pressed firmly against the fence to ensure you get as straight a cut as possible.

• Feed the work slowly and steadily – do not pause, if you can help it.

• Let the fence surround the unused portion of the bit.

• Whenever practical, use featherboards, push sticks and push shoes to guide the work along the fence.

A router table also can be used without a fence. In these cases, a starting pin and a bit with a bearing or a template guide attached is used. This operation is similar to using a hand-held router with a similarly guided bit, but the table operation makes it safer and easier to use larger-profile bits.

The starting pin provides an extra bearing point to allow you to rest against two points while routing, adding an extra level of safety. When using the router table in this setup it's even more important to maintain proper safety and hand clearance from the exposed bit.

DOUBLES AS A JOINTER

Speaking of fences, it would be a large oversight not to mention using a router table as an edge-jointer. Some commercially available router-table fences give you the option to adjust the face of the outfeed table forward slightly (by as much as ⅛") to offset the fences.

With a straight router bit aligned tangentially to the face of the outfeed table, you can run wood across the fence and straighten or thin edges just as you would on a jointer.

If your fence assembly isn't designed to have offset fences, you can achieve the same effect by building up the face of the outfeed table with a piece of laminate or thin ply-

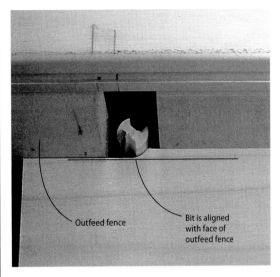

By offsetting the outfeed fence (moving it forward ¹⁄₁₆" or ⅛"), a router table can be used as an efficient edge jointer. The face of the outfeed fence is aligned with the furthest point of the straight bit and, as the wood passes the bit, the outfeed fence supports the cut.

Outfeed fence

Bit is aligned with face of outfeed fence

wood. Adjust the outfeed face to match the bit and you're ready.

FEATHERBOARDS & STOP BLOCKS

Two useful accessories for the router table are featherboards and stop blocks.

• Featherboards are most often thought of as safety devices, and they certainly are, but they also help ensure an accurate cut from the bit. For safety, a featherboard's angled fingers allow the wood to pass the bit and then applies pressure in the same direction you are feeding your work to make it nearly impossible for the piece to kick back (which is when the material is thrown toward the user by the force of the spinning bit). A pair of featherboards used in the horizontal and vertical planes of the router table, as shown in the photograph on page 66, add excellent safety.

Often when using larger-diameter bits in a single pass, the tendency of the bit is to push the material away from it, causing irregular, rippled or shallow cuts. Using a pair of featherboards will keep the workpiece pushed tightly against the fence, table and bit, providing an accurate, smooth and repeatable cut.

• When using a router table, the bit is buried in the wood during the cut and you can't see when or where the cut begins or ends. When making a stopped cut of any type (groove or profile), you need to know the stopping and starting points to make an accurate cut.

One way to determine those points is to make a pencil mark on the fence identify-

Fence face moved forward to act as a stop

Bit rotation

When using a fence, attach featherboards to both the fence and the table to keep the workpiece properly positioned. Featherboards provide firm, even pressure and prevent the piece from kicking back toward you. Also use push sticks and push shoes to feed the workpiece, keeping your fingers out of danger.

You also can use a fence as a stop to prevent creep. However, the fence must be precisely parallel to the miter-gauge slot and you must be feeding the workpiece with the rotation of the bit to pull the piece against the fence.

ing the infeed and outfeed sides of the bit. This helps, but it isn't a positive assurance of accuracy.

That's where stop blocks come in handy. By mounting some adjustable blocks to the fence (using either integral T-tracks or a clamp on the fence) you can be sure you'll always stop and start in the correct spot.

USING A MITER GAUGE

A miter gauge is a simple way of to ensure you get square cuts on the ends of thin stock when using a router table. Just place the stock against the face of the gauge and feed it past the bit as if it was the blade on a table saw.

But there is an important difference – the rotation of a saw blade helps hold the work against the gauge; the rotation of the router bit pulls the wood sideways, making it "creep" across the gauge to the right as you cut.

When not using a fence, there are several things you can do to prevent this:

• Mount an extension (a long, auxiliary face) on the miter gauge and clamp the work to this.

• Clamp a stop to the miter-gauge extension and butt the workpiece against the stop.

• Position a fence beside the miter gauge and let the end of the board ride along the fence as you cut.

• Tape #80-grit or #100-grit sandpaper to the miter gauge face with double-sided carpet tape.

It's also a good idea when crosscutting material on the router table to use a backing board against the face of the miter gauge.

This will significantly decrease tear-out on the workpiece and add some more stability.

MAKING A MOUNTING PLATE

If you buy a router table, many will come with a mounting plate – a thin, flat sheet to which you attach the router base. If you're making your own table, or if the one you purchased doesn't come with a mounting plate, don't worry – making the plate is rather straightforward.

• The material from which you make a mounting plate must be dense enough to absorb the vibrations of the router, but thin enough so it won't restrict the depth of cut. It should also be transparent so you can see what's going on beneath it. I suggest you use ordinary acrylic plastic that's rather inexpensive. Some structural plastics are superstrong, but too flexible. Acrylic is more rigid. I suggest using a ¼"-thick sheet for routers up to 1½-hp and a ⅜"-thick sheet for more powerful routers.

• For safety and accuracy, there should be as little space as possible between the work surface and the router bit where it protrudes through the plate. However, bits can range in size from ¹⁄₁₆" to 3¼". I suggest you drill the opening about ¼" larger than the largest bit you own, then make several inserts to fit the opening. Drill a different diameter hole in the center of each insert so you have a variety to choose from.

• You'll need to fashion some way to hold these inserts in place. Some router bases have metal or plastic flanges to mount guide bushings. If your router is so equipped, you can use these flanges to support and secure the inserts. If your router doesn't have built-in flanges, attach a plastic ring under the mounting plate. The inside diameter of this ring should be ½" smaller than the diameter of the mounting plate to create a ledge to support the inserts.

• To cut an opening in the table's work surface for the mounting plate, first rout a square groove in the surface. Clamp a wooden frame to the table to guide the router and cut the groove so the depth matches the thickness of the mounting plate. (Make this groove about ⅟₃₂" smaller than the circumference of the plate; later, you can sand or file the edges of the plate to get a perfect fit.) Then make the router opening by cutting around the inside edges of the groove with a jigsaw. When the waste falls away, the groove will form a ledge to hold the mounting plate.

• Attach the mounting plate in the opening with several screws. Don't leave it loose, because you don't want it to shift.

• The work surface should be thick enough to permit you to attach the mount-

ing plate securely – short screws may vibrate or pull loose. If the work surface is less than 1¼" thick, build up the area immediately beneath the mounting plate by gluing a hardwood frame to the table.

Because router bits can range in size from ⅟₁₆" to 3¼", you should drill the plate's opening about ¼" larger than the largest bit you own. Then you can make several inserts out of the same acrylic you used for the plate.

A Bit of Advice

A router bit consists of a cylindrical shank (usually ¼" or ½" in diameter) and one or more flutes or cutting wings, usually comprised of a piece of carbide brazed to the metal body of the bit. Throughout this series, we will be providing a closer look at many of the common and specialized bits that can be used with your router. These three bits are great for use with the router table.

Crown-moulding Bit
Designed to make complicated profile shapes in one pass, a crown-moulding bit is a perfect choice for a router table because of its size and the quantity of wood likely to be run.

Table-edge Bit
Because the bit is designed to remove a lot of material in one pass (and run a lot of material at one time) a router table offers power and control for many edge profile bits. Table-edge bits are large and require more power and control.

Raised-panel Bit
Another large bit perfect for router tables is a raised-panel bit for making doors and frame-and-panel cabinetry. The one shown here is a horizontal bit, but vertical bits also are available.

To cut the work surface for the mounting plate, first rout a square groove. Clamp a frame to the table to guide the router and cut the groove as deep as you want the thickness of the mounting plate.

Next, make the router opening by cutting the inside edges of the groove with a jigsaw. This groove will then form the ledge to hold the plate.

Screws work great to attach the mounting plate in the opening, but make sure you do it tightly – you don't want anything shifting while you work.

Router Joinery

by Nick Engler

Although routers were originally designed to create moulded shapes, they can be excellent joinery tools. In fact, they're better in some ways than table saws, professional-quality mortisers or dado cutters when it comes to cutting joints. There are several reasons routers have an advantage:

• **Simplicity:** Setting up hand-held or table-mounted routers is rather straightforward. Tools dedicated to joint-making such as hollow-chisel mortisers are more complex and require more time to set up. Sure, it could be worth the effort to use a mortiser if you're planning to make dozens of duplicate joints. But if all you want to cut are a few mortises and tenons, for example, a router will save you loads of time.

• **Versatility:** You can make a greater variety of joints with a router than with any other joinery tool. No matter if you have a fixed-base or plunge router, you can cut more types of joints than with any other kind of tool.

• **Accuracy:** There isn't a more precise joinery tool. You may find tools just as accurate, but none that surpass the router. Because routers cut quickly, they leave a smooth surface, meaning joints fit better and bonds are stronger.

There are some disadvantages to using your router for joint-making, and I'd be remiss if I didn't mention them:

• Most routers won't stand up to continual cutting as well as heavy-duty woodworking machinery.

• Because you can't make deep cuts in a single pass on a router, it may take you longer to rout some joints than it would to use a mortiser or dado cutter.

• Depending on the joint you want to make, you may be limited by the sizes and configurations of available bits.

These shortcomings, however, are minor. Routers are indispensable joinery tools in any workshop.

RABBETS, DADOS & GROOVES

You can make the most basic woodworking joints – rabbets, dados and grooves – using a simple fixed-base router and an inexpensive set of straight bits.

Rabbets (and the simple tongue for a tongue-and-groove joint) are produced easily with a router. While you may need a variety of rabbet sizes, a single rabbeting bit can accomplish them all. By purchasing a rabbeting bit with interchangeable guide bearings, the width of the rabbet can be changed quickly by selecting and installing a different diameter guide-bearing on the bit.

Rabbeting can be accomplished safely using a router free-hand or in a table. For rabbeting smaller pieces (such as with frames or door mullions) I recommend using a router table. In a table, you can use a simple straight bit to cut the rabbet, or you can use a rabbeting bit with a bearing guide. Even though you may think the bearing guides make a fence unnecessary, you still should use one to limit the amount of bit exposed and to help guide the pieces. Align the fence with the outside edge of

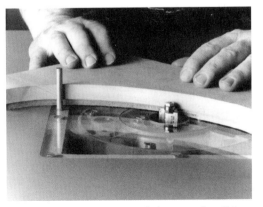

When routing dados and grooves, the joint ordinarily will be the same width as the bit. If you need to make a joint of a larger size, first make a cut that's somewhat narrower than the joint needed (left), then move the fence or straightedge to make a second cut (below), enlarging the joint to the desired width.

the bearing for a seamless process. For improved accuracy and safety, use a fingerboard to hold the material against the fence and table.

As mentioned earlier, a rabbet also can form the tongue for a tongue-and-groove joint. The tongue can be flush to one side of a board (for offset raised-panel doors) or the tongue can be centered on the board. Essentially, the tongue is just a long tenon. Run the groove first, then simply size the tongue to fit in that groove.

Many dados or grooves can be made with a straight bit that is sized to accurately make the joint with a single-width pass. To make a dado or groove that's a non-standard size, choose a cutter that's slightly smaller than the width of the joint and cut the joint in two passes, as shown in the photos above.

Because most basic joints are cut parallel or perpendicular to straight edges, you must guide the router or the work in a straight line. The best way to do this is to use an edge guide, straightedge, fence, miter gauge or a shop-made jig.

If the joint is blind (which means it stops before running through the board) at one or both ends, attach stops to the workpiece or the guides to automatically halt the cut. The location of these stops depends on where the joint is to be cut in the board. For example, to cut a blind groove that stops 6" from the ends of the board, clamp a stop to the outfeed side of the fence 6" from the router bit.

Now, if the joint is blind at both ends, you can determine the distance between the two stops by adding the length of the board to the length of the joint and subtracting the router bit diameter. (For example, if you want to cut a 4"-long double-blind groove in a 10" board with a 3⁄8"-diameter straight bit, position the stops 13⁵⁄8" apart.)

But what if the rabbet must follow a contour? Well, there are a couple of choices, but the only bit that makes good sense for making contoured rabbets is a bearing-piloted rabbeting bit.

For a contoured groove, a different approach will likely be necessary. The answer this time is a guide collar (also called a template guide) and a template. Because a guide collar is slightly wider than the diameter of the bit, the contour cut by the router will not be the same size as the

Stop block

When cutting blind joints – rabbets, dados and grooves that are closed at one or both ends – use a stop block to halt the cut at the blind ends. Note that the end of the stop block is mitered. This prevents sawdust from being trapped between it and the stock, where the dust might interfere with the accuracy of the cut.

When cutting a joint in a contoured edge, use a piloted bit to follow the contour. A piloted rabbeting bit will neatly cut a rabbet in an irregular edge, while a spline cutter will likewise make a groove in an irregular edge a simple task.

template. For inside curves and corners, the contour will be smaller; for outside ones, it will be larger.

There always will be a small gap between the edge of the template and the nearest side of the cut because of the different diameters. To determine the width of this space, subtract the diameter of the bit from the outside diameter of the collar and divide by two. (For example, if you cut a contoured groove with a ⅝"-diameter collar and a ½"-diameter bit, the distance between the template and the groove will be ¹⁄₁₆".)

MORTISES AND TENONS

To make a mortise and its matching tenon, you must combine several techniques. Although it may seem complex, a mortise-and-tenon joint is just a combination of several basic joints. After all, a mortise is simply a groove that's blind at both ends, and a tenon is made by cutting two or more rabbets in the end of a board.

The trick to cutting precise mortises and tenons is to make the cuts in the proper order. Most experienced woodworkers agree that it's easiest to cut the mortise first, then fit the tenon into it.

To make a mortise, you must bore a starter hole and expand it to the dimensions needed. There are several ways to do this using a fixed-base or a plunge router, either hand-held or in a table. However, when you make mortises for mortise-and-tenon joints, you usually want to make several mortises in several different workpieces, all the exact same size and shape. The easiest way to accomplish this is with a simple template.

As a general rule, mortises should be about half the width of the material they're made in. So a mortise in a ¾"-wide piece of wood should be ⅜" wide, with a ³⁄₁₆" shoulder on either side of it. The depth of the mortise should be no less than ¾" to ensure a good joint, but 1" or slightly more usually is a good idea.

The simplest form of template is a piece of plywood that has a hole in it that is the exact size of the mortise you wish to rout.

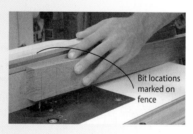
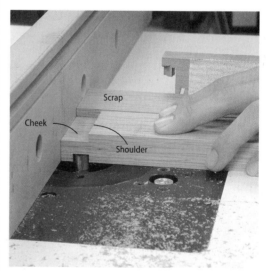

Scrap

Cheek

Shoulder

To make a tenon, cut two or more rabbets in the end of the board – these rabbets will become the cheeks and shoulders of the tenon. To fit the tenon to the mortise, cut the tenon just a bit large, then slowly raise the bit, shaving away a paper-thin layer of stock on each cheek until you get the fit you're after. Guide the cuts with the miter gauge, using the fence as a stop.

Just clamp the template directly onto your work and then form the mortise using a straight bit that has a bearing above the cutting flutes. There are a variety of ways to make the template, from making plunge cuts on a board with a table saw to edge-gluing four pieces of wood together and leaving a gap in the middle that is the size of the mortise. All work just fine.

When cutting the mortise, first plunge straight down in the area you wish to waste away. Then, with the router fully plunged, follow the template's edge with your bearing to shape the mortise to its finished size. (See image on page 70 for how to cut the tenon.)

DOVETAILS

There are three basic dovetail joints: half-blind dovetails, through dovetails and sliding dovetails. The router is the only power tool that can create them all, using a special dovetail bit.

Both half-blind and through dovetails are most easily made using accurate templates. These can be purchased (there are many commercially manufactured ones) or you can make your own.

Tips & Tricks

Let the Wood Get Acquainted With its New Surroundings
When you first purchase lumber, bring it into your shop and let it sit untouched for a few weeks before you use it. This will give the moisture content of each board a chance to reach equilibrium with its new environment. If you cut a board while its moisture content is in flux, the wood may expand or contract unevenly, ruining the fit of your joints and distorting the project.

Connect the Dots to Keep Cutting in Straight Lines
The bit does not always fall in the exact center of a round router sole. Because of this, the cut won't be accurate if the router turns while you're guiding the base along a straightedge. The accuracy also may be spoiled when you remove and replace the sole. To avoid this, put a spot of paint on the edges of the sole and base, one above the other. Keep these spots toward you as you rout, and align them each time you reattach the sole.

Watch Your Tenon Widths
As a rule of thumb, most woodworkers limit the width of mortise-and-tenon joints (where the wood grain must be glued perpendicular to its mate) to 3". Once you exceed 3" wide, you will need to use double tenons.

On half-blind dovetails (above), the joint is hidden from view on one side. This makes it ideal for the fronts of drawers and other applications where you don't want to see the joinery. Through dovetails (right) are visible from both sides and are often used for decoration, as well as joining.

To rout a half-blind dovetail joint (right), secure both of the adjoining boards in the template. The "tail" board is held vertically, so its end is flush with the top surface of the horizontal "pin" board. Cut both the tails and the pins in one pass with a dovetail bit, using a guide collar to follow the template.

When using a fixed through-dovetail template (left) you can't change the size and position of the tails and pins. Rout the tails first, using the tail template, a guide collar and a dovetail bit. Then you can switch to the pin template and a straight bit. Fit the pins to the tails by moving the template forward or back on its holder. This will change the size, but not the location, of the pins.

A drawer-lock joint requires only one bit and one setup. However, instead of reversing boards face for face as you cut them (like in the finger glue joint), you must cut the drawer front with the face of the workpiece against the router table, and then cut the drawer side with the face against the fence. Adjust both the depth of cut and the position of the fence so the members fit together properly.

Through dovetails require two passes and two matching templates. These templates are less common than half-blind dovetail templates and, because of the precision required to make them, can be much more expensive.

Sliding dovetails require no special equipment, other than your router, router table and dovetail bit.

To make a sliding dovetail, first rout a dovetail slot the same way you would rout a dado or groove. Because of the bit shape, however, you must cut the full depth in one pass. Next, cut a dovetail tenon to fit this slot – this must be cut on a router table. The slot, on the other hand, can be cut using a hand-held router. Leave the depth of cut unchanged from the setup you used when routing the slot. Then pass a board by the bit, cutting one face. Then turn the board around and cut the other face. These two cuts form the tenon.

To assemble the joint, just slide the tenon into the slot. If necessary, adjust the fit by trimming a little stock off the tenon's cheeks, either with your router, a small plane or simply with sandpaper.

COPED JOINTS

Perhaps the easiest way to make a joint with a router is to cut a "coped" joint, where both adjoining surfaces are shaped. The most common example of this is on cabinet doors where the rails (the horizontal pieces) meet with the stiles (the vertical pieces). Each joint surface is a mirror image of the other, so the two surfaces mate perfectly.

This has two advantages: the shape of the joint aligns the adjoining parts so the surfaces are flush and the corners are square, and the shape increases the gluing surfaces and strengthens the joint.

Coped joints require special router bits that can be pretty expensive. There are three types of bits, and each must be used in a different manner:

• **Single bit with one cutter:** The male and female cutters are on the same bit, making it a long piece of tooling. You raise and lower the bit in the table to change which set of cutters are in use.

• **Single bit with interchangeable cutters:** You switch from the male to the female cutter by disassembling the bit and changing the orientation of the cutters. There are small shims involved so you need to keep those in the right place as you assemble the bit each time.

Tips & Tricks

Need a Hinge? Just Add a Hole to Finger-jointed Boards
To make a wooden hinge, roundover the ends of two boards with a roundover bit (the radius of the bit must be half the thickness of the boards). Cut finger joints in the rounded ends and assemble the joint. At the center of the rounded ends, drill a hole through the interlocking fingers and insert a wooden or metal dowel to serve as a pivot.

Two Jigs are Better than One, Especially for Dovetails
Many woodworkers keep two dovetail fixtures in their shops – one for half-blinds, one for everything else. For example, I make frequent use of two commercial dovetail routing setups. In one, I have an inexpensive half-blind dovetail jig and an old router with the necessary guide

collar and dovetail bit. Because I rout more half-blind dovetails than any other dovetail joint, this saves me lots of time. Then, when I need to rout through dovetails or other special dovetail joints, I just use my other jig.

Just a Little Bit off the Top, Even when Routing Mortises
When routing deep mortises, remember to make the cut in several passes, routing no more than ⅛" with each pass. If the wood is very hard or tends to chip and splinter, it's better to rout in ¹⁄₁₆" passes. Also, use a spiral straight bit to help clear the chips from the mortise as you cut. This is especially important when you're using a hand-held router and the bit is positioned over the work because the chips tend to fall down into the mortise and clog it.

• **Two bits:** There's one bit for cutting the male part of the joint and a second for the female. This is usually the most expensive route.

There is another type of bit used for assembling boxes that routs the joinery on both edges. The drawer-lock joint – one example of these – is shown on page 72.

LOOSE-TENON JOINTS

Along with all the joints we have discussed so far that require joinery parts cut on the mating pieces, there are a number that use an extra piece to form a loose-tenon joint. The three most common are the true loose-tenon joint, the spline joint and the biscuit joint.

The true loose tenon is exactly what it sounds like. Rather than making a mortise in one piece and a tenon on the other, both pieces have mortises. A third piece (often made in a long stock piece and cut to length) becomes a double-sided tenon, connecting the two mortises. The strength is essentially the same as it is in a mortise-and-tenon joint, but the process is perfect for use with a router, and it is quick and accurate.

The mortises are made as described earlier and can be left rounded on the ends, as created by the bit. The tenon is made from a piece of stock planed and ripped to fit the mortises. Next the four arises are rounded using a roundover bit in your router to make a perfect fit in the mortises. Then you simply crosscut the tenon to fit the mortises.

Spline and biscuit joints are cousins to each other. The spline joint requires a groove (usually about ¼" wide) that you run the entire length of the two pieces to join together. This can be an edge-to-edge joint or an edge-to-face joint. It doesn't matter.

A special router bit called a spline-cutting bit is used to cut the groove. As with a rabbeting bit, the spline cutter uses interchangeable bearing guides of different diameters to adjust the depth of cut. A router table's fence also can be used to adust the depth.

With the mating grooves cut, just glue a spline in place. The spline can be made from ¼" plywood or solid wood, depending on your preference. Again, the spline should be slightly less wide (deep) than the groove to allow some room for glue squeeze-out.

Biscuits follow the same concept, except the spline cutter is used to cut

A Bit of Advice

As stated earlier, throughout this section we will be providing a closer look at many of the common and specialized bits that can be used with your router. These three bits are great when using your router for joinery.

Rabbeting Bit
This handy bit usually comes with a set of different-sized bearings that you can simply swap out to cut rabbets of different depths.

Cope-and-stick Bit
Making decorative frame-and-panel assemblies is a snap with this bit. There are three versions that have different ways of approaching the same operation. In this version, one bit cuts both the male and female pieces.

Spline-cutting Bit
Making grooves in edges is the mainstay of this bit. Newer versions allow you to adjust the size of the groove with shims or by adjusting the cutters.

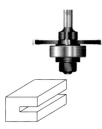

A tongue-and-groove joint requires two matching bits. Rout a groove in one edge of each of the workpieces, then change bits and rout a tongue in the other edge. You must carefully adjust the depth of cut for the second cut to match the first so the faces of the adjoining boards will be flush.

shorter grooves and commercially available biscuits are used to bridge the joint. In essence you've replaced the need to buy a $150 biscuit jointer with a $20 router bit – not too bad.

Use Your Router to Build Boxes & Drawers

by Nick Engler

Woodworkers have been building boxes for at least 5,000 years. For much of that period, boxes were made using a single chunk of wood with the insides dug out to create a cavity. That's because up until about 600 or 700 years ago, turning trees into boards was an extremely expensive process – the boards had to be hand-sawn (or rived) from logs, then smoothed with planes. Consequently, only the very rich owned furniture made from boards.

The invention of the water-powered sawmill in 1328 caused a revolution in woodworking, including the art of making boxes and drawers. The sawmill made it possible for everyone to own boxes made out of sawed lumber, and woodworkers began to build storage units from more than just one board.

This multi-board box remains a rather practical and popular method of construction. While the joinery isn't much of a concern when making a one-piece box, it becomes paramount once you begin building boxes and drawers from multiple boards.

With the advent of multi-board drawer construction, a variety of woodworking planes and saws were developed with box and drawer joinery as their sole purpose. As power tools became more prevalent, the router took over many of the box and drawer joinery duties. In this chapter, I'll take a look at a number of joints that can be created with a router to help you build furniture, drawers and many other boxes.

CORNER JOINTS

A variety of joints formed by routers can be used to attach the rigid corners of boxes and drawers. The best choice of joint will depend on how the box or drawer will be used:

• Will it be a strictly utilitarian storage unit or will it be decorative as well?

• Will it see light duty or will it be subjected to heavy use?

• Will it remain stationary or will it be moved from place to place?

No matter what you decide to use your box or drawer for, we've got the joint for you. Here are some of the most common corner joints (many of these joints were discussed in more depth in Chapter Four):

Butt Joints

These are usually reinforced with screws or glue blocks and work well for light-duty, utilitarian boxes. No routers are necessary here. It's the simplest and weakest corner joint.

Grain can run any direction with plywood bottom

When you make a drawer with a solid-wood bottom, the grain direction should run from side-to-side so the drawer bottom will expand front-to-back. If the bottom were to expand side-to-side, it would press the drawer sides out, making the drawer bind or stick in its opening.

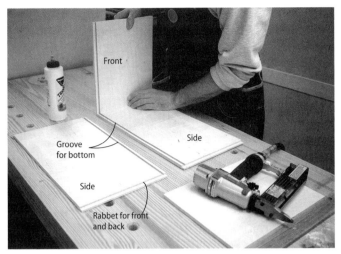

This drawer box is made pretty easily with rabbets. The front and back rest in ½"-wide x ¼"-deep rabbets in the side pieces. The bottom slides into a ¼"-wide x ¼"-deep groove in the sides and front. The back is ½" shorter than the front to allow the bottom to slide in.

Rabbets and grooves are pretty easy to make with a hand-held router. Here you see a router cutting a ¼"-deep groove with a ¼" straight bit and an edge guide.

Rabbets & Grooves:

These look similar to butt joints when assembled, but they are strong enough to be used for medium-duty utilitarian boxes. Rabbets of many sizes are formed easily using a rabbeting bit in a hand-held or table-mounted router. Rabbets and grooves also can be made with a straight bit in a hand-held router if you use a base-mounted edge guide. If the router is in a table, the fence guides the wood to quickly form the rabbets or grooves.

Miter Joints

These are a more aesthetically pleasing option, hiding the end grain on the adjoining boards so that all you see is uninterrupted face grain. However, these are comparatively weak and are best suited for light-duty projects unless reinforced with biscuits or splines. Routers seldom are used to form miter joints, and are used instead to reinforce and decorate them.

Splined Miters

These are much stronger than regular miters and can be used for medium- or heavy-duty decorative boxes. The splines can be hidden or visible, depending on your project's style. They can be made with hand-held or table-mounted routers using a spline-cutter bit, which is essentially a tiny table saw blade with the shaft of the bit serving as an arbor.

Tips & Tricks

Drawer Sides Can Extend Past the Back
Some traditional and modern drawer designs call for the sides to extend ¼"-½" beyond the back of the drawer. This makes the drawer simpler to build and slightly stronger than if the sides are merely flush with the back. For inset drawers, the back ends of the sides often serve as stops to keep the drawer from being pushed in too far. The sides also make more stable stops than the back. Should the back cup or warp, the drawer may protrude from its case slightly. Should the sides cup, the position of the drawer won't be affected.

Size Drawers to Holes, Then Plane Them to Fit
Make the drawers precisely the same size as the drawer openings. They'll be too big to work properly, but you can use your hand plane or belt sander to take just a little bit of stock from the outside surfaces to get a perfect fit.

It May Take Some Time, but Rout the Cavity in Many Passes
If you're making a one-board box with your router, make sure you rout out the cavity in several passes, cutting no more than ⅛" deeper with each pass until you reach the desired depth. Begin by routing the circumference of the cavity, keeping the pilot bearing pressed against the pattern. Then move the router back and forth to clean out the waste in the middle of the cavity. (This technique is used only for small boxes these days – usually jewelry boxes with an odd or organic shape to them.)

Finger Joints

Also known as "box joints," these are strong enough to qualify for heavy-duty boxes and drawers. The interlocking tenons create a vast gluing surface that holds firmly. These were once considered strictly utilitarian (many packing crates in the late 19th and

½" bottom beveled to fit in ¼"-wide groove in sides

Half-blind dovetails

The drawer bottoms in the drawers shown above are ½" thick but are beveled to slip into a ¼" groove, a traditional drawer construction method. Also, you can see the half-blind dove-tails connecting the side with the front.

MAKING DRAWERS

As mentioned earlier, a drawer is a box without a lid that slides in and out of a larger box, chest or case. Most drawers have five parts – a front, a back, two sides and a bottom.

Drawers are classified according to how the fronts and faces fit their openings. They can be "inset" within the opening, they can "overlay" the face frame or front edges of the case, or they can be rabbeted or "lipped" so that only the lips overlap the case.

To a large degree, drawers are made the same way as the cabinets that hold them. The front, back and sides are arranged to expand and contract in the same direction and are joined rigidly at the corners. The bottom usually floats in groove in the sides, free to move independently so its shrinking and swelling won't affect the overall drawer structure.

But there are significant differences between drawers and boxes. Typically, a drawer must withstand more punishment than a box. As you push or pull a drawer in and out, there is a good deal of stress placed on the corner joints. And because the drawer handles or pulls are attached to the front, most of this stress is concentrated on the front corners.

Consequently, drawers commonly are built with extremely strong joints at the front corners, while the back corners and the bottom are assembled with much simpler joinery.

There is another reason people opt to use different joints at the front of the drawer – traditionally, the drawer faces looked a lot like solid boards or panels in a frame. So, the front joinery had to be hidden when the drawer was closed.

The joints listed below are common router-made joints used in drawer joinery:

early 20th centuries were made using finger joints), but in recent years they have been used in decorative applications as well. These joints are best formed with a table-mounted router using a straight bit and a miter gauge or a specially made jig.

Through-dovetails

The strongest of all common joints for boxes and drawers, these are suitable for heavy-duty projects. Similar to finger joints, through-dovetails were once thought of as utilitarian, but today they are used just as much for decorative pieces. Routers make quick work of dovetails using specialized bits and jigs to make precise and tight joinery.

(Note: While some people will use contrasting colors or species of wood when making finger joints and dovetails to make the joinery stand out, just as many want to use the same type of wood for both parts of these joints to make them look more subtle.)

All of these joints can be used to make standard boxes or the more-common open-topped boxes we use every day – known more commonly, of course, as drawers.

Reinforced Rabbets

These are sufficient for light-duty drawers (shown below in the inset drawer). Just rabbet the drawer front, then secure the sides in these rabbets with glue, nails, screws or pegs. This joint also is frequently used to mate the drawer back and sides.

Lock Joints, or Tongue-and-Rabbet Joints

These work well for light- or medium-duty drawers. Cut dados in the drawer sides, and a tongue is formed when you cut a rabbet in

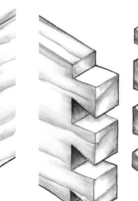

Finger joint   **Through-dovetail**

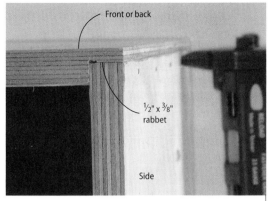

Joining drawer sides to the front and back can be as simple as cutting a rabbet. Then you can use glue and nails to complete the joint.

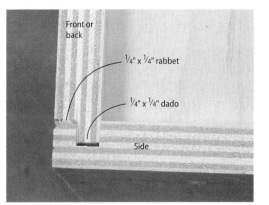

the drawer front and back. Then insert the tongue in the dados. This joint (seen in the photo above right) can be used for the front and back joint in drawers, providing extra strength over a reinforced rabbet. Made using rabbeting, spline or straight router bits, these joints are a mainstay in commercial drawer joinery.

Sliding Dovetails
These are strong enough for medium- and heavy-duty drawers. Simply cut a dovetail groove in the drawer front with a dovetail bit in your router, then cut matching tenons in the sides and slide them together. It's unlikely to be used for any drawer joinery other than attaching drawer fronts.

Half-blind Dovetails
These are the traditional choice when you need heavy-duty drawers. The interlocking tails and pins offer an enormous amount of strength and they are relatively easy to make with a store-bought jig. Because they are "half-blind," they meet the requirement for being invisible with the drawer closed.

Through-dovetails
These are a close cousin to the half-blinds. While they are easier to create, these joints will be visible from the front of the drawer. Because of this, a through-dovetail is often used for the back joinery in a drawer, while the more complicated half-blind dovetail adorns the front.

JOINING THE BOTTOM
The final piece of joinery in a drawer is finding a way to hold the bottom in place in the sides, front and back. Because the bottom

usually floats, your choice of joints is more limited when looking to attach this piece.

Traditional solid-wood bottoms originally were made from ½" material and the edges were beveled or raised similar to the center section on a raised-panel door. This allowed the bottom to be captured in a relatively narrow groove (¼" or so) without losing any strength in the bottom. Raised-

A Bit of Advice
As stated earlier, throughout this section we will be providing a closer look at many of the common and specialized bits that can be used with your router. These bits are great when using your router to make boxes and drawers.

Lock-miter Bit
An excellent joint for mitered drawers, this bit provides extra gluing surfaces and locking strength. The same bit creates both joining edges by cutting one board vertically and the other horizontally with the same set-up.

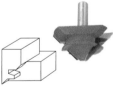

Dovetail Bit
This classic drawer joint adds extra locking strength and also a decorative feature. This bit is available in a number of different angles for use in softwoods or hardwoods.

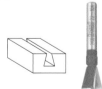

Drawer-lock Bit
This bit lets you form a stronger rabbet joint between the sides and front of a drawer. The drawer fronts are cut horizontally, while the drawer sides are cut vertically against the fence of a router table.

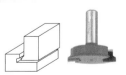

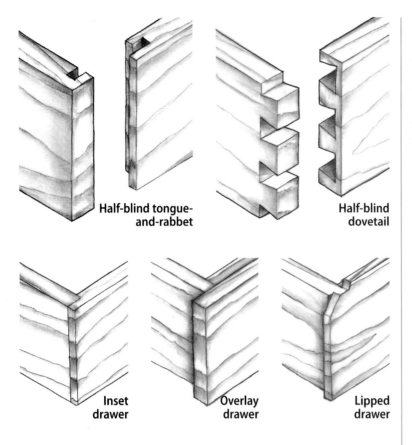

Half-blind tongue-and-rabbet

Half-blind dovetail

Inset drawer

Overlay drawer

Lipped drawer

panel and straight router bits in a table-mounted operation make this joinery safe and fairly easy.

With today's wood technologies, ¼" plywood often is used to create very strong drawer bottoms with no extra milling required.

On many boxes and drawers, the bottom is captured in a groove that is cut in the inside surfaces of the front, back and sides. Just slide the bottom into the grooves at the same time you assemble the box, making

sure you don't get any glue in the grooves. Once the glue has had time to dry, the bottom will be permanently locked in place.

One common variation in drawers is to cut a groove in just the drawer front and sides, cutting the back narrower to stop at the top of the bottom groove. This allows you to slide the bottom into place after the drawer is assembled. Then the bottom is tacked in place on the drawer back. With less mess and haste while the glue is drying, this method also gives you a chance to square the drawer to the bottom.

Another drawer bottom joint can be made by cutting grooves into small strips of wood, then gluing the strips to the inside surfaces of the drawer. The kind of drawer bottom that rests in grooved slips is sometimes called a "French bottom."

Or, if the drawer is so wide that a thin bottom might sag, you can divide the bottom into two or more sections with grooved dividers, also called "muntins."

If your project requires a removable bottom or if you must install the bottom after the rest of the parts are joined, you can rest the bottom on ledges or cleats, or you can screw it to the bottom edges of the box in some cases.

(Note: When you are fitting a solid-wood bottom in your drawer, you must remember to leave space for expansion. How much space depends on the width of the bottom. The rule of thumb is to allow ¼" for every 12" across the grain with plain-sawn wood and ⅛" with quartersawn wood.)

Traditional drawers used raised panels made of solid wood for the bottoms. These are easily made on a router table with a raised-panel bit, then fit into a standard groove in the drawer sides.

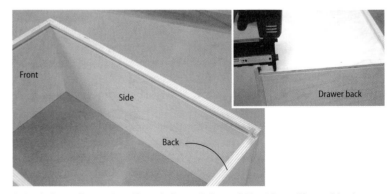

Front

Side

Back

Drawer back

A simple drawer bottom is easily made from ¼" plywood. The sides and front of the drawer are grooved with a straight router bit, ¼" up from the bottom edge. The back is held short at the top of the groove. With the bottom slipped into the groove (shown in the inset photo), you can square up the drawer, then nail the bottom in place into the drawer back.

Edge & Surface Treatments

by Nick Engler

Routers were developed to cut moulded shapes in wood. Although their workshop role has expanded (greatly) during the last century to include joinery and other operations, moulding is still what they do best. They remain the chief woodworking tools for edge and surface "treatments" – cutting decorative shapes.

Before we get into the techniques for making decorative moulded shapes, let's review these shapes and how they're combined. In many woodworkers' minds, this is muddy water. Open any tool catalog to the router bit section and you'll find whole pages of shapes, all in a jumble. But don't worry. There is some order to this chaos.

Despite the profusion of moulding bits, there are really only three shapes in decorative woodworking:

- **Bead (convex curve)**
- **Cove (concave curve)**
- **Flat (straight line)**

Every moulding, no matter how complex, is comprised of beads, coves and flats. If you had only three router bits – one for cutting beads, one for cutting coves, one for cutting flats – you could still produce any shape of moulding, no matter how intricate the shape.

BASIC MOULDED SHAPES

Of course, there's a little more to it. Each of these three main categories is subdivided into a few basic moulded shapes that can be cut with a common bit. All mouldings are variations or combinations of these basic shapes, shown on the following page.

There are no hard and fast rules dictating how you combine these shapes or how you use them. However, you may find these guidelines useful:

- Consider where people will stand when viewing the shapes and present these features at an angle that makes them easy to be seen and enjoyed.
- Vary the shapes in a complex moulding – don't just repeat the same shapes over and over. The classic bead moulding, which incorporates a cove and a bead, has been a favorite of cabinetmakers for hundreds of years – you hardly ever see a moulding with a double cove or a double bead.
- To make mouldings more dramatic, use sharp, crisp transitions between the shapes. Make the curves and flats meet at distinct angles, or you can use fillets to separate shapes.
- If the structural strength of the piece is important, use simpler shapes.

Once you have designed a moulding, you need to plan how you'll make it – what bits to use, how many passes you'll need to make, etc.

Then, consider how to incorporate the moulded shapes in the project you're building. You have two choices: You can cut the shapes into the surfaces of the structural parts, or you can make separately shaped parts (mouldings) and apply them to the piece.

Each of these choices has trade-offs. If you make applied mouldings, you may not be able to match the wood grain and color of the larger piece, but you can use moulding to disguise seams and joints. If you cut the shapes in a large structural piece, you don't have to worry about matching the wood, but you do have to worry if the shape will weaken the piece. Choose whichever moulding design works best for the piece.

This tabletop will see a lot of use, so the woodworker who made it cut a thumbnail moulding in the edge. This relatively simple shape preserves the strength of the edge, while a more complex shape would weaken it and the edge would soon show the wear.

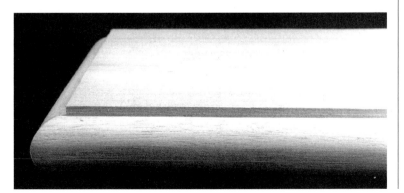

Tips & Tricks

Safe Small Profiles

Small (½" wide or less) profiles and edge treatments can be dangerous to run. To avoid this, use a two-step process. By preparing a slab of wood the appropriate thickness of your profile (let's call it a ½" x 10" x 24" piece of cherry) you can safely run the profile on one long edge, then head to the table saw to safely cut off the thin edge piece. Then head back to the router table and repeat the process. It adds a couple of steps, but it also adds a lot of safety.

Two Sides of Grooves Make Pretty Decorative Panels

Cut a set of grooves in a board that are parallel to each other. Make each groove a little more than half as deep as the board is thick. Then turn the board upside down and cut another set of grooves at an angle to the first set. Where the grooves intersect, they will create openings. The size, shape and spacing of these openings depends on the size, shape and spacing of the grooves.

Simple Cock Beading

Cock beading is a simple edge detail that can dress up doors, drawers and much more. But cutting this detail on a door panel can be a lot of work. The simple option is to run a quantity of ⅛" hardwood through your router table adding a bullnose detail to one edge. Then, simply glue this edging to your panel. Presto – simple cock beading.

CUTTING WITH THE ROUTER

Woodworkers usually shape the edges of a piece. The reasons for this are both aesthetic and practical. Because the edges often trace the outline of the project, shaping the edges emphasizes and enhances the design. Also, the edges are easier to cut than the faces.

The technique for routing moulded edges is simple and straightforward; there's little here that hasn't already been explained in previous chapters. However, a few additional considerations are worth mentioning.

Before you rout a shape in a straight edge, make sure that the edge is as smooth and even as possible. Joint it and remove all the mill marks. If the edge is contoured, make sure all the curves are "fair" – smooth and even. Because one of the purposes of a moulded shape is to emphasize the edge, the shape also will emphasize any imperfections in the edge.

When you're ready to shape the piece, cut the ends (end grain) first, then cut the edges (long grain).

Cut the large parts with a hand-held router, and cut the smaller parts on a router table. With very small parts, leave them attached to a larger board, rout the edge of the board, then cut the parts free. This last technique is particularly important when making mouldings. Most mouldings, when ripped to their final dimensions, are too slender to rout safely. The cutting action of the router may actually tear the thin stock apart.

If you use a large bit such as a panel-raising bit, slow down the speed of the router. The larger the bit, the slower you should

Fillet or listel: use straight bit	Chamfer: use chamfering bit or V-bit	Bevel: use chamfering bit or V-bit	Flat-bottom groove: use straight bit	V-groove: use V-bit	Flute: use fluting bit

Round-bottom: use fluting bit	Cove or cavetto: use cove bit	Quarter-round bead: use roundover bit	Half-round bead or astragal: use beading bit for small beads, nosing or roundover bit for large beads	Cyma recta: use ogee bit (centers of curves are aligned horizontally)	Cyma reversa: use ogee bit (centers of curves are aligned vertically)

Basic moulded shapes

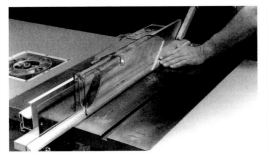

To make an applied moulding or picture frame stock, cut the shape you want in the edge of a wide board, then rip it to the proper thickness, which I'm doing here on my table saw. Don't try to rout a shape in narrow stock – it may chip, splinter or kick back at you.

run the router – otherwise the bit may burn the wood. If you can't vary the speed of the router, you shouldn't use bits larger than 2" in diameter. Even bits larger than 1½" can be troublesome.

SURFACE TREATMENTS

In addition to cutting edges, you can create a variety of decorative shapes in the face of your workpiece. Surface treatments can be cut pretty easily with either a hand-held or a table-mounted router fitted with either an unpiloted or a point-cut bit.

The most common surface decoration is a simple groove – flat-bottom, round-bottom or V-bottom. If the groove is straight, use a straightedge, fence or miter gauge to guide the cut. If the groove is irregular, you'll want to use a guide collar and a template.

For decorative grooves with a more-complex geometry, you can make multiple passes – or use a more-complex bit. For example, by making multiple parallel passes with a point-cut roundover bit (sometimes called a "beading" bit), you can form cock beads and reeds. Or, you can make cuts with a veining bit or a round-nose bit to create flutes. Also, a point-cut ogee bit will rout a wide groove with a double-ogee shape.

MAKING COMPLEX MOULDINGS

When you produce complex mouldings, you often make multiple cuts, combining edge and surface treatments. It isn't difficult, but there are tricks to help you.

• First, you will need to decide which router bits to use to cut the different shapes. Often this is more of an art than a science. There may be three or four bits in your

Tips & Tricks

Subtle Refinement
Edge treatments don't have to be complicated to be effective. A simple roundover bit or chamfering bit in the right locations can soften the look and feel of a piece of furniture, adding an extra level of elegance. And either of these bits work well with a bearing guide in an easy-to-manage trim router.

Keep That Piece Clamped Down Tight
Whenever you're routing something, make sure that either your workpiece or your router is stable and secure – they can't both move. If you choose to move the router across the work, clamp the work to your bench. If a clamp interferes with the operation, rout up to it and turn the router off. Then move the clamp to an area on the workpiece that you've already cut and resume routing.

Back-routing (Also Known as Climb-cutting) Can be Tough
Occasionally you must back-rout a piece to reduce tear-out. This means you are cutting with the bit's rotation, rather than against it. It's much more difficult to control your work this way, so be sure to take shallow cuts and feed very slowly. Keep the router and the work steady, making sure the bit doesn't chatter.

When you're ready to shape your workpiece, first cut the end grain along the ends …

… then cut the long grain along the edges.

This safety consideration also applies to making curved mouldings, such as a classic "gooseneck" moulding. Cut the inside curve in the wide moulding stock, sand it so the curves are fair, then rout the shape in the edge.

When you've shaped the inside edge of the stock, you can cut the outside edge to free the moulding from the piece, as I'm doing here with my band saw.

When cutting straight grooves, you can use a variety of jigs to get a decorative effect. Here, a tapering jig produces a pattern of angled grooves in a table leg. The grooves create the impression of a tapered leg, even though it's straight.

selection that will produce a single shape. Knowing which one will work best is a matter of experience.

• Second, when you know which bits you're using, carefully plan the cuts. Each cut should leave enough stock to adequately support the workpiece during the next cut. If possible, make small cuts before large ones, and remove stock from the interior or middle of the surface before taking it from the sides.

• Third, when you make each cut, use constant, even pressure to feed the work (or move the router) and keep it firmly against the guides. If the pressure isn't constant or if the work wanders slightly, the cut may not be even. If the problem continues over several passes, there may be considerable variation in the moulded shape along the length of the board.

• Fourth, make more moulding than you think you'll actually need, because if you run short, it will be difficult to reproduce the exact same setups you went through.

INLAYING BANDING

You can decorate wooden surfaces by cutting shallow mortises and filling them with inlaid strips of veneer, patches of marquetry and parquetry, slabs of mother-of-pearl, strands of wire and so on.

Template

Some surface grooves are simultaneously decorative and practical, such as the groove around the perimeter of this cutting board. Not only does it collect liquids, but the groove also adds visual interest to an otherwise uninspiring piece. To make this groove, cut a template from hardboard and secure it to the cutting board with double-sided tape. Then you can cut the groove using a guide collar and core-box bit, keeping the collar firmly pressed against the template.

Tips & Tricks

Layers Can Help if You Want Complex Mouldings

Instead of making multiple passes to create a complex moulding, just glue up several simpler shapes. The easiest way to do this is to "laminate" the shapes – or build them up in layers. But you can also "join" the shapes by cutting dados, rabbets or grooves in the moulding stock, then glue smaller strips of wood in these joints. The strips that you glue together don't have to be the same species – you can use contrasting wood, if you want.

How Much is Enough?

To make sure the collet is safely gripping a router bit, insert ¾" of the length of a ¼" shank bit into the collet and insert a full 1" of every ½" shank bit.

Bits Pull Double Duty

Most edge-profile router bits are designed to be run in a specific orientation to the edge. However, if you're looking for an unusual alternative, don't hesitate to think in a different dimension. By running the wood past the bit in a vertical rather than horizontal attitude, the profile is changed subtly. And you get two profiles out of one bit.

Make multiple passes with a beading bit to create decorative reeds and beads in the surface of a board. Because the beading bit is actually a small point-cut quarter-round bit, each pass cuts a 90° arc – one-quarter of a circle. Half-round beads require two passes. The corner bead or reed on this table leg requires three passes because it is three-quarters round.

Point-cut bits with a complex shape, such as this pilotless ogee bit, cut a broad groove with an interesting shape. The sides of the grooves are mirror images of each other.

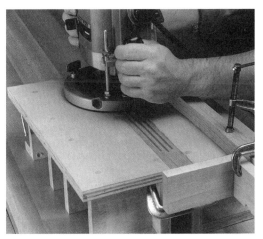

A flute is just a half-round groove – the opposite of a half-round bead. Often, it's blind at one or both ends. Use a veining bit to cut the flute and a straightedge to guide your router. If the flute is blind, it helps to have a plunge router. Attach stops to the straightedge to halt the cut when the flute is the correct length.

Because these inlaid objects often are small and intricately shaped, cutting mortises to fit them requires precision. Not only must the shape be correct, the depth must be accurate and absolutely uniform. That's why one of the best tools for making these small cuts is the router.

Perhaps the simplest type of decorative inlay is the inset wood banding. These simply are ribbons of wood sliced from a board or a sheet of veneer.

They also may be made up of several contrasting colors of wood, forming long strips of marquetry (designs that are made with multiple pieces of wood arranged

A Bit of Advice

As stated earlier, throughout this section we will be providing a closer look at many of the common and specialized bits that can be used with your router. These bits are great when using your router to make edge & surface treatments.

Panel-raising Bit
This bit combines two small wings (which cut downward to shear the top edge) with two large wings (which shear upward for a smooth finish). It's ideal for creating decorative tops and should be used in a router table.

Beading Bit
These bits add an attractive profile to furniture and millwork. They can be used to cut all kinds of material – plywood, hardwood and softwood. They're also available with steel pilots or bearings for similar designs.

Table Top Bit
This bit, designed with sharp curves, helps you generate a strong, uplifting edge, creating a bold effect on all kinds of furniture.

Some banding inlays simply are thin pieces of wood ripped from boards or cut from sheets of veneer. You can make these simple bandings in your workshop, using a saw or a knife. Other inlays can be intricate pieces of marquetry. These are made by arranging different colors of wood in geometric patterns, gluing them together and slicing them into long ribbons. You can make these yourself, too, if you have the patience, but there are many ready-made marquetry bandings available from mail-order suppliers.

Cut recesses for banding with the same setup you would use to cut simple rabbets, dados and grooves. If the workpiece is small, cut it on your router table using a fence to guide the board. If the workpiece is too large to handle on the table, use a hand-held router and clamp a straightedge to guide the router. Either way, a straight bit is the best choice.

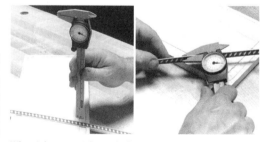

Next, test-fit the banding in its recess. When you're satisfied with the fit, spread glue in the recess and press the banding in place. Wipe away any excess glue, place a piece of wax paper or plastic wrap over the banding and clamp a straight, thick board to the piece over the covering. The board helps distribute clamping pressure evenly, and the covering keeps it from sticking.

When the glue is dry, remove the board and the covering, then scrape away any glue that remains on the surface. But be careful you don't scrape too deeply – you don't want to scrape through the banding.

with the long grain showing) or parquetry (multiple-piece designs with the end grain showing). They are usually straight, but they also may be curved.

To inlay straight banding, first measure its width and thickness. Then rout a shallow rabbet, dado or groove to fit it, using either a hand-held or a table-mounted router. After cutting the recess, just glue the banding in place. For more details, check out the photos at right.

If the inlaid materials are fairly thick, you'll want to rout a recess that is slightly shallower than the inlay is thick. This will make the inlay "proud" when you glue it in place – meaning it will protrude slightly above the surface of the wood. After the glue dries, scrape or sand the inlay flush with the surface.

When inlay materials are thick, you can rout a recess to make the inlay "proud," then sand it flush. When inlay materials are thin, you risk sanding through them if you mount them proud. Instead, use calipers to measure the inlay thickness, then adjust the depth of cut to match.

If the inlaid materials are thin, you risk sanding through them if you mount them proud, as explained above. Instead, you will need to rout the recess to precisely the right depth. Use dial calipers to measure the thickness of the inlay, then carefully adjust the router's depth of cut to match.

Advanced Techniques For the Router

by Nick Engler

The router is an amazing tool that can mimic many of the other tools in your shop, including the table saw, the shaper, the jointer and even the planer. But it's also capable of amazingly delicate profile work, complicated joinery for any type of furniture you can imagine and shaping perfect circles and ovals. For the truly creative woodworker, the router is an excellent tool for making intricate inlay work normally performed by skilled hands alone.

Two things make these and other advanced router techniques possible: jigs and specialty bits. I've devoted more space than normal in this chapter to some of my favorite router jigs because of this. Spending the time to make one (or all) of these fixtures will open up a new world of opportunities for you. I'm sure you can quickly think of many other ways to use these jigs for your woodworking than just the techniques I've mentioned here.

The specialty bits are a different story. In many cases they can be expensive, such as with a rail-and-stile set for making raised-panel doors. Each set often creates only one style of door profile. But if you think about the effort involved to create those profiles in a way other than with a router, you'll quickly see the benefit to purchasing this pricey bit set.

There are other specialty bits that can create multiple profiles with a single bit, and I've listed some to consider in the "A Bit of Advice" section. These also will be able to adapt to your specific woodworking applications.

But please – feel free to try new ideas. If you combine the tilting router table shown with any of the specialty bits, you've made it easier to change the bits, and added a new dimension to your woodworking.

RULE JOINT

A rule joint is not so much a joint as it is two decorated, mated edges between a tabletop

You can rout a rule joint using a simple cove bit. The bit height should leave a flat to match the mating profile's bead.

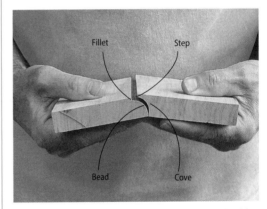

When both rule joint profiles are correct, the pieces should nest together with the top surfaces flush and a very small gap between the profiles.

and a drop leaf. Cut a bead and a fillet in the tabletop, then cut a matching step and cove in the drop leaf.

When the table is assembled, the bead will show when the leaf is down. When it's up, the joint will close and the surfaces will be flush.

The trick to making a rule joint is not as much in shaping the edges as it is in installing the drop-leaf hinges. Each hinge must be mortised into the wood so that its pin is at the center of the arc described by the mating

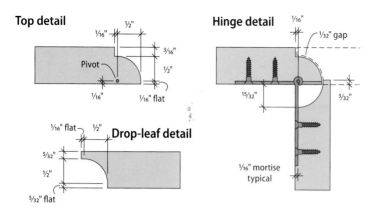

Top detail

Pivot

½"
1⁄16"
3⁄16"
½"
1⁄16"
1⁄16" flat

Drop-leaf detail

1⁄16" flat
½"
5⁄32"
½"
5⁄32" flat

Hinge detail

1⁄16"
1⁄32" gap
15⁄32"
3⁄32"
1⁄16" mortise typical

A great application for the rule joint is to install drop-leaf table hinges. You just need to make sure you think before you act. What seems normal – just placing the hinge barrel where the leaf and top meet, like a door to a stile – is totally wrong. Also, you need to make sure that you don't make the hinges flush with the underside surface. You need a bit of depth there. As with all hinges, the location of the pivot point is the ultimate concern. With the drop-leaf hinge, the pivot point (the center of the pin) must be centered on the radius of the matching profiles.

cove and bead. Just fasten the long leaf of the hinge to the drop leaf, then fasten the short leaf to the tabletop and you're done.

RAIL-AND-STILE JOINT

Rail-and-stile joints require two matched router bits and are normally used to join the shaped surfaces of frame members. Rout the sticking portion of the joint – the portion with the shape that you want to see – in the inside edges of the stiles and rails. Use a fence to guide the stock when routing straight edges, and rely on the pilot bearing only when routing contoured edges.

Rout the coped portion of the rail-and-stile joint in the ends of the rails only. Use a

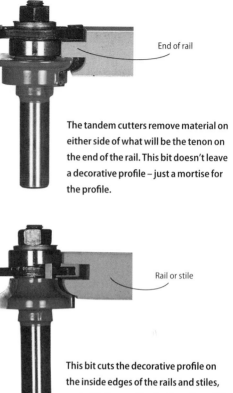

End of rail

The tandem cutters remove material on either side of what will be the tenon on the end of the rail. This bit doesn't leave a decorative profile – just a mortise for the profile.

Rail or stile

This bit cuts the decorative profile on the inside edges of the rails and stiles, and mills the mortise for the rails and the groove for the door's panel.

miter gauge to help feed the stock past the bit. To keep the board from chipping out as you finish the cut, back it up with a scrap piece.

TILTING ROUTER STAND

I've designed more than a dozen whiz-bang router tables in my career, each one supposedly packing a bigger bang than the last. But what finally dawned on me a few tables ago is this: What makes the fixture truly useful has less to do with the tabletop than the stand it rests on.

Whether you build or buy a router table, you're faced with the same dilemma. The router is designed to be a portable power tool. All the controls and adjustments are easily accessible when the router is resting upright on a workbench. Bolt it to the underside of a table to convert it to a stationary tool and suddenly it is a lot less cooperative. Many of us spend a lot of time on our knees in front of our router table, fumbling underneath to change bits and adjust the depth of cut. A woodworker I know calls this "praying to the router god."

Some woodworkers solve this problem by mounting the router to a plate that rests

This door shows a complex version of a rail-and-stile joint. The haunch fills the groove left by the bit. Also, the decorative moulding is mitered at the corner for a classy finish.

Haunch

Tenon

Mitered panel profile groove

Tips & Tricks

Rattle-free Doors

With a solid-wood raised-panel door such as the one shown here, it's important to leave a little room in the grooved frame to allow for panel expansion because of changes in humidity. That's smart, but the extra space can make the door rattle. By adding a strip of rubber tubing or weather-stripping foam in the groove prior to glue-up, the panel won't shift unnecessarily, but the tubing will compress, allowing the panel to expand.

Use a Push Block When Routing Smaller Pieces

When cutting small pieces on a router table, be careful to keep your hands and fingers clear of the bit. You may wish to secure the stock to a push block or a large scrap with double-faced carpet tape to rout it safely.

Use Bearings to Get Perfect Fence Alignment

When setting up a bearing-guided bit in a router table during an operation that uses the fences, the bearing isn't a necessary part of the procedure, but it's still useful to help you set the fence. After adjusting the proper height of the bit for your cut, use a straightedge held against the bit's bearing to align the fences perfectly. In fact, if you don't align the fences correctly, the bearing can protrude past the fence faces, causing your work to ride away from the bit in the middle of your cut.

Small Inlay? Sticky Solution

To inlay a shape, first trace the outline on the wood surface. This can be a difficult task, particularly if the design includes several small shapes. To keep wooden shapes from shifting as you trace around them, stick them to the surface with double-sided carpet tape. To keep hard, dense materials in place, glue them to the wood surface with white (polyvinyl resin) glue. The adhesive won't hold the inlays in place permanently, but it will secure them long enough to trace the outline.

Precision in a Small Package

Rout the inlay recesses with a straight bit and a hand-held router. It's easier to work with small bits rather than large ones. Not only can you cut intricate details with small bits, but they also are easier to control. You may want to work with a small router rather than a large one, because small routers give you better visibility and are easier to control. However, even with a small bit and a small router you may find it difficult to rout a line freehand. For this reason, stop cutting just short of the outline and finish the job with carving tools.

---

in a rabbet, then removing the plate when they need to get at the router. Unfortunately, the sides of the rabbet wear as you pop the plate in and out. As the plate becomes loose in its rabbet, new problems arise with safety and accuracy.

A tilting router stand makes the router easily accessible and lets you secure the router to the table. The table swings up like the lid of a chest, exposing the router and bringing it up to a comfortable working height. You can change bits and make adjustments to the tool while standing upright.

Of course, to get this amazing convenience you'd have to build a complex mechanism and a special table, right? Nope. Most parts are rectangular boards butted together and secured with screws or bolts. The design is easily adaptable to support

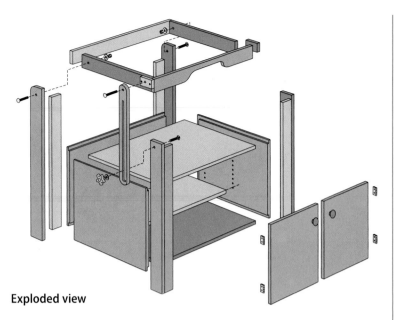

Exploded view

table clips and pocket screws work equally well.

The legs should hold the table at countertop level (roughly 36"). My router table is part of a "work island" – the table saw, workbench and router table all are at the same level. So I cut the legs on my table a fraction of an inch longer than what the drawings show.

A plywood box is screwed to the legs below the table to brace the legs and provide storage for router accessories. There must be adequate room between the top of the box and the bottom of the router table to fit the router when the collet is fully retracted into the router base. I mounted simple plywood doors on the front legs to enclose the box and keep some of the sawdust out.

The most complex part in the table is the support arm. It has an L-slot – a long slot

whatever tabletop you're using right now. You simply need to change the width and depth of the stand to fit.

Begin with the frame under the table. It should be about 6" smaller side-to-side and 4" smaller front-to-back than your router table top. If the table has slots on it to mount the fence, make sure that the frame members won't cover these slots or interfere with the fence movement.

Also give some thought to how you will attach the table to the frame. I used two long cleats, one on each side. However, brackets,

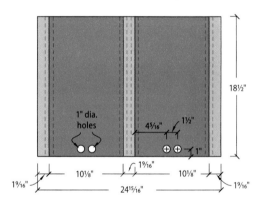

Plan of sliding shelves

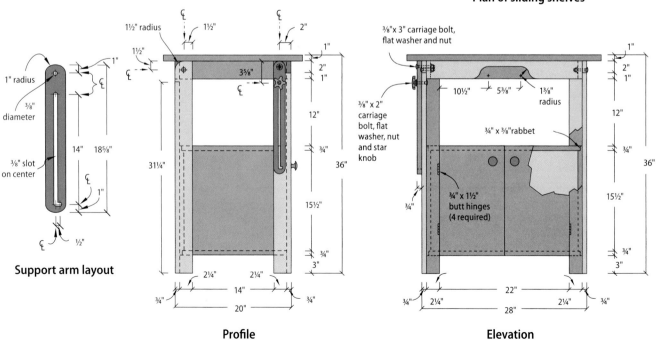

Support arm layout

Profile

Elevation

with a little hiccup at one end. I made the "hiccup" first, drilling a few overlapping holes to create a short slot. I routed a long slot perpendicular to the short one, then cleaned up the edges of the short slot with a file. When mounting the support arm to the stand, the short portion of the slot faces front.

To help organize all my router bits and collars, I mounted two sliding shelves to the fixed shelf inside the storage box. You don't need to buy expensive hardware to get the sliding action. Make narrow hardwood rails to guide the shelves, then cut matching grooves in the sliding shelves and fixed rails. Glue splines in the grooves in the rails, then glue the rails to a fixed shelf. Fit the sliding shelves to the splined guides, enlarging the grooves in the edges and sanding a little stock from the bottom faces so the shelves slide easily. Wax the grooves in the shelves to help them move smoothly. I drilled holes and mounted dowels in the sliding trays to help organize the bits and accessories and keep them in place. The shelves slide all the way out of the storage box so you can use them as a caddy or tray to carry the bits.

To raise the top of the router table, lift it all the way up and push down near the bottom of the support arm to slip the locking bolt into the short portion of the L-slot. Tighten the knob to make sure the top doesn't slam down unexpectedly.

ROUTING OVALS

While circles have a constant radius, ovals don't. The radius of an oval or an ellipse is greatest along the major axis (the length of the oval) and smallest along the minor axis (the width of the oval). Ovals also have two pivot points, each of which is called a focus. See the drawing below for more details.

The technique for routing an oval relies on the same principle as routing a circle,

Oval

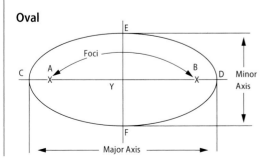

A Bit of Advice

As stated earlier, throughout this section we will be providing a closer look at many of the common and specialized bits that can be used with your router. The bits shown here are great when using your router for some of the more advanced applications.

Keyhole Bit
For hanging a project flush to the wall, a keyhole bit is the answer. It plunges into the wood, then plows a channel, perfectly sized to slip over a screw head.

Multi-profile Bit
One bit does it all. By adjusting the height and the distance to the fence, this one bit cuts a variety of profiles. Mix and match the shapes. The options are limited only by your imagination and the jigs you can use.

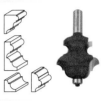

Upspiral Bit
At first you may say this bit just plows grooves. Not true. The spiraling flutes of this bit also remove the waste from the groove, keeping the cut clean and keeping the bit from overheating and working harder than necessary.

Tips & Tricks

Hand Tools for a Crisp Look
After using a power tool to do much of the inlay work, trim up to the line with carving chisels. Use gouges to cut the curved portions of the shape, and use a skew chisel to cut straight edges and corners. Then clean out the waste with dogleg chisels and a small router plane.

Slow Sand to Smooth Finish
After gluing the inlays in, let the glue dry completely before you scrape away the excess. If the inlay is proud, hand-sand it flush with the surface. Don't use a power sander because inlays tend to be very thin and you might sand right through them.

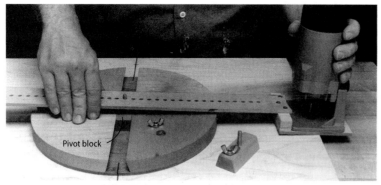

Pivot block

but you must swing the router around both pivots or foci. To do this, make a double trammel – a beam compass with two moving pivots – on which to mount the router. This jig works in the same fashion as a folk toy you might have come across that has a crank handle that describes an ellipse as you turn it. By substituting a router for the handle, you can rout perfect ovals.

Before you rout an oval with a double trammel, decide the length of the major and minor axes, then mark them on the workpiece. Center the double trammel pivot block over the point where the major and minor axes cross (Y), aligning one sliding pivot with the major axis and the other with the minor axis. Stick the pivot block to the workpiece with double-faced carpet tape. Mount the router on the beam, align it with the major axis and position the router so the bit is at one end of the axis. Center the minor pivot (the pivot that moves along the minor axis) over point Y and fasten the beam to it.

Swing the beam 90°, aligning it with the minor axis, and position the router so the bit is at the end of that axis. Center the major pivot over point Y and fasten the beam to it. The beam should now be fastened to both pivots. To check the setup, swing the router once around the pivots with the power off. The bit should pass over the ends of the major and minor axes.

To cut the oval with this double-trammel jig, swing the router around the pivots, pulling gently outward. This slight tension will take any play out of the mechanical system as the pivots slide back and forth in their grooves. Make the cut in several passes.

Trammel Jig – Exploded View

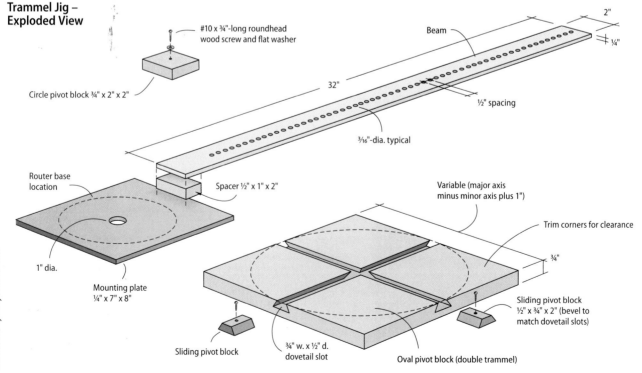

#10 x ¾"-long roundhead wood screw and flat washer

Circle pivot block ¾" x 2" x 2"

Beam

2"

¼"

32"

½" spacing

³⁄₁₆"-dia. typical

Router base location

Spacer ½" x 1" x 2"

Variable (major axis minus minor axis plus 1")

Trim corners for clearance

¾"

1" dia.

Mounting plate ¼" x 7" x 8"

Sliding pivot block

¾" w. x ½" d. dovetail slot

Oval pivot block (double trammel)

Sliding pivot block ½" x ¾" x 2" (bevel to match dovetail slots)

Illustrations by Mary Jane Favorite

Table Saws

Intro to the Table Saw

by Nick Engler

Few tools have revolutionized a craft as much as table saws have changed woodworking. These saws saved tedious hand work and – beyond making single pieces – made it possible to precisely reproduce parts quickly and accurately. This affected how furniture and other woodenware was built and transformed woodworking design.

Tips & Tricks

Cutting on the Table Saw as Easy as 1-2-3-4

No matter how you slice it, there are only four steps to making a table saw cut:
• Lay out the cut on the board.
• Adjust the blade and other accessories for that cut.
• Align the board with the blade.
• Pass the wood over the saw.

Before Making Your Parts, Make Test Cuts on Scraps

After you've made the necessary adjustments, always make a test cut in a scrap piece before cutting good stock. Measure the position of the cut on the board with a ruler or tape measure and gauge the width and depth with a dial caliper.

Think Ahead Before Cutting

When laying out a cut on a board, think ahead to how you will line up the cut marks with the saw blade. If necessary, use a square to transfer the marks to a more visible or more convenient surface. Many woodworkers mark a face and an edge – they use the mark on the edge to align the stock with the blade and the mark on the face to monitor the cut as it progresses. Also, it's best to indicate the waste side of the line so you can see on which side of the line to make the kerf.

The table saw first appeared in about 1800, although historians disagree on who invented it. Some credit a German craftsman, Gervinus; others think it was developed simultaneously by several different people in Europe and the United States. The story I find most interesting was told to me by the late Brother Theodore (Ted) Johnson, a Shaker scholar and member of the Sabbathday Lake Shaker community in Maine.

According to Brother Ted, the idea popped into the head of Sister Tabitha Babbitt as she sat at her spinning wheel at the Watervliet, N.Y., community. (Sister Tabitha, it seems, was from an inventive family – her brother developed Babbitt metal, an alloy still used in bearings and bushings.)

Sister Tabitha happened to be looking out the window at two Shaker brothers as they bucked firewood with a two-man saw. She marveled at how much more efficient her revolving wheel was than their reciprocating saw. Why couldn't the brothers simply mount saw teeth on a wheel?

She asked them, and they decided to try it. They snipped a crude circular saw blade from tin, mounted the tin blade on an arbor and fastened the arbor to a workbench. Spinning the arbor with a hand crank, they found that a circular motion cut much more efficiently than a traditional straight-line, back-and-forth motion. The brothers soon installed an improved version in a water-powered mill to cut siding and flooring to size – the first recorded circular saw in America. From these humble beginnings evolved the table saw.

CHOOSING A TABLE SAW

For more than two centuries, the table saw has remained a simple machine. There are only four crucial components, the same four that comprised the original invention – a table, a blade, an arbor and some means of powering the arbor.

A benchtop saw combines portability for a job site and features to make it functional. But the portability can be a trade-off for performance. The only reason to buy a benchtop saw for woodworking is if you need to transport it or if you don't have the space for a bigger saw.

However, there have been several useful developments along the way. For example, most modern table saws have a fence and a miter gauge to guide the wood past the blade, a blade carriage to adjust the angle and height of the blade, and a blade guard to protect the operator.

There are several different ways in which the basic components of a modern table saw can be arranged. The configuration of these components determines the type of saw.

• On a **benchtop saw**, the motor and blade carriage are encased in the saw body. These are "direct-drive" table saws, meaning the blade is mounted directly on the motor shaft. The body may be mounted on a stand or simply clamped to a workbench.

• The motor of a **contractor saw** is mounted behind the table, making it easier to disassemble the saw and transport it. The motor connects to the arbor by pulleys and one or more V-belts, which help isolate motor vibrations so they don't reach the blade. With more room under the table, the blade carriage can be bigger and beefier, and these big components further absorb vibrations from the saw. As a result, the blade runs smoother and truer.

• Hanging the motor off the back of the saw is OK on an open building site where there's lots of room, but it can take up space in a shop. The motor of a **cabinet saw** is mounted beneath the saw body, encased in the stand. This configuration not only saves room, it's also better balanced. This, together with the mass of the enclosed stand, makes the tool less top-heavy and more stable. Some cabinet saws have a larger blade capacity as well.

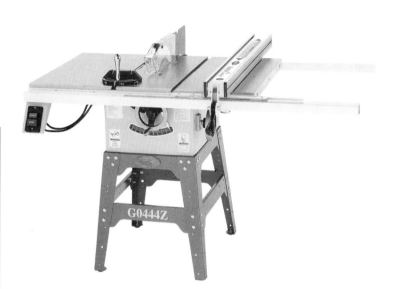

A contractor saw is a great first table saw for most woodworkers. The fence is more accurate, the motor is quiet, reliable and more powerful than that of a benchtop saw, and you can add hundreds of accessories to it. One catch – because the motor extends behind the body of the saw through an opening in the cabinet, it reduces dust collection efficiency.

A hybrid saw is still a contractor saw but has many features of a cabinet saw, including an enclosed internal motor.

• **Hybrid saws** are essentially contractor saws with some cabinet saw features. This is most often a partially or totally enclosed base, with the motor mounted inside the cabinet. Higher performance motors (up to 2 horsepower) are also part of the package, and some hybrids offer beefed-up trunnions that are mounted on the cabinet rather than the saw top, as is the norm in contractor saws.

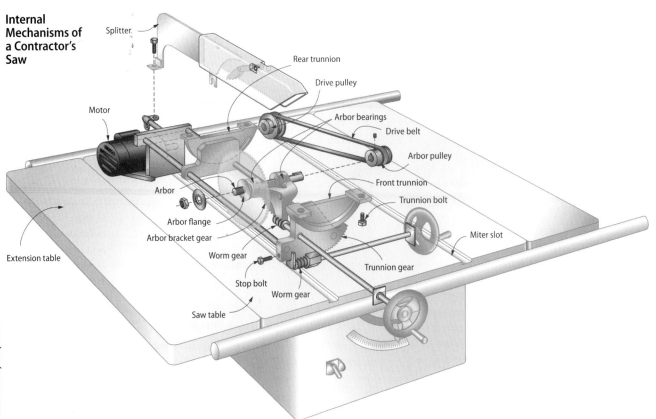

Internal Mechanisms of a Contractor's Saw

Splitter

Rear trunnion

Drive pulley

Motor

Arbor bearings

Drive belt

Arbor pulley

Arbor

Front trunnion

Arbor flange

Trunnion bolt

Arbor bracket gear

Miter slot

Worm gear

Extension table

Stop bolt

Trunnion gear

Worm gear

Saw table

Illustration by Mary Jane Favorite

Regardless of the type of table saw, the internal mechanisms are basically the same. The blade carriage consists of a pair of tilting trunnions and an arbor bracket that raises and lowers the blade. On contractor saws and benchtop saws, the trunnions attach to the saw table. On cabinet saws, they attach to the cabinet.

KEY COMPONENTS OF THE SAW
When purchasing a table saw, carefully match the individual features with your own requirements.

Materials
The materials from which a table saw is made will tell you a lot about its quality. On the better saws, the table and blade carriage are made from cast iron or anodized cast aluminum. Cast iron is considered the best material because it's massive and wears well. Anodizing will make aluminum hard enough to resist wear, but it doesn't add much weight. Table saws made from stamped steel or plastic are on the low end of the scale.

Blade Size
The advertised size of a table saw is the largest diameter blade that it will accommodate. This, in turn, determines its cut-off capacity (the thickest board it will saw through). The larger a blade, the larger the cut-off capacity. It's useful to have a cut-off capacity of at least 2½" – this allows you to cut 4/4 and 8/4 stock in one pass, and 16/4 in two passes. However, there's no sense in buying a saw with a blade that's too large. Large blades require lots of power, and you may not have the necessary wiring in your shop. Saws with 10" blades have adequate cut-off capacity and most can be powered with ordinary 110-volt motors. Also, there is a better selection of 10" blades than any other size.

Arbor Size
Most saws have ⅝"-diameter arbors, so there is a larger variety of blades with ⅝" arbor holes than any other size. Some small benchtop saws have ½" arbors, while some cabinet saws have ¾" arbors. As well as considering the arbor's diameter, you should give thought to its length. If you want to mount a dado cutter or moulding head on the arbor, it should accommodate a ¾"-thick accessory.

Table
Most woodworkers think the bigger the table on a table saw, the better it is. Bigger tables offer more support for the work.

However, bigger is not necessarily better if you have a small shop or do fine work. Pick a comfortable size rather than automatically choosing the biggest. Also check to see that the table is perfectly flat. If it is unacceptably out of true, either don't buy the saw or demand another table.

Blade Carriage
Because this part of the saw will see the most stress, it should be made from massive, well-machined components. Avoid saws with carriages made from stamped steel or plastic components; these often flex under a load. This, in turn, can play havoc with the accuracy of your saw cuts.

Horsepower
The power you need is determined by the type of woodworking you do and the diameter of the blade on the saw. Needless to say, the lighter the work and the smaller the blade, the less power you need. If you own a 10" saw and the jobs you do vary between light and heavy, the saw should have a motor rated for at least 1½ hp. The general rule of thumb is that benchtop saws should be ¾ hp to 1½ hp, contractor saws should be 1½ hp to 2 hp, and cabinet saws should be 3 hp to 5 hp.

Motor Type
In addition to the horsepower of the motor, you should also be concerned with the type of motor, especially when buying a benchtop saw. All direct-drive saws have universal motors, similar to those in hand-held power tools. Universal motors are OK for jobs that can be accomplished quickly, but they won't stand up to continuous use. A table saw should have an induction motor.

Drive
As mentioned earlier, belt drive is better than direct drive because a V-belt helps isolate motor vibrations from the running saw blade.

Fence
The rip fence is the Achilles' heel of every table saw, even on the high-quality machines. Trying to make a piece of furniture with a fussy or inaccurate rip fence is just asking for trouble. There are two common types of fences that should help you improve your accuracy. Benchtop fences

lock at the front and back of the saw and can be difficult to align to the blade. Contractor saws also can use front- and rear-locking fences, though they can interfere with outfeed tables. The most accurate and convenient fence is the front-locking T-square fence, which locks only at the front rail of the saw, is dead-on accurate and is easy to align and set up. [*Editor's Note: We will talk more about fences in Chapter Four of this section.*]

Slot Miter Gauge
The most important part of the miter gauge is the bar or guide. The bar should be solid, machined steel. Avoid poorly machined

To determine if the top of a table saw is flat, lay a level or a straightedge diagonally across the table from right front to left rear, then left front to right rear. If you can see large gaps of daylight anywhere between the table and the straightedge (the maximum amount acceptable is .004" to .008"), the table has been improperly cast or machined. Note: This is the first thing you should check if you order a saw that is delivered through the mail. If the table isn't flat, don't accept the shipment.

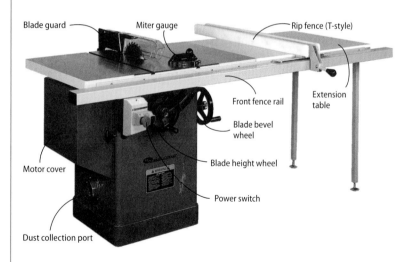

Blade guard — Miter gauge — Rip fence (T-style) — Front fence rail — Extension table — Blade bevel wheel — Blade height wheel — Power switch — Motor cover — Dust collection port

Cabinet saws are a lot like contractor saws, except they are enclosed. Everything is beefier (and generally better) but it's also more costly. One other significant difference is that the trunnions, blade and motor are mounted on the cabinet rather than to the saw's top. This adds stability and reduces vibration. Cabinet saws can be used all day, every day, and provide decades of service. Instead of an open stand, cabinet saws feature a steel cabinet, enclosing the motor and trunnions, which adds weight and improves dust collection. The motor is bigger, is enclosed inside the cabinet and turns the blade using multiple V-belts, so cabinet saws can actually take up less space than contractor saws. But all this comes at a price – an entry-level cabinet saw starts at about $825, but you could spend more than $2,000 in a heartbeat.

Tips & Tricks

'Measure Twice, Cut Once' – It's Not Just a Cliché

Remember the adage "measure twice, cut once" – it describes this age-old technique: Measure the cut, make a mark, then measure the mark. This takes very little effort – just an extra glance at the measuring tool before you remove it from the board.

Take Care to Set the Saw's Rip Fence Correctly

If you've found your fence to be unreliable, here's a good trick. To position the rip fence accurately, first select a tooth. Rotate the blade by hand (with the machine unplugged, of course) until this tooth is near the front of the throat opening. Adjust

the position of the fence, measuring from the inside edge of the tooth to the inside face of the fence. Lock the fence in place, then double-check the setup by rotating the tooth to the back of the saw and measuring again. (*Note: A framing square that is true is the easiest and most accurate measuring tool for this adjustment.*)

gauges – they won't provide accurate results. Many woodworkers prefer T-shaped slots and bars because the slot holds the miter gauge bar flat on the table at all times. Some table saws are now available with miter gauges that offer adjustable-width guide bars. These bars can be tweaked to fit the groove with little or no side play. This feature is also available on a number of aftermarket accessory miter gauges and are a good feature to look for.

Along with the miter gauge (the Osborne aftermarket gauge is shown here), there are a number of other accessories you could add to upgrade your saw. Some of our favorites are, from top, a shop-made push stick, a zero-clearance throat insert, a Power Twist Link Belt and a Biesemeyer snap-in splitter. (For more information on these and other accessories, be sure to check out Chapter 4 of this series.)

Body/Stand

It doesn't matter what materials the body or stand are made from as long as they are rock-steady. It's helpful to have a means of sawdust collection built into the body or stand. This shouldn't be a deciding factor, though, because as long as your saw body or stand is open at the bottom, you can easily build your own.

[*Editor's Note: Of course, one item that we haven't mentioned here is the saw blade, which is the most important piece of the machine. We will focus on the blade in Chapter 2 of this section.*]

Remember that these recommendations are just advice, not absolute gospel. Depending on circumstances, it may not even be good advice. My first table saw was none of the things that I recommend to you – it was inexpensively made and underpowered. It was what I could afford, not what I wanted. Yet I used it professionally for seven years to make musical instruments.

This just goes to show that there are factors that affect the quality of your sawing more than the saw itself – accurate alignment and adjustment, careful layout, proper sawing technique and (most important of all) a good blade.

THREE IMPORTANT ALIGNMENTS

There are many parts to check and adjust on a table saw, and each saw will be slightly different, depending on its construction. However, there are three important alignments that affect the machine's accuracy and ease of operation more than any others – the blade must be parallel to the miter gauge slots, the rip fence must be parallel to the blade and the splitter must be parallel to (and in line with) the blade.

Aligning the Blade

Before you can align any part of the table saw, you must select a base of reference – a line or plane from which you can measure the position of every other part. The reference most often used is a miter gauge slot, because these positions can't be changed.

Use a combination square to measure the distance between a slot and a saw tooth near the front of the blade. Then rotate the tooth to position it near the rear of the table and measure again. These measurements must match for the blade to be parallel to the slot. If they differ, consult your manual

To align the blade, mount a blade and mark a tooth. Rotate the blade so this tooth is near the front. Place a square against a miter gauge slot and slide the rule until it touches the marked tooth. Then rotate the blade so the marked tooth is near the back. Move the square and measure the distance from the slot to the tooth again. If the measurements match, the blade is parallel to the slot.

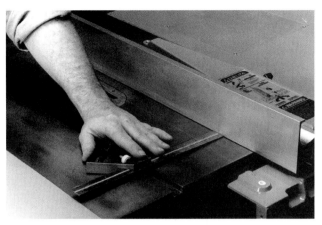

Once you know the blade is parallel to the miter gauge slots, check the fence alignment. To do this, position the fence near a slot. Rest a square against the side of the slot, near the front of the saw. Slide the rule until it just touches the rip fence, then repeat this near the back. If the measurements are the same, the fence is parallel to the blade.

Use a dial indicator to check the flange for runout. It needs to be flat or "true" for the machine to work optimally.

Another important alignment you should check is the arbor flange for runout, as shown at right. Unfortunately, if there's significant runout (about .003"), there's not much you can do about it short of replacing the part.

to adjust for parallel. The steps are different for contractor and cabinet saws.

Aligning the Rip Fence

Position the fence near a miter gauge slot and lock it in place. Use the combination square to measure the distance between the slot and the fence face near the front and back of the saw. If the measurements differ, adjust the fence to be parallel to the slot. When both the fence and the blade are parallel to the slot, they will also be parallel to each other.

Aligning the Splitter

Lay a straightedge against the blade and the splitter to check the alignment. If the straightedge doesn't lie flat against both parts, the splitter is misaligned. Bend or adjust the splitter into position according to your owner's manual.

Tips & Tricks

Miter Gauge Angles can be Tricky to Get Right

To set the angle of the miter gauge, loosen the miter gauge head and place one edge of a square against the gauge face. Slide the tool sideways until another edge touches the blade plate (it must

not contact the teeth). Turn the head until the tool rests flat against the face and the plate, then secure the head.

Drafting Triangles Help You Find the Correct Angles

A set of drafting triangles helps set the miter gauge angle and the blade tilt. The various corners are cut to precise 30°, 45°, 60° and 90° angles.

Don't Get Hit by Kickback

The very act of using the table saw is a vivid reminder of one of its dangers – any tool that cuts wood can cut you. The danger of kickback is not as evident, but it's just as serious. The hole in this concrete block wall was made by a board that was thrown by a table saw blade 15 feet away.

Using the Saw Blade

by Nick Engler

Your table saw is the central piece of machinery in your shop, and the blade (or more appropriately – blades) is a critical aspect of the ease and accuracy of your work. A top-quality blade mounted on a medium-quality saw will cut infinitely better than a mediocre blade mounted on the best table saw money can buy. The reason should be obvious – it's the blade, not the saw, that does the actual cutting.

HOW BLADES WORK

To choose a good blade, you need to understand a little about how blades are designed and how they work. Every blade has several important parts that are generic to all blades.

The plate is the steel center of the blade on which the teeth are mounted. The arbor hole is cut in the center of the plate, and that's where the blade mounts to the saw. The gullets are the spaces between the teeth that allow dust to escape. Often there are anti-kickback limiters between the teeth and gullets, which reduce the chance of wood lodging in the gullet and being thrown at you. Expansion slots are cut along the perimeter of the blade to both quiet and stabilize the cut. And the teeth are the part of the blade that actually does the cutting, but there are lots of teeth variations and arrangements.

Plate and Arbor Hole

For the majority of table saws, the overall diameter of the saw blade (most of which is the plate) is 10". The plates are usually made of a good-quality high-strength steel so the saw blade will remain flat and true. Better saw blades are also machine tensioned to help ensure flatness.

Many manufacturers now offer coatings and polished finishes on the plate part of the blade to help reduce friction during the cut and also to reduce resin build-up and rust. In general, most table saws require a ⅝" arbor hole formed in the center of the blade that fits over the arbor on the saw.

Gullet

As a blade cuts through wood, dust is created and needs to be cleared away from the cut. The gullets (cut in the blade plate) are located between each tooth and allow the dust to be removed. Gullet designs vary by manufacturer and are much smaller today to reduce the chances of material being trapped in the gullet and "kicked back" at the operator. The gullet's size is a careful balance between safety and efficiency. While it's bad for the gullet to be too large, it's also bad if it's too small. Dust can build up during the cut and clog the gullet causing the blade to cut poorly.

Expansion Slots

Expansion slots are usually laser-cut into the plate. While their shape may vary between manufacturers, they all serve a dual-purpose of reducing blade noise and allowing the blade to expand and contract during use as the blade heats and cools. This, once again, helps keep the blade flat.

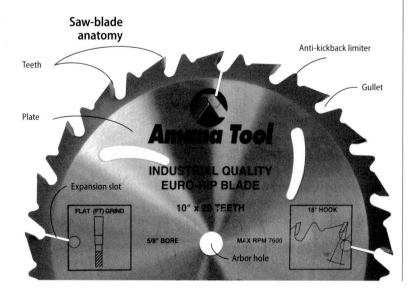

Saw-blade anatomy

Teeth

Plate

Expansion slot

Anti-kickback limiter

Gullet

FLAT (FT) GRIND

Amana Tool

INDUSTRIAL QUALITY
EURO-RIP BLADE

10" x 20 TEETH

5/8" BORE   MAX RPM 7600

Arbor hole

18° HOOK

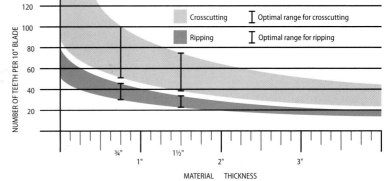

The crosscutting and ripping "swoops" in this graphic designate the optimal number of teeth you should have on your blade when ripping or crosscutting wood of a particular thickness. The areas outside the swoops designate situations in which you may experience a rough cut.

Source: Freud; Illustration by Len Churchill

Teeth

Each saw tooth is ground and sharpened to a specific angle depending on the job it has to do. If you draw a radial line out from the center of the blade through the tooth, you'll find that the tooth is set on the blade at a slight angle. This is called the hook angle. The greater the hook angle, the more aggressive the cut.

On carbide-tipped blades, the teeth are wider than the plate (with the kerf traditionally ⅛" wide) to prevent the plate from rubbing in the cut. This offset is known as the tooth set.

In addition to hook and set, the cutting edge of every tooth has a profile. The edge can be flat or square, beveled left or right, or shaped in other ways to suit its job. Often, the teeth on a single blade will have two or more profiles alternating in a pattern called a grind. The profile determines how each tooth cuts, while the grind determines how the saw blade cuts as a whole.

TYPES OF BLADES

The various aspects of the saw teeth – hook, set and profile – can be arranged to make different cuts or to cut different materials. There are three basic types of blades, (rip, crosscut and combination) each designed to make certain cuts:

• **Rip Blades** have a large hook angle (20°-25°) and, because it's much easier to cut with the grain (ripping a board), they can remove a lot of stock with each pass. Compared to other blades, they have fewer teeth and larger gullets to make room to clear out the big chips. The tooth profiles are usually all flat.

• **Crosscut Blades** have a much smaller hook angle (5°-10°) to remove just a little stock because it's much harder to cut across the grain. Because the chips are smaller, the gullets can be smaller too, and this makes room for more teeth. The profiles of the teeth alternate right bevel and left bevel in

Tips & Tricks

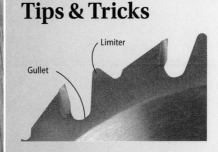

Safer by Design

Most blade manufacturers now offer blades with an "anti-kickback" design. In addition to the ordinary forward-facing teeth, an anti-kickback blade has backward-facing barbs or "limiters" that limit the depth of cut. This greatly reduces the chance that the blade will kick the work back at you, but it doesn't completely eliminate the risk. If you need a determining factor during your next blade purchase, look for this safety feature.

Straight Rip on Rough Edge

If your only choice is to rip a straight edge on a bowed, rough-cut or otherwise crooked board, fasten a straight board to it with finishing nails. Don't drive the nails home – you'll want to pull them out later. Rip the edge of the crooked board, keeping the edge of the straight one against the fence. When you've finished, separate the boards and rip the other edge.

a grind called "alternate-top bevel" (ATB). An ATB grind allows each tooth to slice the wood at a slight angle to the grain, making the cut easier and smoother.

• **Combination Blades** will perform both rip cuts and crosscuts, and their design is a compromise between the two types of blades. The teeth are usually arranged in

Types of Blades

Ripping blade

Ripping blades are designed with flat-topped teeth and an aggressive hook angle to remove wood quickly and efficiently. The action is similar to that of a chisel cutting a groove. While this blade can be used for a variety of cutting actions, its best performance will be in rip cuts.

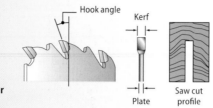

Crosscutting blade

Frequently referred to as an alternate-top bevel (ATB) blade, the beveled crosscutting teeth are designed to slice across wood fibers. It leaves a concave bottom in the cut. This blade's best performance will be in crosscutting, but can be used for other applications and is the preferred grind for cutting plywood.

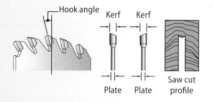

Triple-chip blade

The triple-chip tooth design includes flat-topped and trapezoidal teeth. The trapezoidal teeth are taller and narrower than the flat teeth, making a scoring cut to reduce tear-out. This blade excels for work with laminate and brittle wood materials, including hardboard.

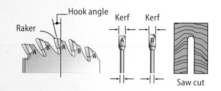

Combination blade

A combo blade uses both rip and crosscut teeth, and can be used reasonably well in either application. There are compromises in quality, but if you're looking for an all-purpose blade, this is it.

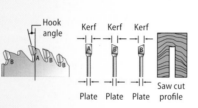

Two examples of alternative-geometry blades. The Porter-Cable (left) combines both rip and crosscut tooth spacing on one blade. The Leitz blade uses variable spacing of the teeth. Both are designed to cut more efficiently and quietly.

sets of five. The gullets in each set of five are the same size as on a crosscut blade; those between the sets are larger, like the gullets on a rip blade. The profiles of the teeth alternate in a five-tooth grind as such: right-bevel, left-bevel, right-bevel, left-bevel, flat. The large gullets are in front of the flat teeth.

In addition, there are several common types of blades intended for specific jobs.

• **Triple-chip Blades** use a special double-beveled-tooth design combined with a raker tooth to reduce chipping in brittle materials. Triple-chip blades can be used in many applications, but are the best choice for work with laminates.

• **Plywood Blades** are designed to make smooth cuts in plywood without chipping the veneer. Cutting the alternating grain in plywood requires both rips and crosscuts. The blade of choice is an 80-plus ATB tooth design, but the hook angle is less than a crosscut blade's.

• **Thin-kerf Blades** usually are carbide-tipped and available in the same styles as ordinary blades (rip, crosscut and combination). However, the plate and teeth are about two-thirds as wide as an ordinary blade. Because the blade removes less stock, the table saw does less work and makes a smoother, quicker cut.

• **Alternative-geometry Blades** change the distance of separation between the teeth. In some cases the pattern is almost random, and in others it's mixing rip and crosscut teeth on the same blade. The payoff is more efficient cutting, less vibration and a smoother finished surface.

• **Dado Blades** mount on the saw arbor like a blade, but make a much broader cut. An ordinary saw blade cuts a narrow kerf (1/8") to reduce waste and the effort required to saw through the stock. A dado cutter isn't meant to saw completely through a board. Rather, it cuts a wide kerf with a flat bottom and square shoulders, and it can create dados, grooves, rabbets and a number of other standard woodworking joints.

The most common dado set is a stack dado. These sets include two 6" or 8"-diameter outer blades (essentially smaller saw blades) and a number of inner chipper blades that may have four or six teeth per chipper. The outer blades are 1/8"-wide, but the chippers vary in width to allow adjustments of 1/32" by rearranging the number and type of chippers used.

WHAT BLADES DO YOU NEED?

With all the choices, what sort of blade should you choose? The answer depends on the type of woodworking you do. However, most craftsmen get by nicely with just three blades:

1. A combination blade for general work. You'll probably keep this on your saw 90 percent of the time. Because you're likely to use this blade more than any other, it should be a premium blade.

2. A rip blade for cutting stock to width. Often, at the beginning of a project, you'll find yourself doing a lot of ripping lumber to size. A rip blade will make this go faster.

3. A crosscut blade for cutting stock to length. A clean, tear-out-free cut when crosscutting makes joinery much easier.

In addition, special types of shop requirements or work will require specialty blades, such as thin-kerf or dado sets. But these can be added as needed.

FOR THE BEST BLADE PERFORMANCE

The table saw is a precision cutting tool. As such, it must be precisely aligned, operated and maintained to get good results.

Small problems can have large consequences. A rip fence that toes in slightly toward the blade, a miter gauge slot slightly out of line with the blade, a tendency to feed the work too quickly or too slowly, or a blade whose teeth have become coated with pitch – all of these seemingly insignificant problems can completely ruin a cut.

Before you make any cut, you must be sure that the working parts (blade, arbor, trunnions, table, fence and miter gauge) are properly aligned to each other. In Chapter One of this section we covered these important initial adjustments.

Another important set-up step that isn't mentioned often enough is how high the blade should be. Most manuals tell you it shouldn't be too high, but the number you need to remember is between ⅛" and ¼" above the wood's surface. This leaves the teeth at an appropriate height to not only make the cut, but to clear the chips and dust from the cut, while not leaving too much blade exposed to pose a hazard.

MAINTENANCE

An old woodworking axiom that is quite true is that your most dangerous tool is a

Two common dado sets are a standard dado (right) that uses shims to fine tune the spacing between the chippers. The dial dado (left) uses a cam dial to fine-tune the width, avoiding the need for shims and allowing for adjustment without removing the blades.

dull one. This certainly applies to table saw blades as well. A dull blade will make you force the material past the blade, making your stance more awkward and increasing the pressure you need to exert toward a spinning blade.

Tips & Tricks

Tip to be Square

To make sure your blade is running square in your saw, you need two measuring tools – a true straightedge and an accurate try square. To check that a straightedge is straight, use one edge to draw a line along its full length. Flip the straightedge face for face and draw a second line on  top of the first, using the same edge. Superimposed, the two lines should appear as one. If they diverge at any point, your straightedge is crooked. To check that a square is square, place the arm against the edge of a board and use one edge of the rule to draw a line. Flip the square face for face and draw a second line right next to the first (shown above), using the same edge. The two lines should be evenly spaced across the board. If not, your square isn't square.

Dado Blade Crib Sheet

Every stack dado set is slightly different when the chippers are in place. Rather than measure each time to set up your dado set, make a sample board using each variation of blades, chippers and shims to make a series of shallow dados. Mark the block as to what combination of blades was used and also mark the resulting dimension of the cut. You may never have to measure your dado set again.

To maintain your table saw in peak cutting condition – and safe – blades must be kept clean and sharp. As you make each cut, wood pitch builds up on the blade and the teeth lose their sharp edge. Here's how to maintain them.

Cleaning

When a blade ceases to cut well, it's not always an indication that the teeth are losing their edges. Usually, the problem is caused by accumulated wood pitch on the teeth. To restore the edge, clean the blade.

There are several ways to do this. Woodworkers swear by all sorts of solvents – ammonia, baking soda dissolved in water, turpentine, mineral spirits and even vegetable oil. My own favorite is oven cleaner. Simply spray the cleaner on the teeth, wait a few seconds and wipe it off with a damp cloth. Then, after cleaning the blade, wax and buff the plate to help the blade run cooler and keep it clean longer.

There are also a number of "environmentally friendly" blade cleaners (often citrus-based) available that also do a good job.

Sharpening

If cleaning the blade doesn't restore the edge, the blade probably needs to be sharpened. Unfortunately, sharpening a carbide blade is not something woodworkers can do in their own shops. There are many facets to the teeth of modern blades, and special equipment is needed to accurately grind and hone these complex angles. It's best to find a good professional sharpening service and take your blades to them as necessary.

Most stores such as Rockler (800-279-4441 or rockler.com) or Woodcraft (800-225-1153 or woodcraft.com) have connections to a sharpening service in your area. You might also try calling a local cabinet shop. They can usually recommend someone in your area to do your blade sharpening.

MAKING CROSSCUTS & RIPS

There are three basic saw cuts – crosscuts, rips and miters. Crosscuts are made perpendicular to the grain, rips are made parallel to the grain and miters are cut at angles. None of these require elaborate jigs or complex techniques; however, each type presents special problems you must deal with to make the cut safely and accurately.

Crosscuts

Of the three, these are probably the most troublesome to make on a table saw. To cut across the grain, you must move the board sideways, perpendicular to its length. The longer the board, the harder this is to do. To make an accurate crosscut, you must use equipment (such as miter gauges) and techniques that improve balance and control.

Rips

These cuts are the easiest because it's a lot simpler to feed a board parallel to its length. Unfortunately, table saws aren't as deep as they are wide, so you need to find a way to control the outfeed to maintain accuracy.

RIPPING LUMBER

Figure 1. Ripping a piece of solid lumber is simpler than ripping plywood, but there is more potential for danger because the stress in a solid wood board can pinch the blade when it's ripped. Roller stands are recommended (you can't see mine in the photos) and should be positioned to support both pieces coming off the saw. To start the cut, you should be positioned at the rear corner

Ripping Lumber

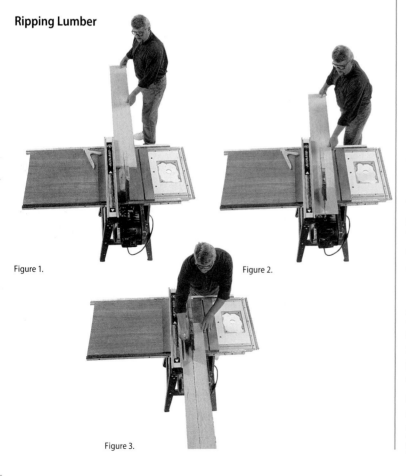

Figure 1.

Figure 2.

Figure 3.

of the board, supporting the back end with your right hand. Your left hand (at the center of the board) provides pressure against the fence, keeping it flush to the fence.

Figure 2. Walk the board slowly into the blade, keeping the edge flush along the length of the fence. When your left hand reaches the edge of the saw, allow it to slide backward along the length of the board, maintaining pressure against the fence. Maintain this support until the back end of the board reaches the edge of the saw table.

Figure 3. Grab your push stick and place it on the back edge of the piece between the blade and fence. Apply pressure forward and slightly toward the fence with the push stick as you continue the cut. Your left hand should only be used to apply minimal guiding pressure on the fall-off piece until the piece is separated, then move your left hand out of the way. Once the keeper board is clear of the blade and guard, turn your attention to the fall-off piece and push it safely forward, again using the push stick.

CROSSCUTTING LUMBER

Figure 1. When crosscutting a board, the substantially thinner width of the piece (and not enough width to ride adequately against the fence) requires us to use a miter gauge rather than the fence. Note the gauge in our photos is not standard equipment. We recommend either adding a backing board at least 24" long to your stock miter gauge or purchasing an aftermarket gauge.

Start by checking to make sure your miter gauge is square to the blade. Then align your cut and support the board against the gauge with one hand on the gauge and the other stretching across the piece to hold it tightly against the gauge. If your piece is too wide to reach across, it's smart to clamp the piece against the gauge during the cut.

Figure 2. Guide the gauge and board into and past the blade.

Figure 3. Once the board is cut through, allow the fall-off piece to lie in place. With your left hand, push the board away from the blade, sliding it along the gauge. Then turn the saw off. Once the blade stops spinning, pull the fall-off piece away from the blade.

Crosscutting Lumber

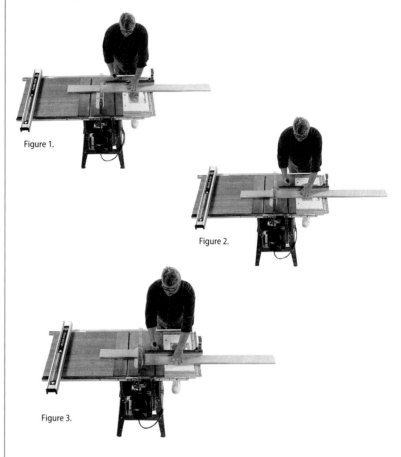

Figure 1.

Figure 2.

Figure 3.

Saftey Tips

One We Hope You Know
There is absolutely no reason for you to ever make a cut (crosscut or rip cut) on your table saw without some type of guiding mechanism. Whether that's a rip fence, miter gauge or miter sled, never make a cut on the table saw freehand. You will most certainly get hurt.

No Rip Fence For Crosscutting
Never use the rip fence as a stop for crosscutting. The cut-off pieces will be pinched between the blade and the fence, and the saw will fling them back at you. Instead, use a stop block – sometimes called a "stand-off block" – mounted to the rip fence behind the blade location to gauge your length and safely make the cut.

Ripping Plywood

Figure 1.

Figure 2.

Figure 3.

RIPPING PLYWOOD

Figure 1. Ripping a 4'x8' sheet of plywood on a contractor saw is possible, but requires finesse. Roller stands are a must, and they should be positioned to support the largest piece coming off the saw, or preferably both pieces. To start the cut, you should be posi-

tioned near the rear corner of the sheet, supporting the rear with your right hand while your left hand provides pressure against the fence and aligns the sheet flush to the fence. With the piece pushed nearly up to the blade, check the fit against the fence again, then slowly walk the sheet into the blade.

Figure 2. As you move forward, keep your eye on the fence to keep the sheet flush along the fence. As the balance of the weight of the sheet is transferred to the saw table you can shift your position to the rear of the sheet, supporting from the back, but still maintaining pressure against the fence with your left hand. Continue to push the sheet forward, paying attention to the point when the sheet contacts your roller stand (to make sure it's riding on the stand, not pushing it over), then continue the cut. My roller stand is not visible in the photos.

Figure 3. At the end of the cut, let the waste piece to come to a rest. Then push the piece between the fence and blade clear of the blade, careful not to extend your reach over the blade. Lift the piece up and over the fence. Then continue to push the waste piece forward and away from the blade until it clears the blade and guard.

CROSSCUTTING PLYWOOD

Figure 1. Crosscutting a sheet of plywood on a contractor saw is a task safely accomplished with the use of roller stands. Here you see one stand positioned to one side of the table saw and another positioned at the outfeed side. When using the rip fence, don't crosscut a piece less than 18" wide and more than 48" long. There is too much chance of the board shifting and becoming pinched. Start by standing in the center. Keep your eye on the fence and keep the board tight against it. Again, arrows indicate where my hands are applying pressure.

Figure 2. Maintain the center position as you push the board through the blade. Keep your eye on the fence. While your instinct is to control the whole board, the part between the fence and blade needs all your attention.

Figure 3. Once the board has cleared the blade, let the fall-off piece lay where it is and carefully push the piece between the fence and blade past the blade and onto the roller stand. Keep the piece flush against the fence until the piece is clear. Then lift the fall-off piece out of the way.

Crosscutting Plywood

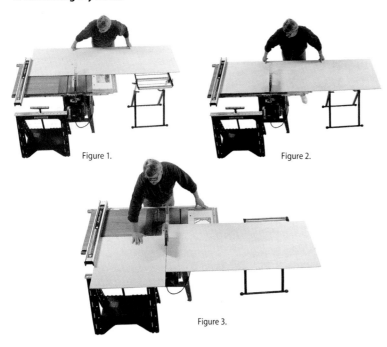

Figure 1.

Figure 2.

Figure 3.

Basic Joinery

by Nick Engler

There are three basic saw cuts: crosscuts, rips and miters. Crosscuts are made perpendicular to the wood grain, rips are cut parallel to the grain and miters are made at angles diagonally across the grain. These are the building blocks to basic joinery on the table saw.

Rips and crosscuts are used to form many joints, including the basic edge and butt joints, which can be used to glue up a tabletop or door frame. These two cuts are also used to cut rabbets, grooves and dados. And a variation of these cuts will create a miter joint.

MITERS

Miters can be the most frustrating cuts to make. Angled cuts are harder to measure and lay out than crosscuts. To make a mitered frame perfect, both the inside and outside dimension of the piece must match on each component. You should start with accurate measuring tools and some basic math, and then you will need to test and retest your setup to ensure its precision.

When you make a miter cut on a table saw, you run into a problem associated with crosscuts – the factory-supplied miter gauge is too small to offer adequate support for guiding most boards. To properly support the work, you must fit the gauge with an extension fence or replace it with a sliding table.

Even when using an adequately sized miter gauge, boards are inclined to creep during a miter cut because of the rotation of the blade into the cut. One way to compensate for this is to add a stop to your miter gauge fence as shown above. Your stop will also help you make repeatable, accurate miter cuts every time.

Accurate angles are another problem on table saws. The stock miter gauge and blade-tilt scale on most table saws – even the best ones – are notoriously imprecise. And you can't use a drafting triangle to set every possible angle you might want to cut. You must use the scales to estimate the degree setting, then thoroughly test the setup until you have it right.

Once the miter gauge angle is properly set, make the miter cuts. If the boards are to be joined by miter joints (such as the members of a frame), you must make mirror-image miters. Note: A single miter joint is comprised of one left miter and one right miter. To do this, flip each board end-for-end, keeping the same edge against the gauge as you cut the ends. Only in rare

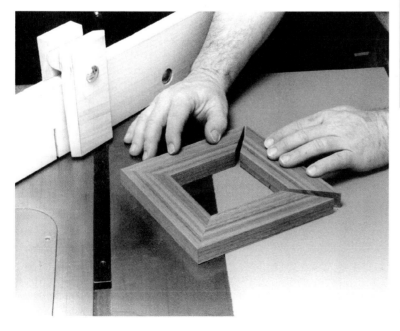

To make sure your miters are perfect, start with a new zero-clearance throat insert on your table saw. Bring the blade up through the insert until the blade height is about ¼" above the height of your frame material. Turn off the saw. After the blade has stopped, use a straightedge to make a mark, extending the line of the blade slot the full length of the insert. This will let you see exactly where the blade will cut. Add a sacrificial fence to your miter gauge that extends past the blade to eliminate tear-out. You can also extend the cut line to the sacrificial fence for extra alignment accuracy.

Tips & Tricks

Setting Between the Lines
Use an angle divider to help set oddball miter angles that you can't measure with a set of drafting triangles or a square. This device, which is available from most woodworking suppliers, looks like an adjustable metal parallelogram.

Right Height, Every Time
When using a dado set and sacrificial rip fence to make rabbets, setting the height of the dado set in the fence is tricky. Make it simple by attaching a new sacrificial fence, then measure and mark the height of the blade (for the perfect rabbet depth) right on the fence face, measuring from the table saw's top. Lower the dado set, move the fence into place, then bring the running blade up into the fence, stopping when you reach your line.

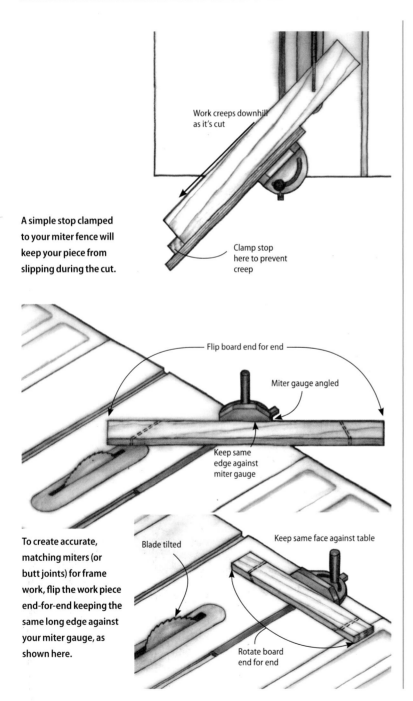

A simple stop clamped to your miter fence will keep your piece from slipping during the cut.

Work creeps downhill as it's cut

Clamp stop here to prevent creep

Flip board end for end

Miter gauge angled

Keep same edge against miter gauge

To create accurate, matching miters (or butt joints) for frame work, flip the work piece end-for-end keeping the same long edge against your miter gauge, as shown here.

Blade tilted

Keep same face against table

Rotate board end for end

instances when you can't flip the board should you have to readjust the angle of the miter gauge to cut left and right miters.

You also can cut a miter by tilting the blade rather than angling the miter gauge. This procedure is similar, but there is an important difference when cutting left and right miters. As you rotate the board end for end, the same face must rest against the table. (Note: You can switch faces if you first switch the miter gauge to the other slot.)

BEVELS
The procedure to make a bevel is similar to the way you make a miter, but you must set the blade at the proper angle, rather than the miter gauge. Measure the angle between the blade and the table with a triangle.

If you rip a bevel or chamfer (as shown below), make sure the blade tilts away from the rip fence. This gives you more room to safely maneuver the board and reduces the risk of kickback. On right-tilt saws, you will have to move the rip fence to the left side of the blade (as you face the infeed side of the table saw).

When ripping an angle other than 0° – cutting a bevel or a chamfer – be sure the blade tilts away from the rip fence.

RABBETS, DADOS AND GROOVES

Although the final results and applications for dados, rabbets and grooves are different, the way to make each is very similar.

• A rabbet is an L-shaped cut of varying widths and depths, cut on the end (cross grain) or side (long grain) of a board. The width and depth of the rabbet can be adjusted to match the piece fitting in the rabbet, such as on a cabinet or drawer side. The joint created is better than a butt joint, but it is stronger when reinforced with more than glue.

• Grooves and dados have the same shape, but they're called different names depending on the direction they're cut on the board. Both a groove and a dado are U-shaped trenches. The depth and width are variable according to the use. This joint is referred to as a groove when it's made parallel to the grain direction of the board. When made across the grain, it's referred to as a dado. This is a stronger joint than a rabbet because the mating piece is captured on three sides, rather than two.

USING A DADO SET

Rabbets, dados and grooves can all be created by making multiple cuts with a single saw blade, or one cut with a dado set.

When changing from a single blade to a dado set, always remember to unplug the saw and carefully handle the sharp blades. Because a dado stack cuts a much wider kerf than the ordinary saw blade, you must replace the saw's throat insert with a special dadoing insert. You can either make your own insert or purchase an aftermarket accessory to fit your saw. It's wise to make or purchase more than one. After you cut the insert to accommodate your widest dado arrangement, it shouldn't be used with a smaller-width setup that will leave gaps between the opening and the blades.

When making rabbets on the table saw with a dado set, a sacrificial wooden face attached to your existing rip fence is a must. This face must have a semicircular cutout that's the same radius as the dado cutter. The cutout face serves two purposes – it protects the rip fence during these operations, and it covers the unused portion of the dado stack when you don't want to cut the full width.

Tips & Tricks

Controlling Large Panels
When using a miter gauge extension to cut off large, wide panels, clamp a block of wood to the extension to serve as a hold-down. This will keep the panels from tipping over the back edge of the table saw as you finish the cut.

Clean in the Corners
After cutting a rabbet with a dado cutter or a saw blade, inspect the inside corner between the side and the bottom. These cutting tools sometimes leave a little waste, or "tang," in the corner. You can quickly remove this with a scraper, chisel, bullnose plane or rabbeting plane.

Because the dado stack makes a wider kerf than the saw blade, you must replace the normal throat insert with one that has a wider opening.

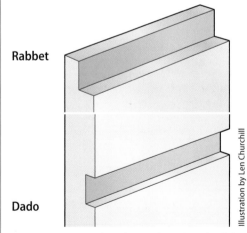

Rabbet

Dado

Illustration by Len Churchill

A rabbet (top) is an L-shaped cut on the end or side of a board. The depth and width can be varied to match a mating piece, or to create a particular type of joint. While the rabbet can be viewed as the female part of a joint, it can also be the male part, as it forms a tongue that can be used in tongue-and-groove joinery. A dado (bottom) is U-shaped and cut across the width of a piece. It can also be adjusted in depth and width. A groove is cut parallel to the board's grain direction. It's always the female part of a joint. Rabbets, grooves and dados can be "through" (run entirely across the board as shown), or stopped at either of both ends, depending on the requirement of the joint.

Your next step is to detach the splitter (and guard, when appropriate) from the table saw and attach a featherboard to the table or wooden fence. Because you don't use a dado cutter to cut all the way through a board, the splitter will just get in your way. Unfortunately, without the splitter and anti-kickback fingers, there is nothing to stop kickback, so be careful. Also, because the dado cutter removes more stock than a standard saw blade, kickback is more likely. To guard against this, use a featherboard.

When making the rabbet cut, the board is most safely run flat on the table saw's top. By virtue of this position, the height of the dado stack should be set to the required depth of the rabbet. The distance from the sacrificial face to the left side of the dado stack (the amount of blade exposed) will be the width.

To make a groove (or dado, but only on wide boards for safety) the rip fence is adjusted to re-locate the groove where needed, and the dado stack height is set for the required depth of the groove.

MAKING RABBET AND DADO JOINTS WITH A SINGLE BLADE

As mentioned, rabbets and grooves can also be made with a single saw blade if you don't have a dado stack.

Rabbets can most easily be made in a two-pass method. The blade height is set for the depth of the rabbet and the rip fence is set for the width of the rabbet (including the blade width in the setup). The board is then run flat on the table surface for the first cut.

To complete the rabbet, the blade height is reset to just shy of the width of the rabbet, while the fence is set to cut away the depth of the rabbet. It's a good idea to have the rabbet size marked on the end of the board to double-check your setup. The board is then run on edge against the rip fence.

The order of these cuts is important. If the board were run on edge first, then on its face, the waste piece could be trapped between the blade and fence, and be kicked back at you at a very high speed. The waste piece falls safely to the outside of the blade after the second cut.

To make a groove or dado with a single blade is more a nibbling away process until the groove is complete. It's easiest to start with the two outside passes that will define the groove's shoulder, then make overlapping cuts between those kerfs to remove the waste material. While this process works, it won't take too many single-blade dados to convince you that the investment in a dado set is a smart one.

EXPANDED TECHNIQUES

In addition to cutting basic dados, grooves and rabbets, there are many other useful ways these joints can be used. Here are just a few of the most common variations:

Stopped Cuts

Sometimes you must halt a cut before it exits the end or edge of a board. To make a stopped rabbet, dado or groove, you must first know where the dado cutter starts to cut as the wood passes across the table saw.

A sacrificial fence attached to your rip fence allows you to accurately use part of a dado set for rabbeting without harming your rip fence. The blade should be run up into the fence while it's securely locked in place to the tabletop. Make sure the blade clears your rip fence.

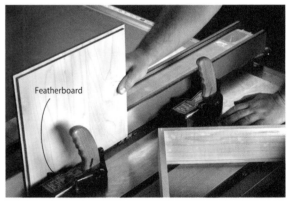

Featherboard

Featherboards, to hold material snug against the fence (and to avoid kickback), can either be shop-made or purchased. The featherboards shown here have magnetic bases to hold them tightly against the tabletop. They should be positioned before and after the blade, but not at the blades' location or the waste will bind against the blade.

To find out, first adjust the cutter to the desired height and position the rip fence. Affix a piece of tape to the fence beside the cutter. Select a scrap with at least one square corner and place it on the infeed side of the table with the square corner against the fence and facing the cutter. Slide the scrap toward the dado accessory as you spin the cutter by hand (with the saw unplugged). When the teeth brush the scrap, mark the position of the corner on the tape.

To find where the dado cutter stops cutting, simply place the scrap on the outfeed side of the table.

Now that you know where the blade stops its cut, you can clamp a stop to the end of the rip fence to halt the cut. Determine the length of the cut required and set the stop block that distance from your infeed blade mark on the fence.

Shiplap Joint

A useful combination of two of our joints in this chapter is shiplapped boards, which are often used as decorative (and sturdy) backs in cabinetry.

The shiplap joint uses two interlocking rabbets (created on the long edges of the boards). The interlocking rabbets form a solid back that still has the ability to expand and contract with changes in humidity, without stressing the cabinet, or opening a gap between the boards. To add a decorative element, bevel the shiplapped boards at the mating edges.

Tongue-and-groove Joint

A mating of a two-sided rabbet (forming a tongue) and a groove run in the long edge of a board forms the tongue-and-groove joint. Offering the same benefit against wood expansion and contraction as the shiplap joint, the tongue and groove also offers great strength as a mating joint. It allows long boards to stay parallel over long lengths. That's why it's most common application is in flooring to lock the board lengths tight against one another. This joint also plays an important role in frame-and-panel doors, but we'll cover that in more detail in Chapter Six of this section.

Rabbet-and-dado Joint

With a rabbet on one side and a dado on the other, this joint makes a strong, but simple drawer joint. While a simple rabbet joint

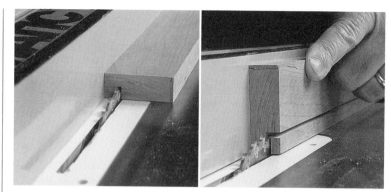

It's possible to create a rabbet on a board with a single blade using only two cuts. The order of the cuts is important for safety, though. The first cut (left) must be made with the face of the board against the saw table. The second cut (right) must be made on edge, with the waste piece oriented away from the fence to allow the waste to fall away from the blade.

With the dado set to the desired height (and with the saw unplugged) the board is pushed forward until the leading edge touches the dado teeth. Mark the board location on the tape. This is the "start" position of the cut.

The tape mark on the fence also indicates where the dado cut ends in the piece. For a more accurate dado, a block attached to the fence (located using the tape mark) provides a positive stop.

can be used as a drawer joint, the addition of a dado allows the rabbet to be firmly captured on three sides. This adds strength and stability to the joint. And this joint isn't only for drawer sides. Many drawer bottoms are slipped into grooves cut in the drawer sides to form an even simpler rabbet and dado. But wait – that makes it a tongue (the entire bottom is a tongue) and groove joint.

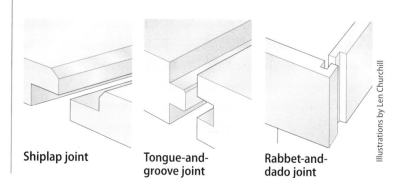

Shiplap joint   **Tongue-and-groove joint**   **Rabbet-and-dado joint**

Illustrations by Len Churchill

Customize Your Table Saw

by Nick Engler

There are dozens of table saw accessories you can mount on your machine to make it safer, more accurate or extend its capacity. Some can be purchased, others can be made by you. By carefully choosing these options, you can soup up your old table saw or customize a new one.

The most common additions are a reliable rip fence, a cut-off system (either an improved miter gauge, miter sled or sliding table) and roller stands or outfeed supports. But there are lots of other accessories, many very affordable, that I'll share with you in this chapter. You can pick and choose what will work best for you on your table saw.

A BETTER RIP FENCE

Perhaps the most beneficial customization is a replacement fence. Many very good rip fences are now available from table saw manufacturers – many as standard equipment. This is a great improvement from more than 10 years ago, but the better fences aren't always included in the base model of the saw, but rather they're offered as an upgrade.

There are also a number of good-quality, aftermarket rip fences that can be added to your new or existing table saw. A good upgrade, or replacement fence, will increase repeatable accuracy and can also increase the usable space on your table saw. Various brands of fences employ different mechanisms for perfect alignment, and most come with precise scales and hairline indicators. When you choose a replacement fence, consider these important features:

• **How long are the fence rails?** Most replacement fences extend the ripping capacity – the maximum distance between the blade and fence. To do so, they use longer front and rear support rails (usually 35" to 50" in length) and a larger table extension, increasing the size of the saw. If you're cramped for space in your shop you may not

While certainly not the only good aftermarket rip fence available, the Biesemeyer is often considered the model to surpass. Accurate, stable, easy to remove and replace, it can be used on either side of the blade.

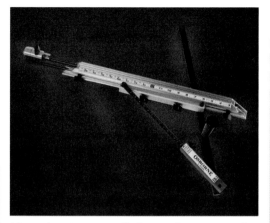

Aftermarket miter gauges offer increased accuracy, capacity and built-in adjustable stops. They also allow the workpiece to remain flat on the table saw surface.

have room for this accessory. But the capacity gained is worth serious consideration.

• **Will the fence dismount easily?** For many operations, you must remove the fence from the saw. This task is easier with some brands than others. Some aftermarket fences have a rear lock that slows removal and replacement. Others connect to the front rail and need to be released or slid off the rail to remove. These mountings can improve accuracy, but they can be a trade-off.

• **Can the fence be used easily on both sides of the blade?** Many factory and replacement fences can be used on the right and left sides of the blade. But on some, the fence face must be removed and reversed when changing sides.

• **Can you easily mount jigs on the fence?** Many table saw operations require you to mount shop-made jigs on the fence. It's easier to drill bolt holes in some replacement fences than others. You may also find a fence that can't be drilled at all – for this, you need to clamp a jig to it. Some fences actually include T-slots in the fence to make attaching accessories easier.

Aftermarket rip fences can cost hundreds of dollars – potentially one-third the price of your saw – so when possible, getting a good rip fence on a new table saw is preferable. If you're upgrading, choose carefully.

MITER GAUGES

Factory miter gauges often are as inadequate as factory fences, but deciding what to replace them with is more complex. How much cut-off work do you perform on the table saw, and how large are the boards that

Tips & Tricks

Keep Things Sliding

No matter how many cool accessories you add to your table saw, if you have difficulties moving the wood past the blade, it's no good. Make sure the table surface is clean and lubricated to provide effortless material movement. There are a number of good dry (that's the important part) lubricants on the market. You can also use paste wax or paraffin wax (canning wax from the grocery store) to treat the top. This doesn't have to be a daily chore, but put your lubricant to work whenever you start a new project.

Cutting Irregular Pieces

Table saw sleds can be used for much more than just crosscuts and miters. At times there are situations where an irregular piece of wood needs trimming. By adding hold-down clamps to a crosscut sled, you can easily trim the wane from a rough piece of wood. You can even square off a cross-section of a log with relative ease, accuracy and safety.

Sled Add-ons

While you can make a separate tenoning fixture for your table saw (I'll show you how in Chapter 5 of this section), your miter sled can also serve as a platform to attach a number of very useful jigs – such as a tenoning fixture as shown above. The fixture is a basic plywood structure to support (and brace) the wood. It's adjustable from left to right (for the width of the tenon) and the supporting brace can even be pivoted for angled tenons.

you must cut accurately? If you crosscut lots of large boards, you need a crosscut (or miter) sled instead of a replacement miter gauge. For small work and an occasional large board, a good miter gauge will serve you well.

Here are a few features to look for in a quality aftermarket miter gauge:

• **The miter bar should be adjustable to allow you to custom fit it to the miter slots in your saw top**. No matter how accurate the miter gauge, if the bar fits sloppily in the slot your work will suffer.

• **Some type of adjustable stop should be included on the fence.** It should be able to be located easily anywhere on the

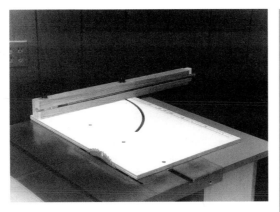

This shop-made crosscut sled has one miter bar and the sled runs right up against the blade. It also adds a mitering feature by adding a sliding track that allows the fence to pivot and lock. A commercial version, the Dubby, is also available at 800-533-6709 or in-lineindustries.com.

crosscut fence. It should be stable, but if possible, a stop that can flip out of the way of the cut without changing the setting is also advantageous.

• **Make sure you look for a fence that is adequate to the task.** A miter gauge should allow you to set a stop for the length of a table leg, so at least 30" capacity is recommended.

When you use a miter gauge, whether a factory gauge or a replacement, there is friction between the wood and the saw table as you push the work across the surface. The larger the board, the greater the friction – and the greater the tendency for the board to twist or creep as you make your crosscut.

A crosscut sled works like a miter gauge, but it also supports the wood and eliminates the friction. Crosscuts – particularly cuts in large boards – are smoother and more accurate with a sled.

While you can't easily make your own miter gauge, a shop-made crosscut sled is definitely an option. There are two distinct styles of shop-made sleds, one that slides on the left of the blade and another that slides on both sides of the blade, with a kerf cut in the sled to allow blade passage. Both have benefits.

The left-sliding sled (shown above) supports the workpiece for square and mitered cuts, but it does not support the waste piece during or after the cut. The "fall-off" piece can truly fall off and without proper caution can become a hazard. This can also cause tear-out at the end of the cut. One solution is to add a second fixed table of the same height as the sled to the right of the blade.

Another option is to use a larger wooden sled that rides in both miter slots, allowing you to support the workpiece on both sides of the blade. It also will always be set for a square, 90° cut, but will not easily accommodate mitered cuts.

SLIDING TABLES

Like a crosscut sled, a sliding table supports the work so you can crosscut large stock accurately and easily. But unlike a miter sled the supporting surface is flush with the saw table. And instead of sliding back and forth in the miter gauge slots, this accessory rolls back and forth on bearings and rails.

A sliding table usually replaces the left table wing on your saw and will require you to relocate, or shorten the fence rails. This

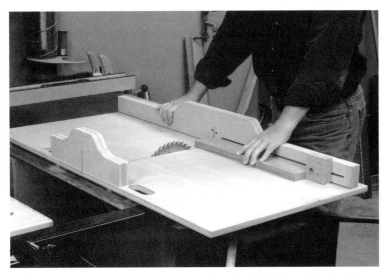

A two-sided miter sled allows equal support on either side of the blade and also functions as a partial blade guard. While stops can also be added into this design (as shown) it doesn't easily allow for adjustable miter cuts.

This sliding table makes crosscutting panels and longer boards simple and accurate. Although they require a bit more space in your shop and are expensive, they can be a valuable addition.

will also limit how far you can position the fence to the left of the blade, so be mindful of this complication.

Most sliding tables not only allow moving larger panels past the blade effortlessly, but they also have stops mounted on the crosscut fence that can accommodate up to a 62" crosscut. The fence can also be repositioned to the front of the table for front-supported crosscuts, or angled for miter cuts.

While very advantageous, sliding tables are expensive and are usually recommended for cabinet saws. If you're working with a contractor saw, you'll likely be adequately served by adding a simple miter sled to your setup.

BLADE GUARDS/SPLITTERS

This is another area where manufacturers have provided what is necessary on the saw, but pricing has kept guard systems at the bare minimum and they're often cumbersome to use. So we recommend upgrading your safety systems on your saw. An aftermarket splitter and guard provide more safety and are easier to use, but they can cost hundreds of dollars. Despite the price, they're a good investment.

Aftermarket overarm blade guards that replace the guards shipped with the saw offer improved convenience and safety, but the convenience usually means you must use both an overarm guard and a splitter for complete safety.

An overarm guard (and there are a half dozen available) usually employs a clear shatterproof basket that covers the blade area and makes it difficult to bring your hand in contact with the blade. Suspended and height adjustable, these guards can be made to operate in most cutting procedures.

Overarm guards are designed to keep your hands away from the blade, but also provide easy and clearly visible saw operation. Able to quickly swing out of the way as needed, this guard also has built-in dust collection.

When a piece needs to be run vertically on the saw, the guard is designed to swing out of the way (temporarily), and swing easily back into place without extensive resetting. Some even include built-in dust collection.

The splitter plays an important safety role. By introducing a thin steel or high-impact plastic plate into the blade kerf after a cut, the splitter keeps the divided piece of wood from pinching the blade, should the pieces be inclined to twist because of internal tension in the wood.

Another part of a splitter is a set of toothed pawls that are spring-loaded and move out of the way as a board passes them. But the teeth will catch on the board keeping it from moving back towards the operator in a kickback.

Typically an integral part of a manufacturer-supplied guard, the splitter and pawls

Tips & Tricks

Bend and Split

For a splitter to work correctly it needs to be perfectly aligned with the blade. Most factory-provided splitters are made from a light-gauge steel that can be easily bent. If your splitter should lose alignment, it's easy to readjust using a hand screw clamp to apply pressure to the splitter bending it back into alignment. Of course, you need to remove the clamp when making a cut.

Nothing Like the Real Thing

While outfeed tables and roller stands can make things much easier when cutting large material, sometimes there's nothing like a helping hand ... when helping correctly. Remember, both operators must be clear of the danger zone. You must each understand what is expected of you during the operation and what you will do if something goes wrong. Hand signals are best. Also, remember that the guy pushing the board is in charge. Don't try and direct the board through the blade. That's his job!

can cause headaches. You must remove them for specialized saw operations such as using a dado stack. Once removed, they can be difficult to reattach. Plus, they can become easily misaligned.

Aftermarket splitter/pawl assemblies that can be quickly detached and reinstalled without using tools are now available. These accessories are just good sense and should always be used in conjunction with an overarm guard system.

ROLLER STANDS AND OUTFEED TABLES

While it might be advantageous to build permanent outfeed tables and side tables to support larger work on your saw, it's not always practical.

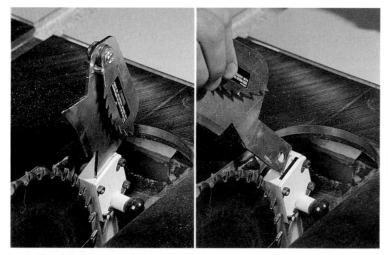

An aftermarket splitter/pawl assembly is shown in position (left) and being easily removed (right), without the use of tools. The splitter keeps a cut board from pinching the blade, while the pawls reduce kickback. The two parts work together to ensure your safety.

Roller stands serve as a simple helping hand when working with wide or long material. The Lee Valley stand shown here uses swiveling casters to support and move the material. It's adjustable for height in both gross or fine increments using separate mechanisms.

There are two distinct types of temporary work support that make handling larger pieces on the table saw manageable – roller stands and outfeed tables.

Roller stands are available for sale in a dizzying array of designs. They all are adjustable in height to align with your saw's table and offer some type of low-friction support head. This can be a set of oversized ball bearings, one or more large rolling bars, or as simple as a tilting, slick plastic surface. All work, but you may prefer one style over another.

You can also make your own roller stands from kits, or from odds and ends in your shop, if that's your preference.

Outfeed tables are more permanent in design and are exactly what they sound like. The tables are usually about 24" wide and about 48" long, and are designed to be about ⅛" lower than the height of the saw's table. These are usually shop-made items and the top surface could be made from melamine or laminate to provide less friction against a moving workpiece.

It's usually handy to make two of these tables (shop space permitting). One serves as an outfeed table behind the saw to catch longer pieces, while the other is used at the left side of the saw to support longer pieces. If necessary, you can get by with one table, locating it for your immediate support needs.

ZERO CLEARANCE INSERTS

All table saws come equipped with a throat plate insert. These usually have a ⅜"-wide slot running the length of the opening to accommodate most saw operations, including bevel cuts. While they work, the slot, which is three times the width of the blade, can allow waste to drop between the blade and the insert where they will likely be splintered.

Don't throw the insert away: Hang onto it and make your own zero-clearance table saw inserts. In fact, make a few of them. Not only will they keep fall-off pieces from being thrown back at you, but when cutting joints, you have more bearing surface for your work to ride on. Another benefit is by providing better support on the underside of the cut, zero-clearance inserts reduce splintering, especially in plywood.

The photo on page 115 shows how to make a simple zero-clearance insert. Once made, run your saw blade down to it's lowest point and fit the plate into the throat opening. Hold the plate in place (either by placing the rip fence over the edge of the plate, or by clamping a board across the edge of the plate) then turn on the saw and slowly run the blade up through the plate.

If you would like to make a throat plate that can be adjusted for height to fit perfectly flush with the saw table, make your blank thinner and then add short wood screws to the plate, located to rest on the tabs inside the throat opening. By adjusting the screws, you adjust the plate.

FEATHERBOARDS

You can increase accuracy and safety with featherboards, which press stock against the fence or table during a cut.

Featherboards work just like the pawls on a splitter assembly, but they're tension-loaded, not spring loaded. As wood is pushed past the fingers, they bend out of the way, but will not allow the material to be pulled back through. This keeps your work tight against a saw table, saw fence or both at the same time.

You can purchase plastic feather-boards or make your own. Evenly spaced kerfs ripped in the end of a piece provide the tension. For less tension, make the cuts longer. For more tension, shorten them up. A straight-grained hardwood is best for featherboards.

Once made, the featherboards are clamped in place. They should be positioned to avoid forcing the piece against the blade. To avoid clamp placement problems, you can also make simple hold-downs to fasten the featherboards in your miter slot.

PUSH STICKS

Push sticks – one of the most important table saw accessories – are often overlooked. When it comes to safety, you can never have enough push sticks handy.

I've known woodworkers to use very simple and very elaborate push sticks. In my opinion both are great, as long as they're being used. And don't worry about nicking your stick with the saw blade. It's much easier to make a new push stick than grow a new finger.

There are dozens of manufactured push stick designs. Some are shipped with new table saws and many other designs are sold

in catalogs and retail locations. All are fine, but consider making your own instead. Use either a solid hardwood or high-density plywood. Either copy a shape from a store-bought design that you like, or design your own. Just make sure you use them.

OTHER ACCESSORIES
Powertwist Belt

If you have a contractor saw, this is a great upgrade. This belt, commonly called a "link

To make a zero-clearance table insert, plane a piece of hardwood to the thickness of your regular blade insert. Trace the shape of the insert on the planed stock and saw it with a band saw, cutting about ¹⁄₁₆" wide of the line. Fasten the metal blade insert to the wooden blank with double-faced carpet tape and rout the final shape with a flush-trim bit. Adjust the height of the bit so the pilot bearing follows the shape of the metal insert while the cutters trim the wood.

Tips & Tricks

Fence Straddler
Push sticks and push blocks are valuable accessories. But sometimes you want even more control than usual. I recommend making at least one fence straddler. When making a narrow rip cut, the stock can be lifted off the table saw as it passes by the rear of the blade. It can also be pinched between the blade and the fence, and then flung like a spear. A fence straddler allows you to both hold the stock on the table and feed it past the blade. Because the U-shape of the jig straddles the fence it adds great stability and the handle on top keeps your hand even further from harm's way.

Everything Handy
This may seem a little simple, but no other single tip will save you as much time and frustration. Five accessories to always keep at the saw: pencil, tape measure, safety glasses, bench brush and calipers or a steel rule. No matter how much attention you're paying in your shop, half the time you end up leaving one of these items somewhere else and have to go chasing it before you can make your cut. This can lead to inaccuracies, poor safety habits and frustration. Find a drawer or even store these items in the hollow front rail of your rip fence, but keep them at the saw.

Low-cost Splitter

The splitter slips into three holes drilled in your zero-clearance throat plate, directly behind the blade.

The drilling guide doubles as storage for the splitters when not in use and attaches to the underside of the throat plate.

One of the most recent and affordable options for making your table saw safer is this polycarbonate plastic splitter from Micro Jig (407-696-6695 or microjig.com). About $20, this splitter installs on any zero-clearance throat plate (which you should have anyway) in about 30 minutes.

The splitter mounts right behind your blade holding the two recently cut pieces of wood apart and greatly reducing the chance of kickback. When you need to make a dado or through-cut, it can be removed quickly and then can be easily dropped back into place after the cut.

Micro Jig makes splitters that will work with standard ⅛"-wide saw blades and also thin-kerf blades. Each package comes with two splitters. Each face of the two splitters exerts a different amount of pressure (in .003" increments) against your stock and the rip fence. This allows the splitter to function as a featherboard, adding accuracy to your rips. Each kit includes the drilling guide (that doubles as storage for the splitters when not in use on your saw), drill bit and instructions.

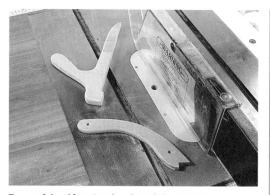

Two useful and functional push-stick designs are shown here. The lower design applies very specific hold-down pressure at the notched tip of the stick. The upper stick is actually more of a push shoe. The entire surface ahead of the notch rides on the material, providing pressure not only behind the wood, but along the length of the wood as well.

Three types of featherboards are shown here. At the top is a shop-made one that can be clamped across the saw table. The "feathers" are created by making repeated cuts on the band saw. The lower left one has a strong magnet that locks it to the saw table and uses flexible plastic paddles. The third rides in the miter slot and uses plastic feathers to apply pressure.

belt," makes your saw run smoother and with less slipping. It costs about $7 a foot (you'll probably need 4'), but it's worth it (available from Woodcraft, 800-225-1153 or woodcraft.com).

Mobile Base
Many woodworkers are challenged by space and one way to ease that is with the use of mobile bases. Even your table saw can be made mobile, though usually cabinet saws are set in place and not moved. If you add a mobile base to your contractor-style table saw, make sure it can be locked solidly in position with no movement. The last thing you want is your saw shifting during a cut.

Dust collection
Table saws are much more friendly about creating dust (at least in volume) compared

to planers and jointers, but the dust they do create is fine and still dangerous. Most cabinet saws offer an effective dust port in the base. Contractor saws require some special effort. The open back makes dust collection less efficient, but it's still worth the effort.

Advanced Joinery

by Nick Engler

In Chapter 3 of this section we discussed basic joinery on the table saw, including miters, bevels, rabbets, dados and grooves. In this chapter we're going to take those concepts a step further. Essentially we'll be using the same techniques. These joints simply require a little more thought before you begin. We'll be looking at compound miters, tenons, dovetails, lock joints and splines.

Each of these joints can be created using tools other than the table saw. Some might even argue that they can be made more easily on other tools. For example, compound miters can be easily created using a miter saw. Tenons, dovetails (with the help of a jig), lock joints and splines can be handily created using a router or a router table.

But why buy extra machinery, tools and jigs if you don't have to? All of these joints can be easily achieved with your best friend, the table saw.

COMPOUND MITERS

To start we'll take a look at compound miters on the table saw. While regular miter joints are a mainstay in picture framing, if you want to make a more complicated, three-dimensional frame you need to cut a compound miter. Useful for much more than picture framing, the compound miter joint is probably most commonly used in forming corners for crown moulding. This joint can be accurately created on the table saw with just a little help from mathematics.

To cut a compound miter on a table saw you need to both tilt the blade and angle the miter gauge for each cut. When two boards are joined by compound miters, the boards slope, rather than rest on an edge or a face. This slope and the number of sides of the frame determine the necessary blade tilt and the miter gauge angle. (See the chart on page 118 to find the settings needed for different frames.)

To make a compound miter, angle the miter gauge and tilt the blade. Compound miters are used to join boards whose faces slope, such as crown moldings.

A standard crown moulding (fitting in a 90° inside or outside corner) commonly has a 45° slope. Reading our chart, for four-sided miters, we come up with a blade bevel angle of 30° and a miter gauge angle of 54.74°.

Before committing to the compound-miter setup called out on the chart, make a sample to check your angle. Cut some small scrap pieces using the recommended angles. Cut enough to complete your test shape. To make matching left and right compound miters, flip each board face for face so that a different edge rests against the miter gauge and a different face rests against the table when cutting each end.

After cutting all the compound miters, tape the pieces together to complete the frame and inspect the joints. If the joints gap on the inside, decrease the blade tilt. If they gap on the outside, increase the blade tilt. If the slope is greater than you expect it to be, decrease the miter gauge angle. If it's less than expected as measured from horizontal, increase the angle. Just make sure

To test a compound miter setup, cut enough sample pieces to form your ultimate shape. Cut all the pieces to the same length so you can complete a small frame. Tape the parts together, then inspect the joints and measure the slope.

TENONS

When it comes to reliable joinery the mortise and tenon is excellent for frames, including table bases, doors and cabinetry. The male part of the joint, the tenon, is easily made on the table saw.

First, the shoulders of the tenon are cut using a miter gauge to guide the workpiece. Depending on the required dimensions of your tenon, you may be able to make all four shoulder cuts without changing the saw setup. Traditionally a tenon is half the thickness of the workpiece. With a ¾"-thick piece of wood that would require a ⅜"-thick tenon. This leaves a ³⁄₁₆" shoulder on the two wide sides of the tenon and that's usually a perfectly good size for the two narrow shoulders as well.

With the shoulders defined, it's time to cut the cheeks. There are a few ways this can be tackled on a table saw, primarily either with the piece held vertically or horizontally. To cut the cheeks horizontally, a dado cutter works well and will accurately center the tenon. Another advantage to using this accessory is that you can cut both a shoulder and a cheek in one pass. If you don't own a dado cutter, a single blade can also

you don't change any one setting more than ½° between tests.

Another way to calculate compound miters is with a scientific calculator (about $9 at most office supply stores) with SIN, COS, TAN and INV buttons. On some calculators, the INV button is labeled FUNC or the key is blank.

Compound Miter Chart for the Table Saw

Slope°	4 sides butted Miter angle	4 sides butted Bevel angle	4 sides mitered Miter angle	4 sides mitered Bevel angle	5 sides mitered Miter angle	5 sides mitered Bevel angle	6 sides mitered Miter angle	6 sides mitered Bevel angle	8 sides mitered Miter angle	8 sides mitered Bevel angle
0			45	90	54	90	60	90	67.5	90
5			45.11	3.53	54.1	2.94	60.09	2.5	67.58	1.91
10			45.44	7.05	54.42	5.86	60.38	4.98	67.81	3.81
15			45.99	10.55	54.94	8.75	60.85	7.44	68.19	5.69
20			46.78	14	55.68	11.6	61.52	9.85	68.73	7.52
25			47.81	17.39	56.64	14.38	62.38	12.2	69.42	9.31
30	49.11	48.59	49.11	20.7	57.82	17.09	63.43	14.48	70.27	11.03
35	50.68	42.14	50.68	23.93	59.24	19.7	64.69	16.67	71.26	12.68
40	52.55	35.93	52.55	27.03	60.9	22.2	66.14	18.75	72.4	14.24
45	54.74	30	54.74	30	62.81	24.56	67.79	20.71	73.68	15.7
50	57.27	24.4	57.27	32.8	64.97	26.76	69.64	22.52	75.09	17.05
55	60.16	19.21	60.16	35.4	67.38	28.78	71.68	24.18	76.64	18.26
60	63.43	14.48	63.43	37.77	70.04	30.59	73.9	25.66	78.3	19.35
65	67.09	10.29	67.09	39.86	72.93	32.19	76.29	26.94	80.07	20.29
70	71.12	6.72	71.12	41.64	76.05	33.52	78.83	28.02	81.94	21.07
75	75.49	3.84	75.49	43.08	79.35	34.59	81.5	28.88	83.88	21.7
80	80.15	1.73	80.15	44.13	82.81	35.37	84.27	29.52	85.89	22.12
85	85.02	0.44	85.02	44.78	86.38	35.82	87.12	29.87	87.93	22.43
90	90	0	90	45	90	36	90	30	90	22.5

Note: The slope is measured from horizontal, with the assembly resting on a bench or work surface.

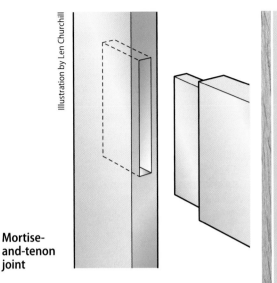

Illustration by Len Churchill

Mortise-and-tenon joint

be used by making repeated cuts to nibble away the waste. It's slower, but it still works.

To cut the tenon in a vertical manner I recommend using a tenoning jig that holds the piece tightly in place, as shown on page 120. Another advantage to a tenoning jig is it also guarantees a centered tenon. The piece is flipped to cut both cheeks, but the jig remains in place, centering the tenon. You should always make a sample piece to test-fit the tenon to its mortise and adjust the setup as needed.

While you can't make a mortise on a table saw, you can make a variation on the traditional mortise-and-tenon joint known as the bridle joint. This joint leaves the mortise and the tenon visible from the ends of the adjoining boards.

While not as strong as a true mortise and tenon, it greatly simplifies the mortising operation and both parts can be cut with a single setup on the table saw using a tenoning jig.

Tips & Tricks

1-2-3 Crown

When adding crown moulding to a cabinet, start by cutting the compound miter on one end of the front piece, then allow plenty of length and rough cut the other end a bit long. Then cut the appropriate compound angle on both short return pieces for the sides, again leaving plenty of length to the back of the cabinet. Use one return moulding to align the front moulding (forming the complete compound miter), then mark the exact location of the second miter cut on the front piece. Attach the front moulding, then simply mark the square cut on the back of each return, make the cuts and attach.

Choose Your Blade

Fitting tenons into mortises can be a little tricky, but by using the right blade you can make it easier. If you know you can cut a tenon to fit perfectly, then using a ripping blade (or flat-bottomed dado) to form the cheeks makes good sense. But if you want to make your tenon oversized and sneak up on the final fit with a shoulder plane, you don't want to have to plane too much material for fitting. Rather, use a crosscut blade to form your oversized tenon. The tooth configuration on the blade will leave a corduroy-type finish on the tenon cheeks with hills and valleys. Planing away only the hills to get a perfect fit is much easier.

Easy, Cheap Clamping

You'll notice I used simple tape to hold together my compound miter test on page 118. Tape can come in handy after the test as well. When you're assembling odd-shaped pieces such as a six-sided compound miter shape it's nearly impossible to put clamps on the piece. Go ahead and use tape instead. Lay the .pieces to assemble with the miters facing down. Butt the joints together and put tape across the joint. Repeat this for all but the last joint. Then carefully flip the taped pieces, add glue and fold the shape, taping the last joint. The pressure exerted by the tape as the joints close will be plenty adequate to hold everything together.

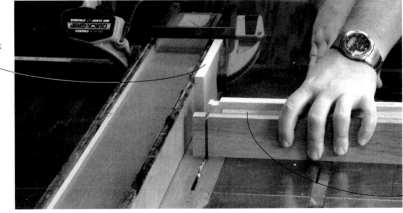

Step-off block

Sandpaper

Defining $3/16$" shoulders on all four sides of a tenon is simple. The piece is run over the blade using a miter gauge. I've added sandpaper to the face of the miter gauge to keep the piece from slipping. I'm also using a step-off block that allows me to set my fence to align the cut, but as the miter gauge moves forward, the block stays behind to avoid kickback if the piece binds.

Cutting a tenon vertically on the table saw is really only safe if the piece is held tightly in place during the cut. A simple shop-made tenoning jig like the one shown here locks the piece in place quickly with the snap of the toggle clamp's lever. My tenoning jig is designed to straddle my rip fence, adding even greater stability and control during the cut.

Toggle clamp

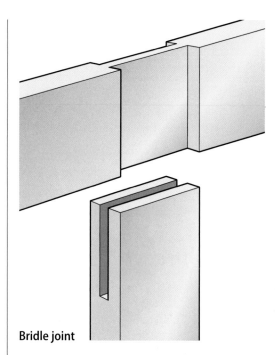

Bridle joint

Tips & Tricks

No-mortiser Mortise

Large through-mortises in furniture can be time consuming and require equipment (a mortiser and appropriate chisel) that you might not own. These types of mortises often occur in table legs and there you're in luck. You can build the mortise into the leg and use your table saw to make it. Most trestle-style legs are too large to be cut from one piece of wood, so a glue-up is required. By running matching, wide dados in the leg halves prior to glue-up, you can make almost any size through mortise with a minimum of effort.

Dedicated Dovetail Blade

If you do a lot of dovetailing on the table saw, you may find it convenient to have a blade modified specifically for the task. Have your sharpener grind the teeth of a rip or combination blade so all the teeth are angled at 10° (be sure to indicate which way your saw tilts). This will allow you to cut right to the shoulder line on the tail board, saving a lot of handwork. You'll still be able to use the blade for most regular work. – *Excerpted from "Cutting Edge Table Saw Tips & Tricks" by Kenneth S. Burton (Popular Woodworking Books).*

The bridle joint shown above is designed for joining a rail to the center of another piece. If the top piece were trimmed away at the left end of the joint, you could easily form the corner of a door frame. All of this can be done on the table saw and without having to fuss with cutting a mortise.

DOVETAILS

Dovetails on the table saw? Not possible! At least you might think so, but if you're making through dovetails (dovetails that allow the joinery to be visible from both sides of the joint), it can be done.

Jim Stack, an accomplished woodworker and author, shared his method for through dovetails on the table saw. The trick is all in a special sled specifically designed to keep everything aligned during the cuts.

You still need to lay out your dovetails as your would with any dovetail jig, but with this method you're not limited by templates and you can make the pins as thin as you'd like without the worry of fitting a router bit into the opening. The page at right shows you how to make the jig and how to put it to work.

Table Saw Dovetails

The table saw is great for cutting dovetails because it can cut straight and square. You can create the look of a hand-cut joint by using this two-sided sled and a rip blade.

1. Use three #6 x ¾" wood screws to attach the hardwood miter guide to the bottom of the base at dead center.

2. Use #8 x 1½" wood screws to attach the angled fences to their mounting cleats and cut a 10° angle on the each end.

3. Draw a line down the center of the base and screw the assemblies to the base.

4. Attach the blade-guard blocks behind the angled fences. Then put the jig in one of the miter slots on your table saw and mark where the blade meets the base. Attach a blade-guard block behind the fence at this location. Put the jig in the other miter slot and repeat the process.

5. Screw the straight fence to its mounting cleat, then screw one end of the mounting cleat to the base, allowing the fence to pivot until you square this fence to the blade. With the jig in one of the miter slots, hold a framing square against the long fence and line up the other arm of the square with the saw blade. Screw the assembly in position.

6. Attach the blade-guard blocks to the straight fence in the same manner that you did with the angled fence. Use glue and screws.

7. Set your saw blade so it's square to the table and about 1" above the base of the jig. Cut a kerf into each angled fence. Don't cut all the way through the blade-guard blocks.

8. Turn the jig around and bevel your saw blade to 10°. Cut this angled kerf into both sides of the straight fence.

— Jim Stack

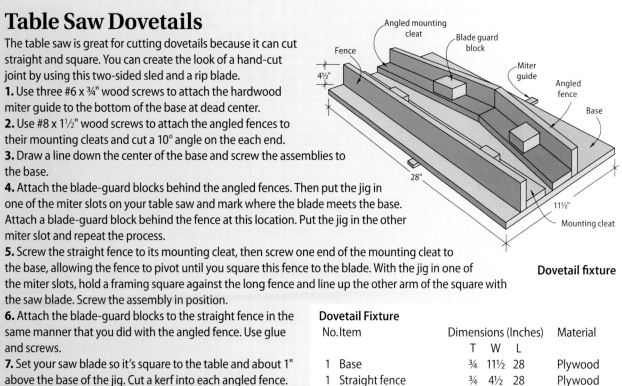

Dovetail fixture

Dovetail Fixture

No.	Item	Dimensions (Inches)			Material
		T	W	L	
1	Base	¾	11½	28	Plywood
1	Straight fence	¾	4½	28	Plywood
2	Angled fences	¾	4½	14	Plywood
1	Straight mounting cleat	¾	2	28	Plywood
2	Angled mounting cleats	¾	2	14	Plywood
1	Miter guide	⅜	¾	13½	Hardwood
4	Blade-guard blocks	1½	2	3	Hardwood

To Cut Your Dovetails:

Lay out the pins on the end and both faces of the workpiece. Be sure to mark the waste material. Set the saw blade height to the thickness of the stock. Using the angled fence on the fixture, make your defining cuts for one side of the pins.

Use the pins as a template to lay out the tails.

Move the fixture to the other miter gauge slot, switch to the other angled fence and make the cuts on the other sides of the pins.

Tilt the blade to 10° and turn the fixture around so the straight fence faces the blade. Raise the blade to the material's thickness. Make the defining cuts on one side of each tail.

Nibble away the waste between the pins with repeated passes over the blade.

Flip the part face for face and make the defining cuts on the other side of the tails. Then clean out the waste. Clean out the corners of the tails with a chisel.

LOCK JOINTS

Similar to half-blind dovetail joints, lock joints (or locking tongue-and-dado joints) cannot be seen from one direction and are often used to assemble drawers. They're much easier to make than dovetails – you can cut them with a single setup on a table saw. The trade-off is that they don't withstand shear stress as well as dovetails (the wood in front of the dado will shear off if you pull too hard on the drawer front). However, they are still a good choice for small drawers or drawers that won't see much use.

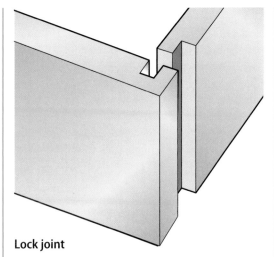

Lock joint

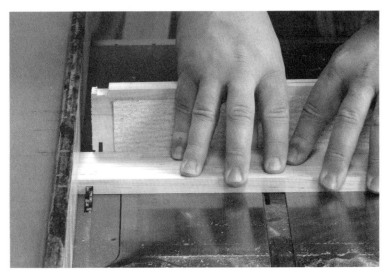

The first cut for the lock joint is made with the inside face of the drawer part flat against the table saw. The piece is slid snug against the fence to locate the dado $1/4$" in from the end. The miter gauge must be set accurately at 0° and the fence exactly parallel to the blade to avoid binding.

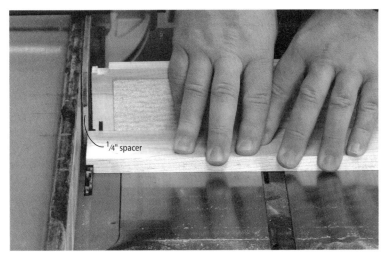

$1/4$" spacer

A $1/4$"-thick step-off piece is used to cut the tenon on the end of the drawer fronts and backs. Not only does this simple block add a bit of safety against binding, but it also allows you to make this second lock joint cut without having to reset the blade or fence.

To make a lock joint, mount a dado cutter on your saw and adjust the depth of cut to equal half the thickness of the board. As most drawer boxes are made of ½"-thick material, make the tongue and the thickness of the dado ¼" thick. This works out fairly well for the dado stack as well, requiring only the two outer blades to make a ¼"-wide dado. And as an added benefit you can actually set the saw and fence once for both cuts.

Using the fence and your miter gauge to guide the stock, cut the ¼" x ¼" dado in the workpiece. The stock is held flat against the saw table and snug against the fence face.

To cut the mating tongue section, you essentially want to shift your dado cut to the end of the board, rather than ¼" in from the end. To do this, use a ¼"-thick spacer against the fence.

Set the tongue board flat on the saw table as before, using the miter gauge again as your guide. Slide the board against the ¼" spacer and then push the board forward toward the blade. The spacer remains behind, leaving a ¼" space between your board and the fence face. Hold the piece tightly against the miter gauge and make your cut. That's all it takes – you have your ¼" x ¼" tongue that should fit your dado perfectly.

SPLINES

A spline is a small board, usually just ¼" to ⅛" thick, that spans the joint between two boards. The spline rests in two matching grooves – one in each board. You also can install a spline in matching rabbets or dados if needed. Splines can be made of solid

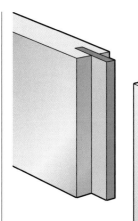

Spline joint for frames

For splines, make a quick carriage to help support the assembly as you move it past the blade. The blade height should be just shy of the joint's inside corner. For flat frames, you can saw right through the carriage's supporting pieces. Just be sure no screws are in the path of the blade. – *Excerpted from "Cutting Edge Table Saw Tips & Tricks," by Kenneth Burton (Popular Woodworking Books).*

wood, plywood or hardboard. Solid wood is best if the spline is decorative and the grain runs perpendicular to the joining pieces. Plywood is excellent when the top plys run with the grain of the joint making a good glue surface while the cross-grain plys add strength. Hardboard, which has no grain direction, is good for any grain direction.

Making a spline groove is no different than making an ordinary groove. Use a saw blade or dado cutter to cut a groove as wide as the spline is thick. Cut the depth about $\frac{1}{32}$" more than half the spline's width to allow excess glue space.

If centering the spline is necessary, simply run the board twice with opposing faces against the fence. Start with the blade near center on the edge, then sneak the fence over till the groove is exactly the right width.

Dry-fit your spline. Half the spline should fit in one groove and half in the other, with just a little side-to-side slop. If everything checks out, spread glue on the adjoining surfaces, the splines and in the grooves, and assemble the joint.

The advanced spline joint is one used to reinforce miter joints. Depending on how a miter joint is oriented, you can run the splines either horizontally or vertically. Also, you can choose whether to cut the spline before or after you assemble the miter joint. Splined miters in which the grooves are cut after the parts have been assembled are sometimes referred to as open spline joints, because both ends of each spline are clearly visible.

Tips & Tricks
Spline Grain Direction
The grain in a corner spline should run across the joint for maximum strength. For a hidden spline, this means the length of the piece will be only about ¾", while the width will be considerably more. Rather than try to cut such a short, wide piece, make the splines from fairly narrow pieces and use as many as necessary to fill the groove. – *Excerpted from "Cutting Edge Table Saw Tips & Tricks" by Kenneth Burton (Popular Woodworking Books).*

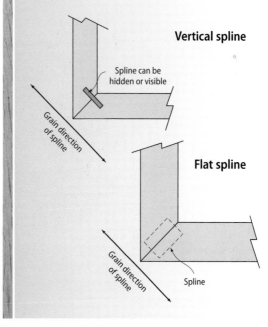

Vertical spline

Spline can be hidden or visible

Grain direction of spline

Flat spline

Grain direction of spline

Spline

Special Techniques

by Nick Engler

Although the table saw was invented to cut large boards into smaller ones, that's not all it will do. With the proper accessories, you can use it to cut a variety of woodworking joints, and an astonishing number of simple or complicated decorative shapes and profiles for your projects.

One such accessory is a moulding head or moulder. A moulder mounts on the saw's arbor similarly to a dado set and also makes broad cuts. But unlike a dado cutter, the kerf left by a moulder is rarely square. There are a variety of knives that fit in the moulding head and each cuts a different shape. With a good selection of moulding knives you can make decorative cuts or complex joints.

In this chapter we also discuss how to cut raised panels for doors and cabinetry. Plus, we show you step by step how to cut delicate tapers for table legs.

Safety Tips

Work Large, Then Small
Many mouldings are created on smaller strips of wood. Don't attempt to mould narrow stock or any workpiece that's too small to safely control on the table saw. Instead, mould a larger board and then cut the smaller piece from it. Another option is to temporarily attach the small piece to a large scrap, mould it, and remove it from the scrap. To attach, use double-sided tape or temporary spray-mount adhesive.

Right at Hand
With all of the special saw techniques in this chapter, safety is even more important. With the blade extended further than normal and when using larger cutting knives, the possibility for accidents is increased. Keep your safety gear nearby. In fact,

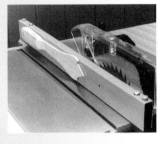

keeping a push stick attached to your saw fence is a great idea. If you have a metal saw fence, inset a couple of magnets in the handle of your push stick to keep it always handy. If your fence isn't metal, hook-and-loop fabric will work just as well.

USING A MOULDER
A moulder is used very much like a dado cutter, with one important difference. While there are only two basic dado cuts (dados and grooves), there are as many different cuts as there are moulding knives. The shape of each moulding cut is determined by the shape of the knives used to make it. Furthermore, you can create hundreds of additional shapes by passing a board over the moulder two or more times, using different knives for each pass.

Although there are many different moulding profiles, they can all be grouped into three categories:

Single-purpose Knives
These knives are designed to cut just one shape, such as a cove, a bead or an ogee. And they do that very well.

Multi-purpose Knives
These knives cut two or more shapes. Usually one side of the knife is ground to cut one shape and the other side is ground to cut another. This saves setup time required to change knives.

Coping Knives
These cut interlocking joints. They come in matched sets – one part of the set cuts one

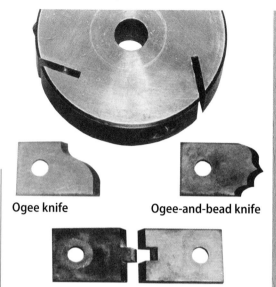

Ogee knife　　　　**Ogee-and-bead knife**

Tongue-and-groove coping knives

The ogee knife is a single-purpose knife because it cuts only the ogee shape. The ogee-and-bead knife is a multi-purpose knife that will cut two different shapes, depending on how you set up for the moulding cut. The tongue-and-groove coping knives are precisely matched – one cuts a groove and the other cuts the tongue to fit it.

half of the joint, while the other part cuts the other half.

SETUP AND USE

Moulding knives normally come in sets of three. This is a good idea because it helps balance out the moulding head. Using only two knives can cause excessive vibration during the cut. Using three knives also improves the quality of the cut, creating more cuts per inch.

Each knife in a set is ground identically to the others. (Coping knives come in six-knife sets containing two matching sets of three.) To mount the knives in the moulding head, slip them into the slots in the cutter-head. Make sure the flat surfaces all face in the direction of rotation. Tighten the screws that hold the knives in the head, then check each screw again. With a standard table saw operating at 3,500 rpm, you don't want one of these knives coming loose.

Set the position of the rip fence and the depth of cut as you would for a dado cutter and cut test pieces to check your setup. If you plan to cut two or more shapes in the same piece (for example, if you want to cut an ogee and a cove in the same board to

Common Moulding Knives

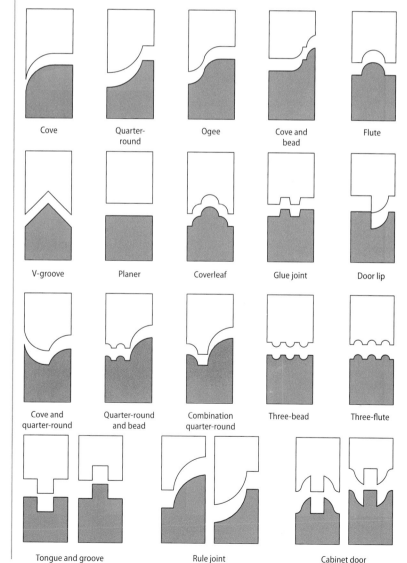

Cove　　Quarter-round　　Ogee　　Cove and bead　　Flute

V-groove　　Planer　　Coverleaf　　Glue joint　　Door lip

Cove and quarter-round　　Quarter-round and bead　　Combination quarter-round　　Three-bead　　Three-flute

Tongue and groove　　Rule joint　　Cabinet door

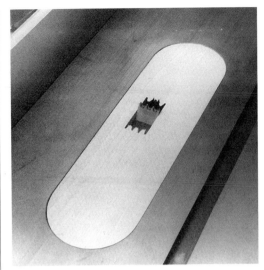

If there are no available throat plate inserts for the moulder you wish to use, you can easily make your own. First make an insert blank by using the existing insert to match the perimeter shape. Then lower the moulder height below the table. Bring the fence over until it covers the insert plate, but make sure it isn't covering the location where the moulding knife will come through. If you're unsure where the knife will come through, you can clamp a scrap board across the insert instead of using your saw fence. Start the saw and slowly raise the cutter up through the insert only as high as needed.

form a crown moulding) cut several test pieces after you fine-tune the first setup. Use these pieces as samples to test successive setups.

As you're making your cut, feed the wood slowly over the cutter – slower than you would when making a saw cut or a dado cut. If you feed the wood too fast, the shaped surface will show ridges or mill marks. By using a slower feed, you allow the moulder to make more cuts per inch so the moulded shape appears perfectly smooth. However, be careful not to feed the wood too slowly, especially when moulding hardwoods. If the moulder dwells too long in any one spot, it will heat up and burn the wood.

The advantage of a moulder over a router or shaper is that it will cut all three surfaces – the face of a board as well as the edges and ends, and it will do it in one pass. Shapers can also cut in one pass, but cut only edges and ends, while the decorative face cuts you can make with a router are limited. To mould the ends or edges, position the rip fence next to or partially covering the moulder (see photos at right). To cut the face, move the fence away or use the miter gauge to guide the work.

When cutting moulded shapes with the board on edge, you must not reduce the width of the board. If your moulding profile shapes the entire edge you need to carefully set the depth of the cut so the moulder does not plane the board. If the moulder removes too much wood, the board will rock forward toward the end of the cut, making the moulded edge crooked. This is especially important when cutting coped edge joints, such as rule joints, and tongues and grooves.

Making Raised Panels

Raised panels are a staple in much traditional and contemporary woodworking. They form an attractive solid-wood panel for doors and cabinet sides, and even can be

To cut a moulded shape in the edge or end of a board, position the rip fence next to or partially covering the knives. Place the face of the board on the table and slowly feed the stock over the cutter. Here, a moulder forms part of a corner bead in the bottom edge of a table apron.

You also can mould an edge with the face of the board against the rip fence and the edge on the saw table. Here, the same apron board has been turned to cut the second part of the corner bead. (Note: If the board is significantly wider than the rip fence is tall, use a tall fence extension to support it.)

When moulding the face of a board, use a miter gauge to guide the board if cutting across the grain and a rip fence if cutting with the grain. Here, a moulder cuts three beads down the center of a table apron using the same knives that made the corner bead shown in the previous photos.

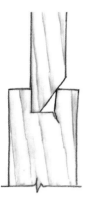

Bevel too steep
Panel splits frame

Bevel too shallow
Panel loose in frame

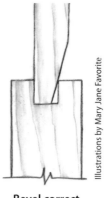

Bevel correct
Panel snug in frame

Illustrations by Mary Jane Favorite

When making a raised panel, the bevel angle is critical. If it's too steep (left) the panel could split the frame that it's mounted in. If it's too shallow (middle) the panel will be too loose and will rattle every time the door is moved. The bevel should be angled so it barely touches the groove's side when the edge of the panel rests in the groove's bottom, as shown above (right). In situations where wood may shrink or expand because of humidity changes, you may choose to leave the panel slightly loose to avoid damaging the frame.

used for most of the pieces (sides, bottoms and tops) required for a variety of boxes – both decorative and functional. They allow solid wood to be used in large physical applications without concerns for wood movement caused by seasonal changes in humidity.

When not in a door frame, raised panels are also used as bottoms in most traditional drawers, allowing a thin groove to support the bottom, while still offering full-width support for larger drawers.

When using the table saw for specialty work, such as raising panels, it's important to remember that pushing a table saw to perform tasks that it wasn't originally designed to do can create a safety problem. If you overextend the table saw, you can easily lose control of the workpiece. This, in turn, makes the operation dangerous, inaccurate or both. When trying new techniques, you must maintain safety, accuracy and control.

Often, the easiest way to do this is to build a simple, sturdy jig to hold or guide the workpiece. A well-made jig is a tool in its own right, with its own capabilities and limits. For raised panels I highly recommend using a tall fence extension. The standard fence on a table saw is just too short to fully support a door panel being run on edge. Along with the tall extension, a featherboard to hold the piece tightly against the fence will make things safer, and also will ensure a quality cut with fewer saw marks.

A raised panel is a board with edges and ends that have been beveled or tapered so the stock is thicker in the center than it is at the perimeter. This panel is usually mounted in a frame that allows it to expand and contract without stressing or distorting

the project. You can raise a panel on a table saw by beveling the ends and edges.

Before you can do so, you must decide what angle to cut the bevels. Most raised panels are designed to fit into grooves in their frames. If you make the bevel too steep, it will act as a wedge in the groove – when the panel expands, the bevel will

Tips & Tricks

Even, Quiet Spacing
Spacing and the proper bevel on a raised panel will make a perfect fit in the door frame. That is, until the panel shrinks because of

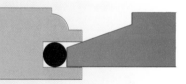

humidity changes. Then the door will rattle and shift in the frame. A new concept (and product) to counteract this (and to make the initial panel-fitting simpler) is called Space Balls.

The concept is to place small rubber balls (.26" in diameter) into the groove in the frame. As the panel is placed in the groove the balls compress, perfectly spacing the panel in the frame. At a later time when the panel shrinks, the balls will decompress, maintaining the panel spacing and keeping it from shifting.

Space Balls are fairly inexpensive (about $5 for 100) and are available at a variety of woodworking supply houses, including Rockler (800-279-4441 or rockler.com). If you're feeling really thrifty, foam strip insulation will also work well for this purpose.

Finish First
Raised-panel doors can create a finishing problem that can be easily avoided. Because the panels are designed to float or move in the frame, unfinished wood can be exposed if the door is stained and finished after assembly. To avoid this, once your door has been successfully test-fit, remove the panels, and sand and stain them to their finished color. A thin coat of clear finish (if you're using one) is also a good idea at this time. It will keep the final staining of the frame from clouding or smearing the stain on the panel.

To determine the proper bevel angel of a raised panel, draw a full-size cross-section of the groove and the panel on edge as shown. Decide how thick the panel should be at the perimeter. (Most woodworkers prefer not to cut it thinner than $1/4$"; if the beveled area becomes too thin, the panel will be weak.) Measure that thickness along the bottom of the groove from the bottom left corner of the groove and make a mark. From this mark, draw a line that just touches the top right corner of the groove. With a protractor, measure the angle between the side of the groove and the last line you drew – that's the bevel angle you want to cut. Tilt the saw blade to that angle.

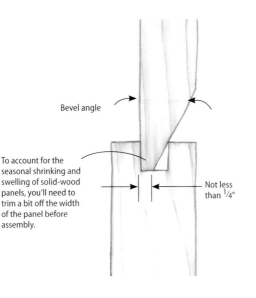

Bevel angle

To account for the seasonal shrinking and swelling of solid-wood panels, you'll need to trim a bit off the width of the panel before assembly.

Not less than $1/4$"

split the sides of the groove. If you make the bevel too shallow, the panel will be loose in the groove. The bevel must be angled to just touch the groove's side when the edge of the panel rests in the groove's bottom. When you've determined the proper bevel, tilt the saw blade to that angle.

Next, decide whether the raised panel will have a step between the field (raised area) and the bevels, and how large that step will be. Most woodworkers prefer to make a $1/16$"- to $1/8$"-deep step (about the same width as the saw teeth). This helps delineate the field from the bevels and makes the visual effect more dramatic.

After it's cut, the step will not be square to the field. Some woodworkers prefer to correct this by trimming it with a second series of saw cuts. However, the step is so small that all it really needs is a little special attention with a file, scraper or sandpaper. If you use sandpaper to correct the angle of the step, wrap the paper around a hard, square block to make the step as flat as possible.

If you decide to make a step on the panel, place the rip fence so that just the outside corners of the teeth break through the wood as you cut. Make several test cuts to get the fence positioned just right, then cut the bevels in the ends and edges of the panel.

Because the blade was tilted when you cut the bevels, the step won't be square to the field. Depending on the grind of the saw teeth, it may not even be flat. Some woodworkers prefer to correct this by trimming it with a second series of saw cuts. But the step is so small that all it really needs is a little special attention with a file, scraper or sandpaper.

When you make your cuts, start with the ends of the panel first, then the long edges. If there's any tear-out while you're cutting across the wood grain, it will be removed when you cut the two bevels that are parallel to the grain.

One other note: On many table saws the blade tilts to the right. This means the fence must be placed to the left of the blade (away from the tilt) when raising panels.

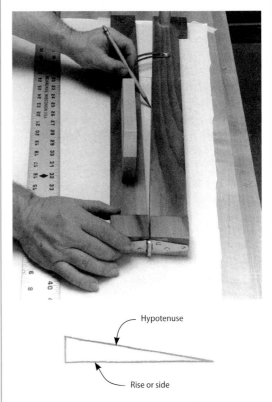

Hypotenuse

Rise or side

On a sheet of scrap paper, draw a large right triangle with the same slope as the taper you want. Use this as a gauge to set the tapering jig to the proper angle: Align one arm with the base of the triangle and the other with the hypotenuse.

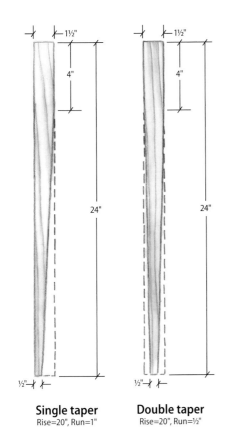

Single taper
Rise=20", Run=1"

Double taper
Rise=20", Run=½"

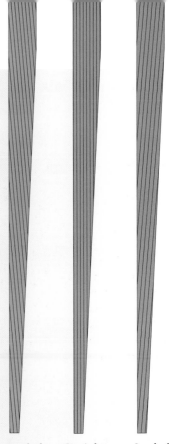

Tips & Tricks
Optical Illusion
When making legs, whether for chairs or tables, choosing your wood carefully can make the difference between beautiful and bizarre. The grain direction in your lumber can make or break the look of a piece. This goes double for tapered legs. If your grain direction is running in contrast or in harmony with the taper on your legs, it changes the look.

The illustrations below help explain this. Angled grain (in either direction) gives your leg a barber pole appearance. Your best wood selection is a straight grain (rift cut) pattern with as little cathedral as possible. This is not only better for aesthetics, it also makes for a stronger leg.

Angled   **Straight**   **Angled**

MAKING TAPER CUTS

To taper a board, you must reduce its width gradually from one end of the board to the other. That requires holding the board with its length at a slight angle to the blade as you rip it.

A tapering jig is the right tool for this job. This jig (detailed in Chapter 2 of this section) consists of two long arms, hinged together at one end. A ledge is glued to one arm near the end opposite the hinge. A metal brace lets you adjust and lock the angle between the two arms. The arm without the ledge guides the jig along the rip fence, while the other holds the stock at an angle to the saw blade.

To set up for a taper cut, you must know the slope of the taper. You also should know whether you will cut a single taper (on a single side or two adjacent sides) or a double taper (with tapers on two or more opposing sides).

Shown above are two tapered table legs, each 24" long. The one on the left has a single taper; the one on the right, a double taper. The foot of both legs is the same width. The rise is equal on both. On both legs, the taper begins 4" from the top and continues to the bottom, making the rise

20" (24" – 4" = 20"). The run is not equal. Although both legs are 1½" wide at the top and then narrow to ½" at the bottom, the single-taper run is 1" (1½" – ½" = 1"), and the double-taper run is ½" ([1½" – ½"] ÷ 2 = ½").

The slope is determined by the length and width of the taper (sometimes called the rise and run). To find the rise of a taper, measure from the starting point to the end. To determine the run of a single taper, calculate the

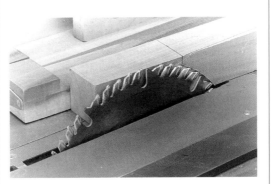

Using scrap stock, cut several test pieces to the same dimensions as the workpieces you will taper. Lay out the tapers on each of these pieces. Place the jig on the table saw with the guiding arm against the fence and place a test piece against the ledge on the other arm of the jig. Position the fence so the inside edges of the teeth brush the layout line that marks the start of the taper.

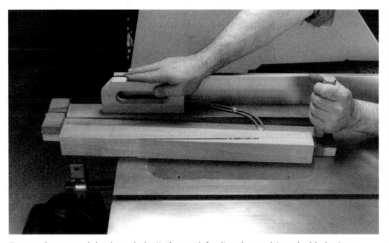

Turn on the saw and slowly push the jig forward, feeding the stock into the blade. As you do so, monitor the cut to make sure the blade follows the layout line. If it does, the setup is correct. If not, readjust the angle of the jig or the position of the rip fence.

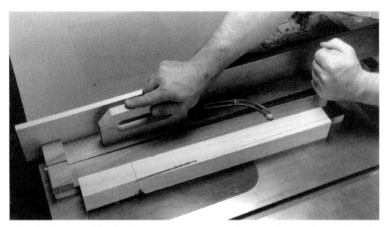

Make the first pass of the double taper as if you were cutting a single taper. Turn the board so the cut side faces the jig and place the shim between the piece and the jig. The wide end of the shim must be flush with the narrow end of the stock. This will hold the workpiece at the same angle to the blade as it was for the first pass. Make the second pass, holding the workpiece and the shim against the ledge on the jig.

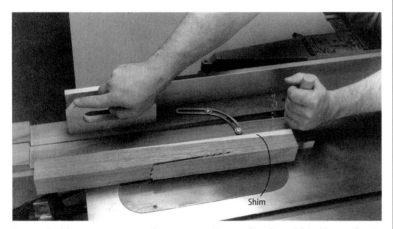

Shim

To cut a double taper, you must make two passes. Use a wedge-shaped shim (shown above) to position the stock on the second pass. The dimensions and slope of this shim are the same as the triangle you drew to set the angle of the jig. Lay out the shim on scrap stock, place the scrap in the tapering jig and cut the shim. Saw to the inside of the layout line.

amount by which the width of the board is reduced. For a double taper, divide that amount in half.

To set the tapering jig to the proper angle, draw a right triangle on a large sheet of paper. The base on the triangle must be the same length as the rise, and the side of the triangle must be equal to the run. Place the jig over the triangle, then adjust it so one arm is parallel to the base and the other is parallel to the hypotenuse (see photo top left). If the slope of a taper is given in degrees, you don't have to calculate the rise. Simply draw the triangle so the angle between the base and the hypotenuse matches that given for the slope.

Next, transfer your taper to a test piece of wood. Place the jig on the table saw with the guiding arm against the fence. Position the fence so the taper will begin at the proper point and make a test cut in a piece of scrap. If the test results are acceptable, cut the good stock.

To cut a double taper, make the first pass as if you were making a single taper. Then flip the board so the cut edge faces the jig. Place a wedge-shaped shim between the workpiece and the jig to hold the stock at the proper angle and make the second pass.

Because the most common use for tapering is table legs, there is one other thing that should be kept in mind during this process. If you will be using mortise-and-tenon joinery to build your table, it's easier to cut the mortises in the legs prior to tapering them. It's much harder to form an accurate mortise on a shape that doesn't have flat sides.

Advanced Techniques

by Nick Engler

In this chapter I'll be sharing some advanced techniques you can use on your table saw to do some amazing things. How about cutting coves for crown moulding? That's just one application for a coved shape, and with a couple of simple jigs you can match any size cove you want.

And how do you get an odd-shaped piece of wood such as a tree slab into shape to move on to the next woodworking step? A couple of tricks with a sled make this advanced technique easy.

Pattern sawing is another trick I'll discuss. If you have a project that requires multiple multi-sided shapes, this technique will save you time.

And finally, my favorite: How to bend a straight board into a curved board without steam bending. I'll show you how to do it all with a technique called kerf cutting.

Once you try these advanced table saw techniques, there's no end to the ways you'll be able to put them to work in your woodworking projects.

CUTTING COVES

The concept of cove cutting on a table saw might sound strange. You're essentially using the side of the blade's teeth to make a dishing cut along the length of a board. While this isn't an operation most saw or blade manufacturers would suggest, it isn't bad for the blade or the saw as long as the cut is taken slowly and in small increments. And it's also plenty safe as long as you use the correct jigs and techniques.

The depth of the cove is determined by the height of the blade above the table. The width of the cove is determined by the angle of the board to the saw. This is where it gets a little tricky. To determine the coving angle, some woodworkers use a trial-and-error method until they get what they want. I prefer something a little more precise, so I use what is known as a parallel rule jig. You can make one for yourself very simply by following the illustrations and instructions on page 132.

Once your jig is made, raise or lower the blade to the desired depth of the cove. Next, adjust the parallel rule to the width of the cove by widening or collapsing the rules. Then place the parallel rule on the saw table so the rule straddles the blade, front and back.

Turn the rules at various angles to the blade while slowly spinning the blade by hand. Find the position where the teeth of the saw blade brushes both rules. Holding the parallel rule in that position, draw two pencil lines across the saw table that trace the inside edge of each rule. The angle formed by the saw blade and either one of these lines is the coving angle.

Using The Right Blade

When cove cutting on the table saw it's helpful to use a blade with the proper tooth configuration. I don't say necessary, because you can make this cut with any type of blade. But it's more helpful to use a combination or ripping blade than a crosscut blade because the inside of the cove will be easier to sand. A crosscut blade uses an alternate, top-bevel tooth arrangement that will leave score marks on the cove. Ripping and combination blades add a flat-topped raker tooth, leaving a cleaner surface on the cove.

Parallel Rule Jig

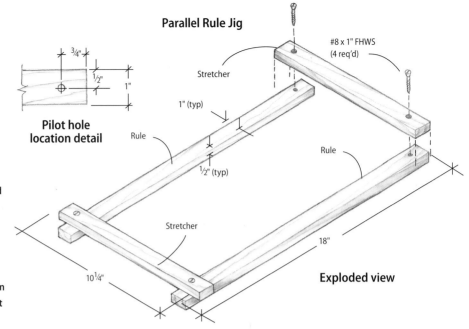

**Pilot hole
location detail**

Stretcher

Rule

1" (typ)

½" (typ)

#8 x 1" FHWS
(4 req'd)

Rule

Stretcher

18"

10¼"

Exploded view

A parallel rule consists of four pieces of wood – two rules and two stretchers. Join them at the ends with screws, making a parallelogram. All the screw holes must be centered between the edge of the rules and stretchers, and they should be precisely the same distance from the ends of the boards. Tighten the screws until they're snug, but not so tight that the parts won't pivot easily.

The next step is to determine the distance from the lines (and the blade) to position your guide on the saw. The illustration bottom right will help you find this.

To guide your cut, you can simply clamp a straightedge to the saw table or you can use a coving fence positioned at the proper angle and distance from the blade, as shown at the top of page 133. (Get plans for a simple coving fence in the free bonus download: Visit shopwoodworking.com/essential-woodworking-jigs and enter the following discount code when you order: WWESSENT.)

You now have all the information and parts to cut your cove. Remember to place the fence or straightedge on the infeed side of the blade. The rotation of the blade helps hold the stock against the fence.

Adjust the saw blade so it projects no more than $\frac{1}{16}$" above the saw table. Turn on

Tips & Tricks

Sprung Mouldings

One of the most common usages for cove cuts is in making crown moulding. This type of moulding is referred to as a sprung moulding because it will lean out from the surface to which it's attached. The two mounting faces of a sprung moulding can be cut at any angle, but the two angles must add up to 90°. To complete the moulding you need to double-bevel the edges of the moulding stock on the table saw. If you cut only one bevel (right) the remaining faces will look odd. The example (left) has been double cut and now looks like a proper crown.

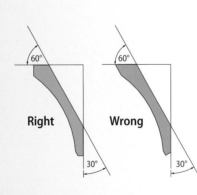

Right

Wrong

Mixing Coves

By combining coves made on your saw and other profiles using a moulding cutterhead you can create complicated mouldings for dozens of projects.

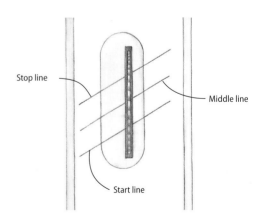

Stop line

Middle line

Start line

Measure the distance between the two lines made with the parallel rule, then draw a third line halfway between and parallel to them. This marks the precise middle of the cove cut. Use all three marks as references to determine both the angle and the position of the coving fence on the saw table. For example, if you want to cut a cove down the middle of a 5"-wide board, the fence must be parallel to and $2\frac{1}{2}$" away from the middle reference line.

Fasten the coving fence to the rip fence and adjust the angle parallel to the three reference lines. Then move the rip fence sideways until it's the proper distance away from the lines. When the fence is positioned, turn on the saw and raise the blade.

the saw and place the workpiece against the fence. Slowly feed the workpiece from the infeed side of the saw and against the direction of rotation. After completing the first pass, raise the saw blade another 1/16" and make a second pass. Repeat until you have cut the cove to the desired depth and width. On the last pass, feed the wood very slowly – this will make the surface of the cove as smooth as possible and reduce the amount of sanding needed.

CUTTING ODD-SHAPED BOARDS

Occasionally, you will need to rip or crosscut a board that doesn't have an edge straight or square enough to hold against the rip fence or miter gauge. Sometimes the board is crooked or warped, other times it's cut or shaped to a particular pattern or contour. The best solution would be to straighten one edge before you cut, but there are times when you can't do this for whatever reason.

To safely cut an odd-shaped board, mount it on a holder that has at least one good guiding edge. This holder doesn't need to be a complex affair; a scrap of plywood with several straight edges makes an excellent holder. Nail the workpiece to the plywood or secure it with double-faced carpet tape. Place the holder against the rip fence or miter gauge, and feed both the holder and the workpiece past the blade.

You also can use a sliding table to hold the piece. The table itself is simply a piece of medium-density fiberboard or plywood with a runner attached that is sized to fit in your miter-gauge slot. Secure the piece

to the jig using the built-in, disc-shaped clamps, letting a portion overhang the sliding table's edge.

Don't let the disc-shaped clamps tilt or tip when you tighten them. If they do, they will put sideways pressure on the workpiece and it may shift as you cut. To prevent this, place a spacer under the clamp, opposite the workpiece, to keep the clamp level. When the workpiece is secured, fit the jig in the miter-gauge slot and slide both the jig and workpiece forward past the saw blade.

This same sled and clamp configuration can help you work with rough-cut log sections, not just flat materials. Simply use longer bolts for the clamps and you can cut up to a 3"-thick chunk of wood. You're only held by the maximum depth of cut of your blade.

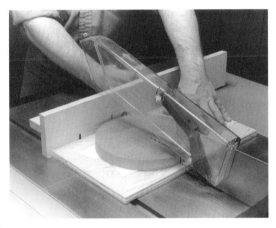

To cut an odd-shaped piece that has no guiding edge, secure it to a rectangular scrap of plywood with nails or double-faced tape. Place one straight edge of the plywood against the rip fence or miter gauge, then guide the piece over the blade, cutting both the plywood and the piece.

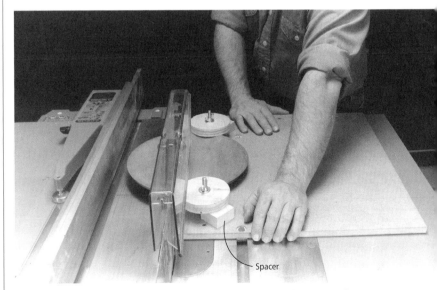

Whether cutting a straight edge on a round object, or adding a straight groove in the center of an oval piece (as shown here) this sliding table holds the odd-shaped piece in place and references off the miter slot to ensure a straight cut.

Pattern-sawing Guide

The mount and the braces are made from hardwood, but the guide is made from clear acrylic plastic. This lets you see the saw blade and monitor the saw cuts as you make them. Cut the parts to size and rout the slots in the mount. Fasten the braces to the mount with glue and screws, then attach the guide with screws. Drill mounting holes in the tall fence extension and bolt the jig to the extension.

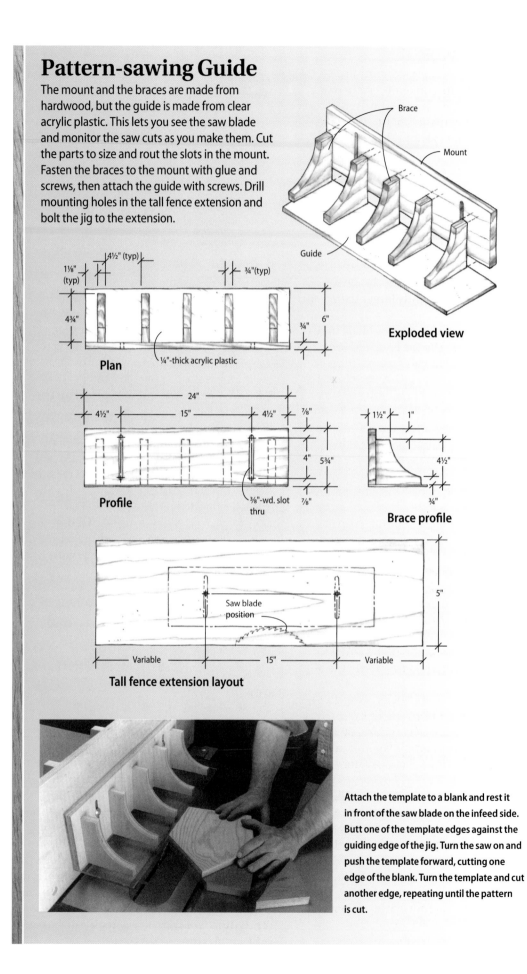

Brace

Mount

Guide

Exploded view

Plan

4½" (typ)

1⅛" (typ)

¾"(typ)

4¾"

6"

¾"

¼"-thick acrylic plastic

Profile

24"

4½"

15"

4½"

⅞"

4"

5¾"

⅜"-wd. slot thru

⅞"

Brace profile

1½"

1"

4½"

¾"

Tall fence extension layout

Saw blade position

5"

Variable

15"

Variable

Attach the template to a blank and rest it in front of the saw blade on the infeed side. Butt one of the template edges against the guiding edge of the jig. Turn the saw on and push the template forward, cutting one edge of the blank. Turn the template and cut another edge, repeating until the pattern is cut.

PATTERN SAWING

Many woodworking projects require that you make duplicate copies of certain parts. This is easy enough when the parts are rectangular – simply rip the stock to the same width, then cut the parts to the same length. But what if the parts are cut to a triangle, pentagon or some other odd shape? As long as all the sides of that shape are straight, you can reproduce precise copies by pattern sawing.

To saw a pattern, first cut a single part to the shape you want. This will serve as the template for all of your duplicate parts. Then cut rectangular blanks for the duplicates, making each blank slightly larger than necessary.

Adjust the height of the saw blade to cut through the thickness of a blank. Mount a tall fence extension to the rip fence and attach a pattern-sawing guide to the extension. I've included plans at left for making a pattern-sawing guide that will work on nearly any table saw.

Align the outside edge of the guide (farthest from the rip fence) with the outside edges of the saw teeth. Then adjust the height of the guide so the bottom surface is ¼" to ½" above the blade.

Fasten the template to a blank with nails, screws or double-faced carpet tape. Holding the edges of the template against the guiding edge of the jig, saw each side. Repeat for each blank until you've made all the parts you need.

It's also possible to cut a curve on the table saw – up to a ¾" arc per foot when cut in ¾" stock. Stock thicker than ¾" isn't recommended as it's pushing the limits of the blade.

You use the same pattern-sawing guide as used with straight cuts. By keeping the curves shallow, the kerf can't bind on the blade because the offset of the teeth keeps the concave side of the kerf away from the blade body.

As with the straight cuts, start with a template affixed to the duplicate piece. If the offcuts will be too large to fit between the blade and the rip fence, trim the offcuts before cutting.

Remember, shallow curves are OK, but if you feel any resistance during the cut, stop the saw and find another way to cut your curves.

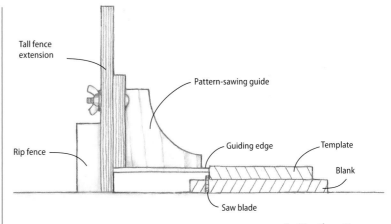

Position the pattern-sawing guide so the outside edge is parallel to the saw-blade plate and flush with the outside edges of the saw teeth. The guiding edge of the jig must be high enough above the saw so that it will contact the edge of the template, but not the blank.

KERF BENDING

Most often when you think of bending wood, pictures of steam bending and lots of clamps come to mind. Steam bending is a good way to bend smaller thicknesses of wood. But when you need to bend a 6"-wide apron for a demilune table there's a better way than steam bending – it's called kerf bending.

You can bend a board of any thickness and width if you first cut several kerfs in one side – usually the side you won't see on the assembled project. These kerfs must not sever the board, but should leave about ¹/₁₆" to ⅛" of stock at the bottom of each cut.

The depth of the cut and the thickness of the stock at the bottom of the kerf will depend on the species of wood – some must be cut thinner than others to bend easily. Experiment with scraps until you can

Calculating kerf spacing

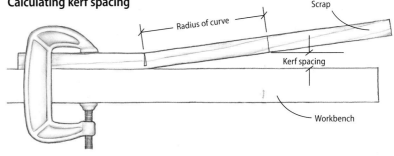

To determine the proper spacing between the kerfs, cut a single kerf in a long scrap board of the same thickness and species as the wood you want to bend. Fasten the board to a workbench, placing the clamps to one side of the kerf. Measure along the board out from the kerf and away from the clamps, and mark a distance equal to the radius of the bend you want to make. Lift the free end of the board until the kerf closes. Measure the distance from the board to the workbench at the radius mark – this will give you the spacing. In practice, I've found it best to space the kerfs a little closer than necessary, so the kerfs don't quite close when you bend the wood. Also, I never space the kerfs any farther apart than 1". If they're too far apart, the bend won't look smooth.

Fasten an extension to the miter gauge, positioning it to pass over the blade when you cut. Cut a single kerf in the workpiece and through the extension. Drive a small brad into the extension to the right or left of the cut (shown above). The distance between the brad and the cut must be equal to the spacing between the remaining kerfs you want to cut. Place the workpiece against the extension with the first kerf over the brad. Cut a second kerf, move the board so the second kerf is over the brad and repeat.

Extra Bending Flexibility

While the whole idea of kerf bending is avoiding steam, a little hot water can help. If the wood is hard to bend or breaks when you bend it, soak a towel in boiling water. Then wrap the kerfed portion of the board in the towel and let it sit for 10 to 15 minutes. Unwrap the towel and bend the wood immediately, before it has a chance to cool.

make a smooth, even bend without cracks or splinters. Even if you cut deeply without cracking or splintering, you need to be cautious of leaving "flats" showing on the curved surface.

Kerf bending isn't only for solid wood. In fact it may even be a more common practice with plywood. This makes lots of sense.

With the cross-grain orientation of the layers in the ply, you can get great strength from two thin layers when you kerf-cut the rest of the layers.

The radius of the curve you want to bend determines the spacing of the kerfs – the tighter the radius, the closer the kerfs. To get a smooth, even bend, the kerfs must be evenly spaced. Gauge the spacing of each kerf by driving a small nail into the face of the miter gauge extension and using it as a stop. (See photo at top, left.)

If you happen to need a curved piece that will be visible from both sides, kerf cutting still works. After kerfing one side, a form is used to bend the piece to the required shape. Then a layer of thin material (usually ⅛" thick) of the same species is glued to the kerfed side and clamped in place.

This is also a valuable technique if you are trying to achieve a free-form curved piece, rather than attaching the piece to a frame. The glued "veneer" will serve as a form to hold the planned shape. This is great for making glass-topped tables and even bookcases.

Cut the kerfs only in the area where you want to bend the wood. After kerfing, carefully bend the wood to the radius needed. To prevent it from straightening out again, brace it or fasten it to the project (see photo at left).

S-curves also are possible by kerfing the wood on opposite sides. This could require adding a veneer layer to both sides of the wood to hide the kerfs, but it can offer a new dimension (or three) to your woodworking designs.

When you bend the wood, you must fasten it to something to hold the curve. If you can't fasten the board to the project itself, fasten a brace to the board.

Casework Construction

Beginning Principles

by David Thiel

To open our seven-part series on casework construction it's probably smart to include the definition of casework. "Webster's Dictionary" (Random House Value Publishing) gives it a one-word definition: cabinetwork. I think that's both a little too complicated and simplistic at the same time. Casework is making boxes. Whether for cabinets, bookcases, nightstands or storage boxes for all your old *Popular Woodworking* magazines, casework is making boxes.

Casework can be as simple as two sides, a top, bottom, back and a door (such as a medicine cabinet). Or it can be a box on a stand with more boxes inside and another box on top of it with doors (such as the entertainment center shown at left).

In this series we'll be discussing casework design, joinery, construction, accessorizing and more. But before we get too deep, let's start with some common definitions so that we're on the same page.

CASEWORK PARTS

Casework can be called cabinetwork, carcase construction and a variety of other things. Similarly, the parts that make up a piece of casework furniture have many different definitions depending on country of origin and who the builder is.

So that we're speaking the same language, I'm going to define the parts of a typical casework piece; and though you might use a different name, we'll refer to them as discussed here throughout the series. Not all of these pieces will occur in every casework piece, but they could. It's similar to the options on your car.

Sides

All casework pieces will have at least two sides and sometimes more if there are upper and lower sections. They can be simple slabs of solid wood or plywood, or frame-and-panel construction.

Bottom

As with the sides, this one's almost a given. There may be specialty situations where a bottom isn't required, but because most casework is designed as storage, having a place to rest your stored items is a good thing.

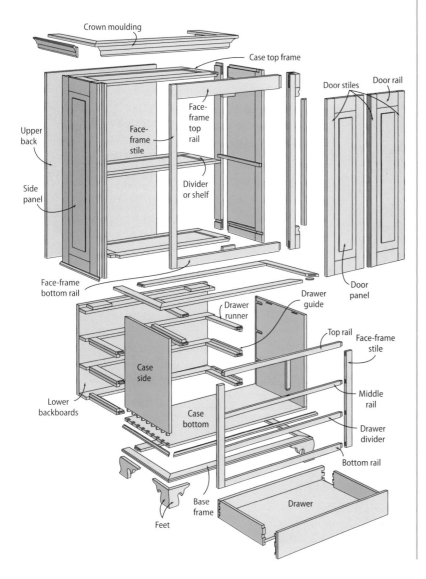

Crown moulding

Case top frame

Door stiles

Door rail

Face-frame top rail

Upper back

Face-frame stile

Side panel

Divider or shelf

Door panel

Face-frame bottom rail

Drawer guide

Drawer runner

Top rail

Face-frame stile

Case side

Middle rail

Case bottom

Drawer divider

Lower backboards

Bottom rail

Base frame

Drawer

Feet

The History of Case Furniture

The history of case furniture actually needs to start with chests that first appeared in Egypt more than 4,000 years ago. The boxes were made from boards joined together at the corners and were used to carry heavy loads when traveling. Around 1,500 B.C. chests found in Egyptian tombs showed improved joinery skills with the introduction of frame-and-panel construction. The interiors often were divided for storage of jewelry and other valuables used in the burial process.

In time, legs were added to boxes used by the Egyptians and these pieces became the first rudimentary case furniture. They were used to store linens, jewelry and toiletries. The next evolution of casework (adding shelves and doors) didn't appear for quite a while.

Furniture designed for holding household goods, what we would call cupboards, didn't appear until late in the Greek and Roman eras. They were still not considered valuable furniture, and were often built using rough wood and crude joinery.

This construction trend continued into the early Middle Ages when the cupboard, known as the press, was often vividly painted to disguise its generally crude joinery. Presses began changing and improving in the Gothic era as more attention was paid to the

This is a 16th-century coffer fort (a coffer fort is bigger than a coffer). The decoration is bitten in with acids so as to present the appearance of its being damascened, and the complicated lock, shown on the inside of the lid, is characteristic of these safeguards for valuable documents at a time when the modern burglar-proof safe had not been thought of.

construction and decoration of the pieces. The form began to change as well, with specific purposes being assigned to the furniture. It was during this period that the armoire and wardrobe furniture styles came into fashion.

True cabinetry started in Italy in the 16th century and the concept quickly spread across the continent. When it came to decorating these cabinets, architecture heavily influenced the designs, much of it classical in nature. During the 17th and 18th centuries, cabinets were the most important and

elaborate pieces of furniture made. Because of the time, effort and skill required to create these pieces, the profession of cabinetmaker became synonymous with particularly fine furniture.

The next evolution for casework was the addition of divided storage. Cabinet pieces with drawers became very popular in America in the mid-17th century. Chests were often filled with drawers (usually four) and were referred to as "cases of drawers." Doors and drawers were soon blended together in pieces to offer a variety in storage options.

And that brings us up to the furniture design that most of us consider traditional case furniture. However, during the mid-20th century, there was a change in case construction that continues to affect the type of furniture we have in our homes – frameless construction.

It's widely accepted that the origin of frameless cabinetry can be traced back to the post-World War II reconstruction effort in Germany. The need for quick, inexpensive furniture using a minimum of materials led to the 32mm assembly-line construction of case pieces. New hardware made it possible to build cabinets without face frames, revolutionizing 20th-century furniture design.

This is a Spanish, 17th-century wooden coffer with wrought-iron mounts and a falling flap, on carved stand. (Basically, it's a fancy box.)

This bookcase design was published in "The Cabinet Maker and Upholsterer's Drawing Book" by Thomas Sheraton in 1793.

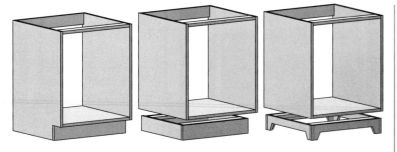

Here are three very traditional casework bases: The version on the left allows the notched sides of the case to run to the floor and a kick plate is added to the front to complete the base. The middle version is a separate base (a box on its own) that is screwed to the cabinet. The case on the right is a similar separate base, but the base is trimmed to make the case appear to have feet.

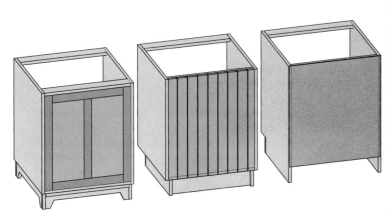

The three backs shown above vary in complexity from left to right. The back on the left is of frame-and-panel construction, adding great stability, but also more time. The middle version is a shiplapped back with each solid-wood board rabbeted to interlock. The far right version shows a simple, but still effective, 1/4" plywood back.

Dividers

These parts can be either horizontal or vertical surfaces. Because they separate the main casework box into smaller sections they're known as dividers. They can be the full depth of the case piece, or they can be partial depth as when dividing drawer sections where the division is important from the front view, but it's not necessary to be full-depth.

Top

This part can be many things. In the case of a nightstand, the top will be a finished, visible piece. But the top doesn't need to be an integral component for strength in the casework piece and can simply be attached to the finished box. In other cases (such as entertainment units) the top is structural and while it's visible from the inside, it won't be seen from above because of the project's height.

Back

This isn't a given, though most pieces will have a back. Some open storage units or bookcases won't, and that adds some difficulties in keeping the box square. Maintaining squareness is the true function of the back. It also makes the piece look more finished.

Backs can be of different thicknesses (more than any other piece in casework), can be solid lumber or plywood and can include joinery of its own, including a frame-and-panel back.

Frame

This is more of a style consideration that we'll look at in later chapter, but it belongs in a parts definition list. Just as with a back, some casework relies on a rigid frame at the front of the piece to add strength and support. If a frame isn't used, that strength needs to come from somewhere else.

Two parts that need defining within the frame are the rails and stiles. The vertical members of a frame are the stiles and the horizontal members are the rails.

Base

A base isn't necessary for hanging cabinets or portable casework, but it's pretty common on casework that will sit on the floor. The base can be a separate construction that attaches to the main case, or it can be built into the construction. A third option is a base that is more similar to feet than a base.

One of the great advantages to a separate base is the ability to level just the base, then add the cabinet in place after. It's a lot easier to adjust a small base than an entire cabinet. It also makes moving the casework more manageable and easier to fit through doorways.

Crown

This part is a finishing touch for many casework pieces. The crown is usually attached to the central case piece at the top and projects beyond the body of the cabinet. It's also possible that the crown could be a separate construction (for transportation ease) that's attached to the case, similar to the separate base.

Shelves

Because most casework is about storage, maximizing the space is important. The shelves can be simple, utilitarian (and hidden), or they can be built in as part of the visual design.

Drawers
These offer more storage. The drawers are simply boxes (without a top) within other boxes.

Doors
These are simply a way to make the storage neat and to dress up the casework. Doors can be a single piece of wood, or they can be an assembly of several pieces. A panel door (raised or flat) will be made of at least five pieces: two vertical members (stiles, just as with cabinet frame members), two horizontal members (rails) and the panel itself. We'll talk at length about the concerns and applications of shelves, drawers and doors in later chapters.

These are the basic parts that make up most casework. There are lots of other parts that we'll discuss as we get into joinery and construction.

CASEWORK STYLES
Casework style needs to be addressed from two directions: function and form. Function is the consideration of how the cases will be used – what storage is required, whether doors and drawers will be added and how casework will be installed. Form is simply the way the finished piece will look. That's not so simple a topic as it covers the balance, proportions, materials, mouldings and even the finish applied to the piece.

Function
In the larger concept, casework can be built using a front frame (sometimes called a face frame) or as a frameless construction. As I mentioned earlier, the frame is useful in keeping the case square and adds strength. The frame can also make the project more complicated. Because the width of the frame extends in past the edge of the sides it interferes with the storage space. Drawers that are mounted inside a frame case can't be as wide as the case itself. There are also issues of how the drawers are attached to the case to compensate for the spacing added by the frame.

Another strong reason for using a frame design is that it makes it easy to use plywood for the case sides, top and bottom. You

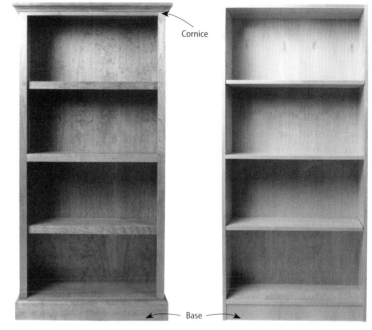

Shown here are two nearly identical bookcases – the version on the left has a face frame, while the version on the right is frameless. These two case pieces are also a good example of different base and cornice options for similar case pieces.

don't want the plywood edge showing at the front of the cabinet, so adding a solid-wood frame will automatically cover all the raw plywood edges without any workaround, such as iron-on edge tape.

Frameless casework lacks a face frame. This allows full use of the interior space, but the case is not resistant to racking forces. Frameless cabinets are often built into a space that allows the strength of the building's walls (and other cabinets) to support

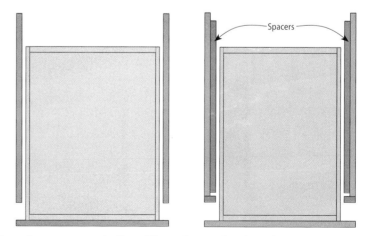

Beyond appearance, one significant difference between frameless (left) and frame cabinetry is the available drawer space. On the frameless cabinet the drawer only needs ½" spacing on either side to handle standard drawer slides. With frame cabinets, spacers need to be added to bring the drawer slides clear of the frame, reducing the interior drawer space by 1½".

The style of door or drawer front you choose for your casework will affect the way the case is designed and built. It will also impact the hardware you use (European or traditional) and you'll need to consider the hardware installation in the process as well.

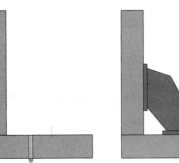

Inset

Full overlay

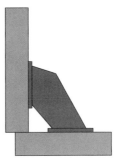

Half overlay   Lipped

the casework. Also, many cabinetmakers will use a thicker back ($^5/_8$" to $^3/_4$") for a frameless cabinet to add rigidity. More substantial joinery also can add greater strength to a frameless cabinet, but this will add time and effort to the construction process.

And yes, you can still use plywood for the case members in a frameless cabinet. But if you do, you'll have to add either veneer tape or a thin, flush-fitting solid edge to the fronts of the members to hide the plywood core.

I'm stepping into the design area here for a second to mention that after determining the type of case construction you intend to use, you'll need to take the door and drawer look and construction into consideration at the same time. Doors and drawers can be built as inset, full overlay, partial overlay and lipped (again something we'll discuss in depth later in the series). How the doors and drawers will look and fit will affect the way you build your cases and what dividers (and what divider dimensions) will be required for the project.

Beyond how the drawers and doors will look, they play an important part in making sure the storage needs are being adequately met by the functional design of your casework. For example, make sure your silverware drawer will actually hold all the silverware. Almost as bad, don't make the drawers so large that they become dumping places that can't be easily sorted or divided.

How the boxes are arranged is also dictated by function. Casework encompasses chests, cupboards, cabinets, wardrobes, secretaries and more. In addition, the basic chest can be arranged to suit specific needs. And a chest can be a chest of drawers, a chest-on-chest design, a chest on frame, or a chest on stand. All of these permutations

allow the casework to match the storage needs. Whether drawers (large, small, deep or shallow), shelving (open or closed) or large undivided space as with a wardrobe, it's all in how you break up the space.

As a last concept in casework function, stop a minute to consider how the piece you're planning will be installed. If it's an entertainment center headed for the second floor, make sure you can get it there. By designing case pieces in, well, pieces, you'll make it easier to move (physically, considering both weight and negotiating corners) and install. And the beauty of building with boxes is that once the pieces are put together, no one will know how many pieces there are!

Form

Beyond function, casework style can be varied and eclectic to match every taste. The style can be as elaborate as a Louis XIV bombé chest of drawers or as simple as the clean, Scandinavian lines of IKEA furniture.

No matter your preference in style, remember the adage of form follows function. Always keep that in mind. It's important first to make sure the cabinetry meets your storage needs. Then you can make it look like anything you wish.

DEALING WITH STRESS

As mentioned already, some of the decisions as to what style of casework to use for a particular project depend on the use of the case. Weight, stresses and even what will be stored will help define what construction techniques best fit the needs.

A bookcase is a perfect example. There are the concerns of the physical size of the books to be stored. The shelves have to be deep enough to adequately support your largest book. But you have to worry about weight as well. Books get heavy quickly and you need to make sure the shelves are not too long or they will sag under the weight.

The construction of the bookcase and of the shelves comes into the equation here. If you're building a bookcase with a substantial back you can help support the shelves from the center of the span. But if it's a $\frac{1}{4}$"-thick plywood back, or there's no back at all, the shelves need to provide all the support.

You can beef-up the shelves by adding a brace underneath the shelf, but that will also reduce the storage space, so there's a balance to be met.

And if you've opted for no back, there's the concern of racking (twisting the case out of square from side-to-side) once weight is added. Without proper structural bracing, or attaching the bookcase to the wall, the whole thing can collapse like a house of cards.

Another way to rack a cabinet is by attaching it to a wall that isn't square. The case can take on the shape of the wall when attached. Also, a case piece can rack because of an uneven floor. Levelling the cabinet upon installation can correct this, but anticipating the problem in your design will make it possible to shim the cabinet to adjust for level without being visible.

Racking not only changes the look of the cabinet, but will also affect the way doors and drawers fit, open and close. So we're back to making sure the case piece is built in a manner that will support the weight and adapt to the location without affecting the function.

One more stress to consider briefly here: wood movement. When wood reacts to changes in humidity, it shrinks or contracts. If you're using solid wood in your case piece, these changes need to be considered. This is mostly a concern with doors and drawers, but we'll get into that in detail later.

ON THE MOVE

The stresses mentioned above are mostly concerns of built-in case pieces. But if your case piece happens to be a mobile filing cabinet, or a kitchen island on wheels, there are more stresses to consider. Moving one of these mobile case pieces racks the box in multiple dimensions, not just from side-to-side.

With a file cabinet you can still use a back and frame to control the stress. But with the

Here are a couple good examples of mobile case pieces. The mobile kitchen island above is an open construction, but the box in the center adds cross-connecting strength to keep the island rigid while mobile, otherwise the motion would rack the drawers and they wouldn't work properly. The tool cabinet at right is designed to carry a substantial amount of weight with tools stored in the open upper section as well as in the drawers. The case is enclosed except for the front, and the upper section's dividers are built into the case construction to add strength.

Shown here are three similar case pieces with upper and lower sections. Each has a different treatment for the cornice, waist and base. All are reproductions in the 18th-century North American style, but each carries the maker's individual touch. The cornice and base pieces are highlighted here. Even though there are similarities, each has subtle design changes to make the piece unique.

kitchen island, there's a very good chance you'd like to be able to access storage from more than one side of the island and that takes away some of your bracing. Adding strong frames on both sides, or adding interior bracing (such as dividers that define the drawer spaces), will tame the stress.

One other "mobile" thought: While you probably know enough to purchase wheels that will be adequate for the weight of the case, how those wheels are mounted is important. If the bottom of the case is simply nailed between the sides and the wheels are attached only to the bottom, the weight of the case will cause that joint to fail. Sure the bottom and wheels will still be standing, but the sides will be sitting on the floor. Carefully planning ahead for such construction concerns will lead to a successful project.

CORNICES, PLINTHS AND MORE

Once the shape and size of your box is determined, and you've considered the storage needs for your case piece, it's time to have a little fun adding some creative aspects.

Throughout the centuries the concepts of dressing up a box have run the gamut from simple to sublime. The most common details to adjust have been cornices and plinths. These parts of furniture actually derive their names from architecture that was originally parts of columns. Both are horizontal decorative additions, with the cornice occurring at the top of the structure (what we would often call a crown on

a piece of furniture today) and the plinth refers to the decorative horizontal addition at the base of the structure.

With cornices, or crowns, the detail is up to the woodworker and can be as simple as

This classic bonnet top by Lonnie Bird dramatically enhances the look of the basic box, which in this case is a tall clock.

a large cove crown (at right), or as elaborate as a bonnet top with even more creative detailing (at right). The odd part about the cornice is that it serves no purpose (no matter how large) other than dressing up the case furniture.

The plinth, what we'd most commonly call the base, can also be simple or elaborate. The detailing on this section can take the form of feet (as mentioned earlier), but that still leaves lots of room for personal expression as shown on the three case pieces above.

But that's certainly not the end of the decorative opportunities. Because we're dealing with boxes arranged with other boxes, sometimes that transition from one box to another is an opportunity for decorative detail. In particular, when an upper and lower case piece (such as the secretaries above) changes dimensions, some transitional detail is helpful. This is referred to as the waist of the cabinet and often waist moulding is used to smooth out that transition. Essentially an inverted crown moulding (as the upper case should always be smaller than the lower case) the waist moulding can also be simple or elaborate.

But the decorative opportunities don't end here. The doors and drawers themselves will add ample opportunity to continue adding to the boxes. The doors can be dramatically figured panels set in frames, or they can be glass doors to allow the items inside (whether rare books or family crystal) visible to all. Even the glass panels can add to the decoration as shown above.

And we haven't even approached the concept of carvings, columns, appliques inlay or marquetry.

This section may be all about the intricacies of building boxes, but there's nothing simple or boring about boxes. They're the cornerstone of most of our furniture, so we'll make sure you get the right information to build perfect casework for your home.

Both of these glass doors are in nearly identical secretaries, but the pattern of mullions on the left offers a simple approach, while the Chippendale design on the right is more refined.

The two waist mouldings shown here help smooth the transition between the upper and lower case pieces. These waist mouldings also help align the upper case and hold it in place on the lower case. The example on the right is obviously doing more alignment than smoothing the transition.

Wood Selection & Prep

by David Thiel

In this chapter we focus on the materials that make up the boxes-within-boxes that are casework.

We'll discuss using solid wood versus plywood, and discuss the properties, both pro and con, for each. Along that same line, we'll consider the concerns of wood movement when using solid wood. For that concern alone, a lot of casework is constructed out of plywood.

Whether it's plywood or solid wood, getting the boards ready to use takes some particular steps to get it right. These steps include proper planing, joining and even gluing techniques. We'll show you the best ways to work in either medium and we'll also take a look at using either power or hand tools for these steps, and a combination of both.

PLYWOOD OR SOLID WOOD?

Case construction is mostly about joining panels together to form one or more boxes. Coming up with the panels is where we start.

Plywood is actually a very old invention. The Egyptians used a crude form of plywood by cross layering thin sheets of wood, alternating the grain direction. Their intent was to make a stronger, more stable piece of wood and that's the same reason we continue to use plywood in our projects today.

We've added veneer to the equation to make plywood an even more valuable building material. Rather than go to the expense of using solid panels of what can be very expensive wood types, a thin veneer of these woods is used as the outer surface of plywood. This gives the appearance of nicely figured, solid wood, with the structural benefits of plywood, and it'll save some money.

That said, solid wood is still a more-than-adequate option for casework panels and we'll talk about some ways to negate the movement issues involved in wood panels. And, of course, solid lumber is still the major component used in case construction as the framework pieces that hold many of the panels in place and tie them together.

CHOOSING PLYWOOD

There are three main grades of plywood we'll discuss here: furniture grade, shop grade and what we'll call high-density plywood. In each category there are sub-categories, but I'll try to keep this from getting too complicated.

Furniture-grade Plywood

Furniture-grade plywood is a plywood that has quality veneer faces on both sides. The inner core can be a variety of materials including softwoods, hardwoods and fiber core. The number of plies, or layers, can also vary. As long as the interior layers are oriented 90° to one another (including fiber core) it still counts as a plywood.

These furniture-grade plywoods are graded by appearance, the best face is graded by letter, with "A" being the best and

Casework can be made from both plywood and solid wood, or a combination of the two, as shown in this blanket chest.

Above are examples of the four most common types of plywood, all in ¾" thickness. At the top is a piece of furniture-grade red oak veneer ply. Below it is a piece of shop-grade plywood veneered on both sides with poplar. This would be a good paint-grade plywood. Directly underneath that is a piece of MDF with birch veneer. While not normally considered a plywood, because the fibers are arranged in a cross-grain pattern it fits in this category and is a useful material for case construction. At the bottom of the stack is a piece of Baltic birch high-density plywood. Notice the number of layers compared to the other two plywoods.

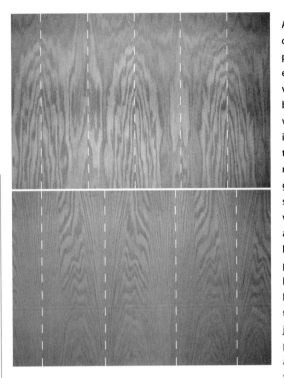

At left are two samples of red oak veneer-clad plywood. Above is an example of rotary-cut veneer, while the photo below is plain-sliced veneer. The plain sliced is a more natural pattern for use in panels, more closely imitating glued-up individual solid boards. The rotary veneer is peeled from a log like an apple skin, leaving a repeating pattern. The dashed lines show the pattern breaks on each piece. As these photos illustrate, just selecting a veneer pattern will not ensure an attractive pattern. Seeing the piece in person is valuable for a reliable appearance.

"D" the worst. The back side is graded by number, with "1" being the best and "4" the worst. For furniture projects you're generally looking for A1 or A2 plywood. The other grades are often relegated to paint-grade projects.

You'll also need to pay attention to the way the veneer is sliced off the log. Rotary-cut veneer is peeled off the log like an apple skin and will have an unnatural appearance to the eye. It's not ugly, it's just not the best pattern.

Plain-sliced veneer is layed-up in sheets as it's cut from the log, from one side to the other, and then seamed – much like you would glue up a panel from multiple boards. This is the veneer pattern that is considered best for visible casework pieces.

Shop-grade Plywood

Shop-grade plywood is plywood without the fancy veneer. It usually includes a veneer, but the material may be a less valued species such as birch or poplar. The usage of lesser materials will extend to the inside of the sheet as well, with more inexpensive materials, and the possibility of more voids and patches acceptable in the plywood layers.

You may have raised an eyebrow when I included fiber-core materials with plywood. Fiber-core, or particleboard or medium-density fiberboard (MDF), are technically plywoods because of the orientation of the wood fibers. In fact, though fiber-core sheets are often thought of as lesser quality, they're actually a better surface for casework. They remain flat and offer more consistent thickness than hardwood or softwood ply-core sheets.

Another benefit to MDF-core plywood is that there is no chance of telegraphing any wood imperfections from the core materials through the veneer. These imperfections are usually something that won't show up until you apply a finish – with very disappointing results.

Shop-grade plywood is often used for just what it sounds like. If your casework happens to be a cabinet for underneath your table saw, or a storage cabinet for all of your pneumatic nailers, this is the sound and economical material for you.

Shop-grade ply can also be handy for less visible case projects, such as built-in closets and cabinetry in utility rooms such as laundry areas.

High-density Plywood

High-density plywood is a valuable, but utilitarian plywood grade. Often branded as Baltic birch, ApplePly or other names, these plywoods use thinner and more numerous interior layers, while a furniture- or shop-grade plywood may have seven interior layers in a $^3/_4$" thickness. By using more plies of thinner wood the plywood offers a more stable and straighter panel.

You won't find MDF-core materials in this category and in general the veneers used for these plywoods are of secondary woods, similar to shop-grade plywood. These "veneers" are usually one of the interior plies that just happens to be on the outside of the sheet and can include foot-ball-shaped patches.

This is a great material for the interiors of your case pieces. Many professional furniture makers will use this ultra-stable material for drawer boxes. And it makes a great sheet product for jigs and workshop fixtures.

CHOOSING SOLID WOOD

Choosing solid wood for a project, whether for panels or for frame pieces, is almost akin to an art form. Where you get your lumber will dictate how particular you can be when shopping. If one of the larger home-center stores is your usual shopping spot, you'll be limited by species, grade and quality.

I'd recommend finding a lumber dealer somewhere near you (check the phone book, or contact a local woodworking shop or woodworking club to find the name of their supplier). Short of that, consider ordering wood by mail or from the internet. We've had good success with these "remote" lumber suppliers, but it still removes you from the lumber selection process, which is what I'll discuss now.

After determining the species of wood you want to use for your project, you must figure out how much wood you need. Unlike plywood, solid lumber comes in random widths, so the calculations are a little involved.

You first need to determine the thickness required. Most case pieces will use $^3/_4$"-thick material. If you're buying lumber in the rough (just sawn at the mill, with no surface planing completed) you'll be looking for 4/4 material. The easy way to remember the "quarter" method of referring to rough lumber is to think of it in terms of $^1/_4$". Four-quarter rough material will measure 1", or four $^1/_4$"s. Six-quarter will measure $1^1/_2$" in the rough, and so on.

If you're buying lumber already surfaced (planed) you should check that it actu-ally does measure the indicated thickness (slightly under or over is possible) and you should also understand some of the terms used to grade and mark solid wood.

S2S: Planed on two faces, with the edges left in the rough.

S3S: Planed on two faces and jointed on one edge, with the opposite edge left in the rough.

S4S: Planed/jointed on all four long edges of the board.

Anticipate a slight upcharge on surfaced lumber, and be prepared to still deal with possible twists or warps in wood that is already the required thickness.

Now back to how much wood you need to purchase: Multiplying each required piece's width and length in inches and then dividing the total by 144 will give you the board feet required for each piece and then you can add all the pieces together. That gives you a gross amount required, but because wood doesn't come that way you need to figure it differently.

If you can go to the lumberyard with your list and calculate what parts will come from each board, you'll be pretty close. Of course, this assumes you have the luxury of

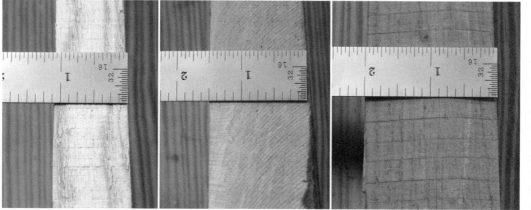

Shown here is rough lumber from a mill. This is how you should think of the "quarter" system when shopping. The left board is 4/4 and measures roughly one inch (you get a little extra on this one and that's possible if you shop carefully), the middle is 6/4 and measures roughly $1^1/_2$" and the right is 8/4 and should measure roughly 2".

picking through the boards for this process. If you're ordering lumber from a local yard or the internet, you can't rely on that.

Your best method is to round up to the nearest whole inch dimension in each direction and then add a little extra to cover loss through planing, checking and other unforeseen occurrences. How much extra? A minimum of 10 percent makes sense and some woodworkers will recommend up to 40 percent. I'd suggest 20 percent, myself.

Now you have your shopping list, it's time to go to the store. You want to consider a number of visual and physical aspects of the lumber beyond size. Color consistency and grain pattern can make or break a project. Unless you're planning on including a sap streak down the middle of your doors, it's best to pick boards with as little sap as possible.

Grain pattern can be a huge factor. Because much of this wood will end up in wide panels for your casework, the idea is to make it look like it came from one board's width. Matching cathedral patterns, or just finding the most straight-grained boards will move you further toward that goal.

Physical aspects to look for include knots, splits and moisture content. If you find a really pretty board with a knot down the middle, don't discard it. Get your cutting list out and decide if you can cut away the knot and still get the pieces you need from the rest of the board.

Most lumber that woodworkers purchase is kiln dried. This speeds up the process of getting the wood into the store, but it can also cause the ends of boards to split, sometimes as much as 10". Check your boards for this defect and calculate it into your shopping. By the way, you shouldn't pay for that section of the board if it's split. Make them take that off the total board footage, or at least discount the price some.

As I mentioned, kiln drying gets the wood into your hands faster than air drying, and it routinely provides a consistent moisture content in the lumber. But it's still a good idea to take a moisture meter along with you to the lumberyard. The wood should ideally be about 7 percent moisture content. A few percent in either direction is acceptable. If your lumber is registering more than 10 percent moisture content, be prepared for some possible warping as it dries to match your

Shown here are two boards arranged to give an example of a good, solid-wood grain match (left) and an example of a bad grain match (right). Even though the boards aren't exactly the same shade, by matching two sections that are long grain, the boards on the left look balanced. The boards on the right have an interrupted cathedral and the cathedral figure on the far right board is pointing the wrong direction.

Board checks are caused by kiln drying and will affect your board yield. Remember to calculate that loss into your plans and don't pay full price for that imperfect 18" of the board!

shop conditions. This may adversely affect the yield of usable wood.

PREPARING SOLID WOOD

This is one of the more time-intensive steps in making case furniture. Of course, if you're experienced in these steps (jointing and planing solid lumber) then you're already a step ahead, but you still need to do the work before making your panels.

By definition you want a panel for your casework to be flat and straight. You need to get your solid lumber in that shape prior to glue-up, and then check it again after.

After checking the lumber for grain match and imperfections, cut the lumber oversized for the needed panel. A few extra inches in length is a good idea, and only one extra inch in width is fine.

The first stop is the jointer. To true a board (make it flat and straight) the jointer

Jointing 101

Start with the board positioned on the infeed table with only light pressure on the board, and your hands positioned back from the cutterhead.

As you feed the board across the cutterhead, maintain light pressure on the infeed side of the board until you reach mid-point. You don't want to try to push the board flat to the table. This will only maintain the board's curvature, and it won't end up straight.

Once the board has passed mid-point over the cutterhead, transfer your pressure (one hand at a time) to the outfeed side of the jointer, keeping the pressure over the outfeed table as you push the board past the knives. Use a push block for this last part to keep your hands away from the knives.

What if your board is 10" wide and you have a 6" jointer? You can actually still flatten the board successfully. You will need to remove the guard for this operation, so be extremely careful and remember to replace the guard once you're done with the operation. Set the fence to a little wider than half the width of the board you're surfacing. Then run the board taking no more than a $1/32$"-deep cut. Allow the board to extend over the jointer bed, but keep steady pressure above the tables.

Then rotate the board so that the part that was hanging off the table is resting on the table. Carefully run the board across the jointer again, maintaining pressure over the tables. Because the knives are cutting at the same depth on each pass you're taking off the same amount of material with each pass. Repeat these steps until the board's face is reasonably flat.

With one face flat, you're ready to run one of the edges to straighten it, and also form a square corner. With the flattened face against the fence, start with all your hand pressure on the board over the infeed table of the jointer.

As when flattening the face, maintain pressure only on the infeed table until the board is mid-way past the knives. Then transfer your pressure to the outfeed table and finish the cut.

This is a view of a board that was too wide for the jointer. You can see the division line down the center of the board, where the cuts overlap. With a couple more passes this board will be ready for the planer.

is a must. You want to make one face and one edge true at this stage.

After the board is jointed, it's time to head for the planer to make sure all the boards are the same thickness. I've added some photos on the previous pages to walk you through these steps.

Of course you don't have to use machinery to true and thickness a board. You can use hand planes. This process is quieter, creates less dust and many woodworkers find it therapeutic. Truing rough stock with hand tools is a bit of a challenge, but it's do-able once you develop a few skills and have the right tools. See "Prepping Lumber by Hand" (page 152) for tips on getting this right.

PREPARING PLYWOOD

One of the reasons I enjoy using plywood in a project (beyond the stability and uniform appearance benefits) is the lack of preparation required to put it into the project. Prepping solid lumber can take a day all by itself, jointing and planing to the proper dimensions. And that's before cutting it to finished size. Working with plywood, it's just cutting to finished size.

Well, almost – you do need to be aware of the fact the plywood is frequently not the full thickness as marked. Three-quarter-inch plywood may be $^{11}/_{16}$" or some other dimension in the thirty-seconds. This isn't a crisis, but you need to be aware of it as part of your preparation to build. Dados, grooves and rabbets may need to be adjusted to make everything fit tightly.

Also, while plywood is manufactured so that the full 48" x 96" sheet can be used, the edges are often dinged, not square to the face and the layers can be uneven at the edges. Most woodworkers plan on having to joint or trim plywood sheets to give an acceptable edge. So, you'll need to anticipate that and probably allow about $^1/_2$" loss in either direction when planning your cutting list.

ASSEMBLING SOLID PANELS

One of the happy situations with joining solid lumber into panels is that a long-grain to long-grain glue joint is the strongest joint possible. There's no need for biscuits, screws or anything. The joint will be stronger than the wood.

Of course you still need to pay attention to the way the boards match up for the best

Planing 101

Planing a board is easier than jointing, but you still need to pay attention to a couple things. Determine which direction the grain is running on the board by running your hand over the surface (top photo). This step is actually like petting a dog or cat. The grain will lay down in one direction similar to an animal's fur. The board should be

run with the grain laying down, starting with the leading edge of the board, to avoid tear-out. Start with the jointed face down on the planer's tables and take light passes until the rough face is mostly leveled (bottom photo).

You're now ready to work down to the final thickness of the board, but it's important to take material from both sides of the board during this step. Because moisture evaporates from wood more quickly on the surface of the board than in

the center, as you expose the board's center the moisture content can shift from face to face. There are also internal pressures in wood that benefit from balanced planing. By flipping the board with each pass you help to maintain an even moisture and stress rate in the board and can avoid cupping and twisting after the board has been planed.

appearance. And you also need to prepare the mating edges to ensure a flat panel. This sends us back to the jointer to – make a joint!

The edge created by a sharp jointer pass is an excellent glue joint. But you need to make sure that the two edges to be joined are darn-near-perfect right angles to the board face. Even after setting the jointer fence, slight imperfections are possible. That's why I like using a little geometry to cheat.

If you take two boards with one edge at 89° to the face and the other edge at 91° to the face and glued the two together, you'd end up with a flat panel. Because the two angles are complementary, they combine to form a 90° relationship.

With your jointer's fence set slightly off of 90° (for any reason) you can form the complementary angle for glue-up by simply reversing the faces of the boards against the fence. Run your first board (seam edge down) with the face against the fence. Run the second board with the face facing away

Prepping Lumber by Hand

Even if you own a powered jointer and planer, there are times that you'll want to prepare boards by hand. Sometimes the boards will be too wide to face-joint on your jointer, or even too wide to surface with your planer. The process requires three planes and a couple other simple tools.

For typical furniture-scale projects, use a jointer plane, jack plane, smoothing plane and two winding sticks – winding sticks can be two matching lengths of straight wood (usually of contrasting colors) or you can also use aluminum angle purchased from the home center.

Use the winding sticks to find out where the high spots are and if the board is twisted. By putting one stick at the front of the board, one at the back and sighting down across them, you'll quickly see any problem areas. Mark the high spots in chalk and knock them down with your jack plane. The cutting edge of the jack plane should be curved and set to remove thick shavings. Check your progress periodically using your winding sticks.

When things look nearly flat, switch to the jointer plane, which should have a slightly curved blade that's set for a finer cut. Work diagonally across the face, then diagonally the other way. Don't worry about tear-out yet. When the face of the board is flat, come back with the jointer plane and smooth the board with strokes following the grain. Clean up all the marks left from the diagonal passes.

One face is now flat. Using a marking gauge, scribe the finished thickness of the board on the long edges and ends – the face of the marking gauge should ride on the board's finished face.

Repeat the flattening process on the other face of the board and work down to the scribed line on all four edges. Finally, use a smoothing plane on both faces to complete your work.

This sounds a bit arduous – it is harder than working with a powered jointer and thickness planer. But if you have your jack and jointer planes set to cut aggressively, you'll be surprised by how quickly the work can go.

Learning to edge-joint a board with a jointer plane is also a good skill to acquire. Sometimes boards that you want to edge-glue into a panel will be too long for your powered jointer.

One accepted technique is called "match planing" (shown below). With this process you sandwich the two boards together in a vise and plane both edges at the same time. Any small differences in the angle of the plane will be canceled out by the fact that the two angles will be complementary. For this process, sharpen your jointer plane with a perfectly straight edge, like that of a chisel or a block plane.

Another traditional technique is to plane each long edge individually and test the boards' edges against one another. For this process, sharpen a very slight camber on your iron. The position of the plane's body on the edge of the work will allow you to correct the angle of the edge. With a little practice, this will become second nature.

— Christopher Schwarz

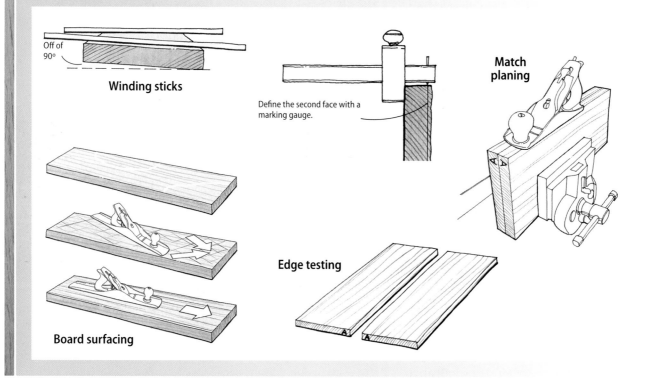

Off of 90°

Winding sticks

Define the second face with a marking gauge.

Match planing

A

Board surfacing

Edge testing

A A

The most important step in gluing up a flat panel is starting with a square edge on each of the mating boards. Accurately setting up the jointer will save lots of headaches. If you're not comfortable with the accuracy of your jointer's fence, cheat by making two complementary angles on the mating boards as discussed in the article.

When working with parallel jaw clamps (as shown) it's not necessary to place clamps on both sides of the panel. The clamp's design holds the panel flat, but it's still a good idea to check the panel to make sure. Align the two (or more) boards' thickness as carefully as possible when applying the clamps. With less offset between the boards there will be less planing or sanding to completely flatten the board.

from the fence. When the two are paired, you'll have a perfect joint.

Gluing up the panel is next. Pre-set your clamps so that you'll have a clamp spaced approximately every 6" to 8" along the board, alternating the clamps from one side to the next to keep the panel as flat as possible.

Apply just enough glue to cover one edge completely with a thin layer of glue. Then put the panels together and clamp just enough to cause the glue to squeeze out slightly. Along with cleaning up the glue, it's a good idea to throw a straightedge on the panel to check for flat.

When the glue is dry you still need to flatten the panel. If you're lucky enough to have a drum sander capable of handling the width of the panel, a few minutes of work will have you ready for joinery. You can also use a random orbit or belt sander to flatten your panel, but take pains to remove material evenly (checking for flat as you go) and be careful not to round over the edges.

If power sanding isn't your first choice, remember how we flattened the single board by hand earlier? It's time to take that same technique to the next level by flattening your joined panel.

ASSEMBLING PLYWOOD PANELS

Making plywood panels is relatively easy if you use the right tool – a biscuit joiner. While not a common task, arranging a veneer pattern to fit your project is possible with this technique. A biscuit joint on a plywood edge isn't very strong, but it will align

accurately and provide stability for use with panels.

Start by using your jointer to make the same type of complementary mating joint as we discussed for solid lumber. Be aware that if your jointer has high-speed steel knives, the plywood can dull or nick the knives. Take light passes.

With the edges prepared, set your biscuit joiner to cut the pockets in the center of the edge and work only from one side of the boards. If your biscuits are placed too close to one face of the plywood, it's possible that the biscuit shape can be telegraphed through the plies and be visible on the face.

Take care when clamping the panel, though the biscuits make alignment easier. Light sanding should be all that's required to finish the panel face.

Using biscuits in plywood panels makes sense to more easily align the faces. But the biscuits need to be in the middle of the plywood edge as shown in the top board here. The lower board has the biscuits cut too close to the top edge. Any swelling in the biscuit will telegraph to the face.

Case Joinery

by David Thiel

In chapter three of our continuing look at case construction we're going to take a look at many of the most practical joinery possibilities for building casework furniture.

As you might imagine, this is a huge topic. Casework runs the gamut from jewelry boxes to kitchen cabinetry, and there are literally dozens of ways to form the cases. Some are traditional joinery methods, such as rabbets, dados and dovetails. Others involve more contemporary mechanical fasteners, such as wood screws, pocket screws and biscuits.

Because of the volume of joinery options, we're only going to be able to briefly discuss the different types, the benefits and deficits of each joint and what casework application each joint is best suited for.

FACE FRAME OR FRAMELESS?

Before we dive into the joinery, let's take a moment to review the two main types of case construction. Case pieces can be built with just the sides, top and bottom, with an optional back – this is called a frameless design. Carcases can also be built with a rigid front frame (formed of stiles and rails) added to the front of the box for extra strength (and it does offer a different look, too).

The type of casework construction you choose, face frame or frameless, will help direct you to the proper joinery. In general, a frameless cabinet requires stronger carcase joinery, while a cabinet with a frame can rely more on the frame for strength and use less stout joinery for the carcase. There are, of course, joints that work for both types of cases.

And because we've mentioned frames, we need to look at two distinct categories of joinery as well: Joinery for box construction (frameless), versus joinery for the construction of the frames themselves.

While a dovetail is an excellent carcase joint, it's not a practical frame joint. Similarly, a mortise and tenon is an excellent joint for frames, but is usually impractical for box building.

BOX JOINERY WITHOUT FRAMES

Let's take a look at some of the joints that are best used when building a case piece that is purely frameless. The chart on page 156 offers a good/better/best comparison of some of these joints.

Some of the joints that aren't represented on the chart are the more mechanical joints, i.e. screws. Screws all by themselves can be used to hold cabinetry together fairly successfully. The difficulty being they're not very attractive. In a utility cabinet, that's not a problem, but it's not what you want in a piece of fine furniture.

The shelf is fit into a dado, resulting in much better strength than a simple butt joint. By adding a peg or two to the joint, you add even more strength and the opportunity to add a visual element to the piece. In this case it's the proverbial square peg in a round hole. A hole is drilled through the side and into the shelf. A piece of square stock cut to the diameter of the hole is then tapered at one end and driven into the hole. When fully seated in the hole, the peg is cut flush to the cabinet side and sanded smooth. The result is the appearance of a square peg and lots of extra strength.

You can countersink the screw and add a plug, but you'll still see the plug. If the arrangement of the pieces allows, pocket screws are an option. By placing the screws on the underside of pieces, the screws essentially disappear. Or, these holes can also be plugged, as with a standard screw hole.

Another mechanical fastener that should be discussed is nails. Whether fired from a pneumatic nailer or knocked in with a hammer, there's lots of commercial furniture that is held together with nails. As with screws, placement is critical for visibility. Nails will add strength to a joint, but not as much as a screw. It's probably better to think of a nail as a fast clamp while the glue dries.

Pneumatic nails do have one benefit over wire nails: The surfaces of the brad nails are coated with an adhesive to hold the clips of nails together. One positive side benefit of the adhesive is that as the nail is driven at speed into the wood, the adhesive heats up, softens and actually serves to glue the nail into the joint.

The more traditional approach to assembling a carcase is to use a wood joint such as a rabbet, dado or dovetail. As you look at the chart, the most obvious piece of information to be gained is that the more complicated the joint, the better it holds. Why? Two reasons. First, as you "complicate" the joint what you're really doing is adding gluing surfaces to the joint. While a butt joint has one surface meeting another, a dado joint has three surfaces in contact between the two pieces. You also gain different grain orientation in the joint, which further adds to the gluing strength.

Second, when you move into the most complicated joints you gain locking strength in the wood itself. Dovetails and locking miters are two very good examples of this strength. Even without glue, the sheer mechanics of interlocking pieces of wood adds significant strength.

You're doing the same thing by adding dowels or biscuits to a joint – increasing interlocking strength and increasing the gluing surfaces.

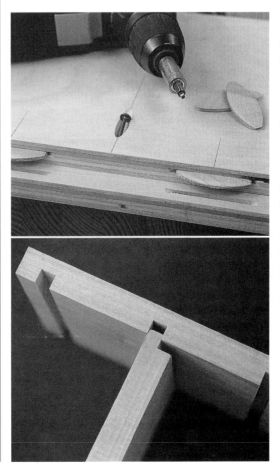

These two examples of joinery would work well for a case piece without a frame. The photo on the left shows plywood construction, reinforced and aligned with biscuits. To add an even stronger touch, a pocket screw is inserted through the bottom and used to pull the joint tight. Veneer tape will hide the plywood edge. At the right, a solid lumber piece is built using a rabbet and dado joint for the top, bottom and shelves.

Casework Box Joinery

Good	Better	Best	A Step Further

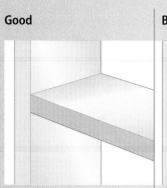

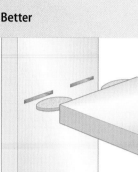

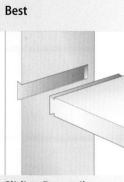

T-Butt

A standard joint for cabinetry, this is a simple but weak joint that requires little investment in terms of time, machinery or tools.

Butt with Biscuit

Adding reinforcement (biscuits as shown, dowels or screws) to a butt joint improves the joint's strength.

Sliding Dovetail

A sliding-dovetail joint effectively locks the two pieces together for great strength. This joint can be stopped (as shown) or through.

Locking Miter

This joint is an improvement over a miter joint, without adding a biscuit or spline. It offers greater gluing surface and strength.

Corner Butt

The same simple joint can be used in the middle of a case piece (top) or to form a corner as shown directly above.

Rabbet

A rabbet joint offers more gluing surface than a butt joint and also adds better support to a corner joint.

Rabbet and Dado

By locking the rabbet in a dado, the strength and protection against racking on this corner joint are greatly improved.

Half-blind Dovetail

No joint provides as much strength as a dovetail. This joint can be partially visible (as above), completely visible or completely hidden.

Miter

This traditional box joint hides end grain. With most casework, the joint will be short-grain-to-short-grain, which offers very little strength.

Splined Miter

Adding a spline to a miter joint increases strength and improves alignment. It also provides the opportunity for an artistic element.

Dovetailed Miter

This joint offers visible joinery, but shows only a miter on the edges of the box, which makes it both attractive and strong.

Groove and Panel

When it comes to adding a back to a case piece, this joint offers strength and convenience. For a removable back, a rabbet is preferred.

One case joint that I want to focus on for a minute is a sliding dovetail. This is a complicated joint to create, but well worth the effort. And with the proper steps most of the complication can be removed or at least minimized.

A sliding dovetail joint adds tremendous locking strength between a divider panel and case sides, or when using a web frame to complete a case. It not only provides strength to pull the two sides together, but protects against racking (corner-to-corner motion).

Full-depth drawer dividers aren't always necessary in a cabinet. To decrease weight, you can use a dividing rail at the front with drawer runners along the side to guide the drawer. But because you're taking material away, it's more difficult to keep the strength in the cabinet. That's where the sliding dovetail comes into play.

By cutting a dovetail-shaped socket in the cabinet sides and a matching tail on the ends of the drawer divider, a much stronger and lighter case is possible.

BOX JOINERY WITH FRAMES

Now that we've shown that frameless case pieces can be built with joinery that provides excellent strength, why would we want to add a frame to the case? Two simple reasons: strength and aesthetics.

This drawer cabinet uses sliding dovetails on the drawer divider rails to reduce weight while maintaining case strength. Sliding dovetails can be tricky to execute, but with the proper setup and a little practice, they're a handy option for a need such as this.

While many case pieces are designed to sit on the floor, such as a dresser or chest of drawers, there are many examples of beautiful wall cabinets that hang suspended without any support below. If your wall cabinet is going to store books or dishes, you're going to need all the strength you can get to counteract gravity. That's one good reason to add a frame to an already strong case.

The second reason is aesthetics. Sometimes a traditional cabinet you're building calls out for a face frame. Even if strength

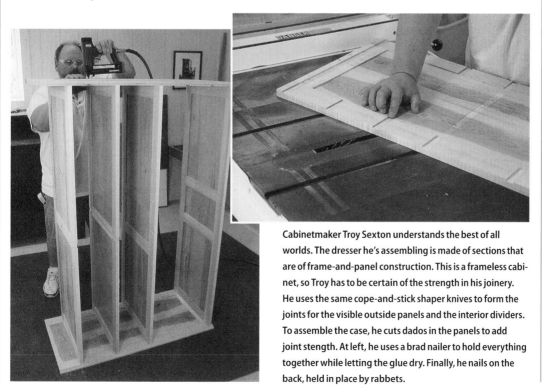

Cabinetmaker Troy Sexton understands the best of all worlds. The dresser he's assembling is made of sections that are of frame-and-panel construction. This is a frameless cabinet, so Troy has to be certain of the strength in his joinery. He uses the same cope-and-stick shaper knives to form the joints for the visible outside panels and the interior dividers. To assemble the case, he cuts dados in the panels to add joint stength. At left, he uses a brad nailer to hold everything together while letting the glue dry. Finally, he nails on the back, held in place by rabbets.

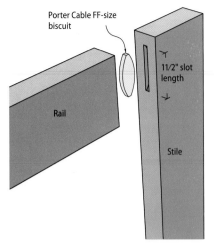

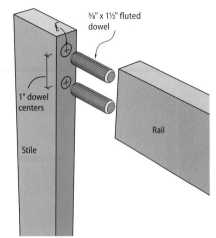

Porter Cable FF-size biscuit

1 1/2" slot length

Rail

Stile

Biscuit joints can work well in face-frame joinery, but don't assume you can use a #20. You need a smaller biscuit so the joint won't show.

3/8" x 1 1/2" fluted dowel

1" dowel centers

Stile

Rail

Stile

Dowels are a decent alternative for joining face frame parts, but they can be tricky to align to get the faces perfectly flush.

1 1/4" self-tapping screw

Stile

Rail

Pocket screws add lots of strength to a face frame joint. And unlike other types of screws, these are easily hidden on the inside face.

isn't a concern, the look of a face frame can dress up what some might call a plain piece of furniture. If you're adding a face frame for looks, then strength isn't your first concern and so the joinery used on the frame itself can be of many different styles.

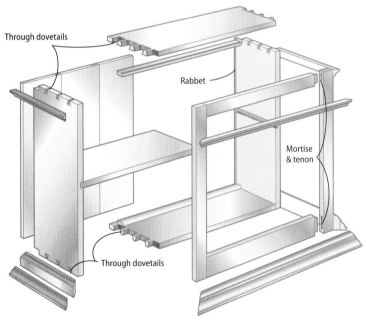

Through dovetails

Rabbet

Mortise & tenon

Through dovetails

Illustraton by Len Churchill

Above is a diagram of a hanging wall cabinet. When a case piece like this is hung on a wall, strength becomes an important factor. With no floor to support the weight, the joints have to be even more reliable. This piece uses strong joints in the box itself, with through-dovetails at the corners of the case. The solid wood back is rabbetted into the case, then fastened by nails. The face frame is assembled with mortise-and-tenon joints in the corners then glued to the box. The frame-to-case strength can be increased even more by pegging the frame in place. There is a lot of strength in this cabinet's joinery.

FACE-FRAME JOINTS

Face frames on cabinets are close cousins to frame-and-panel doors. Many of the same joinery options are available for face frames as are used in making doors. To determine what joint is best for the application, you need to look at the strength and appearance requirements.

In some instances a butt joint is possible on a face frame. This would be one of those aesthetic situations where a case is already plenty strong on its own, but you want the look of a face frame. The frame is then simply glued or nailed to the case and the stiles (the vertical pieces) and rails (the horizontal pieces) are butted together.

While this is frequently done in commercial furniture, I'm going to suggest you go a step further (as a woodworker, you owe it to yourself). The butted ends can move over time leaving a sloppy-looking joint.

Some modern mechanical options for face-frame joinery include biscuits, dowels and pocket screws. All will add strength and even accuracy in aligning the pieces at the joint. Nails (air-powered or not) aren't a good option with face frames as they're likely to split the wood when you work near the ends of boards.

Beyond the mechanical options, some interlocking joints that work well include a half-lap joint or bridle joint. These joints offer a reasonable gluing surface to hold things tight over time, but are still fairly quick to create. The strength is moderate, but certainly better than a butt joint.

Because we're speaking of aesthetics, consider using a lapped dovetail. This variation on the half-lap adds an interesting visual element and also adds some strength to the joint.

But when it comes to making a face frame for strength, the mortise and tenon is the way to go. This joint has been around for millennia – really! And it can be easily created with a router alone, a mortiser and table saw, or with simple hand tools.

To make sure your mortise-and-tenon joints are as strong as possible, here are a few rules to follow:

1. If you're using a mortiser to create your joint, the tenon thickness should be one-half the thickness of the stock piece. So if you're using $^3/_4$"-thick material, the tenon should be $^3/_8$" thick. For creating the joint with a mallet and chisel, one-third the material thickness is preferable.

2. To avoid tearing out the wall of the mortise at the end of the joint, set the mortise (and the tenon) back from the end, leaving at least a $^3/_8$" edge shoulder on the tenon.

3. In general, the tenon length in casework should be no shorter than 1", and $1^1/_4$" is a reasonable length.

If you'd like to consider another option to the standard mortise and tenon, how about a loose tenon? The beauty of this joint is that the mortises can be made in a drill press and the loose tenon pieces can be run

off in mass quantity on a table saw. Then the tenon edges can simply be rounded with a router. This joint offers the same strength as a traditional mortise and tenon without quite as much fuss.

The mortise-and-tenon joint does one other thing that a face frame is very good at: it keeps the cabinet square. A mortise-and-tenon joint (when properly constructed) is a very rigid, square frame and you can actually use it to square up a cabinet that may have joinery that allows more play than is preferable.

I mentioned cope and stick. This is a joinery technique most often reserved for doors because of the edge detailing accompanying the joinery. But this joinery technique can be used for cabinet sides as well, to excellent effect.

With the face frame complete, it needs to be attached to the cabinet. In most cases glue and clamping work fine, but a couple

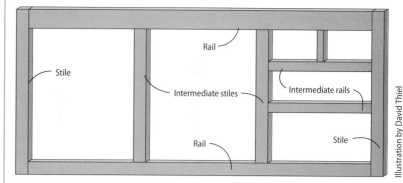

Illustration by David Thiel

When talking about face frames for cabinetry, it's a good idea to know what to call all the pieces. The outer vertical parts are stiles (and always run through), while the horizontal parts are rails (and always run between stiles).Of course, there are circumstances where other terminology is necessary. When stiles and rails are within the perimeter of the frame they are intermediate stiles or rails.

Loose tenons are a simple option over the traditional mortise and tenon. While you still need to machine the mortise (two in fact), this is more easily created on a drill press or plunge router with a straight bit, tools you likely already own. The tenons themselves are easily created in bulk using the table saw and a router.

Casework Frame Joinery

Good

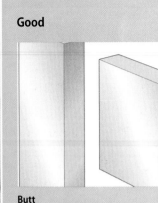

Butt
This joint really doesn't belong in the "good" category. It's structurally weak and provides poor glue adhesion.

Better

Butt with Dowels
Adding a mechanical fastener (spline, biscuit or dowels as above) greatly improves the strength of this corner joint.

Best

Mortise and Tenon
The ultimate in frame strength, the mortise and tenon guards against racking, is strong with lots of gluing surface and is invisible.

A Step Further

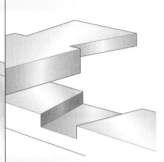

T-Lap Dovetail
Better than a half-lap, the dovetail lap adds locking strength for either a corner joint or mid-rail joinery, but requires even more accuracy.

Miter
A corner miter offers slightly better strength than a butt joint because of the short-grain match, but it still won't hold up to much abuse.

Miter with Biscuit
Biscuits offer improved strength and alignment for what can be a tricky and weak corner joint. Dowels are also an option here.

Miter with Spline
Another way to strengthen a corner miter is with a spline. Beyond the adding gluing surface, a spline can be used as a decorative element.

Cope & Stick
Frames in casework needn't always be plain. A frame-and-panel design dresses up a piece and adds strength.

Half-lap
A good corner joint, the half-lap adds strength and more gluing surface, but requires accurate machining and is a very visible joint.

Corner Bridle
Better than a half-lap, the bridle joint offers greater strength, more gluing surface and security against racking.

Haunched Mortise
A variation on the mortise and tenon, this joint allows a panel to be added into the assembly with less work than a cope-and-stick joint.

Wedged Through-tenon
A great visual element and very strong, the wedged through-tenon takes some practice but adds amazing strength.

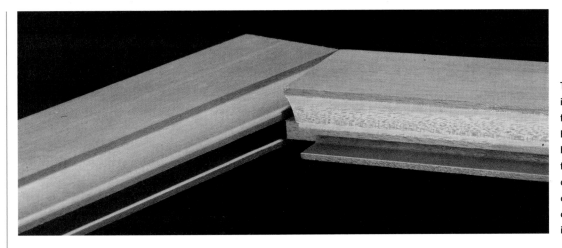

The cope-and-stick joint is a standard for most frame-and-panel doors. But the same joint can be used to create panels for casework. The profile on the cope and stick can vary greatly, but an ovolo, as shown above, is very traditional.

of brad nails can help as well. You could also use biscuits or pocket screws if you feel alignment help or quicker assembly time is a benefit.

BACK JOINERY

One of the most common methods of adding a back to a case piece is by milling a rabbet at the back edge of the sides, top and bottom. The rabbet can be adjusted in width to accommodate $1/4$" plywood backs, or $1/2$" or $3/4$" solid backs, depending on your requirements. One tip: if you're making a large case piece that will be mounted to the wall, it's a good idea to recess the back slightly ($1/4$"). Thus, any imperfections in the wall won't keep the cabinet from fitting tightly against it.

If you're using a solid back, there's joinery that will help span what can be a very large area, while at the same time counteracting any problems with wood contraction or expansion due to changes in humidity. A shiplap joint or tongue-and-groove joint will make using solid wood safe. And these joints leave an attractive back in the case.

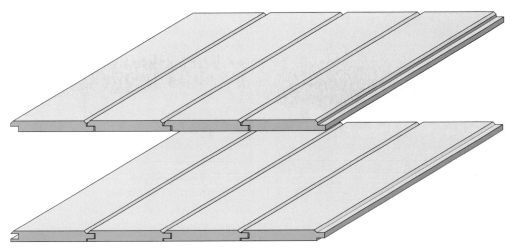

Two joints for solid backs are the shiplap joint (top) and the tongue-and-groove joint. Both allow a solid wood back to move with seasonal humidity changes. The shiplap joint requires slightly less accuracy, but the tongue-and-groove joint offers a locking feature to counteract any warping.

Smart Assembly

by David Thiel

What are we talking about when we say "smart assembly?" In previous chapters, we've discussed a couple of issues that can complicate casework: proper material preparation and choosing the proper joint to make the strongest furniture. Another place to trip up when building case furniture is in the assembly of your components.

Most casework is larger than the average breadbox (although that breadbox is also casework). Because of that large size, cases can be awkward to fit and assemble.

Another complication is that many case pieces are more than just four sides, a top and a bottom. Each side can be as many as five pieces (a frame-and-panel side, for example), and accurately fitting, gluing and assembling all those pieces is like trying to build a jigsaw puzzle without a table.

In this chapter, you'll learn to: test the fit of the pieces prior to gluing; work in stages; and use proper clamping techniques – all of which will help to make your casework construction a more pleasurable and successful experience.

Other assembly issues we'll discuss were briefly touched upon in the previous chapter, but here we'll go into more detail about attaching backs to your case pieces. We'll also spend some time focusing on mechanical assembly options – namely, screws and nails.

TEST FIT YOUR PIECES

This is one of those steps in building furniture that gets forgotten or ignored because we get in a hurry. After carefully measuring and cutting all our joinery for a piece, we hold the pieces near each other, give them a critical squint with our eye, then decide everything looks good enough to add glue. Shortly after that, we're knocking apart a sticky mess because something just didn't fit right under clamp pressure.

As with proper sanding before finishing, test fitting case pieces without glue is always a good idea. As the number of pieces in a project increases, the opportunity for mistakes increases as well. Case pieces have more parts than any other type of woodworking project except intarsia. So take a few minutes to follow these rules about test fitting.

• Work from the outside in. Test fit the case joinery first. This fit will determine the overall shape and size of the case itself. Any

Author Bill Hylton understands the benefits of good joinery (a lock miter at the corners of this piece) and proper clamping during assembly. By using the lock miter joint, the number of clamps required is greatly reduced – as is the complexity.

Fitting each of the interior dividers in this case can take a while, but it's well worth the effort. The plane shown in the right corner of the photo is the correct tool. A shoulder or rabbet plane allows you to fine-tune joinery prior to assembly for a less stressful experience. Once the glue is on the pieces, the mallet is used to tap everything into place.

Having everything on hand for an assembly and knowing the order in which the assembly will progress will help you avoid mishaps. Although we show a door here, the same preparedness is even more important with a case assembly. The pieces are in place and the clamps adjusted. The mallet, square and glue brush are ready to go. What's missing? How about a rag and a bucket of clean water to wipe off the excess glue?

pieces that are attached (drawer dividers or shelves) will need to fit after the exterior fit is finalized.

• With the corners fit, use the back of your case to square up everything. It keeps things in shape while fitting the interior. If you'd prefer to leave the back off for finishing, tack it in place with a couple of nails that can later be easily removed.

• With the case fit and squared, take your interior measurements at the carcase's corners and build the interior structure from those measurements. A common mistake is to fit the interior pieces to the case based on measurements taken from where they will be attached. If your case sides are bowed at the center, you'll only be building that bow into your furniture. That's why you measure at the corners.

• As you fit the interior parts, it's much easier to have the joinery (and the pieces) slightly oversized on purpose. If you try to fit the pieces perfectly beforehand, you stand a better chance of going too far and making the fit loose. It's easier to use a hand plane or sandpaper to fit the pieces perfectly.

• For face frames, don't try to fit the frame perfectly to the case; it's unlikely to work. You're better off building the frame slightly oversized (1/16") in both directions. Then, you can simply take a router with a bearing-guided straight bit and run around the outside of the case to make the frame flush.

WORK IN STAGES

This lesson really is common sense. Rather than try to glue up and assemble a case piece all at once, it's much easier to assemble the case in pieces. There are a few physical limitations that make this technique not only smart, but necessary.

Most of us work in our shops without an assistant. (Even if you do have someone you can get to help, it's unlikely they'll be knowledgeable enough in woodworking to do more than lend a hand.) That leaves us with two hands that never seem to be adequate to the task of gluing and assembling a case piece. There are just too many pieces to juggle at once.

Although glue is great at making things stick together, until it dries it's a pretty good lubricant. That means all the glued pieces have a tendency to slip around. So now you're juggling a slippery collection of parts.

One side comment, choosing the best glue for assembly will help you out. Standard yellow glues dry quickly and works well for assembling panels, but when you're working with so many pieces, a slower curing glue is helpful. There are yellow glues available with longer open times, such as Titebond Extend. Polyurethane glues have a longer open time, but can be messy. Hide glue is a third alternative because it's reversible with heat and water.

When you get all the parts glued and assembled, it's time to put clamps on until the glue dries (leave them on for at least 30 minutes). But what if you don't have 16 3'-long clamps?

Working in stages solves all these problems. Gluing and assembling one end of a case piece is a job that's easily managed with only two hands. And that one end is likely to require only a few clamps – and most woodworking shops have at least a few clamps. All of this results in a more pleasant woodworking experience with fewer chances for mistakes. And those are results worth working toward.

The photo essay below walks you through a typical assembly process for a blanket chest and is representative of the great majority of case pieces.

I'd like to drag your mind back to the earlier topic of dry-fitting for a moment. This is another valuable technique that will make working in stages all the more easy. When you dry fit an assembly, it's an opportunity to find out if you indeed have enough clamps to assemble the case piece. It's also a chance to leave those clamps set to fit the glue-up in question, so you don't have to fumble around once the glue is on the project.

And when you're dry-fitting, it's a good idea to at least pantomime applying glue to the pieces. You may find that you're trying to apply glue to a joint that you can't

Working in Stages

Getting miters perfect is tricky enough when not attached to a panel. With all the joinery prepared, glue them up first.

The back assembly (with pre-finished panels) is already in the clamps, except for the corners. They're the final addition to the back assembly.

Clamping in two dimensions on the flipped back assembly is no problem. Remember not to use glue on the panels so they can float in the grooves. Take the time to check the frame to ensure it's square. With the back clamped up, repeat the process on the front panel.

Next, add the sides. Start by gluing the side rails in place then slide the panels into place. Add glue to the tenons of the ends of the rails.

It's then fairly simple to tap the front of the case into place on the positioned sides and much easier than gluing it all at once.

With the four sides glued and in place, squaring the case as you clamp across the piece is no problem. Because the corners and the two long sides have already been squared during glue up, you have to worry about only a couple of the angles.

adequately reach with the pieces in place. Think of it as a dress rehearsal. Knowing the what, where, when and how before you start makes the actual assembly go more smoothly.

SMART CLAMPING

We've already started talking about smart clamping on the previous page. By adjusting your clamp jaws and having the clamps ready to use within easy reach, you're working smart.

That clamping preparedness carries into lots of areas including what type of clamp to use, where the piece you're going to assemble is positioned, and simple little steps that make it easier to assemble cases when you're working alone in the shop.

Let's start with the clamps. I know this is an area on which it's going to be hard to give absolute advice because we likely all own a very different collection of clamps. Some of us use bar clamps that our fathers or grandfathers used. Many of us have invested hundreds (if not thousands) of dollars on state-of-the-art clamps. While I can recommend an "optimal" clamp collection, chances are you'll make do with the clamps you have. So let's take a look at how to use them.

Clamps exert their force at a specific point on the jaws. Making sure that pressure is placed directly over the area being clamped, and that the pressure is being exerted evenly across the piece, will improve the joint and also keep the case from racking during assembly.

The photo at right shows the clamp holding the shelf on the right positioned with the bar centered on the shelf thickness. The clamp is slid up against the shelf to allow the full length of the jaw to support the shelf. The clamp on the left is kicked to the left at the bottom. This could result in racking the structure during clamping. If the squares weren't being used to hold things at right angles, this could be a problem.

Whenever possible, use a clamp that is only slightly longer than the required clamping size. This isn't something that's going to affect your furniture piece; rather, it's a detail that will affect your ease of clamping. Fighting with a 4'-long bar clamp to clamp a face frame on a 12"-deep bookcase is awkward.

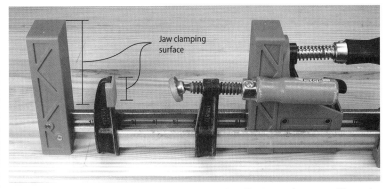

This may sound like an advertisement, and if it does, oh well. It's an endorsement I'll stand behind. When parallel-jaw clamps (at the rear in the above picture) came onto the woodworking scene, they had a huge impact. The jaws allow you to clamp with even pressure anywhere along the length of the jaw. Another benefit is that the design allows the clamp to lay on your workbench, ready to use, without falling over. That's something your standard F-style clamp (propped-up in front) just can't do. Parallel-jaw clamps represent money well-spent for your woodworking shop.

Even with dados run in the sides of this bookcase, gluing and clamping the shelves in place can be awkward because of the shelf length. Here, in anticipation of this difficulty, a couple of speed squares are used to help keep the shelves at a 90° angle during glue-up. The squares are clamped to the shelf and to the lower case side. Then the opposite case side is clamped across the shelf. This not only helps to ensure a square case, but keeps things from wiggling too much while you're assembling the case.

As important as using the right clamps and positioning them correctly is thinking a step or two ahead about where the clamping is taking place. Being able to easily place clamps to provide the best pressure may require moving to a larger, smaller or entirely different work surface.

One of my favorite case-clamping tricks uses some old clamping technology. The

Where you position your work is as important as where you position the clamps. To attach the face frame to this bookcase, a number of clamps were needed to apply pressure around the entire perimeter of the case. If the case were positioned on a flat surface, you wouldn't be able to place any clamps to the inside of the case. A couple of sawhorses work best in this case.

clamps pictured below are most commonly called hand screws. Hand screws have been around for a long time, but they're the clamps I most often use for help with assembly. They take getting used to, but they're very handy when you're working in the shop alone.

These hand screws also make an excellent installation tool for case pieces. Case pieces frequently work like building blocks, attaching to one another to form a wall of bookcases or a run of kitchen cabinets.

This is a strange instance of using clamps for a non-clamping procedure. Many case pieces are simply screwed or nailed together. If you're working by yourself it can be tricky to hold everything in place while you're nailing. By using hand screws to support the shelves during assembly, you've added a shop assistant.

Hand screws

When installing these units, it's often difficult to align the cases while attaching them to the wall. By clamping two case sides together using the sides of the clamps, rather than the jaws, these clamps provide quick, solid holding power across a much larger area to hold cabinets in perfect alignment. Add the screws to hold the pieces together and you're done.

Another handy smart-clamping trick comes into play when attaching backs to case pieces. While a case piece should be checked for square throughout the construction steps, it will still retain enough flexibility to shift out of square. Attaching the back is one of the easiest ways to guarantee that the case stays square, but that means you need to square the case while attaching the back. This is a three-handed job – unless you use a clamp.

Measure diagonally across the back of the case in both directions. Determine the longer dimension and then place a long bar clamp running from corner to corner across the longer dimension. Slowly tighten the clamp until the diagonal dimensions are the same, then nail the back in place. Simple.

ADDING BACKS

Not every case piece has to have a back. But if it does, the most common way to fit the back into the case is by using a rabbet joint on the case sides, top and bottom (although the top and bottom are optional). This hides the back from view and offers an easy reference edge to square up the case.

The rabbet joint also offers the flexibility of using different thicknesses of back. If your case piece is a smaller size and will rest on the floor, a $1/4$"-thick back is adequate. If your case is larger, or will be hung on the wall (often through the back itself) a $1/2$"- or $3/4$"-thick back will be preferable. The back rabbet can be easily adjusted to accommodate any of these back sizes.

Another advantage to a rabbeted back is the ability to temporarily attach the back during construction, but remove it for easier finishing. If a captured back (fit into grooves in the case pieces) were used, it would need to be permanently installed during construction of the case.

The rabbet in the case pieces can be created prior to assembling the case using the table saw or a router. This can require some pre-planning to avoid running a through-

Whether squaring the face frame for your cabinet or the cabinet itself, this is the best way to do it. Using either a tape measure or a wooden folding rule, measure from corner to corner in both diagonal directions. The difference between the two measurements will show you how out of square your piece is. By running a clamp across the piece with the longer diagonal measurement, you can pull up half the difference between the two measurments and make a square frame or cabinet.

A rabbet run on the inside edge of the case pieces is a common way to hide a case back. These rabbets can be created during the initial milling of the case pieces, or created with a bearing-guided rabbeting bit in a router after assembly. When using a rabbeting bit, the last step is to come back with a sharp chisel and square out the corners.

rabbet in a side that might leave a gap where the case pieces meet. Another option is to assemble the case and then run the rabbet on the case using a rabbeting router bit, although this can be a balancing act and creates a small amount of work after the rabbet is finished (see photo top right).

The back itself can be plywood or solid wood. The advantage of plywood is not having to concern yourself with the movement inherent to solid wood. While a stable material, plywood won't look as natural as a solid-wood back – no matter how good the veneer face is. Solid-wood backs look good and the necessary "planking" of the boards to accommodate wood movement can add a pleasing visual element to an otherwise plain expanse of wood grain.

When working with solid backs, there are details to remember in constructing and attaching the back to ensure it will remain intact and continue to look good. The photo above explains some of these important steps.

SCREWS AND NAILS

In the last chapter, we discussed a number of joints used to construct and assemble case pieces. I touched on using nails and screws for assembly, now I want to spend a little time discussing these techniques in detail.

Screws and nails are most often thought of in case construction for utility furniture. The thought is that these mechanical fasten-

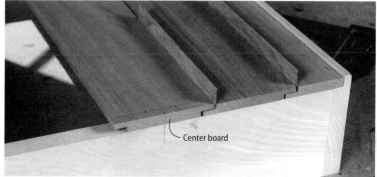

Center board

ers will be visible and the only appropriate place for that is tucked away in a laundry room or garage.

Don't assume these types of joinery are inferior. In many cases, they will prove stronger than a number of joints that take three times longer to create.

And as far as visibility goes, there are two schools of thought. A very popular design style today is more of an industrial look that leaves much of the hardware (and joinery, including bare plywood edges) exposed. By adding little touches to the hardware, you can dress up a simple screw and make it part of the design.

As to using nails as a decorative element, I'm not going to try to stretch that far. Nails should be hidden. Whether installed with a hammer or a pneumatic nail gun, if nails are in a visible part of a cabinet they should be countersunk below the wood surface and puttied.

This simple shiplapped back shows a variation on the pattern. The center board of the back is rabbeted on both edges on one face. The boards to either side (only one is shown above) are rabbeted on diagonally opposed corners, and the end board has no rabbet on one side where it mates with the rabbet in the cabinet side. To allow for movement, the pieces are evenly spaced with some simple scraps of wood. Coins also make fine spacers for shiplapped backs.

Pictured are a few simple ways to dress up a screw and leave it visible … if you consider the look appealing. Not everyone will. At far left is the bare screw. Next is a screw cover that is placed over the screw as it's installed; the cap is then closed over the screw head. Third from the left is a trim washer that is also placed over the screw before installation. At the far right is a self-adhesive wood-grain patch that simply sticks over the screw head. Above it is a plastic cap that taps into the recesses in the screw head. Generally these methods are considered beneath the level to which a woodworker should aspire.

Along those same lines, it's often more desirable to hide screws rather than build them into the design. One method is to countersink the head of the screw below the surface of the wood, then glue a plug into the hole. You can use a decorative plug that actually sticks above the surface, known as a button plug. You see this type of device in a lot of knock-down, assemble-yourself furniture sold today. It's not the hallmark of quality, but it's better than an exposed screw. The best method to hide the screw is to use a plug of the same species and grain pattern, sanded flush. If you make your own plugs (simple to do on a drill press with a tapered plug-cutting bit) from the wood you're using for your project, you stand a good chance of hiding the screw.

Pocket screws are another alternative. There are a couple of ways to hide pocket screws. The first is to place the screw location out of sight. By screwing shelves to the case sides from the underside of the shelf,

the screws will be hidden. Planning how the assembly will work can make this a very effective way to use the strength of screws without the visibility. You can also plug the hole from a pocket hole screw using shaped plugs designed for this specific purpose. Again, you can match species and grain pattern to more efficiently hide the plug.

Another visible option that crosses the wood/metal fastener concept is a dowel. While dowels have been used as fasteners for many years, there is a product on the market now that uses a stepped dowel designed to be used essentially like a nail. By building the look of the dowel head into your design you can save time, build a solid joint and add a decorative element to your project.

To use these dowels you simply clamp the pieces to be joined in their final position, adding glue if required. Next, a stepped drill bit is used to drill through both pieces of the project. Glue is added to the stepped dowel and then it is tapped into place with a hammer. The stepped design of the dowel is slightly larger than the diameter of the hole and the dowel compresses into the space making a tight fit.

It's still a good idea to leave the clamps on the piece long enough to give the glue time to set up, but once that's done the dowel is cut flush to the surface and lightly sanded.

While the old joints are still effective, we continue to devise new and useful methods to improve and simplify the process.

The best use of nails is an invisible application. For a complicated chest of drawers the drawer dividers can be tricky. Rather than use complicated joinery, a well-placed (meaning hidden) nail is driven at an angle through the vertical divider and up into the web frame divider. This angled nailing is called toenailing and works with or without pneumatic tools (but it's hard to swing a hammer in this tight a space).

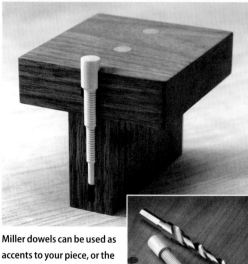

Miller dowels can be used as accents to your piece, or the dowels' wood species can be matched to the project's to hide this useful joinery option.

Doors & Drawers

by David Thiel

Casework, by its very nature, exists for storage. That storage can range from china to rare books, or simply be a place for your children to store their puzzles or you to file your bills. Regardless of the ultimate purpose, casework storage frequently requires hiding the stored materials from view for aesthetics or need. That aesthetic leads us to the topic of this chapter: doors and drawers.

If a cabinet is shallow in depth, simple shelving is a practical method of storage. By adding doors to some or all of the storage areas in the cabinet, the storage is kept tidy to the casual view even if things inside the cabinet are anything but orderly.

If a cabinet is deeper it offers a greater capacity for storage, but the depth makes it difficult to access items that are stored (or accidentally pushed) to the rear of the cabinet. This is when drawers can be valuable. They allow you to store items the full depth (and height) of the cabinet in a tidy fashion, but still allow access to everything with little fuss.

Yes, building drawers does complicate the case construction process, but there's little doubt that the extra work is worth the effort.

Depending on the style of the case the doors and drawers can be complex, both in appearance and construction, or very simple. Most traditional case furniture designs involve frame-and-panel doors that are a small construction project in their own right. Add to that the edge profiles commonly added to drawer fronts and doors, and these storage accessories often carry the larger weight of the final design of the piece.

When a more clean, contemporary look is the goal, doors and drawers are usually required to essentially disappear and blend in to the casework with as little adornment as possible. That sounds easy but in practice allows less room for error.

Shown are a pair of inset drawers designed to close with the drawer fronts flush to the front of the cabinet. The top drawer uses traditional half-blind dovetail joinery to attach the front to the drawer sides. The lower drawer uses more contemporary and commercial rabbet joinery to attach the front. Both styles allow the primary drawer wood (walnut in this case) to be viewed, but the secondary (white pine) wood on the sides remains hidden.

We're going to discuss different types of doors and drawers used in case furniture, as well as take a look at the most common joinery methods to create both. We'll also discuss the proper fitting of doors and drawers, but we'll save the hardware used to attach them until the next chapter.

FITTING THE CABINET

Before we get into details on doors and drawers, let's take a look at a generality for both categories that needs to be addressed. Both doors and drawers can fit into a cabinet in three ways: overlay, lipped or inset.

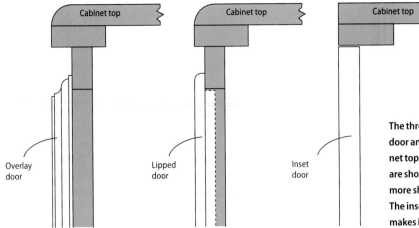

Overlay door

Lipped door

Inset door

The three illustrations at left show an overlay door, a lipped door and an inset door. The views are side sections of the cabinet top and face frame (shown in color). The doors themselves are shown in white. The overlay makes the cabinet slightly more shallow, while the lipped door gains some interior depth. The inset door allows the most amount of interior storage and makes it possible to build without a face frame on the cabinet.

These fittings are a function of both design and application. But that's not to say that one style fits only one type of furniture design. Inset doors and drawers can be found on contemporary furniture as well as Shaker furniture. But their location does affect the appearance of the piece.

The storage aspect is small, but interesting. Both overlay and lipped doors and drawers are designed for use with face-frame cabinets. The frame itself constrains the size of the opening for accessing the storage space. By using a lipped door or drawer you can gain about $3/8$" of storage depth in the cabinet. Again, not huge, but it's extra storage.

The inset door can also be used with a face frame cabinet, but its most significant

advantage is obvious in contemporary frameless cabinets. The inset door allows full access to the top and bottom of the cabinet opening, and can offer a clean, finished look.

Any type of drawer or door construction can be used in any of the three designs, so as we move on to discuss the different doors and drawers we aren't going to focus on that detail, but look more closely at the construction itself.

DRAWER TYPES AND JOINERY

We're going to focus on three types of drawer joinery for this article: dovetails, rabbets and down-and-dirty butt joints. While there are probably dozens more to discuss, these three versions comprise 90 percent of the drawers used in case construction. The purpose of this chapter isn't to show you how to build each drawer, but rather discuss the benefits (and deficits) of each. We will drop a few hints we've learned over the years that will make construction easier.

Dovetails

The first type of drawer is a dovetailed drawer. As mentioned earlier these drawers can be made as overlay, lipped or inset and except for odd occurrences the front joint is traditionally a half-blind dovetail, while the back joint can be either a half-blind or a through dovetail. Half-blind dovetails are more difficult to create because you're carving out a precise three-sided alcove rather than just cutting a two-sided channel. The half-blind type is necessary, however, if you want to see only the primary wood at the front of the cabinet. There's always more

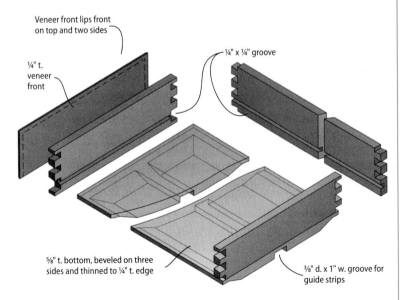

Veneer front lips front on top and two sides

$1/4$" t. veneer front

$1/4$" x $1/4$" groove

$5/8$" t. bottom, beveled on three sides and thinned to $1/4$" t. edge

$3/8$" d. x 1" w. groove for guide strips

This drawing shows a typical dovetailed drawer, but with a twist. Through dovetails are easier to cut than half-blind dovetails. So in this case the drawer is made with through dovetails and a veneer front is added to make the front look like half-blind dovetails.

Drawer Joinery

Half-blind Dovetail
The preferred joint for drawer fronts, providing strength and a quality finished appearance. But also the most difficult to create.

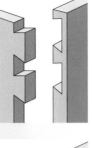

Through Dovetail
Through dovetails also provide good strength, but the joint is visible from both sides making it preferable for drawer backs, not fronts.

Tongue & Rabbet Joint
A good interlocking option that requires less skill to create than a dovetail. The tongue would be on the side piece, and nails and glue are required.

Locking Rabbet Joint
By adding another interlocking element, this joint gains strength by adding gluing surface – as well as an extra step to create.

Rabbet Joint
A simple, but effective drawer joint, the rabbet increases gluing area and adds strength against racking. Glue and nails are a must with this joint.

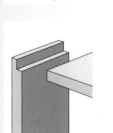

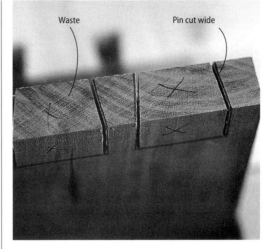

Waste   Pin cut wide

Here are two good tips for hand-cutting dovetails. The photo at left shows how cutting your pins just slightly wide of the line will force them to compress the tails cut from softer wood. The photo below shows the benefit of using a coping saw to clean out waste between the pins. The saw lets you cut right up to the corner cleanly.

than one way to skin a cat, and the illustration at the bottom of page 170 shows a trick for making though dovetails look like half-blind dovetails.

Dovetails are used for drawers because of the great strength offered by the interlocking joint. This is important in a drawer because as the loaded drawer is opened and shut, lots of stress is transferred to the front and back pieces of the drawer as the contents shift against the motion. The interlocking dovetail provides better strength than any other drawer joint. And, of course, they look great, are very traditional and continue to be a hallmark of quality woodworking.

If you plan on making dovetailed drawers there are two general methods of creating the joint available to you. You can cut the joints by hand or you can use a commercial dovetail jig used together with a router. Both will create dovetails and both have learning curves to surpass.

But once you've passed the learning part, which do you use routinely? The answer may be the method you enjoy most, but my rule of thumb is that if I'm going to make one or two drawers for a project, then hand-cutting dovetails is just as fast and effective. If you're making a bank of drawers for a dresser, break out the router and jig!

Rabbets
The second drawer type we'll look at is a more commercially applicable drawer with rabbeted joinery at front and back. While a

Building a Drawer with One Setup

For the front and back pieces, start with a ¼"-wide dado stack in your saw. Set it for ¼"-high and with a ¼" gap between the fence and dado. The first cut trims the end of the rabbet.

The second cut completes the ½"-wide rabbet, with the drawer edge referencing off the rip fence.

Using the same setup on your saw, the ¼" x ¼" groove for the bottom is cut in the sides and front in one pass.

If you're using a ½"-thick solid bottom, you can also groove a rabbet around the three sides of the bottom to allow it to fit easily in the 1/4" groove in the drawer sides and front.

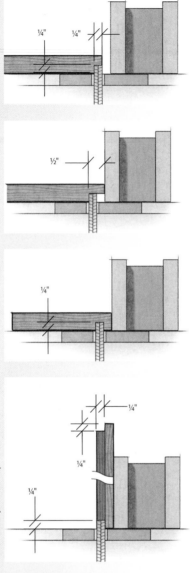

Illustrations by Matt Bantly

Two rabbeted joints are shown on this drawer. Simple in the back, with the rabbet cut only in the sides, while the front joint incorporates a dual-rabbet joint. In either case a nail (with glue, of course) will make the joint much stronger.

drawer, you can vary the location of the rabbet at the back. In either case, you want to make sure you're nailing the joint through the drawer sides into the front and back pieces to provide the greatest strength.

Another option is to rabbet both pieces so they overlap in both directions adding more gluing surface in the joint. This variation is shown at the front joint on the drawer above, while the simpler single rabbet joint is used at the rear of the drawer.

Another rabbeting option that I like is a one-setup joint. Using the simple rabbet joint at both the front and rear of the drawer and a $1/4$"-, or $1/2$"-thick bottom, the drawer can be created with only one setup on the table saw. All you need is a dado stack. (See the step illustrations below.)

Butt Joints

I also want to discuss a third option, the butt joint, that is more utilitarian and serves well in shop furniture for its ease of production and lack of hardware.

While a butt joint is by far the weakest drawer joint possible, if appearance is way down on the importance list while expediency is high, this joint can serve well when backed up with nails.

The drawers shown above have the benefit of using no machined joinery. The four sides are nailed together and the bottom is nailed to the drawer box. The only joinery occurs in the cabinet itself where dados serve as the drawer runners. Simple, quick and efficient.

rabbet joint is more simple to create than a dovetail joint, it also offers less strength and is frequently reinforced with both glue and nails.

While I'm referring to this drawer style as more commercial, I also consider it a perfectly adequate drawer joint for any number of case furniture pieces that you would build for your home or office. There are a couple of different ways to approach the rabbet joint. The simplest is to cut a rabbet on the inside edge of both ends of the drawer front and back and leave the sides straight. While you want to leave the primary wood running across the front of the

One last drawer comment. Another way to make a drawer is to build a drawer box (front, back, two sides and a bottom) using whatever joinery method you prefer, and then add a drawer front to the box. This makes it easier to fit the front without having to fight with the drawer itself and offers other fun alternatives. These are called "false-front" drawers.

DOOR TYPES AND JOINERY

As we start talking about cabinet doors, let me work the opposite pattern as with the drawers. We'll start simple with a slab door and move up to a frame-and-panel door and finally we'll look at a frame door with divided lights for glass.

Slab Doors

The simplest door to make for cabinetry is to cut a piece of plywood or a glued-up solid-wood slab to the correct size and mount it to the cabinet. If it's a solid-wood slab you can leave the edges plain or add an edge profile with a router to class it up a little.

If you're working with plywood for your drawers, the naked ply edge is considered unattractive by almost everyone. So let's look at three ways to dress up that edge. (By the way, the following approaches will work for plywood drawer fronts as well.)

The first method is to use a veneer tape. Veneer tape is available in almost every wood species to match your casework. It's available with an adhesive applied to the back that lets you iron on the tape, or there is also a newer self-adhesive tape that I strongly prefer over the iron-on type.

The tape is sold in rolls and is oversized in width to allow trimming after application. Veneer tape offers a fairly inexpensive option to solid-wood doors and it leaves a clean look to the door, showing only a thin line at the edge.

Another option uses solid wood rather than veneer tape. By gluing a 1/8"- or 1/4"-thick piece of matching solid wood to the plywood edges you create a more visible edge, but it's also more durable than the veneer tape.

Application of the wood edging uses glue and clamps and can take more time than veneer tape, but also offers the opportunity to add a decorative profile. The wood edge can be cut to just wider than the door thickness and then planed, sanded or trimmed

These no-joinery/no-hardware drawers make great utility drawers. The drawer sides are simple butt joints glued and nailed together. The bottom is cut oversized to either side of the drawer to form a tongue that fits into dados in the cabinet sides. A little wax on the tongues and they work very well. The hole in the front even removes the need for a handle. And they're really fast to make!

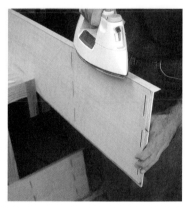

Veneer tape is still most commonly found in an iron-on design. This is effective, but you have to work fast on larger pieces to get the glue to soften and then cure at an even pace along the whole piece. Peel-and-stick varieties are available and a bit easier to work with.

With either tape variety, you still need to trim the excess. While there are a few trimming tools available, I still prefer the look you get using a fast-cut file. Just remember to only trim down toward the tape or you'll end up pulling the tape loose and likely end up with some tear-out along the edge. Just take it slow and smooth.

For solid wood edging, it's been my experience that planing a wood edge to the plywood face is easiest. Sanding can lead to burning through the plywood veneer and routing takes too much setup time.

If you don't miter the edging, a low-angle block plane will help you achieve a smooth fit at the end of the strip, but trim it close on the table saw first or you'll be planing all day.

A classic raised-panel door is shown here. The rails (the horizontal frame pieces) and stiles (the vertical frame pieces) are joined using cope-and-stick joinery, with the decorative profile at the interior corners appearing mitered and perfectly matched. The panel itself is raised (cut on a bevel) from the full thickness to a thinner width at the edge to allow it to fit in grooves cut in the rails and stiles.

with a router to a flush fit against the door face.

One other solid-wood option is cockbeading. The solid-wood edging is cut wider than the door thickness and then a decorative detail (typically a bullnose profile) is added to one edge (with a nosing plane or router). That edge is then allowed to extend beyond the front of the door. Simple.

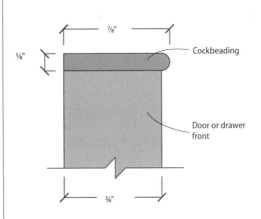

Cockbeading is a great way to make good looking plywood doors in a hurry. Simply hold the back edge flush to the plywood and affix the edging. Mitered corners help complete the finished look. And if you're in a real hurry you can use a 23-gauge pin nailer to attach the edging, avoiding the need for clamps.

Raised-panel Doors

When most people think of cabinet doors, a raised-panel door appears in their mind. As with a dovetailed drawer, the raised-panel door means quality and style. And, as with a dovetailed drawer, they take more work to create.

Panel doors in general are made of vertical (stiles) and horizontal (rails) components joined at the corners using a variety of methods. The long edges of the rails and stiles can be left plain or decorative edge treatments can be added with a shaper or router. The center of the door (panel) can be raised (which really means the edges of the panel are lowered, leaving the look of a panel that is rising to the level of the frame) or left flat and recessed below the plane of the door's face components.

For a decorative panel door a cope-and-stick joint is most often used. This is created using a router or shaper cutter to create mating joinery on the rails and stiles (see the illustration at right). The bits take much of the difficulty out of this process, but they must be accurately set up to achieve a tight, attractive joint.

The panel that is fit into the grooves created in the door frame also requires some special care to create. Because of the wood movement that occurs in solid panels due to changes in humidity, the panel must be fit into the door to allow room for expansion, but also leave a fit that is snug enough to keep the panel from rattling in the door frame when opened or closed.

If this sounds like a lot of work but you still want a frame-and-panel door, consider a flat-panel door. This design occurs often in Shaker, Arts & Crafts and what many call "country" furniture pieces. The rails and stiles are free of decoration and the panel is most often a $1/4$"-thick piece of veneered plywood glued into a stopped or through groove in the frame.

A variety of joinery methods are available for the more simple frame-and-panel doors, including mortise and tenon, bridle and even dowels (see list on page 175 for some of these options). Most are easy to create, but offer varying degrees of strength for the door.

One of the strong benefits to the flat plywood panel is removing the concern of panel expansion. Plywood panels won't move with humidity, so they can be made to fit snug to avoid rattling. And the ability to add a snug-fitting panel allows you to use a frame joint with less strength, relying on the panel to add some stability.

With two of the joints shown below, stability is a concern. The bridle and half-lap joints offer a fair amount of gluing surface,

Door Joinery

Cope and Stick
The preferred joint for doors, the cope and stick provides a strong interlocking joint with matched profiles and leaves a groove to fit the door panel.

Mortise and Tenon
This joint offers great strength, but with a simpler appearance. It can be used at corners or in joining intermediary rails to stiles in multi-panel door frames.

Corner Bridle
Providing lots of gluing surface, the bridle joint leaves visible joinery and can be created on a band saw or table saw.

Half Lap
A quick door frame joint, the half lap offers only acceptable strength and requires careful setup to leave a flush surface on the door frame face.

Dowels
Dowels create a good looking door frame but only offer minimal strength. They also require a good jig and smidgen of luck to do them well.

but don't interlock tightly to offer a self-squaring feature.

To improve either of these joints you can dowel the joint after squaring the frame during glue-up. The dowels can be made of a matching or contrasting wood species as to your preferences. When doweling the joint, always work from the show surface of the door. Tear-out as the drill bit exits the back of the doors isn't attractive. You can also minimize the tear-out by using a scrap piece of wood as a backing board behind the door frame as you drill.

Glass-paned Doors
One type of casework door that seems to strike fear into many woodworkers' hearts is a glass-paned door. Glass isn't a medium that

When making cope-and-stick joinery, a router table is the tool of choice. Make sure the router has a large enough motor (more than 2 horsepower) to supply enough torque to provide a clean cut. Also variable speed is an important feature as these larger bits perform better at slower speeds (16,000 rpm or slower). Lastly, these bits take off a lot of material in a single pass, so it's important to keep the wood steady during the cut and also make sure you are safe from kickback. Appropriately placed and adjusted featherboards will make this process safer and also more accurate.

The most traditional method of creating a cope-and-stick joint for a door frame is by using a cope-and-stick bit set. One bit is designed to cut the edge profile and panel groove on the stiles as well as the inner edge of the rails. The matching bit (the cope part) is shaped to cut the negative version of the edge profile and to leave a tongue on the end of the rail to interlock with the groove in the stile. There are single cope-and-stick bits with interchangeable cutters to switch between cope or stick, and others that have all the cutters in place, but you simply use a separate section of the bit for each procedure.

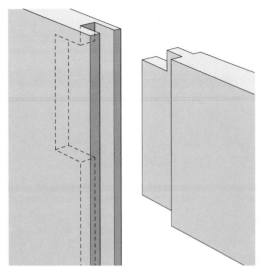

Stopped grooves are complicated to create and require more cleanup time with a chisel than most of us would prefer. But allowing the groove to run through the piece (as shown on the stile above) creates a gap when using a standard tenon. That's where the haunched tenon (shown here) comes into play. By simply removing only part of the tenon's edge a haunch is left that fits in to the end of the groove, hiding the gap.

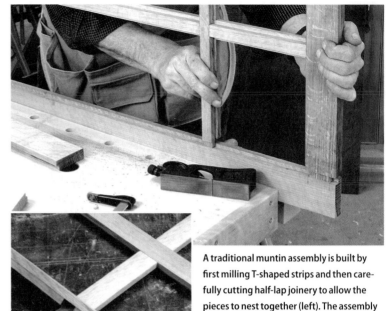

A traditional muntin assembly is built by first milling T-shaped strips and then carefully cutting half-lap joinery to allow the pieces to nest together (left). The assembly is then installed in mortises formed in the door frame (above), making the muntin assembly a permanent part of the door assembly.

woodworkers are always comfortable with, so adding it to their woodworking seems scary. But the truth is, if you're comfortable with a frame-and-panel door, you're only a few steps away from a glass-paned door.

What we're adding to the door's frame are muntins. Muntins are lighter weight strips of wood that divide the glass panes. They can be vertical, horizontal or run at angles. The traditional manner of adding muntins is to form half-lapped frames that fit into mortises formed in the door's rails and stiles. Rather than a door panel groove, a rabbet is formed in the rails and stiles. In cross section the muntins look like a T with the glass panes resting into the corners formed by the T's cross bar. Retaining strips are added behind the glass pane and nailed in place in the rabbets, or glazing putty can be used to hold the panes in place.

Creating the rabbet in the frame pieces is no more difficult than creating a groove, but creating and fitting the muntins does take extra time and can honestly be confusing unless you keep your wits about you.

Glen Huey came up with a shortcut to door muntins that takes much of the time and confusion out of the equation. Rather than create T-shaped muntins and mortises, Glen glues wood strips together to form the T shapes and glues those same strips into

the rabbets to attach the muntin frame to the door.

With Glen's method (shown below) the legs of the Ts are first glued horizontally across the door, resting in the rabbets in the frame pieces. Next, the T crossbar pieces are glued into position vertically in the door, across the first horizontal pieces. Finally the remaining leg and crossbar pieces are fit between the pieces already in place and then glued to those pieces.

This process provides a true divided-light door, but requires only strips that can easily be milled by any woodworker and works more like a jigsaw puzzle than a complicated joinery process.

Glen is placing one of the leg sections of a muntin in place on the already installed crossbar section. At top left you can see an assembled T section.

Cabinet Hardware

by David Thiel

Whether your casework is a bookcase, kitchen cabinet or highboy, the hardware you use to prop up the shelves, hang the doors or make the drawers slide smoothly can make or break the look and function of the finished piece.

We want to focus on three categories in this chapter: drawer slides, door hinges and shelf supports. Then, we'll use a little space at the end to talk about some specialty hardware.

DRAWER SLIDES

For many woodworkers who build traditional 18th- and 19th-century furniture the topic of drawer slides is one that's handled on the table saw. These pieces of furniture use wooden drawer runners and guides that are frequently built into the framework of the piece itself. While these are appropriate and functional, that's not what we're going to talk about here. We're talking about mass-produced metal ball-bearing drawer slides.

Metal drawer slides are two-part hardware, with one part mounting to the inside of the cabinet and the mating part mounting to the drawers. How the two parts interlock and move is specific to the manufacturer and design, but they all use the same concept.

Drawer slides take up some space in the cabinet and that will affect the overall storage space available in the drawers and cabinet. In general you'll lose 1" in width to allow for the drawer slides. But different slide designs will offer different spacing and locations, which we'll talk about further.

Drawer slides can be grouped into two large sub-groups: side mount and under mount. Within these two groups slides can be either three-quarter or full extension. Full-extension slides allow access to all of the drawer's interior, allowing the full drawer box to open past the front of the cabinet. Slides break down even further by weight limit and design. There are truly too many types of slides to discuss all of them here, so we'll hit the most common styles and discuss some mounting tips.

Side-mount Slides

Side-mount drawer slides constitute what could be called traditional metal drawer slides. They've been around for a very long time and have generally provided good service.

Usually attached near the bottom of the drawer side, these slides are available in three-quarter or full extension. Three-quarter-extension slides are most commonly available in 75- to 100-pound capacity and

Putting drawer slides on in the correct location takes a certain amount of careful calculation. Most slides, however, allow a certain amount of adjustability, which provides some room for forgiveness.

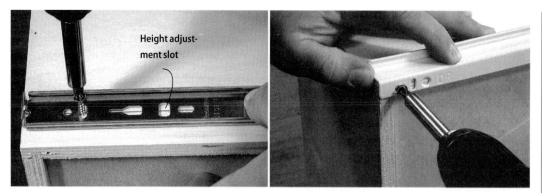

A side-mount slide (full extension) is shown at the left. At right is what is referred to as an under-mount slide. The misnomer on the under-mount slide is that it fastens to both the side and bottom of the drawer (providing excellent support). Both slides mount with the front edge of the slide flush to the drawer box. On the side-mount slide, the height can be adjusted using slotted holes in both the drawer slide and cabinet member. For the under mount, height adjustment is only available on the cabinet member. Notice that the under-mount slide has a "DR" embossed on the member. That stands for Drawer Right and can be a very helpful reminder during installation.

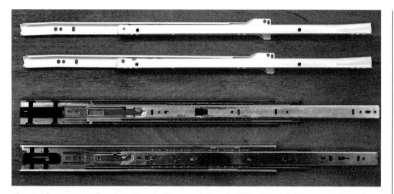

Shown above are under-mount and side-mount drawer slides. The top two are technically under-mount slides, attaching below the drawer side, though they wrap around the side and bottom. Both are three-quarter extension, with the top rated for 75 pounds and the second rated at 100 pounds. The lower two slides are side-mount, full-extension slides that are self closing, meaning the last couple of inches of travel when closing is automatic. They are also rated at 100-pounds capacity. Although from two different manufacturers, they differ only slightly in design.

are used for lighter-duty applications such as small desk drawers and clothing drawers.

Full-extension slides are available in a wider selection of weight capacities, ranging from 100 to 500 pounds per pair. These heavier-duty full extension slides are often used for filing cabinet drawers, silverware drawers, media storage and computer components.

In choosing the correct slide drawer for your application, the weight load and required extension should be your first two factors to consider.

The next factor is the length required. Drawer slides are sized in 2" increments starting at around 12" long and usually topping out at 22" long. If your drawer depth is

15" and you are using a three-quarter-extension slide, you would most commonly use a 14"-long drawer slide. If, however, your case has enough depth to allow a 16"-long drawer slide, you can allow the slide to extend beyond the rear of the drawer box and gain a little extra extension on the drawer.

When using full-extension slides you should try to use the longest possible drawer slide to match the drawer. Otherwise you will be defeating the purpose of the full-extension slide.

Side-mount slides most commonly require $1/2$" of clearance on either side of the drawer to accommodate the slide members. There are some models that require less space, but these are special application slides. Top-to-bottom spacing allowances will be determined by the type of slide used. Most side-mount slides allow the drawer to slide straight in and out of the cabinet, allowing nearly full-height drawer sides and maximized storage space.

Because side-mount slides can be mounted anywhere on the side of the cabinet and drawer box, both the drawer member and the cabinet member offer elongated slots to adjust for height and depth. This offers a fair amount of forgiveness when attaching the drawer slide members. But don't confuse this extra adjustment with a license to be haphazard. Aligning the slides accurately will make the process much more convenient and keep you from becoming frustrated.

Using spacing templates when installing slides will help you evenly space the slides from top to bottom. More important, spacers will help you make sure that the left and right drawer slides are evenly spaced in the cabinet so you don't end up with a "leaning" drawer.

After the drawers are properly fit and adjusted in the drawer space, go back and install the permanent screws in both the cabinet and drawer members. As the drawers are used over time, the slides can shift on the screws in the slotted holes, changing the fit of the drawer.

Under-mount Slides

There are also specialty under-mount slides that mount below the drawer bottom (usually a single slide mounted in the center of the drawer) allowing full-width drawers with no visible hardware. These are frequently more expensive and involve more complicated mounting procedures, including changes to the way the cabinet itself is constructed. You should be aware of them, but we're going to look at the more common undermount enamel-coated slides that mount at the bottom of the drawer sides.

These lighter-duty slides offer good support by wrapping around the bottom of the drawer side (using the drawer itself as support) rather than relying on screws fastened into the sides alone.

I mentioned that these slides are enamel coated. These allow the slides to be made in a variety of colors, including white, almond, brown and black, rather than just bare metal. Many people find this appearance more appealing. Beyond the look, the enamel coating also serves to deaden the noise created by the slides as the drawer is opened or closed.

Because these under-mount slides mount to the bottom of the drawer side as

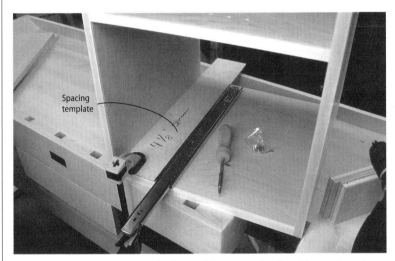

A spacing template makes getting the drawer slides mounted to the cabinet easier and helps ensure that you won't need to do as much adusting to fit the drawers.

Even with careful measuring, sometimes your drawer ends up more narrow than planned. Some slides offer an adjustable (bendable) tab to space the slide (and drawer box) farther away from the cabinet's side for a tighter fit.

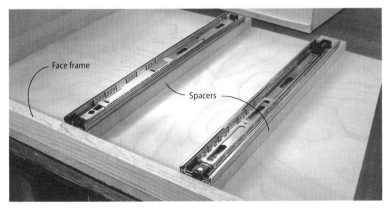

Face frame cabinets have recessed sides on the inside requiring spacers behind the slides to bring them flush to the inside edge of the face frame member.

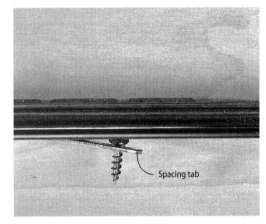

Even if the slide isn't equipped with adjusting tabs, slight adjustments in width are possible. Pieces of veneer tape can be used as shims for a tighter fit. Leave the shims oversize while fitting, then trim to size to hide behind the slide.

Hinge Types

Unswaged Butt Hinge
Requires little work, but presents an unattractive gap between door and frame.

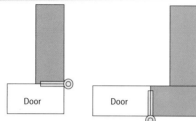

Swaged, Mortised Butt Hinge
Shown in two orientations, this hinge minimizes the gap between the door and hinge, but requires the hinge be mortised into the door and frame pieces.

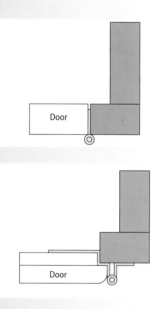

Non-mortise Butt Hinge
By using interlocking hinge leaves, the gap is reduced to 1/16" and requires no mortising.

Lipped Inset Hinge
This wrap-around hinge allows lipped doors to recess within the space of the cabinet frame with little work.

A mortised hinge – the bane of many a woodworker. To avoid an unsightly gap between door and cabinet frame the hinge leaves must be set into the door and frame. As you can see, this requires a three-sided shallow recess. While a router and special jig can make the mortise easier, a chisel is still required.

A wonder of technology – a non-mortise hinge. The leaves of the hinge are built to interlock when closed leaving no more than a 1/16" gap. Even better, all you have to do is screw the hinge in place. Wonderful.

well as to the side, there is no height adjustment on the drawer members of the slides. This makes it even more critical to get the spacing of the cabinet member accurate.

Speaking of spacing, these slides also require a ½" gap on either side of the drawer box to allow room for the slides. In addition, the manner in which the drawer and cabinet members interlock requires you to lift up the drawer to remove or install it in the carcase. This means that the drawer sides have to be shorter than the opening by as much as 1½" to allow for that clearance. Because you have to allow this extra space, that means slightly less storage space in each drawer when using these slides.

DOOR HINGES

As with drawer slides, door hinges is a vast topic to try to tackle in a small area. So we'll focus on the most common types and actually break them into two areas: the more traditional butt-style hinge and the less discussed (but very useful) European hinge.

Butt Hinges

Butt hinges can be used to connect doors to face frame or frameless cabinets and there are hundreds of different styles and permutations. They include swaged, unswaged, mortise and non-mortise hinges and a variety of lipped/overlay/inset hinges for special applications.

Let's talk about the basic hinge first. The hinge is supposed to do two things: make the door swing and allow the door to fit the cabinet in an attractive manner. Swinging is easy; the fit is something else. Butt hinges are sold swaged and unswaged. The two variants are shown in the illustrations on page 180. An unswaged hinge is slightly less expensive, but if mounted without the benefit of mortising can leave a rather unsightly gap between door and cabinet. If mortised into the pieces the gap will shrink, but will not close to what I would consider acceptable proportions.

Swaged hinges will leave about a ⅛" gap between the door and case if used without mortising. Better, but still not preferable. Mortising will allow an airtight fit, but will require time with a router and chisel, or just a chisel. It can also be tricky to get the mortise the perfect depth to accommodate the hinge leaves.

Which brings us to non-mortise hinges. These hinges have interlocking leaves that allow the door to close leaving just ¹⁄₁₆" gap between door and cabinet. That's an acceptable gap requiring only that you screw the hinge in place.

These non-mortise hinges are available in a number of styles to fit many different door profiles. Speaking of which, standard hinges wander into a dizzying array of choices when they become "wrap around" hinges. These hinges are designed to accommodate inset, offset, lipped and overlay doors. Shown at left is only one type of option in this area. Your best bet is to match the door profile to the hinge. And I mean match. Fit the hinge to the door. I can't count how many times I've purchased what I was sure was the correct hinge, only to head back to the store.

With all these hinges I recommend drilling pilot holes to accurately center the screws in the holes. Otherwise a slight shift of the hinge can throw the door alignment out of whack.

European Hinges

European concealed hinges are quite a bit different from butt hinges, and the differences in design and function can be bewildering. Once you understand how they function, the choices you have, and a few quirks, you can use them to quickly and consistently hang doors on both face-frame and frameless cabinets.

The biggest difference is that no part of the hinge is visible on the outside of the cabinet. A base plate attaches to the inside of the cabinet, or to the face frame. The hinge arm fits in a 35mm diameter hole bored in the back of the door.

Different thicknesses of base plates and different types of arms allow you to have the doors inset within the opening, or partially

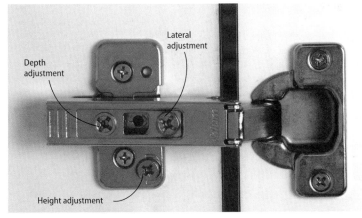

European hinges are adjustable in three directions after installation. In this hinge, two screws lock the position of the base plate, and the height adjustment screw acts as a cam to move the hinge up and down. The other adjustment screws are also cams. The depth adjustment moves the hinge toward or away from the front of the cabinet. The lateral adjustment moves the hinge to the right or left when facing the cabinet. These adjustments allow you to fine tune the fit of the doors, but the doors and their openings must still be carefully made. You won't be able to make an obtuse door square, or a small opening larger by adjusting the hinge.

Use a jig – either a shop-made one or a commercial jig as shown – to precisely locate the holes for the hinge base plates. This jig from EZ-Mount (ez-mount.com) lips on the cabinet front and gives a 3" offset from either the top or bottom of the cabinet. The jig allows you to hold the hinge plate accurately in the jig while using a Vix bit to pre-drill the screw holes. Different jigs are required for offset versus overlay hinge locations. The hinge type is imprinted on the plastic of the jig to avoid mistakes.

A drill press with a fence and the right size Forstner bit consistently locates the holes for the hinge cups. A rabbet on the bottom edge of the fence will keep chips from building up that would hold the edge of the door away from the fence. Adjust the fence and drill test holes to get the hole the right depth and distance from the edge of the door.

When the fence and depth stop are set, use a small square to mark the location of the center of the bit on the fence. Measure from that point both left and right and mark the distance from the edge of the door to the center of the bit. When drilling the holes in the doors, line up each end of the door with the mark you made on the fence. When you mount the hinge arms in the holes, make sure that the flat area of the arm is perpendicular to the edge of the door.

If all the parts are placed in the right locations, using European concealed hinges will let you hang a lot of doors very quickly. The hinge arms clip into place on the baseplates. If the alignment is slightly off, loosen the height-adjustment screw on the baseplate to allow the hinge to clip on.

or fully overlaying the front of the cabinet box.

The trade-off for the speed and adjustability of concealed hinges is twofold. They take up some space on the inside of the cabinet, and they don't open as far as butt hinges. Instead of swinging freely, European hinges will stop opening at 105° to 176°.

The big advantage to these hinges is that you have built-in adjustments as shown in the photo above. After you hang the doors you can move them in or out, up or down, or right and left by turning a screw. You still need to work carefully to get the doors and their openings square and the correct size, but the ability to adjust can be a lifesaver.

Most retailers sell prepackaged combinations of plates and arms designated by the application and type of cabinet. They also have pretty good instructions either in the packaging or on their web sites. Successful installation is mostly a matter of placing the holes exactly where you want them, and making sure they are the right diameter and depth.

One issue with European hinges is that they are manufactured in metric dimensions. Laying out the work and following instructions is faster and easier if you switch to working with millimeters. Converting from fractions to millimeters and using the nearest "inch size" bit instead of the correct metric one can lead to problems. It's a lot like working on a car that uses metric fasteners – a $1/2$" wrench doesn't really fit a 12mm nut, and a 35mm diameter hinge cup doesn't really fit in a $1\frac{3}{8}$" diameter hole. You don't have to work with millimeters for your entire project, but a metric tape and rule will help you immeasurably.

The location of the hinges and plates vertically is the one variable that isn't locked in. Between $3\frac{1}{2}$" and 4" from the top and bottom of the door works well in most cases. If you are working on a project with varying door heights, it's easiest to place the hinges consistently on the doors, and locate the base plates in the cabinet boxes to match.

The base plate holes are always 32mm apart, and 37mm in from the front edge of the cabinet for overlay doors. With inset doors, add the thickness of the door to 37mm to locate the base plate holes. These holes need to be precisely located so it makes sense to use a drilling jig as shown on page 181. You can buy one, or you can make your own.

The hole in the back of the door is generally 35mm in diameter, and is best drilled with a Forstner bit. Before drilling a real door, check your drilling setup on some scraps. It's important that the depth of the hole is correct, and the distance between the hole and the edge of the door determines either the amount of overlay or the gap on an inset door. You can use a drill press (shown on page 182), set up with a fence so the edge-to-hole distance is consistent, or use a jig and a hand-held drill.

Because the hole for the hinge cup is close to the edge of the door and relatively deep, a moulded profile on the edge of a solid wood frame and panel door may intersect the hole. Run the profile on some scrap material and drill a test hole to make sure this doesn't happen. Many router bit manufacturers make low-profile bits for this application.

If you're only hanging a few doors, you can mount the hinge arms in the doors, place the door next to the opening, and mark the centers for the base plate holes directly from the door. If you have a project with many doors, make or set a jig to locate the holes in the cabinets. You can then mount the baseplates in the cabinets and the hinges in the doors.

Once you have both pieces of hardware in place, the end of the hinge arm clips on to the base plate as shown below. Start by locating both hinges in the notches at the front of the plate and push the arm back until it snaps into place. If they don't quite line up, you can loosen or change the height-adjustment screw to get them to snap on.

While European hinges are designed to be used in frameless cabinets, you can also use them with traditional cabinets that are built with face frames. Special baseplates are made for this application, or you can add some wood behind the face frame to provide a flush surface to mount standard base plates.

When you have all the doors attached to the cabinet boxes, you can use the adjustment screws to get even gaps between doors, and an even overlay at the edge of the cabinet. I generally set the height first, then the depth and make certain that the door swings freely. Once this is done, adjust the

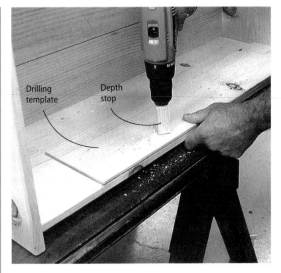

Drilling template

Depth stop

Two tips to drilling for shelf supports are evident in this photo. One is a simple drilling template that will always index off the bottom of the shelving unit. The other is a simple depth stop slipped over the drill bit to guarantee the proper depth for the shelf pin.

doors side to side. You may need to go back and readjust to fine-tune the finished look.

SHELVING SUPPORTS

While most woodworkers are aware of the fact that they're adding shelves to their cabinetry, they may not plan very far ahead as to how those shelves will be supported in the carcase.

As you can see from the brief selection of shelf supports shown on page 184, there are lots of things to consider. And there are lots more than those shown.

The critical things to consider when selecting a shelf support are stability, visibility and flexibility.

If you're loading your shelves with 150 pounds of books you would be best served to consider metal rather than plastic supports. Another stability factor is whether the shelf will shift on the supports. The straight pins shown are attractive, but have very little bearing surface against the bottom of the shelf and will allow the shelf to slide forward easily. It only takes a 2" shift to drop the whole shelf off its back pins. Supports with a flat bearing surface offer better support, and a rubber pad will eliminate any slide.

Visibility is always important. If you build an attractive piece of furniture you don't want to junk it up with lots of support items. The "standards with clips" are mostly shown as a bad example and in my opinion should be relegated to laundry-room storage. A number of supports space the shelf away from the cabinet side, leaving a gap that's unsightly and sloppy looking. The

Shelf Supports

Standard with Clip

One of the most common, inexpensive, versatile and ugly supports available. Easily adjusts in ½" increments. The track should be grooved into the case side, requiring a router or table saw operation.

Reinforced Support

Inexpensive plastic support, slips into single or series of evenly spaced holes in the case side. Because of the back flange this support holds the shelf away from the cabinet side by as much as ⅛".

Right-angle Support

This support is almost invisible once the shelf is in place. The optional rubber pad helps keep the shelf from sliding. This support still holds the shelf away from the side of the case, leaving a gap.

Straight Pin
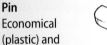
Offers low visibility (only seen under the shelf) and requires no gap between shelf and case side. Holes must be drilled to accurate diameter or the pin can slide out of hole and make the shelf unstable.

Spoon Pin (with sleeve)

A refined version of the straight pin. Can be used with or without sleeve. No gap between the shelf and case side and the flat "spoon" holds the shelf better than the straight pin and also is less visible beneath the shelf.

Low-profile Pin
Economical (plastic) and invisible support requiring a single hole. A series of holes is also possible, but this would defeat the invisibility. Extra machining (stopped grooves in the shelf edge) are required.

Hidden Shelf Wire
A metal version of the pin above, it offers an invisible means of support with no gap between the shelf and case side. Again, a stopped groove in the shelf edge is required. The metal is stronger, but the single support requires an accurate fit in the groove.

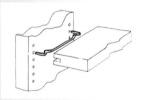

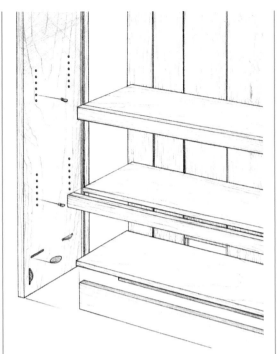

Planning for the future is an important part of drilling for shelves. While you may know what will be on the shelves today, next year you may require different spacing. By drilling a series of evenly spaced holes you will have room to grow in either direction.

"low profile" and "hidden shelf wire" supports offer very clean looks, and the fact that the supports are trapped in the shelf itself also offers great stability.

Versatility is a double-edged sword. While you want to plan ahead for usage changes and make it easy to move a shelf an inch or two in either direction, a row of shelf pin holes can be fairly unattractive. The diameter of the holes required for each of these supports vary, with the straight pin and hidden wire supports requiring very small holes.

Alternatively, the spoon pins are available with matching finish metal sleeves to dress up the holes, so even though they're visible, they blend in.

SPECIALTY HARDWARE
The specialty hardware category will fill a book and already fills dozens of pages in most woodworking catalogs. Here are two that have significantly improved casework for our staff.

Casework pieces usually fit against at least one wall, and leveling the piece so that it aligns properly with the surroundings can be tricky. Shims, scribing and any number of other techniques are used daily, but the little piece of hardware shown right is well worth the extra expense. The leveler (actually four, if you're doing it right) is installed beneath the lower shelf and behind the kick plate of the cabinet. A small hole in the shelf allows you to adjust each leveler until the cabinet sits correctly.

While the photo shows this hardware installed in an assembled cabinet, you can also use this hardware on a base built separately from the cabinet. This method allows you to level the smaller (and more manageable) loose base, then simply slide the cabinet in on top of the base. No holes in the cabinet are necessary when using a loose base.

While many case pieces use drawers that have integral fronts, many use a false or added drawer front. False fronts allow you to leave space for drawer slides without having to delve into complicated joinery to mate the drawer sides to the front. False fronts also let you adjust the drawer boxes so they are level side to side and front to back in the cabinet, then adjust the drawer fronts to align perfectly with the cabinet.

This last aspect is significantly important when aligning inset drawer fronts where the spacing around the fronts should be perfect to offer the best appearance. For years woodworkers have used double-stick tape or even hot-melt glue to affix the false front in place on the drawer box, adding the permanent screws once all is aligned. The one problem is that tape and glue space the

Leveling a cabinet is always a tricky process, but this clever piece of hardware makes it a snap. Built into the space behind the base is a leveling foot that can be accessed through the bottom shelf once the cabinet is in place. When level, a plug or cap is used to hide the access hole.

front away for the drawer box somewhat and don't allow room for easy adjustment.

The drawer front adjuster shown below solves the space problem while still offering plenty of room for adjusting the false fronts.

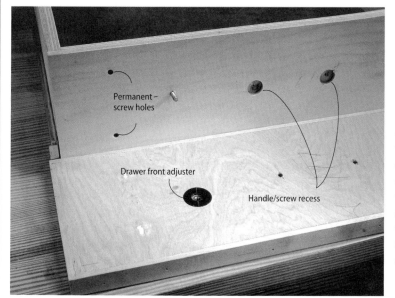

Permanent screw holes

Drawer front adjuster

Handle/screw recess

Added drawer fronts are very common and add significant convenience. But aligning the front once the drawer is in place is usually a slide-adjusting nightmare. The round device mounted in the front is a drawer front adjuster. The inner sleeve allows the drawer front to move $1/8$" in all directions while in place on the drawer. Once things are aligned, the permanent screws can be added. Also shown is a recess in the drawer box so the handle will mount only to the drawer front, again easing adjustment.

Special Applications

by David Thiel

This computer armoire has a slide-out keyboard tray that brings the working surface to the user. Storage is provided for the printer, monitor and paper products, as well as drawers for CDs and storage of other peripherals. When the computer is not in use, the doors can be shut and all the untidiness is hidden away. (Plans for this project were featured in the June 2003 issue #134 and while the computer shown is vintage, the storage still works for today's electronics.)

O ver the past six chapters of this section on Casework Construction we've focused on how case pieces are built: the joinery, materials and construction techniques that are unique to this type of woodworking. And we've also looked at the doors, drawers and hardware that make case construction both decorative and functional.

In this final chapter we get to wander away from the ordinary and take a look at some of the special applications for which casework is used. In particular we'll discuss casework for computer and audio/visual (A/V) applications, and we'll take a look at some special storage considerations for clothing and small kitchen appliances.

COMPUTERS AND AUDIO/VISUAL

Since the first stereos, televisions and home computers were sold, there's been a constant struggle to store them in the home so that the components are convenient, but not in the way. Heck, remember console televisions? The whole idea was to build the television (and sometimes the stereo) into an attractive piece of furniture.

Beyond the physical presence of the components, there are issues of connecting the pieces (wire management) without running cables all over the place. Additionally, there is the concern of keeping the components cool during operation.

We're going to look at computers and A/V equipment simultaneously. While there are some different requirements between the two categories, there are many more similarities.

What I want to focus on here is the special hardware and accessories that can be built into your cabinetry to maximize space and performance.

A television is most commonly a standalone component, although today's setups often include a cable or satellite decoder box and a DVD player, and will often also be hooked into a sound system. While you may have a stand-alone stereo receiver, you need speakers to make it work and it's likely

There are still plenty of televisions out there that need to tuck into a storage space. While that's good for storage, it's not so good for viewing. That's when a turntable makes sense. This slide/turntable allows the television to pull forward and rotate to present the best viewing aspect to the seating arrangement in the room. These swivels are rated for hundreds of pounds and will easily support a large unit. The pocket doors (seen tucked back into the cabinet) are another way to hide the television when it's not in use, and special hardware keeps the doors from interfering with the view while you're watching.

While the two photos at left are an obvious marketing ploy, they're effective. The photo on the left shows a tangled mess of wires that are not only confusing, but likely to become tangled and disconnected. One wire management solution is shown above on the right, channeling all the loose wires through a central conduit that allows access along the length of the conduit. One other problem is reaching the wires to keep them tidy. The picture above shows a pull-out mechanism that allows the components to slide out of the cabinet and then rotate to provide easy access.

that there's also at least a CD player tied in somewhere.

The multi-component requirements of A/V systems are similar to those with a computer. There is usually a central processing unit (CPU), printer, keyboard and monitor that all work together. Some newer computers have combined the CPU and monitor, but a printer and keyboard are still separate components.

The trick with A/V or computer components is making them easy to use, and attractive at the same time. The case piece shown on the preceding page is a good example of storing all of your computer needs in an accessible cabinet, but still having the option of simply shutting the doors to hide all the components quickly and easily.

Flat-panel screens on both televisions and computers have changed the storage needs in a positive way for both types of systems. While most stereo and computer components measure a reasonable 12" to 15" in depth, the monitor of tube-style television can require 20" of depth, dramatically affecting the appearance of a storage unit.

Designing cabinetry around components is a topic in its own. So I'll just say that making sure you have adequate space (for now and the future) is a critical first step in storing A/V and computer components. One accessory that's available for televisions

is a slide/swivel unit that makes storage convenient while still making viewing user-friendly. And while most televisions these days are flat screens, the swivel unit is still useful.

Once you've addressed the location and organization of your components, it's time to tackle the wiring. This can be a huge mess – one that you'd probably prefer to do once and never have to tackle again. Unfortunately that's not usually how we work. There's always a reason to replace or relocate a component, and that means pulling a cabinet away from a wall, crawling behind it and disconnecting everything (and hoping you remember where everything goes).

Managing the wires and cabling so that it's organized is good for appearance, but even more important because it doesn't take much to accidentally disconnect a wire when shifting components. There are a number of different wire-management systems available, but most are flexible plastic conduits that corral the wires in a single tube, as shown on the previous page. Some of these conduits are left to hang free, while others are mounted to the cabinet to more efficiently direct the wiring.

That's half the battle, but you still have to get to the back of the components to make changes. One of the most convenient options we've seen is a pull-out mechanism

While an enclosed cabinet provides a clean look, it makes it difficult to manage wires and to allow proper ventilation. Shown here are a few products to keep things cool and organized while not affecting the look of your cabinetry too much. At top left are a couple of wire grommets. Holes are cut in the top or side surfaces of your cabinets and the grommets slip into the hole. While the round grommets take up less space, they are often too small to handle larger computer cable connectors. That's what the oval grommet is for. Also shown are a couple of ventilation grommets that are installed the same manner as the wire grommets. They allow air to circulate in the cabinetry while offering a "finished" exterior.

that slides the components into the room and then swivels to make access a snap (this device is shown on the previous page).

Wire conduit connects the components when they're close together, but there are lots of situations where components aren't near each other. The printer for your computer may need to be on a separate shelf or compartment and that means running cable through the cabinet sides, top or shelves. Cable grommets are a tidy way to dress up the wiring holes in your cabinet. While the hole is still there, the grommet helps blend the hole with the cabinet and even allows the larger connector on the end of the cord to pass through, but can then be

closed to allow an opening large enough for just the cord itself. Neat.

Other useful grommets include those for ventilation. Whether it's a computer or a stereo system, the components heat up, and not only when they're running. To keep things cool, air needs to be able to circulate inside the cabinet. Cutting ventilation holes in the cabinet back or sides is one ventilation method and there are grommets to help "dress up" these holes as well.

There are also small ventilator fans that can be mounted in cabinet sides to not only allow air to circulate, but to create air movement to quickly dissipate the heat. All of these options will extend the life of your expensive components.

That takes care of the components, but we still need to store the discs. Whether on DVD or CD, your movies, music and software can take up a fair amount of space in your cabinets. Storage options can be as simple as a set of shallow shelves at the sides of a main cabinet, or as complicated as drawers designed with a variety of manufactured inserts to perfectly fit your discs.

Shown below is an option that provides hidden storage while still offering maximum capacity and convenience. The drawer is built to open to the side rather than the top, and is built into a storage unit. Manufactured inserts keep the discs separated and in place.

When preparing storage for any medium, remember to measure the discs and cases as appropriate. While there are standard sizes, DVD movie "collections" and compact disc anthologies can throw all of your careful storage plans right out the window.

CLOTHING STORAGE

While closets aren't exactly casework, the specialty accessories designed to improve closet space can be incorporated into custom cabinetry serving as clothes storage. In fact, many newer homes incorporate walk-in closets that just beg for custom storage and organization. How can you say no?

We've come a long way from a bar for storing clothes stretched between two walls in an alcove. Today's storage makes allowances for hanging or folded clothes, and even hanging clothes can be made more readily accessible with pull-out storage bars to make it easy to find what you're looking for.

Media storage is another big part of keeping things organized and tidy. Whether it's your collection of compact discs or your DVDs, there are dozens of inserts for vertical or horizontal storage of all these music and video formats. The inserts shown here are built into a drawer at chest height. When the drawer is pulled open, it's easy to view and access the discs you want.

From wire racks to cedar-lined rolling shelves, your folded clothes will be better maintained and easier to select. And closet-component designers haven't forgotten your shoes and ties. There are lots of available ways to store these items.

All of these accessories are designed to improve convenience and access – and they do. But it won't take long for the price of the accessories to quickly add up to the amount of money you spent on the cabinetry itself. And as you consider the many ways in which to arrange the interior of your closet, you'll find that you're designing the space to match the accessory sizes, which may or may not be the most space efficient.

As a woodworker you have the option of buying these niceties ready to install, or you can make your own roll-out shelves for the price of a piece of edged plywood and a pair of drawer slides. It becomes a balance of convenience and expense. And, as with all things custom, being able to make your own closet fixtures gives you the flexibility to design the interior to perfectly fit your needs and space.

It may be smarter for you to take a look at the accessories available, decide what will work for the storage design you have in mind, then supplement the plan by building the other units that aren't available. This blend of commercial and custom should allow you to maximize space – and money.

KITCHEN MAGIC

Twenty-five years ago when I built my first custom kitchen, the importance was in providing the correct balance of drawers, shelving and open space to best accommodate the homeowner's needs. Today's kitchens include commercially available accessories that make a kitchen cabinet a shining example of efficiency. Many of these items can be built-in as part of the original kitchen. But most can also be added years later. So don't despair if you've got an older kitchen. That complete remodel you've been considering may only need to be a rehab.

Upgrading most kitchens is about maximizing storage. Because of the layout of many kitchens there are dead spaces that aren't accessible, or just haven't been properly divided to allow access. That's what all these cool accessories are about.

Let's start with the pantry. Most pantries are a tall, skinny open-shelving arrangement.

Shown above are just some of the available accessories for upgrading and organizing a closet space. The items shown are from KV (knapeandvogt.com) and include a pull-out clothes rod (left) that allows easy access to hanging clothes in a small space, some pull-out storage baskets for shoes (center) and even a small laundry hamper (right). It's simple to mix and match the accessory items to accommodate the space and needs in your home.

You can stuff a whole lot of bottles, cans and boxes onto a shelf. The problem is, you can't find what you've stored without taking everything out again. Even the most obsessive-compulsive storage system will leave items stored at the back of the shelf. There are a number of pantry-organization accessories that allow you to incorporate pull-out shelves, or entire rack systems that let you swing out the shelving to maximize organization and accessibility.

And while we're talking about inaccessible areas in the kitchen, the corner dead space is one of my least favorites. Lazy-Susan storage has been around for a number of

The pantry system shown at left is the Cadillac of storage. The swinging and nesting shelving allows you to access small items quickly, but still benefit from the full-depth storage of the cabinet. There are similar wire rack systems available, but I wanted to give you this image because if you're ambitious, you can make it yourself!

A vertical storage rack allows easy access to just the item you need, but still maximizes storage space.

many ways to maximize and organize your kitchen drawers.

The items stored in kitchens range in size from toothpicks to blenders. In general, people tend to store same-sized items in the same area. Pots and pans are a good example. Most kitchens have some type of inefficient nesting arrangement where the largest skillet is on the bottom of the stack. If you're really organized, all the lids are stored in the same area as the pots. Because these cooking items are designed to hold food, they're essentially empty storage units themselves, making them bulky and awkward to store without take up an awful lot of valuable space. Storing "flat" items on their side takes up less space and also leaves the items easily accessible without having to unstack and restack. This not only applies to pots and pans, but dishes and cooking sheets as well. Think vertical.

As for appliances, there's a tricky balance between storing mixers, blenders and other bulky items efficiently, but still

years. But the opportunities for maximizing use of this problematic space continue to expand.

Drawers are usually the best way to store items in a kitchen. They allow convenient access to the back of the storage space and handle small items fairly well. But when it comes to small items, organization can quickly change a junk drawer into a spice drawer. Below are just three of the

Cookware can be tricky to store efficiently and even more tricky to access conveniently. Rack systems such as that shown at the left store items vertically, allowing good use of space and easy access. Other items that are difficult to store include mixers. Once stored it can be a hassle to get out and then you have to find counter space to use it. The mechanism shown here allows you to easily raise the mixer (or other appliance) out of its storage space on a simple lift. When at the maximum height, it locks in place and serves as a sturdy work surface.

You can do dozens of things to maximize drawer storage. The spice rack at left is not only space efficient, but lets you easily see the labels on all the spices. The silverware divider trays shown at center are very space friendly, offering a top layer for the most used items, with a second layer below. And bread boxes aren't "hip" anymore, but I'll bet you could use a bread drawer! Designed to keep things fresh and off the counter, it's a great idea.

leaving them accessible. The counter top is not usually the best answer, especially if you have limited counter space. Special drawer inserts and hardware provide storage options for these bulky items, that allow you to easily bring them into use, as shown in the photo on page 190.

In almost any kitchen, space for storing garbage is given up reluctantly. While you want the garbage can handy, you don't want it sitting out in the open (it's a little unsightly, even if you're the tidiest of house-keepers). Storing the garbage can behind cabinet doors has become fairly common, but it doesn't leave the can very accessible. There are literally dozens of accessories available to allow the garbage container to pull out like a large drawer for easy access. They're designed for many different-sized cans and even make allowances for separating recyclable items from plain old trash in separate bins.

And speaking of things that you'd rather keep out of sight in the kitchen, how about towels and sponges? The location for storing towels in a kitchen is a bit of a personal preference, but there are some clever towel-rack systems that keep them stored out of the way, but easily accessible. The sponge storage "drawer" is actually my favorite. Designed to utilize more "lost space" in the kitchen, the false drawer in front of your sink can now become useful storage with minimal work (shown above, right).

CABINET LIGHTING

While much casework is designed to hide the items inside, some is created to showcase the items – in which case good lighting is key.

Can lights, rope light, curio lights, halogen or incandescent – all of these are easy to build into a china cabinet or other visible piece of casework. Some simply require mounting the light fixture to the cabinet with a couple of screws. Others require cutting the fixtures into the cabinet or, in some cases designing the cabinet to build in the lighting. There are some battery-powered options, but I don't strongly recommend them. There are likely too many batteries to replace in your house already, and the light is harder to control.

Most cabinet lighting fixtures are considered ambiance lighting and provide just enough illumination to accent the pieces

The waste container at left rests inside what is essentially an inverted drawer box, with the drawer slides mounted out of sight. The box mounts to the cabinet door, making it a drawer front. For recycling concerns, other units offer separated containers. The unit on the right is mounted on a pull-out rack for stability.

These are two of my favorite kitchen-storage accessories. At left is a towel rack that is mounted to what is essentially a single drawer slide mounted inside the cabinet. Open the door and pull out the rack when you need it. Tuck it back in when you're done. The tip-out storage unit shown at right takes dead space and the false drawer front mounted at the sink and turns both into a functional storage area for sponges, soap and any other sink items that are a little less than picturesque. Very cool.

stored in the cabinetry. Some of the lighting styles are so unobtrusive that until they're turned on, it's not obvious they're there.

As mentioned, some of the fixtures require a little pre-planning for the best results. Can lights (that shine down on the interior) are usually cut into the top of the cabinet with the majority of the light mechanism stored outside the cabinet. Other lighting fixtures with a similar effect are often called puck lights (they look a lot like a hockey puck) and are designed to mount to the inside surface of the cabinet.

While can lights are less visible from the inside, they require something to mask the components on the outside of the case – such as crown moulding around the cabinet top.

Rope lighting throws a very pleasant light on its subject and can be adjusted for length to perfectly fit the needs of custom cabinetry, but it isn't very attractive to look at. In most cases it's a good idea to plan on building channels into the cabinet for the rope lights. The channels will allow the light to shine on the preferred objects, but hide the lights themselves from view.

The image above shows the difference between an inset-lighting fixture and a surface-mount fixture. Both require a hole through the cabinet, but surface-mount lights don't protrude through the cabinet as some inset-lighting fixtures do.

Above is a great example of the effect a little lighting can have on a cabinet. The lights shown in this case are inset mount incandescent lights.

Rope lighting also gets used in cabinetry to provide accent lighting in the room. By adding rope lighting above wall-hung kitchen cabinetry, a soft glow is thrown on the ceiling and walls, providing nice accent lighting.

Undermount lighting is a lighting concept, but it's also a phrase used to commonly refer to self-contained lighting fixtures that are mounted under kitchen wall cabinets. The fixtures are larger and are designed to mount to a cabinet surface. They're used primarily as task lighting for shadowed or difficult-to-light areas such as the sink or counter. The light fixtures themselves can be multi-bulb halogen or incandescent lights, or fluorescent fixtures. While rope lighting could also be used for this application, the light from undermount fixtures is designed to be brighter and can be directed down on the work surface, rather than splashing across a large area.

Every lighting fixture will offer slightly different effects in your cabinetry. But I guarantee that a piece of furniture designed to display items is much more effective and dramatic when a little light shines on the subject.

CONCLUSION

As I mentioned early in the chapter, the specialty items shown throughout the chapter are only a small selection of the accessories that are now available to upgrade, specialize and customize your custom casework.

But all of these special accessories are only icing on the cake. The information provided throughout this series will allow you to build sturdy and beautiful casework for every room in your house. Don't be afraid to experiment and have fun along the way.

At right is a section of rope light. It's a lot like holiday decoration lights encased in a plastic tube. These lights provide soft, even illumination of their subjects.

Even when planning ahead isn't an option (such as when you're upgrading a kitchen), attractive and beneficial undermount lighting can be added to cabinetry without looking clunky. The three-fixture halogen unit shown here mounts below the upper cabinet and provides bright but unobtrusive lighting to a commonly used area.

Sources

Of the dozens of items discussed in this chapter, these are but a fraction of the specialty items available to customize your cabinetry. We've listed five sources below that carry most of the storage and lighting items discussed in this article (and they provided the pictures), as well as hundreds of other items that may work for your cabinetry needs.

Lee Valley: 800-871-8158 or leevalley.com
Rockler Hardware: 800-279-4441 or rockler.com
Woodcraft: 800-225-1153 or woodcraft.com
Woodworker's Hardware: 800-383-0130 or wwhardware.com
Woodworker's Supply: 800-645-9292 or woodworker.com

A Better Way to Work

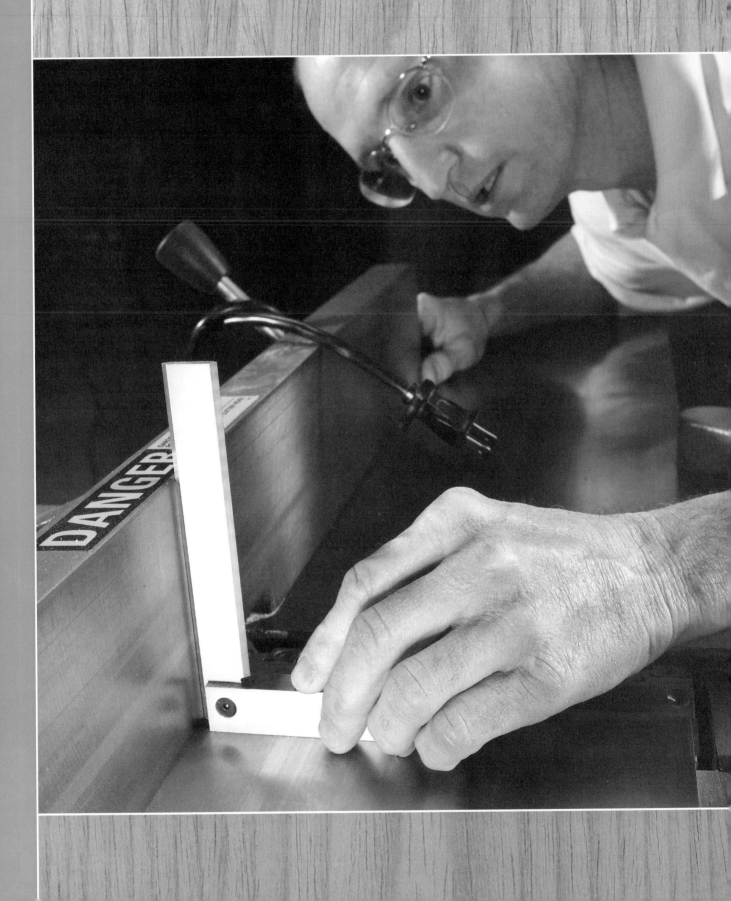

Learn the Skills to be Safe

by Marc Adams

Controlling your stock in a safe manner will also improve your confidence and the accuracy of your results. By learning a few simple rules to work by, you won't be cut by your machinery.

I can't tell you how many times I've introduced myself as a woodworker and had the first response be, "Let me see your fingers."

Why has our craft become known for being so dangerous? Why is woodworking considered as hazardous by those who don't do it? Why do certain professionals such as musicians, surgeons and NFL quarterbacks stay completely away from woodworking? Why is it that tool manufacturers don't help promote safety better – especially because they bear the brunt of liability issues? Or better yet, why don't they require some kind of user-competency test before you can purchase their products?

Why has the SawStop met with so much resistance from manufacturers when the technology is so great? What is the real reason that school systems across America have eliminated woodworking classes from the curriculum? Why do some of the most comprehensive books on woodworking not even mention safety? Is safety just not an important issue or is it taboo?

The answer to each of these questions is, simply, "risk." Safety has always been an issue of defense instead of offense. The corporate world would rather address the issue when it becomes an issue. As a craftsman and educator I choose to take a contemporary approach to safety education: Be aggressive instead of passive.

In my experience, safety is a "skill." That's right; safety is a skill, a fundamental in technique, just like cutting a dovetail. It does not occur through happenstance or luck; it happens through planning, understanding and proper execution, just like the "fit" of a tight dovetail joint.

Most accidents occur because of improper techniques, bad habits, haste, fatigue, inexperience and overconfidence. It's hard to teach an old dog new tricks, but a few simple adjustments in the way you work at each machine, coupled with a few rules about control and exposure, along with understanding that you and the tool both have limitations, can make woodworking enjoyable for years to come.

BEFORE MACHINES RULED THE SHOP

In great-grandpa's days, before the Industrial Revolution, woodworkers rarely got hurt in the woodshop. That's right, serious accidents didn't happen when the user provided the power. You're thinking, "Now wait – I've always been told that a chisel is a very dangerous tool." But that's only the case when it is being used or stored improperly. Yes, hand tools have risks – but those risks are minimal in comparison to power tools.

Woodworking changed the day that tools started to rotate under their own power. This rotation and excess power caused unbelievable risks to the user. Old-world craftsmanship had to change; a new generation of woodworking had to be developed with many new and unforeseen challenges.

The Occupational Safety and Health Act (OSHA) was enacted in 1971. The purpose of this law was to ensure safe and healthful conditions in the workplace. This act of Congress caused manufacturers, employers and all high school, college and vocational programs to re-think the entire process of hazards in the shop. Their focus on woodshop safety shifted to more on guarding and less on the attention to sound fundamental procedures to using all equipment safely. Although OSHA requirements work well to protect us in the workplace, they have no effect on how we work in our private shops, and I believe this has added to the complacency of safety.

The purpose of this section is to explore safety for today's woodworker, explore how specific stationary tools work and why they can bite, kick, throw, grab and pinch – and what we can do to minimize these actions through control and preparedness. Before operating any power tool you must become thoroughly familiar with the way it works and the correct procedures to follow. As you learn to use a machine the correct way, you will also be learning to use it the safe way.

SET THE STAGE FOR SAFETY

It's not a bad idea to start off with a look at general shop safety. I remember in my old high-school shop class the instructor said that you should always remove your rings and watches before you use any power equipment. It's a great rule, but if your hand is so close to something that your ring or watch are going to catch and pull you in then you've already put yourself at risk. I remember the safety speech in high school about keeping your fingers away from the blades on the jointer because they can cut you. What? That was my entire safety lesson! I also remember bits of the other common-sense rules that included: dress properly, watch your hair (not

Machines offer awesome power, but they also ask something of you. You have to know when certain operations become unsafe, such as when your stock becomes too thin to pass through a standard planer.

a problem for me today), keep the shop clean, no horseplay, don't carry screws or nails in your mouth, unplug the machine before you make any adjustments and so on. Great common-sense rules, but we need more.

When it came to the technique side of how to use stationary tools, everything was according to the textbook, but it wasn't enough. We were never taught the theory of the machine, the actions of the machine and the results of those actions. We never learned anything about where the control points were to maintain safe handling at and through the point of contact, nor did we learn the best ways to minimize exposure. This is the perfect place to begin safety in today's shop.

LEARN THIS WORD: CONTROL

All woodworking machines operate by rotating or reciprocating motion, or by a combination of these motions. Each machine is engineered to provide control that counters the actions taking place – especially at the point of contact. There are three concerns for control at each machine: the direction of the rotating/reciprocating cutter, the position of the wood at the point of contact, and the execution of the movement of wood through the process.

A well-designed machine uses control to counter the kicking and grabbing forces that naturally take place with rotating/reciprocating cutters and provides the user with a clear range of motion through the entire process. For example, a power miter saw does a great job using control to its advantage. The motion of the blade rotates away

Miter saws offer good control points. The spinning blade pushes the stock down and against the fence during the cut.

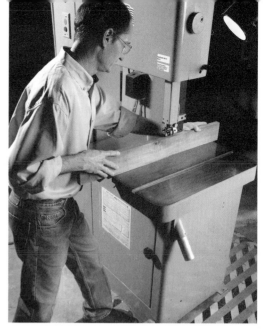

Band saws also offer excellent control points. The rotating blade pushes the stock against the control of the table, which eliminates the problem of the work kicking toward the operator – as long as the work is supported by the table.

from the operator toward the fence, which causes the blade to actually push the wood, while being cut, against the control of the fence. At the same time the motion of bringing the blade down into the wood forces the wood down to the control of the table. The point of operation on a power miter box is at the bed and the fence. Because the wood is held stationary during the cutting process, it makes control easy to manage, unlike a table saw. Another great way to describe control is by examining the cut that takes place on a band saw. As the blade rotates downward toward the table, all the force behind the blade is pushing the wood directly on the table. As long as the wood is flatly supported on the band saw table, at the point of contact, there will be no kicking or grabbing because the control is the table at the point of the cut.

Control can also be added to machines by the guarding, hold-down devices, fences, fingerboards, push sticks and other devices. Machine control and ways to create additional control will be discussed with each individual machine throughout this section. But remember this: No cut should ever be made without the use of the control surfaces.

LIMIT YOUR EXPOSURE

I like to give two meanings to the word "exposure." The first is obvious: How much cutter are you presenting at the point of contact? For example: How high should the blade be above the thickness of a board when using a table saw? I've lectured at trade shows for nearly 20 years and still shudder at how irresponsible "pitch men" selling blades

and saw accessories can be. No guards, no splitter, blades as high as they go.

Face it, we live in a world where "guards removed for clarity" is an acceptable way to work in the shop. That's just wrong. There is no advantage to seeing the actual cut take place when it causes the user to be at risk. We know what wood looks like when it's cut. When it comes to how much blade should be exposed, the rule is to minimize not maximize. Like the late Roger Cliffe use to say: "How high the blade should be above your work is a definition of terms, the difference between amputation and laceration."

The second type of exposure is in terms of repetitiveness. Each time you make multiple cuts or passes you put yourself at more risk. For example there is no sense in making several passes over a table saw blade to make a wide cut when you could have done it in one pass with a dado blade. As you expose yourself to extra passes or multiple moves, you expose yourself to more risk. Exposure, however, can cut both ways. I believe it is better to make two passes at $1/16$" on a jointer to remove $1/8$" of stock rather than to make one pass with an $1/8$"-deep cut. There will be less blade exposed, less kicking force and if the grain tears out on the first pass, it is easy to correct it on the second pass. This second point of exposure merely causes you to think about the safest way to approach each cut on any given machine.

THREE TYPES OF LIMITATIONS

There are three types of limitations to consider. The first two are common-sense: your physical limitations and the limitations of your shop space. Everyone has difficulties handling a sheet of plywood, jointing the edge of an 8'-long board or band sawing the corners off a large tabletop. There is nothing wrong with asking for or waiting for help to arrive. Just make sure that you and your helper work together as a team and if necessary do a dry run of the motions along with body and hand positions before the cut is performed.

Always dedicate one person to guide or direct the work while the other obeys commands – it's hard to have two people steer a car at the same time.

The second common-sense limitation is determined by the space in your shop. Small shops will require a lot of pre-planning and strategies for large or heavy wood.

The third limitation, which is definitely the most important limitation to understand, is what each machine is capable of doing or not doing. Every machine has a limit as to the size of material that it can cut or handle safely. It's important to understand that there is always an alternate way to cut, size, shape, dimension and sand wood.

Some machines have very defined limitations while others don't. We automatically know the width, depth and thickness limitations of a planer because the bed is only so wide and can be adjusted up and down only so much. When using a planer, you have to know when a board is too short or too long. You have to know the proper feed rate for the depth-of-cut. And you have to know to what thickness stock can be planed before you need to add a carrier below your stock before the knives become dangerously close to the cast iron bed of the machine.

Other machines have equal concerns. You just can't go to a jointer and safely joint a board that is only 3" long or cut a 1" cube in half on a power miter saw. One common-sense guide to the limitations of any machine is if you don't feel comfortable before making a cut, or if any safety device has to be removed or altered, then let that uncomfortable feeling be your guide. Search for another method of cut. Each tool has limits and most often those limits are not listed on the front of the machine. It is a great idea to establish some guidelines to follow, such as my 12" and 3" rule. This will easily help you determine when you are working beyond the capabilities of each machine.

THE 12" AND 3" RULE

The 12" and 3" rule should always be addressed at every machine every time you use that machine. This rule should be the Golden Rule of shop safety. No exceptions. If you are ever in doubt about the control, exposure or limitation of any machine, this rule will clarify and establish boundaries to make its use safer. Because it is a two-part rule it is best to explain each one individually.

The 12" part of this rule states that if your wood is less than 12" in length, you should pause to ask yourself if it is too short to safely run through this machine. For example, a board shorter than 12" might be too short to run through a planer, but long enough to cut on the band saw or power miter saw. The 12" rule is just a way to evaluate the risk of short lengths at each station-

It's riskier to take five small cuts with a standard-kerf saw blade when one cut with a dado stack will do the job. Unnecessary repetitive cuts expose you to more danger.

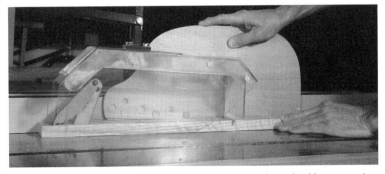

When a cut will take your hands within 3" of the machine's guard, you should use strategies (such as push sticks) that will keep your stock under control and your hands at least 3" away from the guard.

ary machine. The key to determine if 12" or shorter can safely be cut on any machine will also be dependent on the 3" rule.

The 3" rule, which is by far the more important of the two, is a boundary that you should observe: Always keep your hands at least 3" away from any guard, shield, pulley or pinch point. Let me clarify: Your hands should always be 3" away from the front, sides, top and back of any guard on any machine. Because the blade is contained within the guard or shield, that gives you a little extra distance from the cutter. Any time the cut requires your hands to be within this boundary, that's when it will be necessary to use push sticks, hold-down boards or some clever fixture to aid the cut.

Here is how the 12" and 3" rules can work together. Let's say that we have a board that we want to cut in half that is only 8" long. If you choose to cut this board at the chop saw, you can follow the 12" and 3" rules because the hand that supports the wood on the table can still easily be 3" or more away from the shield that covers the blade.

Here's another example: Let's say that we have a board that's 4" wide and we want to rip it in half. Although this cut is within the limitations of a table saw, it will place my hand or hands inside the 3" boundary of the guard. When it comes to pushing this

piece of wood through I would definitely use a push stick.

But if the piece of wood is wide enough so that my push hand can be more than 3" from the guard, I will not use a push stick when ripping on the table saw. I will explain when and when not to use push sticks later in the section. Just as a hint: When using a push stick you surrender a degree of control.

PERSONAL SAFETY

Even though your home shop isn't regulated by OSHA, it makes sense to observe the same safety rules used in industry to protect workers. Personal safety – which includes your eyes, ears, lungs and hands – is priority one.

I recommend that you always wear ANSI-approved eye wear while working in the shop. It's also good to have goggles as well as a face shield in the shop for when the chips really fly.

I recommend dust masks that are NIOSH rated for woodshop dust particulate and can be reused from day to day under normal working conditions. Replace these when they start to loosen up and no longer fit properly or when they become so used that they no longer are easy to breathe through. It's a good idea to store these overnight in a plastic bag. These "particulate respirators" are not suitable for solvents, oils, resins and finishing.

For finishing I always use a high-quality NIOSH approved mask that has charcoal cartridges that filter out toxins from finishing materials. These masks must be properly selected, based on the contaminant and its concentration level. They must be properly fitted and used in accordance with all the manufacturer's instructions.

Ear protection in the shop is important – especially with routers. Some people use the foam ear plugs and some use the ear muffs. Be aware that foam ear plugs have to be inserted properly to work and ear muffs can get awfully hot. There have been times when I have used foam plugs along with ear muffs for extra protection.

The issue of gloves is important. I definitely recommend that you wear heavy-duty rigger's gloves when handling large timber or stacking wood and when carrying heavy sheet stock such as plywood, particle board or MDF. But I would never wear gloves while using power equipment. Any saw that rotates or reciprocates can grab the glove

When you need assistance at a machine, make sure one person is in charge and the other is only following orders.

and pull you into the machine. With heavy gloves you lose tactile ability that is important. Your fingerprints have a sticky quality that's important when pushing a board forward or back.

When it comes to solvents, finishing materials and resins, a good rule is if you stick your hands in it then you should stick your hands in gloves first. Be aware that some solvents and resins affect rubber and latex gloves differently.

There are health hazards associated with working with different woods, glues and finishes. By being aware of some of these potential hazards you can better prepare yourself for their contact.

Woods

1. Trees produce resins, chemicals, bark and even antibodies to protect themselves from diseases, insects and fungi. These natural safeguards may also have a profound effect on people who come in contact with wood.

2. Be aware of allergic reactions to wood. If you develop a runny nose, watery eyes or hives, you should make a note of the type of wood that seems to bring on these symptoms. Contact your doctor and seek some advice.

3. If you experience any reaction to wood dust make sure you limit your exposure. Wear a mask.

4. Be aware of the mold and spore effects of spalted or decayed wood. Some people have severe reactions to the fungus and spores in these types of wood.

5. Do not work with (or burn) treated lumber in your shop. This wood may have been treated with creosote or arsenic. This stuff is for the outdoors.

6. Man-made or composite boards (plywood, particleboard, MDF and laminates) contain resins that can be hard to breath and can also be eye irritants. Protect yourself while using these materials.

7. Be aware that some woods contain tannic acid, which could be an irritant to some people and can cause your hands to turn temporarily black.

Resins and Glues

1. White and yellow glues, as well as hot hide glue, are usually non-toxic, and clean up easily. However, urea formaldehyde (resin glue), cyanoacrylate (Super Glue), epoxy,

Your push sticks and hold-downs should be designed so you can obey the 3" rule. These push sticks look different than traditional ones, but they offer advantages.

For dusty jobs with lots of flying debris, you should have additional equipment in your shop, including a face shield, an effective dust mask and ear plugs.

polyurethane glue and contact adhesives (laminate glue) are all poisonous, and should be handled and cleaned up with care.

2. When you use resin glues, cyanoacrylate, epoxy, polyurethane glue or contact adhesive, you should wear gloves and a dust mask. After you apply the glue, make sure you immediately clean up any spills or drips. Do not let these glues get into your eyes, nose or mouth. Each glue cleans up with a different type of solvent, so make sure you know what the solvent is and that you have some on hand when you start mixing or spreading it.

3. Always wear eye protection when you are scraping glue off the wood, floor, bench or wherever it is.

4. Cyanoacrylate (Super Glue) has a special concern – try not to glue yourself to your project. If you use this glue, keep a bottle of solvent on hand.

5. Some glues cannot be mixed on plastics or with plastics. Make sure you learn the correct procedures when gluing anything other than wood.

Finishes

1. Almost all woodworking projects need to be finished to protect and preserve the wood. Finishing materials, if used recklessly, can be dangerous.

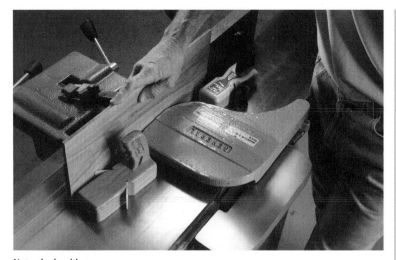

Not only should you have safety equipment in the shop, but you should use it regularly. Always perform operations in the same safe manner. Rushing or cutting corners can get you cut.

2. Pregnant women and women who are breast feeding should avoid finishing projects. Exposure may be especially dangerous during the first three months of pregnancy.

3. Correct storage and disposal of finishing products must be observed. If you are not familiar with what that means you should contact your local fire marshal.

4. Most of the finishing products for wood are made with some kind of organic solvents. Most of these chemicals attack the central nervous system, and some can damage the lungs, liver, kidneys and blood as well. They may irritate the skin, eyes, nose and throat, producing acute and chronic effects.

Be aware that some of these chemicals can cause chemical burns. Some strippers contain lye or bleaching agents such as oxalic acid. If you come in contact with these materials, immediately flush the affected part with water for at least five minutes. If the area blisters, especially if it involves the face or hands, see a doctor.

5. Make sure that you protect yourself. To prevent these adverse effects from happening while working with these chemicals, make sure you wear gloves (either rubber or latex), an apron, face shield and an organic vapor respirator.

6. When working with wood-finishing products make sure the area is well ventilated. Open the windows and create air flow that helps remove the fumes from your working environment. Wear a close-fitting air respirator with organic vapor cartridge filters (charcoal filters). And be certain to wear a face shield and rubber gloves.

7. In addition to health risks, most of the materials used to finish wood are highly flammable. Following some good housekeeping practices can help prevent your shop from burning down. Keep all finishing materials in their sealed metal containers. Store the metal containers in a fireproof cabinet. Make sure you properly dispose of rags and paper towels saturated with finishes in either a sealed metal trash can or better yet get them outside your shop and lay them out flat to dry. Do not wad any rags up when using them or after. Rags saturated with linseed oil may spontaneously ignite. Always lay your rags out flat to prevent fumes and heat from accumulating in the wrinkles. Always have a fire extinguisher nearby. Never run a heater when finishing.

8. Be careful of how you dispose of finishing chemicals. Dedicate a "satellite" container into which used solvent, paint and stain can be disposed. Check with your fire marshal to determine the best way to dispose of these chemicals. However it is possible to recycle some of the used solvents by pouring them into another container and letting the solids settle out, then re-pour the clear liquid back into another container to use it again. Mineral spirits and turpentine can be use this way. Some solvents can be poured into a shallow pan. This will allow the solvents to evaporate leaving the hard solids, which can then be put in the dumpster.

9. Always cover your workbench with cardboard or newspaper to protect it from spills. If you spill on the floor, clean it up as soon as possible.

Preparedness

Safety in woodworking is largely a matter of common sense, awareness and being prepared. Most shop accidents occur as a result of either being over confident, tired or inexperienced. When you work in your shop don't rush; nothing good can come from it. Woodworking on power equipment is primarily a mechanical process. Try to always use a machine in the same manner. Do not do it differently from time to time. If safety is a fundamental part of the routine of machining wood, then working wood will always be safer.

CHAPTER 2

Practical Safety Devices

by Marc Adams

I recently ran into an old woodworking friend of mine who had his hand all bandaged up, and the first thing he told me was: "I have new respect for my router table."

He went on to say that he was doing something that he knew was dangerous, had done it before and was sure he could get away with it again. The workpiece was definitely too short and sure enough it caught and pulled his hand into the cutter. The first thing I asked him was, "Were you using a push stick and was the guard in place?"

His head sank while his eyes looked at the top of his shoes and he uttered an embarrassed "no." He knew better and he was going to pay the price with a scar for the rest of his life. And even though his fingers were mauled and sore, he knew the accident could have been much, much worse. Throughout the years I have probably heard as many woodworking horror stories as anyone, and I have always found the explanations of what happened to start off one of two ways. Either: "I was doing something stupid," or "It was late and I had just one more cut." But I have never, ever had someone tell me that their accident happened because of a properly working guard, or because of a properly functioning safety device or apparatus, or because of proper techniques. But sometimes accidents happen because the user simply chooses the wrong machine. For example, when trying to cut a 1" x 1" block of wood in half, the power miter box would be the wrong machine; a scrollsaw or a fine hand dovetail saw would be a much better and safer choice.

Remember the 12" and 3" rule from the first chapter of this series. If the work is shorter than 12", ask yourself if that piece is too small for the capacity of the machine you have chosen. And you should always follow the 3" rule, which causes you to set a boundary limit of hand clearance of 3" or more away from any guard, shield, pulley or pinch point.

Machines used in woodworking can be dangerous, particularly when being used improperly or without proper safeguards. Often, machines are asked to do a variety of tasks. Sometimes these tasks are within the limitations of the machine and sometimes they are not. More than likely, when a machine is being asked to do something

To be safe in the shop, you need three things: guards that work, practical safety devices to assist your cuts and good rules to work by.

The clear Lexan shield on this cut-off sled is durable and does not restrict your line of sight. The block of wood at the end of the shield covers the blade at the end of the cut, making this jig quite safe.

complicated, such as cutting cove moulding on a table saw, or cutting very small pieces on the band saw, the standard guard will not work and might even make the process more dangerous.

However, it is important that you provide additional safety devices such as guarding and push sticks to establish control and to protect yourself. Guards, whether the original to the machine or homemade, play an enormous role in safety and should always be considered before any cut is made. OSHA explains guards this way: "A guard should prevent employees from contacting the dangerous parts of the machines, and it should be secure. Workers should not be able to easily bypass, remove or otherwise tamper with the guard. In protecting the worker, however, the guard must not create additional hazards, nor prevent the worker from performing the job."

Although OSHA rules do not apply to hobbyists or the one-man shop, they do set practical and reasonable standards that everyone should follow.

POINT OF OPERATION

The point of operation is the place where work is performed on the material. This is where the stock is cut, shaped, bored or formed. Most woodworking machines use a cutting or shearing action that is produced by rotation or reciprocation. These actions, when under power, are dangerous regardless of the speed, size or surface of the

moving parts. It is at this point that considerations have to be taken to guard or protect the user from accidental contact.

There are two aspects to consider when it comes to safeguarding machines at the point of operation. The first is to use some type of guard to help cover the cutter and prevent physical contact with the dangerous part of the machine. The second safeguard is to set shop standards such as the 3" rule. It is important when setting boundaries of awareness such as the 3" rule to understand when to use safety devices such as push sticks, push blocks, featherboards, combs and special aids to assist in feeding stock through the process.

TYPES OF MACHINE GUARDS

There are three types of guards that are used on woodworking machines: fixed, adjustable and self-adjusting.

Fixed guards provide a permanent barrier on a part of a machine. Usually fixed guards are used to cover pulleys and belts, cutterheads on a planer and protect the on/off switch from being accidentally activated. These types of guards require little to no maintenance and provide maximum protection.

Adjustable guards provide a barrier that may be adjusted to facilitate a variety of operations. These guards are set by the operator before the cut is made and they maintain that setting throughout the cut. There are a few downsides to adjustable guards in that they don't stop your hands from entering the danger zone and that they can also limit visibility.

Self-adjusting guards provide a barrier that moves according to the size of the stock entering the point of operation. A self-adjusting guard stays in place when the machine is at rest then adjusts for the wood while the cut is being made. These are the types of guards found on most all woodworking tools such as table saws, jointers and power miter boxes. These guards can require frequent maintenance and they can limit visibility.

Remember: An important part of woodshop safety is that you must guarantee safety for two – you and the machine. It is therefore important to understand the choices you have in deciding which guards will work best. There are three options. The first is to use the standard guards that come with the machine without any alteration. However, there are times when those guards can be cumbersome, difficult to work around or just plain in the way.

The second way to safeguard a machine is to purchase one of the great aftermarket guard systems such as the Biesemeyer, Excalibur or the Brett-guard. (I have always used the Biesemeyer table-saw guard with both the splitter and overhead shield, and have been very happy with its effectiveness on my table saws.)

The third way is to make your own guard or shield. Yes it's perfectly legal to make your own safety guard in your shop. Remember: OSHA does not regulate the individual homeowner's shop. With any homemade guard, it must be well engineered, securely fixed in position and allow safe operation of the equipment. If you have employees using this equipment, then OSHA rules apply and they require that guards be designed and installed by technically competent and qualified persons. OSHA might also require that the manufacturer of the equipment review the proposed guard design to ensure that the guard will adequately protect your employees.

MAKING GUARDS

I recommend that guards and shields be made out of the best material you have available. That might include solid wood, such as the spring-type guard and hold-down, or the wooden block to protect the user from the blades after the cut has been made that are shown on page 44. Baltic birch, MDF and particleboard are all good guarding materials except they can restrict your vision. I recommend you drill a few holes to allow a little peek into what's happening at the point of contact.

The last and probably the best material to use whenever possible is Lexan, a polycarbonate plastic made by General Electric. It is said to be 200 times stronger than Plexiglas. It is worked easily by the band saw, table saw and drill press. It is a bit expensive so I recommend that you buy it as scrap or off-fall from your local plastic dealer. Because Lexan is a polycarbonate material, it can be glued together, but I suggest that you ask your plastic dealer which adhesives he recommends. It's possible to order a two-part adhesive specially formulated for polycarbonates that is made by IPS

Corp. The product is a high-strength clear polyurethane glue called Weld-On 55.

PUSH STICKS AND OTHER SAFETY DEVICES

Push sticks are the ultimate sacrificial tool. If you have one that doesn't have at least one nick or cut in it, then you aren't using it enough. They are used on table saws, band saws, jointers, router tables and shapers to push short or narrow lengths of material through the cut. Some push from behind the work, some hold and push from the center of the work, some are very thin, some are made of plastic and some will be forfeited to make a very specific cut. They are always replaceable. Push sticks are valuable tools regardless of their shapes and sizes. However, there are specific ways to use them and

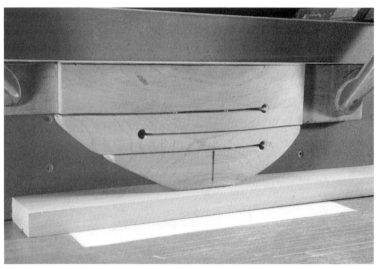

The beauty of this shop-made device is that it performs two essential functions on a router table: It holds the work down and denies your fingers access to the spinning cutters.

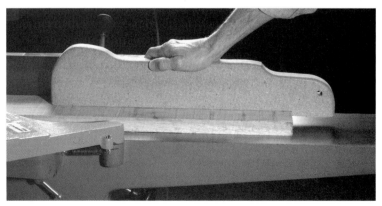

The hook at the end of this push stick protects your thumbs from a common injury on the jointer; plus, it changes the vector of the forces applied to the board to give you more control during the cut.

some push sticks are better for certain cuts than others.

It is important to understand when to and when not to use a push stick. As long as you have your hands on a board when making a cut, you will always have a great degree of control. As soon as you use a push stick, you lose a great degree of that control. I would always recommend that you choose to use your hands for pushing your work when you have more than a 3" clearance from the guard – you simply have more control.

However if your hands will be within 3" of the guard then a push stick is definitely necessary. Again, be aware that you will lose some control. Push sticks should not be used at the beginning of a cut on a long board – your hands have more control and will not be at risk. I keep my push stick handy, and when my push hand gets to that 3" limit, with one hand holding the board firmly, I let the other hand pick up the push stick and finish the cut.

There is one catch to push sticks. We've all seen the old-style push sticks – you know the kind you had in high school shop class that look a bit like a snake with an open mouth. Well, those are the ones I would use as a second choice. These types of push sticks have a pushing vector that is almost straight down at the back of the board. With too much pressure applied at the

wrong time it could cause your board to tip upward. However it is always a good idea to have a variety of different styles of push sticks available. Here are my recommendations for making a first-class push stick, which works more like a push block.

1. You can make push sticks out of any scrap material in the shop, however Baltic birch would be the best choice because it has great internal structure, is rigid and can bear a great pushing load. Particleboard and MDF would be lesser choices because they have no internal structure and can fracture easily. Still, if particleboard or MDF are all you have, they will make acceptable push sticks.

2. Never make a push stick with a handle grip (similar to a handsaw grip). Although this seems like a good idea, it can cause your hand to be trapped, and if for some reason the push stick gets grabbed or thrown, your hand will be caught and could be seriously injured.

3. Push sticks should always be thinner than the width of wood being cut. If the push stick is too wide, it will not clear between the guard and the fence. It is a good idea to make several push sticks of varying thicknesses.

4. Push sticks should be designed to hook the back of the board, however, I think it is very important to have the push stick also sit on top of the wood. This will change the vector of push from the back of the board to on top of the board and will greatly improve the amount of control. Again, it would be a good idea to have push sticks of varying lengths for different-sized work.

5. Good push sticks that sit on top of the board (such as the one for the router table pictured above) can be used both on the vertical and horizontal, which make them very handy.

6. Be aware that sometimes push sticks can slip off of your work causing a very dangerous situation. Always keep your push stick hooked firmly over the edge or side of your work.

PUSH BLOCKS

Push blocks are very similar to push sticks but they permit you to apply considerably more forward pressure throughout the cut. There are two types of push blocks. One simply sits flat on the top of the board; the other sits on top of the board but also hooks

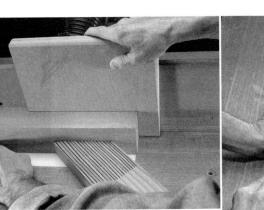

Good push sticks for the router table can be used vertically or horizontally on the table. Note how the hook helps push the work through the cut with no danger to your fingers.

The push blocks that came with your jointer are useful if you use them correctly. Don't grasp the handle as shown above left. This traps your hands. Instead, wrap your hand over the push block as shown at right. Don't forget to replace the pad's foam with a piece of sandpaper.

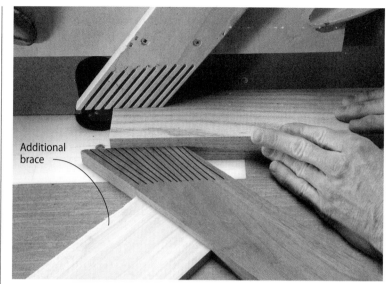

Additional brace

Here I'm employing two featherboards to keep the work under control. Note the additional brace in front of the featherboard that's flat on the router table.

over the back. One of the big struggles we all have with push blocks that don't hook over the back of the board is that they can have a tendency to slip. I recommend that you take a piece of sticky sandpaper and attach it to the bottom of your push blocks (replace the foam). This will give the push block more grip and less slip.

I think it is important to understand the correct way to use push blocks with handle-type grips because your hand can become trapped if you grab through the handle. Unfortunately, all the plastic push blocks have this type of grip. The grip also is at an angle to allow the pushing vector to force the wood to move in a specific direction. I recommend that you hold this type of push block with your fingers over the top of the handle in order to avoid being trapped. It is also important to make sure that the angle of the handle grip is forcing the work against the fence or in the direction you wish the force to be directed.

When using the table saw to cut thin stock, I prefer to use a push block that straddles the fence. This will give the push block more control.

HOLD-DOWNS AND RESTRAINTS

Featherboards, spring boards, combs, anti-kickback fingers, spreaders and magnetic hold-downs are all methods to hold the work down or against an edge. Shopmade featherboards and combs should be made out of solid wood. They are usually cut on

one end at an angle of about 45°, with slots cut in the same end to make the board somewhat flexible. These do a great job of providing side or top-down pressure with resistance to the wood being thrown backward toward the operator (similar to anti-kickback fingers). It is important that featherboards, combs and magnetic hold-downs not be placed to create side pressure behind the blade for ripping on a table saw or band saw. If one of these devices is placed toward the back of the blade it will cause a binding that could result in the start of a kickback. Sometimes featherboards are asked to hold down and push in at the same time. This can easily be accomplished in one of two ways.

The first is to simply use two feather-boards: one in the horizontal position and one in the vertical position. A second option might be to use a featherboard that is cut from thick material. It can be made like a regular featherboard with the exception that on the 45° leading edge, you cut a bevel that will help push and hold down the stock at the same time. There are sometimes challenges to overcome with clamping feather-boards to your cast-iron tables. If a simple clamping solution is not readily available, you might try placing high-strength, fiber-woven carpet tape on the down side. This will hold the featherboard to the table but will not quite give the "stay put" holding power that you can get with a screw or clamp.

USE STOPS FOR SAFELY REPRODUCING PRODUCTION CUTS

Stops for production cutting or cutting duplicate parts can be set up on just about every machine except the planer. The requirements for stops vary from machine to machine and depend on the actions that are taking place at the point of operation. Stops are most commonly used for three purposes. The first is for repetitively cutting wood to a consistent length. The second is for acting as a control during a start cut where the wood is engaged in the center of the board. The third way is to prevent wood from kicking back during operations. The resulting action of the cut will determine how the stops are to be placed and how they are to be used.

Don't use the rip fence as a stop block for crosscutting. The better way to make repetitive crosscuts on a table saw is with a sled and a double-clamped stop block.

A loose stop block will spoil your accuracy and cause you to lose control of your cut. Whenever possible, use two clamps on your stop blocks, such as this stop on my miter saw's fence.

There are very specific rules for stops. For example, using the fence on a table saw as a stop for crosscutting could be very dangerous if done improperly, while using a stop on the fence of a jointer might be perfectly fine. Because there is an infinite number of stops and ways they can be set up and used, it is better to have some simple safety guidelines to follow with their application. Keep in mind that placement of all stops might depend on whether the cut is made across the grain or with the grain.

1. Stops must be set up to create no binding whatsoever. They must not interfere with any guards or safety apparatus and should not restrict the user from safe operations.

2. Never crosscut on a table saw when using the miter gauge and fence at the same time. The cut-off work can be captured and twisted between the fence and blade and can be thrown back toward the user. This will create a dangerous kickback.

3. When stops are used, the wood captured between the stop and the blade must be held securely. For example, on a chop saw the wood between the stop and the blade must be held firm and still until the blade comes to a complete stop in the down position.

4. Be aware of the rotation of cutters, bits or blades when choosing the location of a stop. For example, whenever using stops on the drill press, you need to remember that the chuck spins in a clockwise direction so the pulling or kicking force will be in that same direction.

5. Whenever possible, stops should be double-clamped into place to prevent movement of the stop and to make sure it doesn't come loose during operations.

6. Stops must be designed so that sawdust does not build up and interfere with the accurate or safe use of the stop.

7. Stops can also be used to prevent wood from being kicked back, such as the stops used on a jointer when cutting tapered legs. These types of stops must always be tight and can be used as a way to prevent kickback when the cutter fully engages the wood.

Power Jointers

by Marc Adams

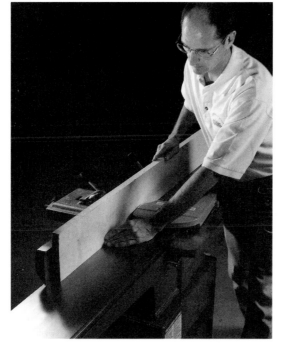

The power jointer is one of the most useful woodworking machines – but it also is one of the most dangerous. Proper procedures and guards are important.

One of the very first lessons of working wood is how to "S4S" a board – surface it on all four sides. One small caveat to the process is that the board also be flat and true after the process. There are many ways to get from point A to point B in the S4S process, but in today's shop you can bet that one of those ways will include the jointer. Edge-joining is the simplest and most common job performed on a jointer and serves both as a way to straighten edges before ripping and as a great way to remove saw marks after ripping to help create an inconspicuous glue line. But it is also an excellent machine to help flatten the face of boards in the beginning of the milling process. Jointers are terrific for removing twist, bow, cup and crook. They can also be used to cut rabbets, chamfers, tapers, spring joints and even tenons. A jointer is nothing more than a stationary version of the hand-plane, but it will do the job much faster and in most cases more accurately.

While invaluable in the shop, the jointer is also one of the most dangerous tools as well. Everyone talks about how dangerous table saws are, but if a true hour-by-hour, usage-to-accident ratio were to exist between the two machines, I bet we would find that more people are injured on jointers per hour of usage than on table saws.

Although the jointer has a guard that is fairly user-friendly, it still affords an opportunity for exposure to the cutterhead. Usually accidents occur because of one of four reasons: 1) Jointing wood that is simply too small, too thin or too short for the machine to safely cut. 2) Kickbacks due to improper control or too much cutter exposure. 3) Failure to use push sticks and other appropriate safety devices along with failure to follow the 3" and 12" rule. The jointer does provide good control surfaces (the 90° pocket between the fence and table) and as long as your stock is well supported within this control, with clear and unrestricted access, you will minimize your risks. 4) Failure to understand what can reasonably go wrong and where your hands will end up when it does.

I would also like to go on record as saying I believe that the fence system on jointers shouldn't be able to tilt or angle. Fence systems should be welded to a perfect 90°. Here's my logic: Most all fences can tilt toward the guard, presenting a "trap" point making it harder to handle stock and obscuring your view of what's taking place at the point of contact. Manipulating wood through the machine with an angled fence is difficult, and the degree of accuracy and consistency isn't that great.

One of the best woodworking lessons is learning what machines to choose for each operation. You always want to use the safest machine with the most control. In order to cut angles, bevels and chamfers you can use a jointer, table saw, router table, shaper or handplane.

Today, with all the choices in router bits, it would be much easier and safer to cut chamfers and bevels on the router table at nearly any angle. In the past 15 years at the school with more than 150 of the best woodworking instructors of modern time, we have never had an instructor use or demonstrate cuts on a jointer other than at 90°. My belief is that manufactures should make all fences at 90° and sell a sub-fence that can be attached to the fence that has the tilt feature. For those people who insist on jointing wood at angles, they could buy an aftermarket accessory fence that still allows the jointer fence to tilt.

Using the jointer can be a very safe process when you fully understand the machine, its purpose and the correct technique to safely manipulating a board throughout the cut.

JOINTER LIMITATIONS

There are several different sizes of jointers, and it never fails that the one you own will be just smaller than the width of the board that you want to joint. The size indicates the length of the knives or the width of stock that can be cut. The 6" and 8" machines are the most common sizes in today's shop. The second capacity factor is the machine's maximum depth of cut. The depth of cut is determined by the height of the infeed table relative to the cutterhead. This can range from 0 to ½" with a typical depth of cut being ¹⁄₁₆" to ⅛". Cuts deeper than ⅛" should

be made by making multiple passes over the cutterhead.

Jointers definitely have limitations on what they can safely cut; this is where most woodworkers get into trouble – not understanding those limitations. However, common sense coupled with good intuition should be your guide. Remember the 3" and 12" rule. Your hands have to be 3" from any guards, shields, pulleys or pinch points. And when your board is less than 12" in length you should take a moment of pause and evaluate if that piece of wood is too small or beyond the limits of that machine.

The jointer has several concerns that involve small, short or thin wood as well as end-grain cuts and those where you have to watch the grain direction with care. I simply set size rules that have become the law for using my jointer. Remember these sizes are at the limits of the minimum size I like to deal with – all on the small size. Obviously, all size requirements assume that the width of stock being cut is less than the blade length. In other words, if you have a 6" jointer, then your stock must be 6" wide or narrower. We will discuss ways to hold or support these small pieces later.

1. Never face joint pieces less than ⅝" in thickness. If a board is too thin, under ⅝", it can chatter when being cut, it can flex or distort under pressure, and could be more susceptible to kick-back and tip-in. It might be better to consider alterative ways to

Nearly every jointer cut occurs with the fence at 90° to the bed. So why do we as consumers insist that the fence tilt? If I had my way, I'd weld the fence at 90° and sell a sub-fence that allows angle cuts. I bet that very few people would actually use them.

The jointer's guard on North American machines is fairly friendly to the user. It swings out of the way during a cut and keeps the knives exposed to your hands to a minimum. What's important is that you use the guard and push sticks and push blocks. The guard alone is not enough.

machine thin stock, such as handplaning, sanding or using a stationary planer.

2. According to the Powermatic and Delta manuals, material that is being face jointed should be no less than 3" wide. In other words, if you are face joining narrow-width boards, under 3" in width, alternatives for cutting should be considered.

3. Never face joint or edge joint short-length boards; my rule on jointers is to avoid jointing boards under 12". However, with good safety devices and proper push sticks, which can put your hands beyond the 3" limit, it would be possible to joint boards slightly less than 12" long. Small pieces have a tendency to "tip" into the cutter, which could cause the wood to kick back and expose the user to the cutterhead. I definitely would not joint boards less than 8" in length under any circumstances.

4. Edge jointing is the most common type of cut made on a jointer and with a properly working guard can present the least amount of blade exposure. Edge jointing requires that the stock be held tight to the fence and down on the table, which will place the stock in a sound control pocket. It's possible to edge joint materials on their edges down to $\frac{1}{16}$" in thickness, as long as that thin material is rigid in nature, such as Formica. For thin stock it is important to use some type of additional holding support such as a magnetic featherboard.

5. Edge jointing can be considerably dangerous when the workpiece becomes narrow or thin. For thin and narrow stock, push sticks and hold-downs must be used, but should not be restrictive. There are no written rules about how small stock can go for edge jointing, but if you put all the above rules into effect it would give us a fair idea of what limits we should impose. Stock less than $\frac{5}{8}$" in thickness is out. Stock narrower than 3" and shorter than 12" in length will require precaution and the use of additional safety devices.

6. End-grain cuts are dangerous and usually involve short lengths. Never joint the end grain of a narrow piece of lumber – always follow the size limits listed above. When end-grain cuts are necessary on properly sized wood, I recommend that you make a small cut on one end, approximately $\frac{1}{2}$" in – avoid tipping into the cutter. Then turn the board around and make a pass in the other direction. This will help prevent tear-out along the edge of the board. In general, however, I try to avoid all end-grain jointing.

7. Try to keep each pass to $\frac{1}{16}$" to $\frac{1}{8}$" in depth. This creates an issue. In the first article of this section I mentioned "exposure." Exposure has two concerns: First is the amount of blade exposed during the cut, and the second type of exposure relates to the number of unnecessary repetitive passes. In this case, I believe that it is better to make two passes at $\frac{1}{16}$" to remove $\frac{1}{8}$" than it is to remove all $\frac{1}{8}$" in one pass.

THE WORKING PARTS OF A JOINTER

Jointers, regardless of the make, features and size, all have the same basic components. These components include a heavy metal base, an infeed and outfeed table, fence, guard and cutterhead.

On quality jointers, both the infeed and outfeed tables can be moved up or down by either a lever or hand wheel. A cutterhead typically has three or more knives and rotates at a speed of 3,500 to 4,500 revolutions per minute (rpm). The fence is used to guide the stock through the cut and to provide control at angles from 90° to 45° in both directions. The guard covers the cutterhead except for the portion that is opened during the cut.

Infeed Table

The infeed table is where you place your work to start the cut and is what I call the "push" side of the machine. It is imperative that the infeed table be flat and parallel to the cutterhead, have a positive depth-of-cut adjustment and a locking device that keeps the setting secure. The infeed table also offers the rabbeting ledge. It is the infeed table that sets the depth of cut. Although it is nice to have a long infeed table to help support the stock, there is no real advantage to having a longer infeed table than outfeed table.

Cutterhead

Cutterheads can have two, three or four straight knives (or dozens of replaceable square-shaped carbide inserts) that should be set perfectly level and at the same protruding height as each other. For the jointer to work properly the cutterhead must be parallel to both the infeed and outfeed tables. Today it is possible to upgrade the standard cutterhead with an aftermarket cutterhead.

These new heads offer quick-change blades that are absolutely accurate in their height and location relative to each other. Changing blades goes from taking hours to just minutes and does not require any set-up devices. They are affordable and fairly easy to install. Costs on a new cutterhead can run from $300 to more than $1,500, depending on if the head offers straight knives or helical knives. These upgrades are worth every penny.

In order to wear the blades uniformly, I suggest that you move the fence often to allow better wear. As a matter of fact, I recommend that you try to use your blades in three divisions. I always use the first 1" closest to the fence as the sharpest part of the blade and will use this inch only when jointing glue edges. I use the center part of the blades as the general jointing section, and use the very front edge, closest to the

guard, as the side of the blades over which I can run particleboard and plywood.

Get to Know Your Outfeed Table

The outfeed table is the most important part of the jointer and is what I call the "pull" side of the machine. If you have ever experienced a snipe or an undesirable taper in the cut, it is more than likely an outfeed table issue.

The outfeed table should be set at exactly the same height as the arc of the knives at their highest point during rotation. If the outfeed table is set too high, you won't be able to feed your stock through. If the outfeed table is set too low, you will get snipe at the end of your board. If the outfeed table is set just a few thousands of an inch higher or lower than the arc of the cutter, it can create either an undesirable taper in the cut or a slight spring in the cut (a spring cut is a situation where more wood is removed in the center of the board than on either end).

The Fence You Won't Adjust Much

Most fence systems are centered at the cutterhead and have two levers that allow the fence to adjust in two directions. One lever allows the fence to adjust in and out across the width of the blades, which determines the amount of knife exposure when cutting. The other lever allows the fence to pivot at an angle in order to cut bevels and chamfers. The fence is usually about three-quarters of the length of the overall size of the infeed and outfeed tables combined. Its placement goes halfway over the outfeed table and halfway over the infeed table. Some fences are designed to be both parallel with the infeed and outfeed tables or set at a skew angle to the blades to create more of a shear action when cutting gnarly woods.

The main purpose of the fence is to help control the stock when being fed through the point of contact, however the fence does serve different purposes when face jointing versus edge jointing stock. When face jointing (making the face of a board flat) the fence provides no bearing to the quality of squareness of cut and is used for control only – it doesn't matter if the fence is perpendicular to the table. However, when making edge joints the fence provides both control and a way to ensure that the edge is square. The best place to check for square between the fence and the table is just

When I bring a jointer into the shop at the school, the first thing I do is remove the stock cutterhead and add a Terminus cutterhead, which makes changing knives a simple process instead of a chore (visit terminus-stl.com).

Many new jointers are equipped with sweet carbide-insert knives, as shown here. These last longer than standard steel blades. You get four fresh edges on each insert. For some woodworkers, that can be a lifetime of work.

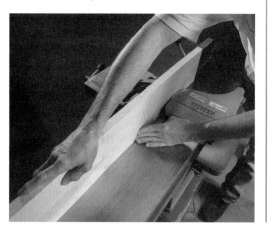

I'm surprised by how many people don't pull their work across the cutterhead from the outfeed table. Keeping the stock under control on the outfeed side of the table is absolutely key to getting straight stock.

beyond the blades, right at the edge of the outfeed table.

On Guards

American guards are quite different than European guards but both work well and should only be removed when rabbeting, which I don't recommend. (European jointers don't have the rabbeting ledge.) The American style of guard (sometimes called a "pork chop") swings from the outside of the jointer toward the fence and is typically spring loaded.

The European guard is set just above the thickness of the wood and stays over the blades at all times. During the cut you adjust the height of the guard so that the wood will fit under it during machining. Make sure either style of guard is working properly before using your jointer.

THE TECHNIQUE

Because the jointer has two common cutting actions, edge jointing and face jointing, it is important to understand that each action will require a little different handling technique. These techniques can also change according to the length and weight of the material being cut.

One important technique is that you never hook your finger or thumb to the back edge of any board at any time. If the board were to kick back it would break your thumb, and if the board for some reason drops into the cutterhead at the end of the pass, you could get seriously injured. Also, as long as your hands are beyond the 3" rule, I would not recommend push sticks. I know that is not what you are taught, but I firmly believe that you have more control with your hands than you do with push sticks. I would never use my hands to push wood through a jointer when they will be at risk – under the 3" rule. That is when I would definitely use some kind of push stick or safety device.

UNDERSTANDING PUSH AND PULL

It is important to define the difference between "push" and "pull" on a jointer. Of course, cuts should always start on the infeed or push side of the jointer.

When your hands are in a position to push wood into the cutterhead they are always at risk. If by accident they were to

Many woodworkers hook their thumb over the end of the board during face-jointing, even with thin material. And they are putting themselves seriously at risk. Use a push stick, as shown at left, which will stand in for your precious digits.

slip off the board, more than likely they will fall in a forward direction, with force, directly into the cutterhead and result in a serious injury. This is the dangerous side of the cut; it also happens to be the kickback side of the machine.

Because the board on the infeed or push side has yet to reach the point of contact, it is more than likely not square and could even still be rough, bowed, warped or cupped. Because these conditions more than likely will exist on the board on the push side (at the beginning of a cut) it really doesn't make any difference how square the fence is on this side (jointer fences are typically warped and not square along their entire lengths). On the infeed side of the cut the fence is almost always used more as a control surface than a squaring surface. This is why it is not necessary to check that the fence is perfectly square at the very front when edge jointing. The best place to check that your fence is square to the table is closer to the point of contact or just after the point of contact.

The outfeed, or pull, side of a jointer is by far the most important and critical to the accuracy of the cut and is the safer side of the machine. When your hands are in a position to pull wood on the other side of the cutterhead they will always be at less risk. If by accident they were to slip off the board, because they are beyond the blade, they will fall forward – away from the blades resulting in no injury. I teach students to get their hands to the outfeed side of the machine as soon as possible and learn how to "pull" your board through the process.

Once a board reaches the point of contact and the cut has occurred, from that point on as long as the board is maintained in a controlled position it will stay flat and tight to all control surfaces (both the table

Note how my feet are positioned so I can step forward in an easy and natural manner with my work if necessary.

This is the wrong way to stand at the jointer. My mobility is greatly limited and I can trip myself.

and fence). In other words, focus on technique and hand placement are most important once the cut takes place and then after. This is why the focus on pull is more important; it helps you to maintain the stock tight in the control pocket after the board has been machined. If you push a board concentrating on hand placement at the infeed side, your cuts will never be as accurate because the board itself is not accurate at this point.

BETTER EDGE JOINTING

Always stand to the left of the machine on the infeed side. Your feet should be parallel with the machine in order to allow you to take a step or two forward if necessary. Never stand flat-footed facing the machine. Always put the flat face of the stock against the fence when jointing.

It is important to understand that using a jointer accurately and safely is all about good technique. Good jointer skill begins by understanding the three actions/motions that have to take place to edge joint a board. First the board has to be held down to the table. Second it has to be held tight against the fence. And third it has to be pushed and

pulled forward. This is where 95 percent of all bad technique occurs. Three actions – two hands, the math just isn't quite right. The best way to solve that problem is to dedicate hands. Have one hand be the "hold-in hand" against the fence. Designate the other hand as the pushing/pulling and hold-down hand. I use my right hand as the push/pull and hold-down hand, and my left hand as the hold-in-to-the-fence hand.

I grip the board with my right hand (as long as it is within safe size limits) at the halfway point – never at the end. Remember, do not hook your finger or thumb over the edge at the back of the board. This becomes the push/pull hand and keeps the board down against the table. This hand will be responsible for as much of the forward motion as possible. It is perfectly fine that this hand stay on the board throughout the entire cut as long as it maintains the 3" rule.

I try to position this hand and my body to make one motion from start to finish without having to re-grab or reposition. If the board is long enough that you have to re-grab or reposition, I always make sure that the repositioning happens on the pull or outfeed side of the jointer.

Remember: The best-jointed edge happens when the motion is continuous. If you must re-grab to complete the cut, try to do it as smoothly as possible – it will be necessary in this case to have the left hand continue to pull the wood until you can get your right hand back into position – both hands should be on the pull side of the jointer at this time. This is also the reason that your feet should be facing parallel to the machine so that you can step forward with the board throughout the motion.

The left hand or the hold-in hand is what keeps the stock supported against the fence and can provide a little push/pull and hold-down when necessary. There is definitely a correct way to position this hand and it must go to the outfeed table as soon as possible in the process. Most people place their left hand with the fingers facing down. This is absolutely wrong and dangerous. In this case your fingers are facing down toward the table and if you slip off they will more than likely fall into the cutterhead.

Instead, I place my fingers facing the fence with my thumb completely off the work. Because my main vector of force is not toward the table with my fingers, they can't

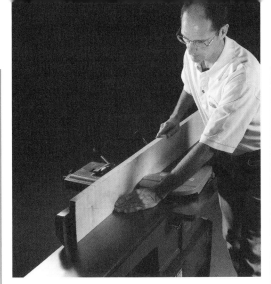

Each hand has a job. My left hand's job is to push the work against the fence. My right hand's job is to move the work forward and down.

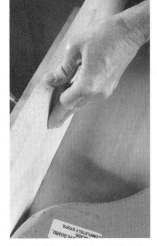

If you hold your left hand like this (above) and you slip, there's a chance your hand will drop into the cutterhead. Don't do it.

With your fingers positioned like this (at right), the force is directed at the fence and your hand is much less likely to slip downward toward its doom.

slip down. If there is a need for downward force, I'll just move my thumb to the top edge of the board. This puts my hand in a position that is less likely to slip off the stock.

The function the left hand serves is very important to the quality of the cut and should stay close to the point of contact, but not violate the 3" rule. I start with this hand on the infeed side to help get the stock into the control pocket. Once the stock is just beyond the cutterhead, I move this hand just beyond the guard and place it on the outfeed table and position it just like a featherboard.

This hand now focuses on keeping the board tight to the fence and the hold-down force now becomes the total responsibility of the right hand.

EDGE JOINTING SMALL STOCK

When jointing stock that is still within the size limitation of the machine, but small in size, it will be vital that safety devices be used. I prefer to use magnetic feather-boards and push sticks that hook over the back but still allow me to position my hand at the center of the stock. If the stock is long enough (but too thin or narrow) I set the push stick on the back side of the fence so it is ready to pick up once my hands have pushed the board to the point where the 3" rule will be violated. I pick up the push stick then to finish out the cut.

FACE JOINTING

Face jointing is where the entire face of the board makes contact with the blades. This contact can remove cup, warp and twist

from one face of the board. The fence in this case is used only for control and does not need to be perfectly square to the table. Remember wood under ⅝" thick is too thin to face joint. Hand position for this cut is different than edge cutting. Both the right and left hand perform the same task. They are both used to hold the wood down to the table and push/pull the wood forward and through the cutterhead. Consistent speed and uniform pressure make face jointing a little safer than edge jointing. Remember: As the board passes beyond the cutterhead there will be a great deal of blade exposure before the guard can spring back closed. It is fine to pass your hands over the cutterhead as long as you are using safety devices.

I never place my hands directly on the wood – regardless of the thickness. I always use a paddle grip in my front hand, which will be my left hand. The back hand, which will be my right hand, uses a push block that grips the back of the wood, but allows my hand to be over the wood.

As far as the paddle grip goes, I always replace the foam on the machine's push pads with sticky sandpaper to give it better grip. I never hook my hands into the handle grip. If the stock were to kick back and pull the push pad, my hand would be trapped. I always place my hand on top of the handle, but not in the handle.

Miter Saws

by Marc Adams

Power miter saws, for the most part, are saws of our generation. They were first introduced to the hobbyist market in the mid-1970s but really took off in the 1980s. They have become so popular that they have all but replaced the radial-arm saw.

Power miter saws are about the handiest of all power saws because they are:
- portable
- easy to set up
- relatively inexpensive
- very accurate
- available in a variety of sizes (both in blade size and horsepower).

Above all, miter saws have a high degree of precision, consistency and repeatability; you can shave off just a little bit until you get the perfect cut. And when used properly can be very safe.

One of the greatest attributes of power miter saws is that not only do they do a great job making perfect 90° cuts, they also can make angle and compound cuts up to 45° to either side of the blade. Most saws have built-in brakes that help stop the blade after the trigger is released. And there are specific miter saws with specific blades (and techniques) that can cut through most anything, including plastic, metal, paper products, composites, stone, solid-surface materials and, of course, flesh and bone.

THE LIMITATIONS OF MITER SAWS

There are some things that miter saws can't do. They can't rip wood or crosscut wide boards. Besides these obvious limitations, they are not made for dado blades or moulding heads and cannot (or should not) make special surface cuts, such as flutes, reeds, tapers, rabbets or tenons. Power miter saws also cannot make horizontal cuts such as rotary planing, shaping or sanding.

So the million-dollar question is: Why have these simple machines all but eliminated the definitely more versatile radial-arm saw? The easy answer is accuracy. The practical answer is safety. I started on a radial-arm saw and have routed, shaped, ripped, turned and drilled on that machine, and fortunately I never got hurt – but not a one of those operations was safe or very effective.

There are other machines in today's workshop that simply do a better job for each of those specific tasks. And when you get right down to it, most people simply use radial-arm saws for crosscutting only.

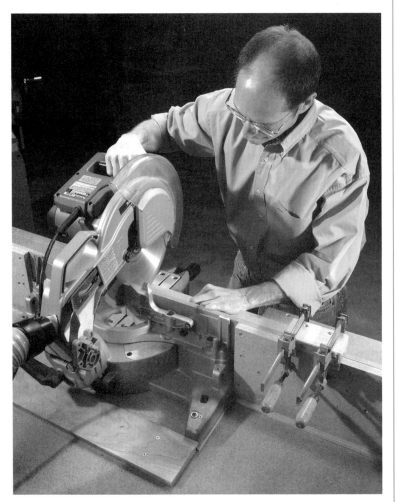

When properly set up and used, the power miter saw is an accurate and safe machine.

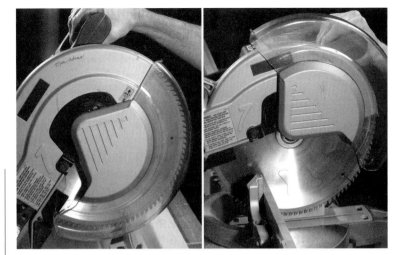

The motion of the blade lurching forward when cutting, the lack of accuracy in the finished cut and the cumbersome size of the machine, along with alignment and control issues, have made the radial-arm saw a dinosaur in today's woodworking shop. Today, clearly the saw of choice for crosscuts and mitering is the power miter saw.

Because power miter saws weren't around when most of us took high-school shop class, the majority of woodworkers were never taught the correct and safe way to use this unimposing machine. It's a saw that should demand as much respect as any other stationary power tool in the shop. Through a better understanding of the actions that take place when using this machine, along with safe and sound rules, this saw should perform perfectly every time.

FACTORS TO CONSIDER

This saw often goes by the nickname "chop saw." The word "chop" reminds me of words like "hack" and "split" and "slash." It also makes me think of a "fast" action to cut one board into two boards, which unfortunately can add to haste. I agree that there are jobs when simply cutting one board into two boards, without regard to accuracy, is necessary. But swiftness should never take precedence over technique. Whenever I make a cut on a power miter saw, whether it's of the highest degree of accuracy or simply cutting a board to a more manageable size, I use the same cutting technique with total and absolute regard to safety.

Most power miter saws have a small degree of runout, which is a bit of wobble in the arbor. If you are one of those people who keeps changing blades in hopes of finding that perfect cut, be aware it's more than likely not in the performance of the blade – it's runout from the saw.

Here's a test. Unplug your saw, firmly grab the blade and try to move it side to side.

More than likely you will feel a little "play" or "slop." Most saws have runout, which is why I prefer to use a 10" power miter saw for all my fine, highly accurate cuts and my 12" saw for general cutting. (This of course assumes that the width of wood is within the limits of the cutting depth of the saw.)

An 8" or 10" blade will distribute this wobble over a lesser diameter than a 12" blade, which in turn creates a finer and cleaner cut. Unfortunately, I have no solutions on how to eliminate a mechanical problem with your saw. Just be aware that most power miter saws do have this characteristic.

Also remember that a fast action when cutting will always create a sloppy cut, and cuts that are too slow will burnish or burn the wood. Take your time during the cutting process and let the blade cut at its pace – not yours. The same blade will cut differently through wet wood versus dry wood and dense wood versus softwood and so on. You must compensate by learning to listen and feel how a blade reacts to the material it is cutting.

COMPOUND CUTS COMPOUND THE SAFETY ISSUE

Today almost all power miter saws offer the "compound" feature. With compound miter saws, the motor not only pivots left and right but it also can be tilted to either side to make beveled cuts. This feature is great for projects that require cuts to take place in two planes, such as a box with corners that are mitered and tapered or cutting crown moulding, which adds to the versatility of the machine.

Since power miter saw manufacturers added the compound-cutting feature, the guards have had to expose the user to the blade more. Note how much blade is evident as the motor carriage is pulled down. It goes from fully covered (left) to fairly exposed (right).

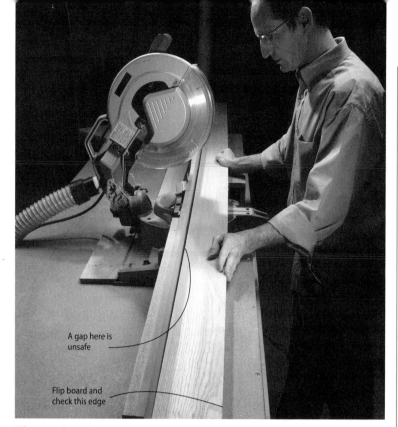

A gap here is unsafe

Flip board and check this edge

When you place a piece of stock against the fence of the power miter saw, always put the straightest edge against the fence. If the stock is rough, make sure that the board contacts the fence for a distance that is equal to the length of the saw's built-in fence on one side of the blade. Shown is a board that should be flipped over.

This pivoting of the motor, however, has caused the engineers to reconfigure the tool's guarding system. The old guard on a power miter saw was a simple yet effective shield that enclosed the blade at all times. The user always had the plastic shield between his or her hands and the blade. But when manufacturers added the pivot feature, which allows for compound cuts, the guard system had to be completely re-engineered. This new guard is much less effective than its predecessor, but it is the only solution to offering some type of protection on a saw that moves in multiple planes.

Today, it makes no difference if you are making square, angled or compound cuts. The guard on all power compound miter saws exhibits a lot of blade exposure during any cutting procedure. As a user of these types of saws, you must be aware of this potentially dangerous exposure and how it affects the process of using this machine.

My best guess is that most hobbyist woodworkers, cabinetmakers and furniture makers make square or angled cuts more than 98 percent of the time when using power miter saws. That means that less than 2 percent of the cuts will actually involve the "compound" feature. Now that we know that the guards on these machines are designed to accommodate the compound feature, and knowing that it creates more

blade exposure, that would mean that 98 percent of the time, (under normal cutting circumstances) you are at more risk from blade exposure due to a guard that is designed for less than 2 percent of the cuts you will make. That's not a very fair trade for general safety usage.

The other issue that goes along with compound saws is that you now have to keep a vigil on both the X and Y axes of a compound cut – unlike on a regular miter saw where the Y axis is permanently set.

The compound feature can also spoil your accuracy with straight cuts. You should always be careful when carrying or lifting these compound machines by the motor because it can change the stop settings for the compound feature.

At times it might be convenient to make multiple cuts at the same time by stacking lumber. This can safely be done by making sure that all the boards are tight against the fence and, if different in size, stacked from the largest on the bottom to the smallest on the top. Be aware that there will always be some risk of inconsistencies in the size of each piece as well as accuracy of the angle of the cut. If your saw is slightly out of perpendicular it will cause the board on top to be different than the board on the bottom. When accuracy matters I would never stack-cut.

HOW TO ADD ACCURACY AND SAFETY

Lumber with bows, twists, cups or warps can be especially challenging to cut on a miter saw. Remember: There are rules for keeping your stock under control. If your wood has a bow or an edge that is not straight, it is very important that the board be situated so that the flattest or straightest part of the board is at the point of contact with the blade. This will prevent pinching. Never make any cut unless the material is secured on the table and against the fence (see the photo above).

Be aware that boards with edges that are not true will more than likely not produce perfect 90° cuts. The miter saw performs best when cutting boards with straight edges along the saw's built-in fence system. If your board has cup or twist, it might help to shim under the high points to keep the board from rocking while the blade is pushing through the wood. This will also help to prevent the blade from getting pinched in the work.

Stops are an important part of using miter saws, and I recommend that they be placed to the side opposite to the motor side or opposite where the handle and trigger are located. An accurate stop should always be double clamped to triangulate pressure and to ensure that the stop will stay in place.

It is a good idea to design your stop so that dust will not interfere with the cutting accuracy. I do this by setting my stop about the thickness of a penny above the saw table. And most importantly, always support or hold the piece between the blade and the stop as long as it allows you to follow the 3" rule (which states that your hands should always be at least 3" from any tool's guard). Always make sure the blade has completely stopped in the down position before it is raised back up – especially when stops are being used. If the blade is still rotating as it comes back up through the wood that's trapped between the blade and the stop, it could lift the trapped wood, ruin the blade, possibly damage the wood and more than likely knock your stop out of place.

Power miter saws can be used with either hand running the trigger. These machines are ambidextrous. It is very important that you never cross your arms when making any cut. There is nothing wrong with positioning yourself to use your left hand on the trigger or positioning yourself to use your right hand on the trigger. As a matter of fact, several brands have a dual trigger switch that adapt for both right- and left-handed people.

Because all guards are made out of some type of plastic, it can be hard to get a clear and undistorted view of the blade when aligning the cut. Some manufacturers place slots in the front edge of the guard, which is designed to give a clear, straight-on view of the blade for easy alignment.

MAKE A DISPOSABLE FENCE

One of the best ways to enhance the accuracy and quality of a cut on a miter saw is to add a disposable/sacrificial sub-fence. This sub-fence can do three things to help enhance the performance of the cut. First, it will help eliminate all potential kickbacks (with proper cutting techniques).

Second, it will help eliminate tear-out on the back edge of the board. And third,

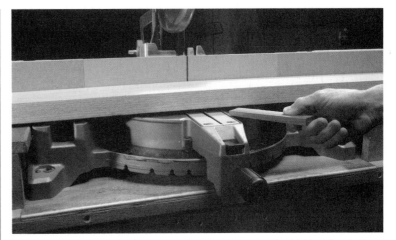
If a rough board won't sit flat on the table of your miter saw, you should shim it from below to prevent it from rocking during the cut.

once the sub-fence is cut, it will identify exactly where the right- and left-hand sides of the blade are. This helps setup and locates board placement for very accurate cuts. It will eliminate guessing where the blade will cut; you now will know exactly where the blade will be.

Here is what I do to make my saws perform better. I use a scrap piece of ½"-thick MDF or particleboard that is at least as long as the two fences on the saw and as tall as possible while still allowing the motor/handle to be drawn completely down into the tool's cutting pocket. I use exterior-grade carpet tape to hold the sub-fence in place. Once a cut has been made through this

Some blade guards get dusty or distort the location of the spinning blade. I prefer guards that have open slots so you can get a clear picture of where the blade is.

Here is a proper setup for a good crosscut. Note that my stop has two clamps, which ensures it will stay put if the work gets kicked about.

sub-fence, it is ready to go. Remember: This fence is disposable. I suggest that when you change angles on the saw that you dispose of the existing fence and put on a new one. Imagine how easily this new fence will help you to align those 45° cuts. It is also possible to place a sub-table on your saw if you are experiencing tear-out on the bottom of your boards.

MITER SAW LIMITATIONS

Miter saws are not commonly used or recommended for ripping lumber. They do, however, do a perfect job at crosscutting in a range of 90°. Unfortunately these saws do have limitations. The user must always be aware of all three dimensions – length, width and thickness.

The length limitation can be considered at both the long and short ends of the scale. In terms of long, you will be limited only by your physical surroundings. In terms of short, you must follow the 3" rule. It is possible to safely cut wood down to 4" inches in length as long as your holding hand is 3" away from the guard. If your work is shorter than 4" and your holding hand is closer than 3" to the guard, then it will be necessary to use some type of hold-down or safety device to keep the wood from moving during the cut.

The width limitation is where most problems occur with miter saws in terms of limitations, and if you are using a sub-fence it will even reduce the potential depth of cut. Obviously the larger the blade the larger the width of cut, but most 12" saws will cut through a 2 x 8 at 90° with a little room to spare. As the miter changes from perpendicular, so will the limits of the cut.

There are a few ways to get more width from your saw. Both ways have some risk. The first is to simply lift the edge of the board once the cut has been bottomed out. With the blade still rotating and in the down position, the leading edge of the board can be lifted slightly to present the board being cut to more of the diameter of the blade. This might give you an extra ½" of cut, but it will also cause you to forfeit a fair amount of control.

The second way is to take advantage of the diameter of the blade by raising the table to capitalize on the diameter. This is a safer method than the first method because it keeps the board stable during the cut.

The thickness limitation is again affected by the blade size. Generally speaking, most 10" saws will cut through 2½"-thick wood and 12" inch saws will cut through 3½"-thick wood. However you will find that if you are

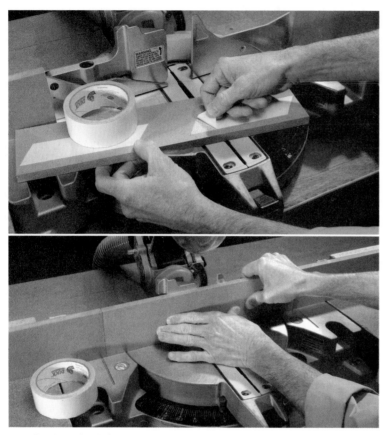

I install replaceable sub-fences on my miter saw to control tear-out and increase my accuracy. Here I'm installing one with exterior-grade carpet tape (top). Then I simply press it into place (bottom).

With the sub-fence installed, I'll make a straight cut into it (left). Now I know exactly where my saw will cut when crosscutting my stock. I simply line up the mark on my board with the kerf in the sub-fence (right).

If you need to cut a board shorter than 4″ long, one safe solution is to use a second block that is notched out to hold your work in place.

Sometimes we need to squeeze out a little more crosscut capacity from our power miter saws. One strategy is to lift the work into the spinning sawblade (left), a technique I do not recommend. The safer way to do this is to place your work on a thick piece of scrap, giving your work access to the larger diameter part of your blade (below).

cutting very thin stock it might be best to support or place under the piece a sacrificial board to prevent small stock from shattering or tearing out.

IMPORTANT SAFETY STEPS: THE PROCESS

The following is how I teach students to accurately and safely use a power miter box. If you follow these steps and make them a part of the cutting process, then your cuts will always be accurate, you will prevent unnecessary wear to your saw and you will be safe.

1. Wear protective personal safety gear for your eyes, ears and lungs. Make sure all loose clothing is secured and away from any action that could pull it in – no gloves. Always stay alert.

2. Keep the guards in place and in working order. Make sure there are no chips or cut-offs in the guard housing.

3. Use proper blades that are sharp and well maintained. Make sure that all moving parts on the saw are free and clear. Maintain a regular maintenance schedule and read the important user information in the owner's manual.

4. Never cross your arms. When cutting either right- or left-hand angles, always position yourself to the obtuse side of the machine, which will allow you to pull the blade handle away from your body. Make sure there is nothing in the path of the blade that you don't want to cut (cords, a push stick, off-fall, fingers and so on). Never overreach, and always make sure your footing is secure.

5. Always follow the 12″ and 3″ rules (discussed in Chapter 1 of this section, "Learn the Skills to be Safe") and be mindful of your control surfaces. Never cut freehand or cut wood without using the fence or the table as your control surfaces.

6. Always start the saw in the uppermost position. Let the motor run up to full speed before bringing the blade into contact, and never force the blade during the cut. Use a controlled and consistent motion. Never start the saw with the blade against the workpiece.

7. Once the cut has been made, keep the blade down and in the pocket, and then let off the trigger. Make sure the blade comes to a full stop before lifting the blade up. This is by far the most important safety issue with running a power miter saw. Force yourself to develop this habit. It will eliminate almost all hazards with this machine.

8. Never attempt to remove small pieces while the blade is coming to a stop in the pocket. Never stick your hand in the

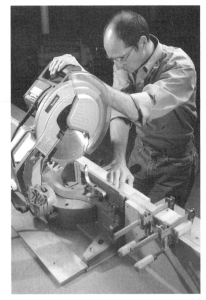

Here's one of the most important rules for a miter saw: Never cross your arms when working with the tool as shown above. An accident is almost inevitable.

guard or around the blade. Never reach around the saw. If it is necessary to touch the blade or the inside of the guard housing, or to reach around the saw, unplug the saw first.

9. When the workpiece is too large or too small, make sure you use appropriate

clamping or hold-down devices. All work must be supported either on its face or edge.

10. Always position your body to give you the best view and the safest grip. Remember: The machine is ambidextrous, either hand can be used to run the trigger and grip of the tool.

11. Do not become distracted; concentrate on the process of the cut and the action that is taking place.

12. Make sure that the table's locking mechanism (if the machine has one) is tightened and secured before you make any cut.

13. At all times, you should use either a good vacuum system or the dust-collection system that came with ⸴he machine.

14. If you are using a stop-block for production cutting, make sure that you hold or clamp the workpiece between the blade and the stop-block. It's this piece that can bind between the blade and stop if it moves. Keep a firm grip on this piece until the blade stops. And don't forget to use two clamps on your stop-block, which will keep the stop in place if your work kicks.

15. There is no substitute for common sense. Remember that these are only general guidelines and that you should stop using your saw at any sign of abnormality.

When the table of the miter saw is angled, never stand in the acute part of the angle (shown above). This forces you to put your hands closer to the blade. Instead, position yourself so you are in the obtuse part of the angle (right).

I always double-clamp my stop to keep it in place in case my work gets kicked by the saw. The coins (removed after clamping) raise the stop to help with dust removal.

Band Saws

by Marc Adams

The band saw can be used for straight cuts of course, but it's also handy for cutting cabriole legs, dovetails, mortise and tenons and much more.

I once toured a very large custom cabinet-making shop and noticed that they had no band saws. When I asked the owner what his reason was for not having one of these saws, he responded by saying, "Band saws are for curves, and when we need to cut a curved line we use either a scroll saw or a saber saw." I was shocked to think that a multi-million dollar manufacturer of wooden products did not have one of the most valuable and versatile tools in the shop.

As a matter of fact, I have since toured many production and home shops that do not have band saws either. How can that be? I think the band saw is one of the most versatile woodworking tools. Yes, it can cut curves and irregular lines, but that is just the beginning. Band saws can be used to cut thick materials, re-saw lumber, make compound cuts such as those used for creating cabriole legs, reproduce or make duplicate parts with a high degree of accuracy, cut a variety of joints including dovetails and mortise and tenons, cut circles, square notches, make angled cuts, and of course they can cut any type of a straight line – both with a fence and freehand.

The band saw gets its name because the blade that cuts the stock is a narrow steel strip where the ends have been welded together to form a continuous band. It is usually not the first machine purchased by the home woodworker, but it can be one of the most useful machines in the shop. Band saws are not typically used in the final milling process to make boards square or S4S (surfaced on four sides) but they can be wonderful tools to help cut rough lumber to length and width before starting the milling process.

They are sold in a variety of sizes. I have heard over the years that the size of a band saw is determined by the wheel diameter or the distance from the blade to the throat. This measurement is the limiting factor on how wide wood can be cut to the left of the blade. Most home-shop band saws are 10" to 14" in size. However, this measurement or size limitation is only one part of the equation. The other consideration when determining the size of a band saw is the depth of cut it can make.

The depth of cut on a band saw is determined by the overall distance from the table to the guides when they are at their highest point. Generally, the larger the machine the more powerful it will be and the more capacity it will have. Bigger machines can typically accommodate larger-width blades which could be desirable for certain applications of re-sawing. All saws should be able to handle narrow blades.

The size of the table is usually not a consideration when buying a band saw, but the larger the table, the more support and control the saw will afford. Today, some manufacturers such as Powermatic offer extension tables that fill the void between the left side of the table and the upper arm. The size of the table will determine how much it can tilt to both the right and left of the blade. Most band saws can tilt 45° to the right and about 10° to the left.

The purpose of this chapter is not about how to select blades or whether or not to de-tension them when not in use. It is not about how to align the wheels or discuss the difference between bearing guides or cool blocks. Nor is it about the techniques of how to re-saw lumber, cut cabriole legs or how to make and use the variety of jigs and fixtures that make fancy cuts. There are a lot of good articles and books that have already been written on those topics.

The purpose of this chapter is to explain the proper and safe techniques for using this saw. For the purpose of proceeding, from this point on we will assume that the mechanical function of the saw such as blade tracking and blade tension, as well as the adjustment of the guides, are all in proper working order and adjusted correctly.

Band saws are quite easy to use and fairly safe, as long as you understand two basic fundamentals of the machine: the action of the cut and how to plan the cut.

CUTTING ACTION

Band saws do not create a kicking or throwing motion toward the operator. Instead they have pinch points. Because the cutting action of the blade is created by a downward motion, all cutting forces are directed toward the table. This all but eliminates kickback toward the operator. It can, however, pull the stock, especially small offcuts, through the throat plate toward the bottom guides. This in turn could possibly break the blade, damage the throat plate, wreck the guides and throw off the tracking, any of which could create risk to both the machine and operator.

So what should you do with all those small offcuts? It is tempting to tap them away with another piece of wood or with your fingers. However, this would put your hands within the 3" rule – which is in violation of safety rule number 1. These small offcuts cause no harm until you put them in motion. More than likely, the next piece of wood to be cut will push those small pieces out of the way. When the last cut is complete, wait for the blade to come to a complete stop before removing any offcuts next to the blade.

It is also important to know that the blade on a band saw will only cut on the front edge and not the sides or back. Since the sides and back have no teeth, wood that comes in contact with these parts of the blade will not be cut or pulled in any direction. Even if the sides or back of the blade do cause some kind of force to the stock, it will be minimal and more than likely not cause any risk. This is where some confusion comes in with the guides. The guides do not act as guards. Remember, the guides keep in close proximity to the side and back of the

If you have to make a sculptural cut that will result in wood that's not flat to the table, be aware of pinch points, and plan the cut to minimize this problem.

blade, yet they leave the business side of the blade totally exposed.

In order for a band saw blade to cut, the stock must be pushed or pulled into the descending teeth on the blade's front edge. Band saw blades will not cut stock that is idle. The cutting action requires that the stock be placed in motion toward the rotating teeth. With stock sitting flat and supported on the table, it is fine to "let go" of the stock to reposition your hands while cutting. Once you stop pushing, the cut at the point of contact stops. This safety feature allows the operator to always be in control of the cutting action/motion.

It is not recommended to do sculptural work, round or unsupported freehand cutting on the band saw without providing some type of control under the work. For example, round stock at the point of contact is unsupported, which in turn can cause the stock to start to spin and be pulled into the blade. I recommend that a V-block be used to support all round stock to prevent this from happening.

Although it is not advisable to do sculptural work on a band saw, there are considerations that must be taken into account when doing this type of cut. It is important to set your work on the table to create the least amount of angle or "tip" between the stock, the blade and the table. When cutting wood that is "tipped" off the table, the support is gone and the blade will want to grab the wood and slam it toward the table. This pulling will be sudden and can create a major pinch point. If you ever make this unadvisable type of cut, set your work so that the angle of the pinch point is minimized.

PLANNING THE CUT

Usually, the correct cutting position for operating a band saw is to face the blade. However, you can operate it by standing to the right-hand side or the back of the saw if it places you in a better position to see and control the work. (Be aware that if the blade breaks and is thrown from the saw, it has a tendency to whip to the right-hand side as you face the band saw.) Make sure you keep a well balanced stance. Think about your body position at the starting point of the cut as well as at the finish point of the cut to avoid overreaching.

Before the saw is turned on, the upper guides have to be adjusted for the height

When cutting round stock, the initial point of contact between the blade and workpiece is unsupported. Exercise caution, as your stock may start to spin and be pulled into the blade.

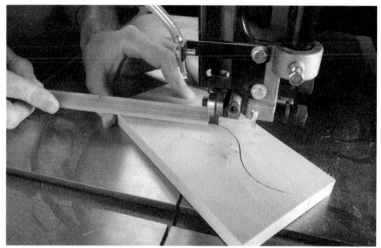

If you need to back the blade out a of curved cut, turn off the machine and wait for the blade to come to a complete stop. Then, use a stick of wood to steady the blade as you pull the workpiece out along the kerf.

of the wood being cut. A good rule is to set the guide about ¼" above the top edge of the stock. Keep in mind that the upper and lower guides are not guards, but are guides. The function of these guides is to support the blade and to help it run true. They also keep the blade from drifting and deflecting during the cut.

Two things are basic to properly functioning guides: feed rate and the amount of pressure applied to the stock as it is pushed into the cutting path of the blade. Both feed and pressure will depend on the kind and thickness of wood, and the size of the blade and speed that it is traveling. If the feed is too fast, the saw blade will chatter and squeak as the back of the blade is pushed against the ball-bearing blade support at the back of the guide. If the stock is fed too slowly into the blade, it could cause burning. Pushing too hard with one hand or the other could cause the blade to be pushed sideways, resulting in wear on the side guide system. This could cause the blade

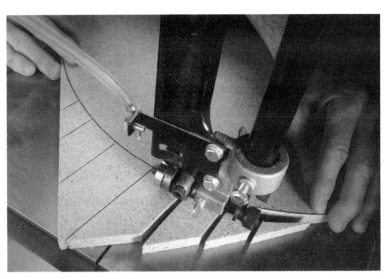

If you're cutting an inside radius, make the initial cut at the drill press or mortise machine before moving to the band saw.

On outside radius cuts, it's a good idea to first make a series of relief cuts in the waste area of your workpiece.

to dull or break and will more than likely result in an uneven cut.

When the work is so large or heavy that it causes you to pay more attention to supporting it than cutting it, an extra hand or support system would be a good idea. Always let the machine build up to full speed before starting.

Before you cut wood it will be important to think about the path of the cut. Some pieces will swing in such a way that they will not clear the main upper arm support. Without a plan, you might find yourself in a position where backing out of the cut might be necessary.

There are a few simple rules for backing out of cuts: It's OK to back out of straight cuts but not OK to back out of curved cuts. When backing out of short, straight cuts, the blade remains unaffected in the cut path and the stock has little chance of catching the back of the blade. But when trying to back out of a curved cut, the stock can catch the back of the blade and pull it off the wheels. If you find that you need to back out of a curved cut, simply shut the machine off and use a stick to steady the motionless blade while you remove the stock. If your project requires that cuts be made from two sides, always make the shortest cuts first. This will make backing out easier. Whenever possible, it is better to cut through the waste rather than backing out.

Cutting inside corners that are either radiused or rounded can best be accomplished by pre-cutting on either the drill

press or the mortise machine. This is an especially handy idea when you have tight radii or need a high degree of accuracy. When cutting outside radii it would be a good idea to make relief cuts to help keep the back of the blade from binding in the kerf. These relief cuts allow waste stock to fall away as you are cutting to provide more room for the blade to turn.

HAND PLACEMENT

One interesting fact about the band saw is that cuts are usually made freehand, by good old hand-eye coordination. Making accurate cuts depends on the tension and tracking of the blade along with good feed direction. The basic cutting rule is to keep the blade on the line that you have drawn. Most woodworkers push wood into the blade when making cuts on a band saw. This seems to be the natural and usual way to cut either curved or straight lines. However, I teach students that sometimes it is better to cut by "pulling" the wood into the blade by positioning their hands to the outfeed or back side of the blade as soon as possible. Make sure to allow for the 3" rule. If you watch the hand position of professional scroll saw craftspersons, you will see that they have a tendency to place their hands to the back of the blade. This gives them better control, allows for better sight of the line and, most importantly, keeps their hands away from the front of the blade.

Remember: The back of the blade does not have teeth so if by accident your hands were to somehow slip or contact the blade, nothing would happen. If you keep your hands on the infeed side of the cut, if you slip, your hands could fall directly into the blade side with the teeth.

Whenever I resaw, I place both hands to the pull side as soon as possible and try to avoid using my thumb as a hook on the end of the board. Sometimes when resawing if there is a lot of stress in the board, the last few inches of wood could pop open suddenly and if your thumb is hooked on the back it will immediately continue, with force, into the front of the blade resulting in a serious injury.

There are no real guards on the band saw other than the guard that prevents undue blade exposure. This guard is usually well above the guide system. It's important that you establish a boundary of 3" around this guide/guard system and make it a rule that your hand not encroach this area. If you're cutting very small or short pieces, use double-stick tape to adhere them to a larger board that places your hands beyond the boundary. Never flick away small pieces with your hands; I've had several people over the years tell me they got cut on their band saw by inconsequential hand movement.

Another rule about hand placement is that when you are pushing wood from the front side of the blade, the farther away your hands are from the blade, the better leverage you will have to turn and make corrections. It seems natural to place your hands as close to the blade as possible to gain control of the cut, however, I believe you have better control with your hands farther away. Try this for yourself. Take a large piece of scrap plywood (at least 24" x 24") and draw a curvy line down the center. If you keep your hands close to the blade, just beyond the 3" limit, you will find it difficult to control the turning motion of the cut. Now place your hands at the back edge of the board and notice the gain in control. I recommend that you either learn to pull wood through the cut by placing your hands to the back of the blade, or that you position your hands as far away from the blade as possible to gain leverage.

IMPORTANT SAFETY STEPS – THE PROCESS

The following is how I teach students to accurately and safely use a band saw. There are so many situations that we simply can not cover in this chapter. All of these rules will apply in most situations. The key is to learn good common sense. If you follow these steps and make them a part of the sawing process, then the "skill" of using a band saw will always be accurate and be safer for the user.

1. Wear protective personal safety gear. Remember your eyes, ears and lungs. Make sure all loose clothing is secured and away from any action that could pull it in – no gloves. Always stay alert.

2. Keep the guards and guides in place and in working order. Make sure there are no chips or offcuts that could affect the performance of either. Make sure the upper and lower wheel guard doors are closed tightly before turning on the saw.

When resawing, try to move your hands to the other side of the blade as soon as possible – and avoid using your thumb as a hook.

The only "guard" at the band saw is the one that moves up and down to minimize blade exposure. Make sure you follow the 3" rule around this guard and the guide blocks.

To cut small pieces at the band saw, first secure them with double-stick tape to a larger board that allows room to hold the work safely throughout the cut.

3. Use proper blades that are sharp and well maintained. Be aware of proper blade tension, tracking and alignment. Use the correct blade for the type of cut being made. The narrower the blade, the sharper the curve it will cut. Wider blades should be used for larger curves and re-sawing.

4. Make sure that all moving parts are free and clear. Maintain a regular maintenance schedule and read the important user information in the owner's manual.

5. Since the main guard on a band saw is used to prevent excess blade exposure and is located above the guide systems, it will be very important to establish a boundary limit of 3" from that blade that your hands will not enter.

6. The upper guide system should be set to approximately ¼" or less above the height of the work surface. If the guide is too high, the blade will not have the proper support and that could cause the blade to twist.

7. Be aware that the right-hand side of the saw is where broken blades have a tendency to travel. Keep bystanders away from this area.

8. Always keep your fingers and hands away from the path of the blade. Avoid using your thumb(s) to hook behind your work to push the work forward.

9. Always use push sticks, featherboards or any other necessary safety device when cutting small or short stock, or as a way to gain control. Remember that double-stick tape is a great way to hold small parts to larger, more manageable materials.

10. Do not attempt to cut stock that does not have a flat bottom surface (such as round stock) unless a suitable support is used or your work is clamped to a sound surface of some sort. Always remember that the table is your control surface.

11. Hold the material firmly and feed it into the blade at a moderate speed – never force the cut. Allow the machine to come to full speed before making any cut. If the motor starts to slow down and drag, you are feeding the stock too fast.

12. As a general rule, it is OK to back out of short straight cuts. Turn off the machine if the work is to be backed out of curved cuts. It is a good idea to make release or relief cuts before cutting long curves. Without relief cuts, the blade could become pinched in the work; this will dull or break the blade.

13. If the blade breaks, shut the machine off and stand clear until the machine comes to a complete stop. Unplug the machine and wait for the motor to stop rotating before you open the doors.

14. Keep a balanced stance while using the machine. It is possible to move from the front of the saw to the back to pull your work through, because there are no kickback forces. It is recommended that you get help if your workpiece is too large for one person to safely handle.

15. Never try to pick up or push away small offcuts that are next to the blade. Because there is no kickback hazard, learn to leave these pieces alone. If they are in the way, shut off the machine and wait until the blade comes to a complete stop before removing any such piece.

16. Do not overfeed or force your stock into the blade. It can reduce blade life and cause blade breakage.

17. When cutting with the table at an angle, be sure to block or clamp the workpiece to prevent it or the offcut from falling off the table.

18. Give the work your undivided attention. Make sure you shut the machine off when you are finished. Never leave a running band saw unattended.

Thickness Planers

by Marc Adams

The planer is the most unassuming machine in the shop. Simply set the depth of cut and the machine does all the rest. All you have to do is put the wood in and let the machine take over. The cutterhead and all other moving parts are well guarded, there is plenty of control surface for safe operation and the machine limitations are well defined. So what would be the reason to discuss safety of such a simple and unpretentious machine? I believe that if an accident were to occur on a planer, it quite possibly would be the worst accident that can happen on any woodworking machine in the shop. Think of it: The planer pulls the wood into the cutterhead with unforgiving power. Imagine if it were your clothing or – heaven forbid – your hand.

Though planers seem simple and safe, there are some serious operational and safety issues to consider. Follow these rules and your work will be better and you won't get hurt.

Because the machine does all the work, it is easy for the user to daydream or lose focus, especially when running lots of lumber. And most often accidents occur because the operator isn't paying attention. Because the cutterhead, infeed and outfeed rollers do not have a quick braking system, the machine would still continue to run and pull towards the cutterhead – even as it slows down after the stop button has been engaged. Not to mention that planers generate kickback, have tremendous pinch points, make terrible noise and generate a huge amount of dust. All of a sudden, this unassuming machine becomes one of great concern.

The basic function of the thickness planer is to smooth rough stock or to reduce the thickness of any piece of wood. The planer will not correct or straighten warped stock because the pressure of the infeed roller will press the warp out of the board as it passes into the cutterhead. As soon as the board passes beyond the outfeed roller, the board will resume its warped shape.

Most planers cut from the top and are built rugged enough to take the shock and stress of cutting wide, rough lumber. The size of the planer is determined by the knives or the widest stock it can surface.

Most of today's small shop planers have a cutting width of between 12" to 20" and can handle wood up to 6" thick. Depending on the size of the motor and the type of stock being machined, it is recommended that a typical pass be less than ⅛" in depth of cut, with the average cut being around 1/16". Some machines have limiting bars that restrict the depth of cut from pass to pass. But there are those monster machines that can take off up to ½" depth of cut at each pass. There are also planers that are designed to do moulding operations, straight-line ripping and even planers that convert into jointers. No matter what kind of planer you have, the rules of safety for the machine will be the same.

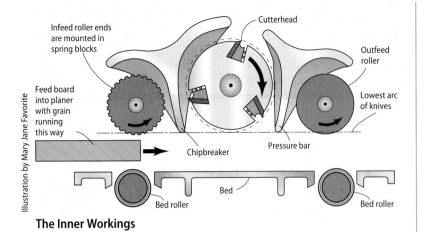

Infeed roller ends are mounted in spring blocks

Cutterhead

Outfeed roller

Feed board into planer with grain running this way

Lowest arc of knives

Chipbreaker

Pressure bar

Bed roller

Bed

Bed roller

Illustration by Mary Jane Favorite

The Inner Workings

Because the planer does all the work when it comes to moving and cutting the stock, the best way to understand the safe application of the machine is to understand its moving parts.

THE INFEED ROLLER

The function of the infeed roller is to push the material into the machine and it is the workhorse of the planer. It is spring-loaded, which helps hold the board against the control surface of the bed and relieves kicking forces. Infeed rollers are usually spirally corrugated to give the roller grip and add to the muscle of the pushing motion. It is important that when sending multiple boards through at the same time that they be very close to the same thickness. On high-dollar planers the infeed corrugated rollers are also segmented to allow boards of different thicknesses to be sent through at the same time. These segmented rollers can accommodate wood variances of up to $\frac{1}{4}$".

To provide proper drive, the infeed roller should be set so that the bottom of its arc is just below the arc of the cutterhead knives. Definitely read the owner's manual to get the exact recommended setting, but it will be around $\frac{1}{32}$". Remember: Both the infeed and outfeed rollers have to be parallel with both the bed of the machine and the cutterhead knives. Otherwise your work will have a tendency to skew one way or the other when it's feeding.

OUTFEED ROLLER

The outfeed roller continues to feed (pull) the wood through the machine after it leaves the infeed roller. Outfeed rollers are smooth and some are even rubber coated to

prevent damage to the surface of the wood. Because the outfeed roller is smooth it does not have nearly the muscle of the infeed roller. You may even find that you have to help pull that last bit of your board from the planer. If your boards are really having problems being pulled from the machine, either wax the bed or adjust the outfeed roller. The correct free position setting of the outfeed roller is $\frac{1}{32}$" below the arc of the cutterhead knives. Verify this by reading the owner's manual.

ANTI-KICKBACK FINGERS

Not all planers have anti-kickback fingers, but they are an important safety feature. They are out of the way and are adjusted at the factory. They operate by gravity and should be inspected frequently to make sure they are free of pitch and gum and that they move independently of each other.

CHIPBREAKER

Between the infeed roller and the cutterhead is the chipbreaker. The chipbreaker serves several important functions including: breaking chips into smaller pieces, to help avoid splintering out of the wood, helping keep thinner stock from bouncing and directing the flow of the chips out of the machine to the dust collector.

The edge of the chipbreaker is set fairly close to the knives of the cutterhead and can be adjusted up and down. Chipbreakers are usually spring-tensioned or free-floating. If the chipbreaker is set too low, it may prevent stock from feeding into the machine. If it is set too high, snipe could occur on either end of the board.

THE PRESSURE BAR

High-end planers have pressure bars located just behind the cutterhead and situated fairly close to the knives, just like the chipbreaker. The purpose of a pressure bar is to hold the material down after it passes under the cutterhead until the stock reaches the outfeed roller. It helps eliminate chatter marks.

Because most planing problems can be related to the pressure bar, some manufactures choose not to put them on their machines. Instead they move the outfeed roller a little closer to the cutterhead. If your planer has a pressure bar, it must be set at the exact depth as the arc of the cutterhead knives. If it is too high, you will get a snipe in the last bit of the board. If it is too low, the stock will not feed.

BED ROLLERS

Many planers have bed rollers. They reduce the friction of the stock on the bed as it feeds through the machine. On high-dollar planers the bed rollers can be quickly adjusted with a lever. On most middle-of-the-line planers these rollers are set at the factory.

Bed rollers can be both good and bad. If your lumber is thick, rough and twisted, the extra rollers help move the stock through the machine. However, as the stock gets thinner and is able to "flex," the bed rollers become a major problem. Here's why. If you look at the drawing on page 228, it shows the typical setting of the bed rollers. They are slightly higher than the bed. Remember that the infeed and outfeed rollers are spring-tensioned and have a tendency to "pinch" the wood to the table. It just so happens that the infeed and outfeed rollers are pretty close to the same location of the bed rollers. That means that as the stock is "pinched" between the top and bottom rollers, the stock that is directly under the cutterhead is unsupported. As each knife of the cutterhead strikes the wood it causes the thin stock to "bounce." This can cause some wood to shatter. This is why I always use a sub-table when planing thin stock.

FEED-SPEED CONTROL

The cutterhead normally operates at a fixed rate of about 3,000 to 3,600 rpm, but most planers have a quick control for changing the feed rate from rough to finish surfacing. The feed rate is affected by the speed of the infeed and outfeed rollers. The feed rate should be varied with the width of stock, the kind of wood and the desired quality of the surface of the stock after planing. Wider boards and harder woods should be fed at a slow speed, and narrower pieces of softer wood at a higher rate. Because the infeed and outfeed rollers are typically powered by the same motor as the cutterhead, when the machine is under exceptional load the rollers usually slow the feed rate as well.

BE AWARE OF PINCH POINTS

Other than the obvious pinch points such as belts, pulleys, chains and cranks, the infeed and outfeed rollers present a special kind of pinch point. Remember these

It's good practice to remove material from both faces of your work (once both faces are planed flat). To keep your board's grain direction oriented correctly, flip each board end-for-end after each pass.

rollers are spring-tensioned and have a tendency to force wood to the bed. If your hands are caught under the board when the infeed roller engages the wood, they will be smashed. I make it a habit to try to hold my boards from the top side as I load them onto the bed of the planer. When planing rough boards you may be tempted to wear leather gloves to protect your hands from the rough-sawn edges. I hate splinters as much as anyone, but under no circumstances would I ever wear gloves when running a planer. Never let your fingers slip into any knot holes, grooves or any other irregularities on the board.

In an effort to extend the beds on planers for more support some manufacturers include an extension roller that can be added to either the infeed or outfeed side of the bed. These extension rollers are dangerous – especially on the outfeed side of the bed. Imagine that your mind drifts and as you reach to the outfeed side to grab the board, your hand gets between the extension roller and the wood. Once the board pinches your hand, it will continue to feed and will cause a serious injury. If you have these rollers I suggest you add a sub-table board that is long enough to cover the danger of this overlooked pinch point.

The bed of the planer should be a serious source of concern – it's an easy place to get pinched. The wrong way to feed the work (top) is to hold the board from underneath. The correct way (above) is to hold the board by its edges whenever possible.

Remember the 3" rule. On the planer your hands should be at least 3" from the front or back opening of the machine along with any guards, shields, pulleys or anything that can grab or pull you in.

PLANER KICKBACK

Kickback on a planer can occur for many reasons. If wood does kick back it will more than likely be thrown toward the infeed

Planers can kick back at you – and quite violently. Never stand directly in front of the machine while operating it. Stand to the side. The tape on my shop floor is a good reminder of where not to stand.

side. However, if a piece of wood shatters in the process of cutting creating a kickback, these bits of shrapnel could ricochet on the inside of the machine and fly out the either the front or back of the machine. This is why rule number one is to never stand behind your work. Always stand to one side of the machine on both the infeed and outfeed side. Never stoop down to watch a board being surfaced. Never stack boards on top of one another and run them both through the machine. Kickbacks most likely will occur because of one of the following reasons:

• **Knots.** Knots are not always solid. Loose knots can be pulled or knocked loose from the board. Once they are free inside the machine, they can easily come in contact with the rotating knives and be thrown out.

• **Short stock.** Never run stock that is shorter in length than the distance from the infeed roller to outfeed roller through the planer. The shortest board that the machine can handle should be 2" longer than the distance between the infeed and outfeed rollers. That way stock will always be supported by one of the feed rollers. If the stock is shorter than that distance, it can get trapped between the two rollers with no support at the point of action, creating a kickback. When surfacing several pieces of short stock, (short meaning stock that it is still longer than the distance of the infeed and outfeed roller plus 2") they should be fed by butting the ends. These butted pieces will help push each other out of the machine.

• **Wood that shatters.** Thin stock can easily shatter under the force of the rotating knives. The grain direction and character of the grain, such as curly, swirly or burl wood, or wood with serious defects, can shatter while being planed. If the chipbreaker is set too high, the stock can tip up into the cutterhead causing the stock to split or tear unevenly. Forcing the feed or taking too much of a cut can cause the wood to shatter.

• **Nails or debris.** Always check the wood before planing to make sure that it is not embedded with foreign material. Even dirt or small bits of sand can nick the knives, which in turn could grab the wood awkwardly and possibly cause kickback. Be especially careful with old lumber that may have hidden nails or debris. Glue lines or wood that has an existing finish on it could cause undue wear on the knives, and dull knives can cause potential kicking forces.

DISTORTED STOCK

Wood that is warped, cupped, twisted or bowed could cause inconsistent contact with the blades, which in turn could cause kickback. It is best to joint these boards on one face before planing. Never feed two or more boards through the planer at the same time that are not consistent in thickness. When surfacing a number of pieces to a given thickness, it is a good idea to run the thickest pieces first. Once these thicker boards become equal in thickness to the remaining boards, you can then run them all together at the same setting.

LIMITATIONS

Planers do have obvious limitations. They are limited by the length of the knives and the opening depth of the machine. You will be limited by how long a board you can send through the machine by the walls in your shop. If your planer is portable then length will not be an issue. And remember, the shortest length of board you can send through your planer is based on the distance between the infeed and outfeed roller plus 2".

How thin stock you can plane will be determined by whether or not you use a sub-table board. Most planers are designed so that you cannot lower the blades into the bed. If you use a sub-table, you can plane your wood all the way to oblivion. Most often you will find that as your stock gets thinner, it will have a tendency to shatter. At some point, planing very thin stock should give way to a better machine such as an abrasive planer or drum sander. It might help to send smaller stock through at a slight skew angle to provide a smoother feed and to create a shearing cutting action.

Planers are also limited on how much material can be removed per pass. The thickness of the cut is usually determined by the width of the stock, the hardness of the wood, the feed rate and the finish desired. Although planer manufacturers recommend that passes be limited to less than ⅛", ⅟₁₆" is probably the most common pass setting.

CLEARING JAMS

Periodically, wood will have a tendency to jam somewhere between the infeed and outfeed rollers. Jams can occur because of many reasons including: improper machine settings, wood that is inconsistent in thickness

When planing short stock, you should always butt the ends of the boards against one another as you feed them into the machine. This will reduce kickback and snipe.

or width, knots or debris, roller malfunctions or distorted stock. When a jam occurs the safe thing to do is to stop the planer, stand to the side and wait for all moving parts to come to a complete stop. If the jam requires that you stick your hand into the machine make sure you unplug it first. Once the jam has been cleared, evaluate and correct the cause, then resume action.

If the board is thicker at one end than the other and jams during feeding, you do not need to shut off the machine. You can slowly crank open the adjustment wheel until the board resumes feeding. The reason this situation will not create kickback is because the infeed and outfeed rollers are totally engaged in the wood. Lightly lowering the bed position will relieve the bind that created the jam. However, it is always better to stop the machine, make the adjustments, then start it up again.

DUST COLLECTION

Planers produce a large amount of dust, chips and fine shavings. It is definitely recommended that an adequate dust-collection system be used. Be aware that chips from the planer are passed at a high rate of speed and in the right conditions can cause a static charge. Make sure to properly ground your planer's dust collection system.

Your planer has limits as to how thin it will plane your work. If you need thinner stock, you need to use a sub-table board to get your work thinner. Note that this can shatter your work.

Table Saws

by Marc Adams

It is estimated that nearly 80 percent of all woodworking requires some type of sawing. The power, accuracy and control of the table saw has made the process of sawing wood a lot more productive and a lot less physical. It's arguable as to who first invented the circular saw, but one thing is certain – it has revolutionized our craft. I've often wondered if plywood as we know it today would have ever been invented if we didn't have a way to productively cut it. I also think about the skill shifts of the traditional apprenticeships. At one time it took years of practice and great skill to handsaw wood accurately. The table saw changed that process to an almost rudimentary procedure.

Table saws can make myriad cuts including rip cuts, crosscuts, coves, mouldings, dados, kerfs, rabbets, miters and bevels. It is a precision-cutting tool that requires that the machine be set up accu-

rately, maintained properly and be used competently. Small problems can have huge consequences. R.J. DeCristoforo summarized using a table saw better than anyone when he said, "measure twice, saw once" and "think twice before sawing."

My goal with this chapter is not to review the different types of saws available today, or discuss their characteristics. I'm not going to explain the difference between blades or how to make fixtures to cut tapers or tips and tricks or troubleshooting or maintenance schedules, and I don't want to compare European to American saws. All that information already exists in myriad books and articles.

I have decided to stay away from the topic of dust control because we all know the dangers of dust and the importance of controlling it and, again, there are volumes of books and magazine articles on the subject. My intentions with this chapter are to focus on the techniques, methods and mechanics of safely using the table saw. After all, it is very well documented that more accidents occur on table saws than any other machine in the shop.

In Ian Kirby's book "The Accurate Table Saw," there is a brief introduction written by Les Winter who is a forensic engineer. He explains the essence of danger by defining two components: hazard and exposure. A hazard has the potential to cause injury. Exposure is the likelihood of coming into contact with the hazard. It is the combination of hazard and exposure that make something dangerous. If you can reduce the exposure then the hazard becomes less dangerous.

In my very first chapter in this section, "Learn the Skills to be Safe." I set the stage for the rules that apply to using all power equipment by defining control, exposure and limitation. These three factors are exactly what the user needs to know to reduce the hazards of a table saw.

If you cannot do an operation without the stock guard or an effective shop-made one, you should use another machine.

Pushing vectors

Good table saw technique begins with your stance. Always stand to the left of the blade and gain additional support by bracing yourself against the saw.

Notice how my right hand has fingers lipped onto the fence. This registers my hand in relation to the blade. Also notice the push stick positioned for use to finish my cut.

CONTROL

At the table saw, you must always be in control of the work. Control occurs through a combination of sequences and involves both managing the material and understanding how the machine is designed to give the user as much support as possible through the point of contact. The following is a list of six factors that are important to gaining better control at the saw.

First, you as the operator must have a firm stance at the machine. Your starting position will vary depending on the size of material and type of cut being made. I definitely recommend that you stand to the left of the blade with a pushing vector toward the fence and away from the back of the blade. I like to firm up my stance by placing my hip against the saw itself; this gives me better support.

Never stand directly in front of the blade or in direct line of potential kickbacks. It is not uncommon to see both novice and experienced woodworkers standing to the right of the fence. Although this does protect you from being in the direct line of a kickback, it causes you to have to reach over the fence, which could put you off balance. The natural tendency when pushing wood is to push it in the direction that you are leaning. Leaning toward the blade from the fence side could cause the pushing motion to be

directed more toward the back of the blade, and nothing good comes from the wood making contact with the back of the blade. Plus, your hand position for pushing from this side of the fence is awkward.

Second is how to maintain control while pushing the stock through the saw. Never cut freehand on a table saw. A freehand cut can deprive you of most of the protection a table saw affords. For most of us, pushing wood through a table saw is instinctive. However, there are real mechanics to the pushing process. The wood must remain flat on the table and tight against the control surfaces, such as the fence or miter gauge.

When ripping wood, I dedicate my hands so that my right hand provides the forward push and my left hand pushes the wood against the fence – make sure to maintain 3" of clearance from the guard with both hands. When ripping wood, I also like to hook a finger or two on the top edge of the fence to keep my right hand from accidentally being thrust toward the guard. It is OK to stop feeding a board during the middle of the cut to reposition your right hand or to pick up a push stick – but you must never let go of the stock with your left hand during this transition. Once the cut is complete you need to make it a rule and habit to not reach over the saw blade to pick up and bring the stock back to the front of the saw – even with the guard in place. Never clear scraps away with your fingers while the blade is rotating; always let the blade come to a complete stop first. Make sure that you always push the stock that is between the blade and the fence so it is beyond the back of the blade; always use good follow-through after the cut.

Third is maintaining good eye contact. Learn to keep your eyes in tune with the fence and the guard (instead of the blade). Most people want to stare down the blade as it's cutting the wood, but with the guard over the blade the cut is obscured and will tell you very little. As long as you keep pushing the wood the cut will take place. You must be aware of the entire work area; be alert and keep your eyes moving over the entire table but concentrate mostly on the control between the work and the fence. Visualize where the 3" rule is and develop a good awareness of this zone. Be aware of where your hands are at all times; watch to make sure your fingers stay way beyond this zone.

Fourth is how to control oversized material. Large and heavy wood can have a tendency to tip or fall off the machine. It's very hard to control large and awkward stock. I know most shops are limited on space, but it sure is nice to have extra table surfaces around the sides and especially the back of the saw. If you have someone

helping you with large stock, make sure you practice first and make sure you are in control of the cut. The helper should just act as a table extension. It does not work to have two people trying to steer a piece of wood through the saw at the same time. If a helper is not available, use a roller support to help support long stock as it is being ripped.

The fifth factor of control on a table saw is the feed rate. The rate you feed the stock in the cut can be affected by many factors including the differences between ripping and crosscutting, the type of blade being used and its sharpness, the type of material being cut, and the power of the saw. Sometimes just listening to the cut will tell you more than anything else. You should never force the cut to the point where the blade stalls. If you notice the edge of the board is burning, that's a pretty good indication that you are feeding too slowly, that your blade is dull or that the fence is misaligned – or possibly all three. If the edges of your boards are showing signs of burning, try to speed up the feed rate a bit. If that doesn't improve the burning then the blade is probably getting dull or needs a good cleaning. Verify that the fence is parallel to the blade.

And finally, the sixth factor of control is built into the saw itself. On a 10" table saw the blade is rotating at approximately 4,000 rpm. As wood makes initial contact with the blade there is little kicking force because the cutting force is straight down toward the table, just like with a band saw. As the wood continues in the cut to a point where the stock is about halfway past the blade, the wood will start to encounter a forward vector of force that in turn will cause the wood to react by moving in the direction of the rotating blade or toward the operator (the action of kickback will be explained in my next article).

To counter these forces, engineers have built in "control" as a way to manage the undesirable effects of the wood when it contacts the blade. The table itself, the fence, a miter gauge, standard guarding, specialty devices such as push sticks, featherboards and hold-down devices, are all great ways to control the stock as it meets the point of contact on a rotating blade. A well-designed machine provides or has available some type of "control" to counter the kicking and grabbing forces that naturally take place with rotating cutters and provides the user

Stationary tables to both the left and right of my table saw make this area more user friendly, but nothing increases safety more than a proper outfeed table.

with a clear range of motion through the entire process.

THREE KINDS OF EXPOSURE

Going back to Winters' explanation of hazard and exposure, he says that by reducing the exposure, you will reduce the danger level. Less exposure means less danger; more exposure means more danger. It almost doesn't get easier than that – and that should be the golden rule of operating all power equipment in the shop safely. Exposure at a table saw can have three meanings: blade height when there is no guard being used, blade height with the guard and repetitiveness. (For the sake of argument let's just say that these rules apply to all blade types.)

BLADE HEIGHT WHEN NO GUARD IS USED

Let's face it: No matter what rules we establish for the table saw when it comes to using your guard, most woodworkers, both professional and novice, will at some time remove the guard(s) to make certain types of cuts. If you do decide to run a table saw without a guard (which I do not advise), then you must set some kind of rule as to how much blade exposure you will allow.

It is recommended that when you are making unguarded through-cuts that the blade be set about ⅛" to ¼" above the stock. However, keep this in mind: At a lower blade setting there are a considerable number of teeth in the cut that are moving in a substantially forward direction. Kickback forces can be transferred into the wood most efficiently with a low blade, and with a lower blade there is a greater distance between the rear of the blade and the splitter. Plus more teeth means more friction, which in turn heats the blade and increases the risk of burning the wood.

Let's just make this whole issue simple: Always find a way to guard the blade; never use a table saw without the guard. The point of the two photos above right is to demonstrate that at the low blade exposure, the blade will have three teeth in the work at the rear of the blade. At full exposure, only two rear teeth are in the work. The trajectory at the low setting will have the teeth of the blade leaning 60° off vertical, directed at the operator while at full exposure, the trajectory of the teeth is only 30° off vertical.

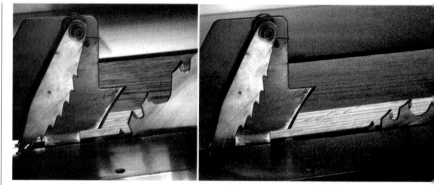

In the photo at left you can easily see the trajectory of the blade's teeth and the closeness of the blade to the splitter. Above, the teeth trajectory is forward, toward the operator and the distance between the blade and the splitter has widened.

BLADE HEIGHT WHEN GUARD IS USED

This may take you by surprise but a higher blade height helps the blade to run cooler. At the same time, it helps the motor to run more efficiently while using less power. I've been told that if the saw is adjusted just right, you will also get a cleaner cut with a higher blade. This is why at trade shows you always see the "pitch man" running the blade as high as possible when demonstrating his blades. Why don't they use their guards – bunch of dummies!?!

Think of this as well: With fewer teeth in the cut, the transfer of forward energy is less efficient and a higher blade presents less of a gap between itself and the splitter. All of a sudden, it sounds like I'm recommending that you run your blade as high as possible, but that's not the case. Keep in mind that a higher blade setting produces more exposure and a greater danger level – only if the guard is not in place. And this discussion is about blade height with the guards in place. With a guard acting like a barrier, the likelihood of the blade contacting your hand(s) from any direction, except straight in, is low. No pivoted or aftermarket guard can prevent you from sliding your hand straight into the blade. So what's the answer? The answer is that a well-guarded blade can be set slightly higher than an unguarded blade.

REPETITIVENESS

The second type of exposure is in terms of repetitiveness. Each time you make multiple cuts or passes you could be putting yourself at more risk. For example, there is no sense in making several passes over a table saw blade to make a wide cut when you could have done it in one pass with a dado blade. As you present yourself to extra passes you expose yourself to more risk.

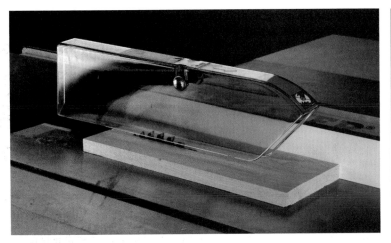
It's important that a guard be clear and not distort the view of the blade as the cut is being completed.

LIMTATION

There are two types of limitations to consider. The first are common-sense items such as your physical limitations and the limitations of your shop space. Everyone has difficulties handling a sheet of plywood or cutting heavy or long wood. And small shop space can sometimes require a lot of planning and strategy before making a cut. There is nothing wrong with asking for help.

The other type of limitation, which is definitely the most important factor in understanding any machine, is to know when that machine is not capable of safely performing an operation. At some point you have to determine when the table saw has reached its limits. My rule is simple: I use the guard as my determining factor. If the guard on my saw will not permit me to make the cut that I desire or if I can't effectively make or obtain a guard that will work, then the table saw is not the machine for that operation. There is nothing wrong with walking away from the table saw when it's the wrong machine. Actually, I find the challenge of figuring out a second approach to be a great learning experience and believe it has made me a better woodworker – not to mention it's helped to keep me out of the emergency room.

UNDERSTANDING GUARDING AND HOW IT RELATES TO THROUGH & NON-THROUGH CUTS

Guarding simply is the act of positioning barriers or other safety methods so that hazards are inaccessible to the user. I'm probably going to take a hit for this next statement, but I think that most table saw manufacturers make guards that are ineffi-cient and not very user-friendly. Yes, they do meet the provisional requirements by OSHA (1917.151 (c) (1,2,3)) for having an enclosure, splitter and anti-kickback fingers, but they lack real design ingenuity.

What makes a table saw so versatile is it can make both through and non-through cuts. Standard "off-the-showroom-floor" guarding doesn't make it easy to move between these two actions and worse yet, most manufacturers have attached all three guards together to act as one unit. If you remove one, then you've removed all three. It can be a lot of work to remove a guard – followed by a lot of work to put it back on. After doing this a time or two, frustration sets in and it won't be long before it becomes a habit to just leave the guard off altogether.

Ask any woodworkers today if they still use their guard and watch how quickly they look at the top of their loafers and say, "... uh, no." Then ask them if they even know where their table saw guards are – most usually don't know that either.

I truly believe that everyone who uses an American-made table saw today would use their guard system, no questions, if the guard systems were user-friendly. This is why aftermarket guarding is becoming so popular today. Aftermarket guards separate the enclosure from the splitter, which allows you to remove one and leave the other in place.

Plus, most aftermarket guards have a degree of adjustability, which gives them a better range of protection and they can be taken off and put back on in a matter of a few seconds. But even with that, aftermarket guards can't accommodate every possible cutting action on a table saw – but they sure are better, and I definitely recommend that you look at upgrading your standard guarding.

Every table saw that I've owned over the last 15 years has had the standard guard replaced by aftermarket guarding systems. Make sure the aftermarket guard you purchase has at least the blade enclosure and a splitter. More than likely the splitter will come with anti-kickback fingers attached to it.

In order to fully understand guarding on the table saw, you have to understand the differences between the three guards, their purposes and how they function during through and non-through cuts.

BLADE ENCLOSURES

The blade enclosure, which is sometimes referred to as a shield, hood or top guard, is the most visible part of the guarding system on a table saw. A good enclosure should either rest on top of the wood or be set as close to the wood as possible. It should not allow your fingers to get between it and the wood or near the blade and should not have pinching forces. Enclosures that do not pivot act to a small degree as a way to help hold the wood in control and to limit any potential lifting of the stock just in case it grabs or catches on something. It should provide good coverage on all four sides of the blade.

I use the enclosure as a starting point for my 3" rule. A good enclosure should not obstruct your view through the point of contact and must aid in deflecting chips away from the user and direct them toward the dust collector, or at least down toward the table. One of the biggest drawbacks to conventional or standard enclosures is that they are not adjustable from side to side or front to back, which can cause problems when trying to rip narrow or short stock. Although aftermarket guards do allow some adjustability, they also have limits before the guard obstructs the path of motion. If the cut requires that the enclosure be removed, remember my simple rule: If the guard on my saw will not permit me to make the cut or if I can't effectively make or obtain a guard that will work, then the table saw is not the right machine for that operation.

When making non-through cuts, enclosures or top guards can sometimes be more of a hindrance than asset. They can limit the motion, restrict control and create binding. Non-through cuts will require creative ways to protect yourself from unnecessary exposure to the blade.

SPLITTER

The second guard on a table saw is not quite as obvious as the enclosure or top guard but is the most important part of the guarding system. The splitter, sometimes referred to as a spreader or riving knife, is directly behind the blade and is used for through cuts. Splitters are most effective when they are the exact width as the kerf of the blade and are in perfect alignment with it. The splitter separates and prevents material that is being cut from coming in contact with the back of the blade. That minimizes the

A blade guard can be as simple as a piece of Lexan attached to a scrap. When clamped to your fence, it provides safety by limiting potential contact with the blade.

chance of pinching and kicking back. Typical American-made splitters will not work for non-through cuts, which will require that they be removed. It is important to realize that even with a splitter properly installed, kickback can occur if through some circumstance the wood should make contact with the back or top of the blade and just before the splitter. Be aware that the closer the splitter is to the blade, the more effective it will be. Splitters should be used for both ripping and crosscutting.

There are two types of splitters – static and dynamic. Most new saws come equipped with the typical top guard/splitter/anti-kickback-finger combination-guard

Due to typical American-style splitters extending above the top of the blade, making any cut except for a cut completely through your stock is not possible.

Standard splitters do not follow the blade as it raises or lowers. Therefore, the gap between the two can be wide. This opening is an area where pinching and kickback can develop.

system. This combination guard system is attached just behind the blade arbor and just to the back of the saw table. They do not move once they are installed. Standard splitter/guard systems can vary in how close the splitter is located to the blade, but can be as far back as 2" or more. The larger the gap between the splitter and the blade, the more potential there is for a piece of stock to come in contact with the back of the blade. Be mindful that with a static splitter, the gap will vary as the blade is raised and lowered. Static splitters must also be removed when making non-through cuts.

A better type of splitter is one that is not connected to the enclosure or top guard, but is connected to the arbor casting itself. On European saws this type of splitter is called a riving knife. It is located just barely behind the blade and will raise and lower with the blade. The gap between the two never changes and is typically as close as ¼". A good riving knife is set just a little lower in height than the arc of the blade. This allows you to make both through and non-through cuts, which makes you safer and more productive. Riving knives should not be used with dado or moulding-head cutters. For the

record, I would much rather have a riving-knife type of splitter on my saw.

ANTI-KICKBACK FINGERS

Anti-kickback fingers are sometimes referred to as non-kickback fingers, dogs or pawls. Their job is to oppose the tendency of the saw to pick up material and throw it toward the operator. Overall, I'm all for any thing that can make a saw safer. From an engineering point of view, anti-kickback fingers seem to be a good concept but they come with quite a bit of controversy as to their effectiveness. European saw manufacturers don't use them at all because they deem them to be virtually ineffective with little positive gain. As a matter of fact, European saws can't have anti-kickback fingers because of the dynamics of a riving knife. Anti-kickback fingers can sometimes get in the way. For example they can limit and even interfere when ripping narrow stock. I've had on numerous occasions the anti-kickback finger limit the motion and even obstruct my push stick.

A splitter is a nice safety addition to a crosscut sled. However, you will have to remove your anti-kickback fingers if you use a splitter with your crosscut sled because they will create a hang up when you pull the sled back after the cut. Although anti-kickback fingers do work when using a miter gauge for crosscutting, they are virtually useless with stock less than 6" wide. Remember: A standard guard/splitter combination is set back from the blade, which causes the anti-kickback fingers to be positioned even farther from the back of the blade. When crosscutting, the cut is completed when the trailing edge of the board clears the front of the teeth. This will leave the unsupported cut-off board right next to the back portion of the blade and just before the anti-kickback fingers. Because anti-kickback fingers are attached to the splitter, they follow the same rule for through and non-through cut applications as the splitter.

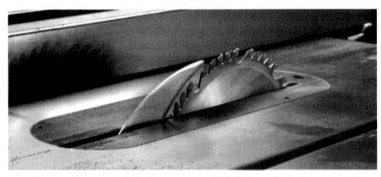

Riving knives add a great deal of safety to any standard blade cut. The knife travels with the blade to maintain a close fit to the blade and reduce the possibility of pinching.

A cutoff of nearly 6" is not captured by a traditional splitter or anti-kick-back fingers, but a riving knife positioned close to the blade would keep the cutoff away from the back of the spinning blade.

 Published by Popular Woodworking Books, an imprint of F+W, A Content + eCommerce Company, 10151 Carver Rd. Blue Ash, Ohio, 45242. First edition.

Distributed in Canada by Fraser Direct
100 Armstrong Avenue
Georgetown, Ontario L7G 5S4
Canada

Distributed in the U.K. and Europe by
F+W Media International, LTD
Brunel House, Ford Close
Newton Abbot
Devon TQ12 4PU, UK
Tel: (+44) 1626 323200
Fax: (+44) 1626 323319

Distributed in Australia by Capricorn Link
P.O. Box 704
Windsor, NSW 2756
Australia

Visit our website at popularwoodworking.com or our consumer website at shopwoodworking.com for more woodworking information.

Other fine Popular Woodworking Books are available from your local bookstore or direct from the publisher.

ISBN-13: 978-1-4403-4370-4

19 18 17 16 15 5 4 3 2 1

Editor: *Scott Francis*
Designer: *Daniel T. Pessell*
Production Coordinator: *Debbie Thomas*

a content + ecommerce company

Read This Important Safety Notice

To prevent accidents, keep safety in mind while you work. Use the safety guards installed on power equipment. When working on power equipment, keep fingers away from saw blades, wear safety goggles to prevent injuries from flying wood chips and sawdust, wear hearing protection and consider installing a dust vacuum to reduce the amount of airborne sawdust in your woodshop. Don't wear loose clothing or jewelry when working on power equipment. Tie back long hair to prevent it from getting caught in your equipment. People who are sensitive to certain chemicals should check the chemical content of any product before using it. The authors and editors who compiled this book have tried to make the contents as accurate and correct as possible. Plans, illustrations, photographs and text have been carefully checked. All instructions, plans and projects should be carefully read, studied and understood before beginning construction. Due to the variability of local conditions, construction materials, skill levels, etc., neither the author nor Popular Woodworking Books assumes any responsibility for any accidents, injuries, damages or other losses incurred resulting from the material presented in this book. Prices listed for supplies and equipment were current at the time of publication and are subject to change.

METRIC CONVERSION CHART

Inches	Centimeters	2.54
Centimeters	Inches	0.4
Feet	Centimeters	30.5
Centimeters	Feet	0.03
Yards	Meters	0.9
Meters	Yards	1.1